Patriarchy and Families of Privilege
in Fifteenth-Century England

University of Pennsylvania Press
MIDDLE AGES SERIES
EDITED BY EDWARD PETERS
Henry Charles Lea Professor
of Medieval History
University of Pennsylvania

Patriarchy and Families of Privilege in Fifteenth-Century England

Joel T. Rosenthal

upp

University of Pennsylvania Press
Philadelphia

Copyright © 1991 by Joel T. Rosenthal
All rights reserved
Printed in the United States of America

Library of Congress Cataloging-in-Publication Data

Rosenthal, Joel Thomas, 1934-
    Patriarchy and families of privilege in fifteenth-century England / Joel T. Rosenthal.
        p.   cm. — (Middle Ages series)
    Includes bibliographical references and index.
    ISBN 0-8122-3072-8
        1. Family—England—History—15th century. 2. Patriarchy—England—History—
15th century. 3. Upper classes—England—History—15th century. I. Title. II. Series.
HQ615.R67   1991
306.85′0942′09024—dc20   91-17228
                                                                                                                   CIP

for Dora and Hilmar
Rose and Morris

Contents

Tables and Figures

Tables

Figures

Abbreviations

Bedford	Margaret McGregor, ed., *Bedfordshire Wills Proved in the Prerogative Court of Canterbury, 1383–1548*, Bedfordshire Historical Record Society, 58 (1979).
BIHR	*Bulletin of the Institute of Historical Research*
Buckinghamshire	E. M. Elvey, ed., *The Courts of the Archdeaconry of Buckingham, 1483–1523*, Buckinghamshire Record Society, 19 (1975).
CCR	*Calendar of the Close Rolls, 1377–1509*
CFR	*Calendar of the Fine Rolls, 1377–1509*
Chancery	Calendar of the Inquisitions Post Mortem Preserved in the Public Record Office, Henry VII, vol. I. HMSO, London, 1898.
Chichele	Ernest F. Jacob, ed., *The Register of Henry Chichele, Archbishop of Canterbury, 1414–1443*, vol. II. Oxford, 1938.
CP	George E. Cokayne, et al., eds., *The Complete Peerage*, 12 vols. in 13. London, 1910–59.
CPpL	*Calendar of Papal Letters*
CPR	*Calendar of the Patent Rolls, 1362–1498.*
DNB	*Dictionary of National Biography*
Emden, *CU*	Alfred B. Emden, *A Biographical Register of the University of Cambridge to 1500*. Cambridge, 1963.
Emden, *OU*	Alfred B. Emden, *A Biographical Register of the University of Oxford to 1500*, 3 vols. Oxford, 1957–59.
Fifty	Frederick J. Furnivall, ed. *The Fifty Earliest English Wills*, Early English Text Society, o.s., 78 (1882).
Lancashire I	William Langton, ed. *Abstracts of Inquisitions Post Mortem*, Chetham Society, o.s., 95 (1875).
Lancashire II	William Langton, ed. *Abstracts of Inquisitions Post Mortem*, Chetham Society, o.s., 96 (1876).

Letter Book	Reginald R. Sharpe, ed., *Calendar of the Letter Books . . . of the City of London* (London, 1899–1912): Letter Book I, 1909: Letter Book K, 1911: Letter Book L, 1912.
Lincoln	Andrew Clarke, ed., *Lincoln Diocesan Documents, 1450–1544*, Early English Text Society, o.s., vol. 149 (1914).
Nottinghamshire I	K. S. Train, ed., *Abstracts of Inquisitions Post Mortem Relating to Nottinghamshire, 1350–1436*, Thoroton Society 12 (1952).
Nottinghamshire II	Mary A. Renshaw, ed., *Abstracts of Inquisitions Post Mortem Relating to Nottinghamshire, 1437–1485*, Thoroton Society 17 (1956).
Oxfordshire	J. R. H. Weaver and Alice Beardwood, eds. *Some Oxfordshire Wills, Proved in PCC, 1393–1510*, Oxfordshire Record Society, 39 (1958).
PCC	London, Public Record Office: Wills of the Prerogative Court of Canterbury.
RP	*Rotuli Parliamentorum*, 6 vols. London, 1832.
Sharpe	Reginald R. Sharpe, ed. *Calendar of Wills . . . in the Court of Hustings, London, A.D. 1258–1688*, 2 vols. London, 1889–90.
SMW I	F. W. Weaver, ed. *Somerset Medieval Wills, 1383–1500*, Somerset Record Society, 16 (1901).
SMW II	F. W. Weaver, ed. *Somerset Medieval Wills, 1501–1530*, Somerset Record Society, 19 (1903).
TE	James Raine and Jaimes Raine, Jr., eds., *Testamenta Eboracensia, I, II, III, IV*, Surtees Society 4, 31, 45, 53 (1836–69).
TRHS	*Transactions of the Royal Historical Society.*
VCH	*Victoria County History*
Yorkshire	William Paley Baildon and John W. Clay eds. *Inquisitions Relating to Yorkshire of the Reigns of Henry IV and Henry V*, Yorkshire Archaeological Society, 59 (1918).

Preface

These essays are offered in the hope that they will be suggestive, adding a further dimension to what we know about the lives of the prominent and a further direction and context to what we can glimpse of the lives of lesser men and women. Then as now, family life was a many-faceted affair, a kind of moveable feast that we share now with some, now with others, and with differing degrees of pleasure and spontaneity in different situations. It is still hard to escape the idea that fiteenth-century England was the last medieval century, and the appeal of a waning civilization remains strong; tarnished glory, at best, as a harbinger of things to come. Certainly, fifteenth-century sources are sparse and laconic, compared to the explosion of records and expression that marks Tudor England. They retain an air of mystery and of challenge to those who work to explicate them.

In the introductory chapter I explain at some length how and why I wish to present a series of investigations into family forms and structures so as to offer a brief for their diversity. Each life comprised its own unique tapestry, and in generalizing about typical if not universal life experiences I have drawn heavily upon the historian's license to move from individual(s) to group and back again. There is a universal similarity in the human condition, of course, and the fifteenth century can be seen as more like our world that we might think at first glance, especially once we cease to approach it by way of the morbid dramatizations of Huizinga or the sentimentality of popular historical fiction. It was not a century of *fin de siècle*. On the other other hand, "the historian is in no sense a free man," as Marc Bloch reminds us, and I have tried to shape my orchestration of late medieval behavior, institutions, and social interaction so as to include a fair run of *their* words, *their* ideas, and *their* perception.

This book has but slowly worked its way to the end of its road. The idea of a series of separate if related essays on the varieties of family life first occurred while I was mulling over a conversation with Compton Reeves as he worked on his *Lancastrian Englishmen*. Many other projects, interests, and commitments have interrupted my progress: University and departmental administration, work on Anglo-Saxon England, research on old age and the aged in the fifteenth-century, and watching baseball with my children and "L. A. Law" with my wife are among the serious diversions that have claimed a share of my time and energy.

Since I first turned my thoughts to an oveview of the late medieval English family, many colleagues have offered their versions and variations of the larger topic. From recent books by Barbara Hanawalt and Judith Bennett we have seen how much of peasant life and of peasant lives as a "lived experience" can be reconstructed. Colin Richmond has shown how to approach old topics with a novelty of perception and a sense of personal empathy for the long-dead. From David Herlihy has come both the large and the small; a wealth of micro-cosmic insight, in concert with Christiane Klapisch-Zuber, and the broad brush approach in a book on the medieval household that I have read with pleasure and taught to (or studied with) undergraduates with a sense of challenge and of stimulation. We speak with more confidence about households, private and domestic religiosity, and the elasticity of kinship and cooperation, both for England and the continent, than we did a mere decade ago. And medieval widows, I am happy to say, are virtually a "growth industry"; Michael Sheehan and Sue Sheridan Walker are among the many now focusing inquiries that have been uncoordinated, if not unpublished, for far too long.

I wish to thank friends and colleagues who have heard some of my ideas and whose encouragement has always been welcome and often necessary. Ralph Griffiths, Jo Ann McNamara, Caroline Barron, and Carol Rawcliffe are among those who have been patient and supportive, and many others who are recognized by way of footnote acknowledgments could well be mentioned here (not least of whom are my editor and the readers for the University of Pennsylvania Press). Nor are my debts confined to people. The Institute of Historical Research of the University of London, in its own monumental way, is a familiar home away from home: its librarians, staff, seminars, and tea room have all played their part. The library and staff of the Melville Library of SUNY Stony Brook have invariably been helpful. My own department has provided a congenial atmosphere. Though life at Stony Brook is not quite up to bee-keeping (or hiking, for that matter) on the Sussex downs, it has offered a goodly measure of stimulation and reflection. My university has also been generous with that peculiar academic commodity, free time. The National Endowment for the Humanities must be thanked: a senior research fellowship was both a vote of confidence and an opportunity to read and to write with few(er) distractions. To all these, and to many others who have helped—friends, family, correspondents, students at many levels and in many courses, and to other citizens, old and new, of the far-flung empire of historical inquiry—I add a final word of gratitude.

Introduction

These essays are an exploration of the theme of variety. They examine *some* of the forms of family life and family structure within which men and women, primarily from families of privilege and property, lived and interacted. They are offered as a brief for diversity and plurality—of the structure and the function of family organization, as well as of individual roles over the course of the life span. Some of the variety was simultaneous, some set serially through the stages or segments of life. This argument for the coexistence of various forms of family life pushes against two avenues of explanation that have sought to achieve a quasi-orthodox status in social history and in recent family studies. One is the line of exposition that presents a particular form or model of the family as the dominant form of social organization at any given time. The other portrays historical changes in the family as operating in a single and compelling direction, as though there were a developmental or evolutionary model to which or within which the Western family must conform.[1] In presenting the case for diversity we endeavor here to argue against efforts to impose more coherence upon the multiplicities of human existence and of the social structure than the matter admits of, and other scholars have struck a similar tune and also demonstrated how the concept of family is a mix of the corporeal and the fictive and symbolic.[2] Just as individual lives operated within as well as beyond the family framework, so in turn that very institution that we sum up and pre-package as the family had various forms and purposes, depending on the questions posed and the data offered for the examination. There was diversity of form and structure, and within a single form there was further diversity, for a given individual, at various points along each particular life line.[3]

Just because they lived in "traditional" and "preindustrial" society, there is little reason to believe that the men and women of fifteenth-century England failed to enjoy the freedom to participate in divers human relationships as well as in divers *forms* of relationship. Out of this diversity, those relationships centering around those whom they (and we) identify as kinsfolk, and the interactions between ego and ego's kin, are singled out for detailed examination. In making this choice, we do not mean to imply that such interactions were the only critical ones of the personal, socio-economic, and political world, nor were they necessarily or invariably the most important. Other studies can be (and have been) written focusing on the bonds created by voluntary unions—political, economic, cultural, military brotherhoods, guilds and fraternities, and so forth—by means of which society was held together and collective activity given shape and meaning.[4] In some cases these other forms of social organization *also* happened to embrace many whom we know to have been related as kinsmen and kinswomen, and in other instances they did not. However, family ties were virtually universal ones, in fifteenth-century England, as elsewhere. Though they might often contain powerfully negative currents, as a counter or balance to their more obviously positive ones, they were among the main ligatures that wove separate lives into what we, from our safe and convenient distance, have no trouble identifying and labeling as the social fabric. If the family is one of the larger institutions within which we examine that peculiar blend of individual biography and collective behavior, it is as two-edged as life itself. The "haven in a heartless world" could also be the tool by means of which the older generation, and not infrequently the dying and even the dead, could impose their dictates upon those still to make their mark in this world. We will talk from time to time about social control, as well as its limitations, but we will rarely scale the heights of cynicism that H. R. Trevor-Roper reached when he turned his thoughts to the Pastons: "Why must the tomb be prefabricated, the masses prepaid? It is because, in spite of all this lip-service to the family, no one really trusted anyone else, not even his sons, once his power over them was gone. In reality the family was not cultivated as such: it was a necessary alliance from which every man hoped individually to profit."[5] On the other hand, romanticization of the family is not likely to be our shortcoming.

A further caveat is in order before we proceed. An examination of the household in time past has greatly enriched recent work in social history.[6] However, studies of the household are separate from those of the family, though few students on either side of the line could draw a boundary with great confidence. The data presented and discussed below are carefully segregated from the ambiguous if beguiling problems of fifteenth-century domestic arrangements and all those intriguing issues raised by the consideration of how shared space affects the collective life of those who share, and their hierarchy of social values.[7] In the context of historical studies of the household, the dwelling unit and its aggregations of residents naturally receive the main focus of attention. The social (as opposed to the physical) distinction between the "nuclear family" and other forms of family organization within the place of residence (from castle to hut) is obviously of paramount importance in such studies. Village and urban studies have both exemplified the role of proximity and propinquity as factors in material and inter-personal relations.[8] But for our purposes the examination of various forms of family structure and interaction are pretty much separated from questions of who lived with whom and of the links between different collections of folk who shared a common (patriarchal) roof. These essays are not about the household, per se, in so far as such a distinction can be drawn, and our focus on families of privilege—while ignoring child care and fostering—makes residence of less concern.

Had we different data, or even a different perspective on the data we use, we might see an altered picture. Frequent contacts within a confined space might be read as reinforcing the link between close kinship and close affection, though we are also told, by both poets and historians, that absence can make the heart grow fonder, and it is no less than the young Margaret Paston who says to her husband: "I had never so heavy a season as I had from the time that I knew of your sickness till I knew of your amending, and yet my heart is in no great ease, nor shall be, till I know that ye be really well."[9] Indeed, physical propinquity might only serve to highlight the disparity between the formal ties of close kinship and the powerful affective bonds that could be forged with more distant kin. Studies of violence hardly endorse the idea that one loved one's neighbors; at the same time we should remember that violence was anomalous and one act of aggression might come after years of cooperative intercourse.

In addition, were we to explore our agenda through the records of village and manorial society, it is not certain that the same conclusions would present themselves: patriarchy was in some measure a construct related to the control of and the power to transmit property, while lineage may have meant little if we descend below some given point on the social pyramid. However, we have not relied very much on the records of the more humble, and our case rests primarily on the behavior, modes of expression, and experiences of the titled aristocracy and the propertied gentry. Some dip into municipal records and urban lives does occur, but again we have not done more than skimmed such materials, and we have hardly explored all the niceties of urban custom or burghal tenure where such conventions turned the life experience in a different, or distinctly urban, direction.

When he looked back upon his survey of western civilization, H. A. L. Fisher said, with perhaps less than total candor, that "one intellectual excitement has, however, been denied me. Men wiser and more learned than I have discerned in history a plot, a rhythm, a predetermined pattern. These harmonies are concealed from me."[10] Tongue-in-cheek or not, similar thoughts come to the fore here. Some scholars look at the western family, in the long duration between the high middle ages—Marc Bloch's "second feudal age"—and the full industrialism of the nineteenth century, and see it evolving from one structural paradigm to the next: from patriarchy to shared enterprise to a privatized concern of affection and reciprocal interest. Others see individualism, in both its economic manifestations and in murky realms of ego-identity, as cropping up long before we once thought of it as an idea whose time had come.[11]

My purpose here is not to argue against various theses, but simply to assert a claim for variety. The multitudinous interpretations we have been offered, if not true or correct, are certainly helpful explanatory mechanisms for the dissection and rearrangement of large bodies of inchoate material about everyday life, family interaction, and self perception. As hypotheses, they have at least stimulated if they have not invariably convinced. If I seem to deal with some recent opinions in a cavalier fashion, in my efforts to get on with the orders of the day, I mean neither to belittle nor to deny the role of many important contributions to scholarly debate and to historical understanding. Change over time is always very hard to identify and to describe from ground level; indeed, it is almost impossible. As we read the tale, there is little in the fifteenth-century evidence that allows us to argue for evolution in either family structure or in the calculus of affective relationships. There seem to have been neither more nor fewer categories of expression and behavior, personal and collective, in 1500 than there had been in 1400. Moreover, there is much that argues for a continuing and sustained diversity in function and in types of interaction. Admittedly, a century is an arbitrary construct to impose on data that reflect small group and private behavior, and it stands as a relatively short period for a student of "traditional" society. It is far too small a span for significant change to emerge and catch the eye of the distant observer. This is particularly so when we choose to follow that most conservative of historical paths, the one trampled by the words and the views of the ordinary people—if not in social class, seemingly in ideology and conformity—as they trekked through the interconnected courses of their private and public lives. Such records as they have left about these matters are generally outside (and subterranean to) the boundaries of what they themselves would have recognized as the historical record. The ephemeral, the personal, and even the legal were not designed, at the time, to talk explicitly to questions of social structure, any more than to questions of private feeling and belief. Society was seen as a stately pageant, a ritualistic drama with an unchanging script: new characters would enter as old ones exited, no doubt, but rarely with a flourish of hautboys and trumpets to catch our flagging attention. Without major changes in the modes of production, without a shift in the global balance of economic and political power, and without a change in residential patterns that transformed society from rural and village to urban and industrial, a basic change in either the family or in human perceptions of the family is unlikely to be identifiable. Fifteenth-century families resembled nothing so much as other fifteenth-century families, and they mostly were content to place themselves within this static tableau, even if they were not above throwing an occasional elbow in an effort to jostle their way forward in the queue.

We propose to argue that people could and usually did live, simultaneously, within and through a variety of family structures or contexts.[12] One of these is the patriarchal family—the nuclear family that "once" was—molded and cast so it could bear its heavy burden of ideology and normative behavior as well as the worldly baggage of economic and sexual convenience, child rearing, and the ties of affection. The second is the horizontal family, that sprawling and flexible network of kin, from siblings outward until the circles were lost on the horizon: Cooperation, competition, and much of the life experience often fell, in high, middling, and low society, within such a framework. The third "structure" is widowhood, a distinctly female experience. And at the end we will turn, briefly as part of our conclusion, to some family "situations" that came apart. General and miscellaneous data (some of it quantitative), along with some fortuitously chosen case studies will be summoned, like the ghosts who flit across the stage of Shakespearean melodrama, to turn our thoughts in the right direction and to point the moral of each tale.

One danger of the approach adopted in this study is that it makes fifteenth-century men and women seem much like us. Perhaps a more felicitous way of expressing this is to say that the approach we have adopted emphasizes those aspects of *their* lives that are most like *ours*. Given the weight of different social settings, there seems to be more similarity between the father-son or the parent-child relationships across the span of the centuries than between late medieval political and economic ties of subordination and superordination and their modern analogues. In many ways, fifteenth-century England indeed was our (British and U.S.) world, writ 500 years ago, and many aspects of "the world we have lost" can be seen as social artifacts or constants that we have simply covered over by dint of centuries of continuous residence on the same site. As we look at the varieties of family life, we note that many of the distinctions between the late medieval and the modern world are barely visible at the level of microanalysis. The earthquakes of the Reformation, of the growth of the European world system, and of the rise (and decline) of industrial capitalism and colonialism can all be readily digested within the avaricious maw of a patriarchal last will and testament, or by the affectionate and unvarying terminology we sometimes find linking the dying husband and the surviving wife. While we are constitutionally reluctant to say that "the more things change," we must beware of a temptation to see too much of the present in the past we recreate in our own image. In addition, there is the problem of circular reasoning: *once* we have asserted the prime importance of the family in fifteenth-century life, we find support—in almost all the sources, and in all the examined forms of interaction—for our case.

Thus a great risk of this approach is that it isolates the smallish unit of structure and of interaction, and then it accords that unit a primacy of focus because all other data and explanations have been organized around it; center defines periphery (and vice versa). But the other side of this coin is a reminder that large social changes are built on small ones, and that sometimes very basic small units are not so much transmuted as merely rearranged. Families are both powerful forces with an internal dynamic, and impressionable structures upon which change is etched. They are resilient and multi-dimensional. Their potential for encompassing, if not masking, ambivalencies is a major theme of Old Testament history, of Greek tragedy, and of the Christian mythology and iconography, as well as of the Paston Letters and of the petitions flowing out of England to the papal chancery pleading special cases pertaining to sex and marriage. A healthy measure of ambivalence and ambiguity was familiar, in oral, visual, and written form, to the men, women, and even children of pre-Reformation Europe.[13] Why should we try to deny to those of the fifteenth century their share of and contributions to such rich psychic and sociological material? To some extent the vast universe of differences and changes in material culture, in religious and philosophical world view, and in technological conditioning mean that we are dealing with people distinctly different from ourselves. Even the most cursory look at late medieval millenarianism and mysticism drives home the width of this distinction. But on the other hand, the people of the fifteenth century coped with the daily realities of choas and of order, and with the bitter-sweet flavors of their close interpersonal relationships. They were often driven to respond in a fashion we still find comprehensible and even moving.

Another danger of the case study approach to an analysis of historical social structure and behavior is its heavy reliance on upper and middle class data. Their lives and deaths are better known, and consequently can be better studied, in both individual instances and by means of statistical aggregations and calculations. This is a fact of life, just as surely as were the better life styles, the higher incomes, and the more grandiose family tales of those to whom God had been pleased to give (much) more. The crucial question for us—in studying this universe of uncertainty and inequality—is whether better recorded lives were significantly different in regard to either the quantity or the quality of family relationships and interactions. The scale of the upper class map on which their manoeuvers was enacted was clearly more detailed, but that alone does not necessitate differences in the nature of the terrain or its basic physical characteristics. The family quarrels of the Berkeleys, or of the Poynings brothers with their sister, were over sizable patrimonies, with their perquisites of castles, manorial holdings, and titles.[14] But such animosity could be, and no doubt often was, reenacted in miniature over cottagers' plots and the villeins' chances of a slightly preferable strip in the fields and the home gardens. So again, our approach not only tends to find similarities between late medieval families and contemporary western ones, but it compresses or deemphasizes gross distinctions between classes. It begs the question of the link between socioeconomic rank and the emotional and affective framework within which life is enacted.[15]

By minimizing class distinctions it is possible that sex and gender become more important distinctions than they otherwise would have been. It is not difficult to accept that the social boundaries between fifteenth-century men and women were perhaps less important than those between rich and poor, the propertied and the propertyless, though they were clearly immutable.[16] But once again, what we find in historical inquiry is largely a result of what we search for and what we contribute or bring to the search. An investigation into family relationships produces data that then help shape our view of past reality until those very data become—at least to us and to our historical comprehension—a basic element of that lost world. An inquiry into military bonding and martial brotherhoods in the Hundred Years War introduces us to one kind of truth about the social relationships of men at war. An inquiry into the transmission of theological and philosophical arguments within the schools opens windows into prosopographical networks that linked the men of Oxford, Cambridge, and Paris. And so if our original working hypothesis is that family links are critical ones and that they provide at least one entree into a dimension of late medieval life and social interaction, it then should come as no surprise if our conclusions, supported by mountains of material culled from consequent research, serve to confirm the validity of the original premise. The extent to which family was more or less important—either in regard to other fifteenth-century social ties and institutions or in comparison with those of the twentieth century—is an open question. Moreover, the fifteenth-century answers varied for different fifteenth-century people, just as they do for different observers today, as well as for the same people at different times. The dialectical relationship between the subject and the object is an issue of great fascination to the modern historical expositor, and to offer another example of its complexities is by itself a considerable return for research. To discover or to assert that virtually all fifteenth-century men and women for whom documentation exists give indications of caring for and about the family is hardly an improbable finding, and it is one we will continuously find bolstered by the data we discuss and analyze.

Part of the fascination of an investigation into the family is that it enables the modern student to straddle that high and often narrow ridge separating the world of involuntary relationships and proscribed bonds from that of volition and free choice regarding colleagues and networks of affiliation. In a strictly definitional sense, one did not choose ones relatives (except perhaps for the marital partner[s]). But in terms of working social relationships and interactions, there was scope for a considerable amount of volition. One might have brothers, and one might choose to or be compelled to work closely with them, at least some of the time. But on other occasions one could choose not to: there was a balance, an ebb and flow, that might serve to keep relationships comfortably warm rather than too hot (or too cold), life from appearing to be just constriction and social control. One presumably had some freedom to turn, at least some of the time, away from brothers: perhaps to other relatives in the horizontal network, perhaps to non-relatives. But mostly, we suspect, one simultaneously interacted with some relatives and with some non-relatives. Such groups of colleagues were rarely totally distinct or mutually exclusive. When we look at any collection of fifteenth-century wills, we quickly see that most large lists of testamentary executors embrace both kinsmen and kinswomen and non-kin, as do most large aggregations of testamentary beneficiaries. Most legal compacts for enfeoffment and for quitclaim agreements embrace similar mixtures, if they run to any fair size. And on the darker side, much criminal activity, at least of the systematic and semi-organized sort, involved men linked through blood or marriage as well as through social proclivity and residential proximity.[17] Society was an amalgam of groups, interests, and forces: that kinship links were among the stronger ligatures behind an event is hardly unlikely, especially given the breadth of defined kinship and the general practice of socially endogamous marriage. Detailed studies of individuals and of individual families often reveal that the elements of competition and rivalry could be nicely contained within, as well as without, the family.

But such rivalry was not often based on any pre-determined principles of social organization or of family structure. Compatability of temperament and the harmony of interests could count as heavily as formal links, if not more so. In situations where we can identify members of secular networks and of voluntary associations, we find that many were related to some of the others, a few to all, and perhaps relatively few to none. We find such mixed affiliations in the House of Lords and on the fields of the Wars of the Roses, as well as in manorial court quarrels over inheritance, common debts, and the communal duties of the village and the rural world. The family was a little like home in Robert Frost's poem: it was where you *could* go when you felt you had to. One could return and operate from it as a base, but without the necessity of forsaking all other kinds of entanglements, other strategies for mutual support and aggrandizement.

Interaction is both a critical term and a relative one. In this study it is the shorthand for those points or moments of intersection for the individuals within the family. As a busy highway intersection is the junction of numerous thoroughfares, each (in geometrical terms) going in its own logical but different direction, so a point of family or personal intersection can bring a fair number of individuals together for some variable period of time and some length of a common course. That they come from different directions and to some considerable extent were to have separate destinations does not negate the value of examining what happens at the intersection itself, as well as to those who pass through it. Ultimate divergence is an important factor, no doubt, but so is the fact of convergence and the measure of the common course.

Interaction is also a relative concept. Its value as an insight or a tool of analysis is a factor of our level of information and of our assessment of such variables as the physical and emotional proximity of the individuals involved, the frequency of their interrelationships, and by the psychic and the material levels of their mutual exchanges. Parents and small children or husbands and wives could interact, then as now, far more often than the historical record can meaningfully follow. Their daily relationships are lost in the vast welter of frequency, of routine, and of unrecorded habit and custom. Nor are many of such interactions worthy of much note, certainly not from the distance of five centuries. From our vantage point we look, instead, for those occasions in time and space, of the most signficant intercourse. These distinguishable and well-lighted intersections of the various life lines become the *events* of family and social history, the elements from which we construct the complex molecules of historical synthesis and vicarious interpretation. Where information is extant, such events as marriage, the birth of the heir, the stipulation of the last will's provisions and conditions, and the funeral can all assume the desired degree of importance, of necessary larger impact. They can be identified and analyzed, the distant but still distinct and measureable moving stellar objects that lie within the scope of our instruments.

Families were aggregations of linked individuals, yoked together by the way in which society defined and incorporated biology. When the parts came into contact, they interacted with and upon each other: such critical moments were the *events* of social or family history. When we can actually plot and analyze such crossings in the heavens or in the collision of particles, the historic family is transformed from the static or fictive one of the genealogical table into the dynamic one of collective identities in action. We think of family interaction as being essentially face-to-face. But it might be formalistic, or at a distance. The birth of a son and heir could deeply affect the lives of three older, already-married sisters, though they might never even see the new male heir. And in this case, the interaction is negative: his mere existence now bumps them from their prior and preferred position as heiresses. But on the other hand, their loss of legal status might be compensated to some extent by a greater share of personal and sentimental bequests in the father's will, since the girls were now less likely to share the basic patrimony or to have a title to transmit via their husbands to their own children. In this hypothetical case a change in structure of the nuclear family could lead to a compensatory shift in affect. So the interaction, the *event* in family history, for example, the belated birth of the male child, could be worked out in many guises, at many levels, both positive and negative. But whatever its configurations, the event—the moment of intersection or historical interaction—stands as a point of special significance on the line of historical inquiry. And such points become the trenchant data for the world of family history, as surely as battles and constitutional crises were of the political and national.

The interaction of the separate members of the family groups represented, in aggregate, that mixture of voluntary and involuntary association that comprises the fabric of social life and that maps both the private and the public hemisphere. The interactions between people of the same and the opposite sex, between people of different generations, and between near and more distant kin, were partially controlled by custom and etiquette or by mannered behavior, partially by individual preferences and personal initiatives. The interactions between a father and his son were different, in multitudinous ways, from those he had with his brothers or with his sister's children. And often, of course, the relations with closer relatives were more frequent and more complex: they were also "closer" in that more was sometimes given, sometimes demanded. The scope for ambiguity and ambivalence in the closer relationships that lie within the inner circles of kinship was correspondingly greater. As a counter against too much fluidity and individual volition or definition there stood the firmer secular walls of custom and defined expectation, built and maintained to help govern and formalize events such as marriage and marriage portions, dower settlements, testamentary divisions of personal and real wealth, and burial ceremonies. Lives were a dramaturgic procession wherein the demographic and the biologically possible set the stage upon which personal preference and external values wove an elaborate dance that could extend well beyond the grave. But over time and given a large number of people, the preferences reflected by statistical incidences can also be isolated and examined. The worlds of individual volition build up into larger worlds, about which we can speak in such terms as "most" and "usually."

One open issue concerns the extent to which demographic factors shaped the psychological outlook of the fifteenth-century individual. In a world where at least a minor fraction—if not more—of the children were likely to die before reaching age 10, was there a corresponding freeze on emotional links, a hoarding of psychic capital by the parents, only to be expended—later, if ever—upon the survivors?[18] Not only are such questions really beyond resolution, but it is hard to see what kinds of data could be introduced to support the case. We are not impressed by arguments that seek to minimize the personal investments devoted to bad risks within the family. On the other hand, there is no doubt that life experiences then were unlike those usually encountered in the industrialized west today, and we cannot be too dogmatic in asserting that such objective differences did not necessarily have subjective consequences. The average person, even in the seventeenth century, was apt to have a very different set of experiences to look back upon, from the vantage point of (relative) old age: "Born into a family of five children, of whom only half reached the age of 15, he also . . . had five children, of whom again only two or three were still alive when he died . . . [at 52]. [He] survived in his immediate family an average of nine persons: one of his grandparents (the other three having died before his birth), his two parents, three siblings, and three of his children."[19] Obviously demographic realities did not take all the emotional powder out of family life. But did they lead to a greater reserve in personality and style of expression? Both individuals and their larger family units would seek to build defenses—personal, legal, and spiritual—against mortality. One way in which such almost-inevitable blows were cushioned was by the construction of a definition of family that embraced the living *and* the dead. As an ongoing unit across time, family boundaries were not wholly circumscribed by physical mortality. Christian dramaturgy, expressed in iconography, in the liturgy, in the visible ceremonials of popular religious life, lent itself to a belief in and an identification with a transcendental family. The roads both to spiritual salvation and to personal solace were engineered to breath life into and identification with this abstraction. Chantries and prayers for the dead can be seen as parts of the spiritual and emotional continuum of obligations and mutualities that each generation performed for those now dead and then likewise imposed upon those yet to come. Any single life span or any single generational cohort within a family was but one leaf in a series of overlapping, unending family obligations. The dead were explicitly remembered, the line between their corporeal remains and those duties owed their incorporeal essences deliberately kept as thin (and as undefined) as possible. The family boundaries were not wholly of this world, and the exact edges of definition were allowed to fade into the mists of time and of spiritual values. In a similiar fashion, those relatives on the outer branches of the genealogical tree might be within some of the functional definitions of the family, as they might be beyond others.

The evidence of chantries and of prescribed prayers for the dead reinforces the idea that the family was indeed a unit created to surmount temporal and mundane parameters. On this extra-worldly stage it is hard to say whether children were immediately grasped to the bosom or held at some distance until their membership was validated as serious and sustained. They were born into a world where the family enterprises and priorities—at all social and economic levels—not only antedated the personal relationships of marriage, but sometimes never yielded their primacy to the softer and more intimate ties. So in this sense children can be seen as part of the *business* of family life, as well as the emotional pillars and hostages to fortune that each generation left to the one to come. In this context it becomes harder to determine whether they were or were not loved just because they might die young. There were so many other reasons, as well, why they might or might not be loved: neither can we be so certain how survival per se was correlated with affection.

In similar fashion, did the bonds between husband and wife stop short of full confidence and mutuality because about half the spouses, of either sex, would survive and go on to marry more than once? We will see examples of close partnership between a man, marrying for the third time, and a widow who had already buried two husbands. The variety of behavior, as revealed below in the analysis of widows and widowhood, was so great that it must have contained ample scope for a full range of emotional links, both positive and negative, when the concerned parties chose to so invest it. What is true regarding variation and volition within the simple (nuclear) or primary family was also true for the horizontal family, between siblings, or for those such as uncles, nephews, and cousins, though the levels of relationship were often more diluted in these outer reaches. To go so far as to deny that demographic probabilities (of survival, of infant mortality, or of widowhood) had any effect on interpersonal relationships is to deny fifteenth-century men and women a full awareness of what went on in their world, as well as a conscious freedom to try and shape it so as to shelter themselves from its most hostile blows. But to say that affection only followed or was primarily dependent upon the odds for survival is to impose a kind of callous demographic or behavioral and statistical determinism on feelings and thoughts. These people shaped their lives through some conjunction of the possible and the preferred, and towards such efforts separate temperaments and chemistries played no inconsiderable part. So too did proscribed expectations about what a man owed an unmarried daughter, or a younger son, or a pregnant widow. The mix of personal idiosyncracy and probability was presumably shaped to fit contemporary expectations as well as our historical comprehension.

To what extent were they like us? The data for family structure and family interaction have been presented from the premise that their families, in definition at least, were quite similar to modern western ones. Relationships were defined pretty much then as now, and families were likewise bilateral and extending to affinal as well as to consanguinous kin. The church was at some pains to clarify and to elaborate these ties, for the ecclesiastical rules surrounding marital partners were the widest functional definition of family. The church also helped foster the interest in genealogy that figures in such secular considerations as the search for an heir at law when there were no direct blood descendents. The functional family of affection and of interaction—when birth and survival proved cooperative—usually ran to three generations vertically and out to first or second cousins and nephews and nieces when calculated horizontally: not so different from its customary working boundaries today. It is possible that if the data were collected in a different fashion, organized on some other principle, the fifteenth-century family might seem much less familiar to us than in the presentation below. But in a realm where there is no revealed truth or no single truth, the form of the explanatory construct becomes a critical aetiological key. The modern definition of family at least seems adequate to explain their links and their behavior. Furthermore, little in the historical record about their family lives looks to be beyond comprehension, once we have begun to work backwards from the modern definition and from modern views of interaction. This even covers a good deal of the anomalous and fractious behavior that crops up with some regularity. The premise of basic similarity between the fifteenth- and the twentieth-century family at least *looks* valid. It supports the data about structure, function, and interpersonal relations. It is at least a good tool, if not a metaphysical or historical constant.

To help organize the material about family life we have imposed three main organizational categories upon the data, as we said above. The first focuses on the relations between fathers and sons, especially between the patriarch and his son-and-heir. This relationship highlights the special ties between the chairman of the primary family, within each generation, and his special successor. Nor are we solely concerned with birth, gender, and survival. As Michael Mitterauer and Reinhard Sieder remind us: "*Pater* and *mater* are notions that express not genealogical connections but dependence on authority . . . The position of *pater familias* has, in fact, nothing to do with natural fatherhood. It derives, rather, from a specific position of authority. The *pater* was originally the master of the household."[20] Patriarchy stands up for examination in terms of the ideology that supported it and in terms of its biological and social bearing on family continuity and upon the preservation and transmission of the patrimony. This combination of the internal and the external, the largely conceptual and the obviously tangible, is what family history should aim for in recognition of the two-faced reality (biological-demographic and social) of human institutions and situations. There are many reasons behind the medieval cultivation of the concept of patriarchy: the transmission of land by primogeniture, the political and economic value of impartible inheritance, the use of the father figure as the intermediary between the collective expression of the public will and the small social units, and the paradigmatic links with biblical and heavenly models. Whether the triumph of the patriarchal family over the clan was a genuine historical phenomenon of the high middle ages, or whether it was a triumph at all, or whether it even occurred, are not issues at stake here. Suffice it to say that by beginning our family analysis with the patriarch and by then following his behavior and his self-expression in his dealings with his male heir (and his children in general), many bonds and types of relationship between the generations become comprehensible.

Patriarchy is the keystone to the idea of the family as a combination of a peculiar set of human responses to biological links and to some perennial categories of social relationships. The examination of the full meaning and operation of patriarchy incorporates demographic material as well as a consideration of interpersonal relations. There could be no father-son relations if there were no sons. And when there were sons, the tie between the father and his son-and-heir was usually the most important of all family (and human) ties—more important in a definitional if not in a practical sense than that between husband and wife—and it could be strengthened still more by deliberate institutional and emotional reinforcements. In this context younger sons are cast as understudies, as alternative heirs whose role might remain in doubt even beyond the death of the father and the succession of the elder brother. In the quest for patriarchal succession and patrilineal continuity, if all went well, such lesser sons were either expendable or they were available as extra human capital, perhaps to be invested in new ventures. Their roles might remain peripheral, their own lives kept in suspended animation, perhaps even in penury.

The kernel of the family might be the bonds between the father and the next male heir. But both in terms of daily life and of an individual's involvement with kin, many other relatives beyond the (male) children played a part. They are referred to collectively as the horizontal family, the family network, and they served many purposes and played a diversity of roles. A study of a given family network starts from a center point, the ego in the midst of those concentric circles that mark the degrees of relationship roughly corresponding to the rings of social and personal intimacy and interaction. Bands of relatives of roughly equal distance from the center encircle each individual, as we proceed from spouse and children outwards to distant cousins and to such as great nephews and great nieces. Separate interactions become lost, and some of the case studies elaborated below show the arbitrary and limited value of seeing any one man's set of cycles and epicycles as a fixed cosmos. Siblings and their children and all the other participants were busy creating their own webs and circles and networks, and these could all double back to embrace the original ego but rarely to accord him a high degree of centrality in their own circles. The various and miscellaneous members of the horizontal network, like the younger sons of the patriarchal family, might have a back-up role if there were no children to succeed: a distant and perhaps once cloudy alternative who now, perforce, becomes the next of kin. Or this heir might be a real substitute for or a parallel to the primary family. The network could also figure, through some of its members, in those realms of activity where choice of association was at least partially under one's control, regardless of whether the issue was piracy, breaking and entering, or creating webs of testamentary benefaction. Most men with networks of relatives led public lives that intersected with those of at least some of their relatives, as best we can chart such activities. Levels and incidences of intimacy within such networks probably varied even more than they did between members of the primary family. But if there were more from whom to choose, and as distance weakened obligatory or expected ties, so freedom to pick and choose as one wished could compensate for the decline in intimacy and the more tenuous biological links.

A woman was almost always the second best, the other, in a world of men and of men's historical sources and records. She entered life as an inferior, regardless of her social status, and there was little she could do to alter, let alone reverse, this depressed condition. In the course of her life, if she stayed in the secular world, she was apt to marry and to bear children. Beyond this, in time, she had a better than even chance of becoming a widow. And in this latter status she at least was essentially different from her brothers: she now potentially or hopefully occupied a position regarding property and emancipation that no male could emulate. Widowhood could be an abject fall, or it could be the vestibule leading her forward to a life of unprecedented freedom, influence, and financial independence. In any case, it brought women into a kind of peculiar semi-autonomy with which the freer life course of the men had no exact analogue. Created out of grief and bereavement, widowhood could also carry its opportunities: it might be the gateway to a sisterhood comparable to the blood brotherhood of warriors. For some women widowhood really was a desolate spell, largely bereft of resources, companionship, and social and family utility. For many, if not for most, it was a mixed lot. Its potential for freedom and even power has been exaggerated and romanticized. Chaucer's Wife of Bath is, and should remain, a fictional creation. The historical records generally portray a more sober picture, with perhaps some slap, tickle, and pilgrimage, but nothing like the good wife's endless zest for remarriage and her scorn of normal restraints upon body and tongue. Her monumental and affluent existence has cast too long and too rosy a shadow, great creation though she is.

An examination of patriarchy, of extended family networks, and of widows and widowhood offers us some family vignettes, mainly along a vector in time. In addition, we shall look very briefly, at the end, at some people who had trouble fitting into or holding on to their place within one of the customary modes or forms of family structure. In these analyses, with their general information and their case studies, we crudely mix the diachronic and the synchronic, the push and the pull of kinship studies. We yoke people who, in some senses, were going in different directions but who happened to be in the same space at a given time, or vice versa. They often had different interests. We define them as part of a common social universe to which we assign a collective or common name and interest, albeit some were more critical to and involved in the joint enterprise than were others. In addition, some were dedicated to its ends, some indifferent, and others perhaps even hostile, caught up though they might be by its powerful magnetism.

The picture of the fifteenth century family can easily become a static one. Change over time is not the theme here, nor is it a theme whose presence can be readily detected. But it might always be lurking around the corner. If the change was not apt to be one of social structure or of family function within a larger economic and social tableau, there was always the change of personnel. Like the rivers of the pre-Socratic philosophers, one could not put a foot upon the same family tree twice. Birth and death, marriage and remarriage, baptism and god-parenthood and co-sponsorship, and the fluctuating temperatures of personal relationships meant constant alteration, new departures to balance new entries, new networks to compensate for new feuds and new factions. Some of the relationships considered here were important in terms of intergenerational ties. Others existed within the same cohorts and between rough contemporaries. Still others coupled those permanently within a family or lineage with those who were but passing through. There is no true family or real family, no correct and permanent list of members to which we can refer in order to set the record straight. Rather, in its diversity of forms and with its divers purposes the family was an ever-changing creature with many goals and purposes. It was no more focused on a set end or a declared teleology beyond itself, than it could fall back upon a fixed list of *dramatis personae*. If we see the family as a larger reification of personal relationships between blood relatives and affines, we must also remember that it too is an entity that shifts and re-orients itself at critical times and junctures. It also can change, slowly and imperceptibly, while apparently crossing even the calmest of waters.

The family embraces many purposes and many people. But in itself, it was not an end in life. Its sheltering arms must not be turned by the modern imagination into the sentimental, all-nurturing forces we are accustomed to expatiate upon, scattered so liberally throughout traditional society. Some people were badly squeezed by its grip, others were barely held at all, even at times when they most needed such comfort. The interpersonal ties of pre-industrial society could be supportive and comforting, but they could likewise be most unfeeling. Many an adult with every reason to think that life was now safely contained within a functional family unit built to endure unto death, if not beyond, suddenly found himself or herself out in the cold. The marital link had been snapped, or it had been built from the beginnings on a false premise, its protective cover but a facade for hostility and even violence. There were numerous reasons for the "broken family." In some instances one or other of the parties was clearly at fault and can be stigmatized with full responsibility for the social and domestic fracture. In others the problems bore a more innocent origin, for example, ignorance of ecclesiastical definitions of relationship. Ones status could change because of others actions over which one had little control, and such changes were rarely advantageous ones. Often the truth behind the collapse of the primary or even of the extended family network can no longer be extracted from the extant records of litigation and of mendacious and partisan allegation. If men and women did not invariably lie in presenting their case, they were certainly apt to tell their version of the episode, their share of the truth, and such partisan fragments are often all that remain. Entry into marital life, we shall see, was no guarantee of stability, and behavior often deviated widely from the prescribed standards. Not even the broad boundaries of family life were always adequate to encompass all the hostility that proximity and jealousy regularly generated. Animosity could overspill. When family ties turned sour, the aggrieved parties—then as now—often expressed their woes with a special sense of bitterness, of a strong feeling of personal betrayal and personal inadequacy. The family, one of our great institutions for the definition of the ego, for the normalization of sexual and personal expression, and for the linking of the individual to the larger social unit, could turn to bite those who fed it and who had been taught, by all the values of the accepted spiritual and secular structure, to believe in its protective embrace.

Notes

1. Important recent books that are culprits in their desire to narrow the scope and to argue against diversity include Lawrence Stone, *Family, Sex, and Marriage in England, 1500–1800* (New York, 1977), and Edward Shorter, *The Making of the Modern Family* (New York, 1975). Stone's views on partriarchy and the evolutionary line of development are conveniently summarized in his "The Rise of the Nuclear Family in Early Modern England: The Patriarchal Stage," in *The Family in History*, ed. Charles Rosenberg (Philadelphia, 1975), pp. 13–57. Perhaps the most judicious overview written with fifteenth-century England in mind is (still) to be found in Francis R. H. DuBoulay, *An Age of Ambition* (London, 1970), pp. 80–127 (the chapters on "Marriage and Sex" and "Household and Family"). And behind most of these studies, and an inspirational if not an invariably convincing text, is Lawrence Stone, *The Crisis of the Aristocracy, 1558–1641* (Oxford, 1965), especially in the monumental Chapter XI, "Marriage and the Family" (pp. 589–671).

2. Reviewers of Stone, *Family*, have been more than willing to stress the importance of explanations that tolerate diversity of forms and multi-causal analysis. See, in particular, Alan Macfarlane, in *History and Theory* 18 (1979), 103–26; Edward P. Thompson, *New Society* (September 7, 1977), 500–501; J. E. C. Hill, "Sex, Marriage and the Family in History," *Economic History Review* 2nd series, 31 (1978), 450–63 (for a review that also discusses Peter Laslett, *Life and Illicit Love in Earlier Generations*). Christopher Brooke refers to Stone's *Family* as "a book which is perhaps excessively given to find change where only variety can be seen": "Marriage and Society in the Central Middle Ages," ed. R. B. Outhwaite, *Marriage and Society: Studies in the Social History of Marriage* (New York, 1981), p. 18; for other pithy comments on Stone, see Brooke, *The Medieval Idea of Marriage* (Oxford, 1988), especially chaps. 1, 6, 8–11. See also Michael Anderson, *Approaches to the History of the Western Family, 1500–1914* (London, 1980), p. 14: "there can be no single history

of *the* Western family since the sixteenth century because there is not, nor ever has
been, a single family system . . . [but instead] diversity of family functions . . . diversity in attitudes toward family relationships . . ." For a related but different approach, and another useful corrective, see Randolph Trumbach, *The Rise of the
Egalitarian Family* (New York, 1978). There is now a useful and judicious survey of
recent work, Ralph A. Houlbrooke, *The English Family, 1450–1700* (London, 1984).
One last caveat: Anthony R. Wagner, *English Geneology* (Oxford, 1960), pp. 178–79,
makes the important distinction between "family" and all one's kin as "elements in
family history."

3. See Michael Mitterauer and Reinhard Sieder, *The European Family*, trans.
Karla Oosterveen and Manfred Hurzinger (Oxford, 1982), especially pp. 43–44.
David Herlihy, *Medieval Households* (Cambridge, Mass., 1985), and Frances Gies
and Joseph Gies, *Marriage and the Family in the Middle Ages* (New York, 1987) both
offer a useful synthesis and data relevant for our tale.

4. For some studies that deal with some of the "other" forms of social orga-
nization, see Maurice Keen, "Brotherhoods in Arms," *History* 47 (1962), 1–17; John
Bossy, "Blood and Baptism: Kinship, Community, and Christianity in Western
Europe from the Fourteenth to the Seventeenth centuries," *Studies in Church His-
tory* 10 (1973), 129–43; Bossy, "Some Elementary Forms of Durkheim," *Past and
Present* 95 (1982), 3–18; Philip Niles, "Baptism and the Naming of Children in Late
Medieval England," *Medieval Prosopography* 3, 1 (1982), 95–108; Michael Bennett,
"Spiritual Kinship and the Baptismal Name in Traditional European Societies," in
Principalities, Power, and the State, ed. L. O. Frappel (Adelaide, 1979), pp. 1–13;
Christine Klapisch-Zuber, "Parrains et Filleuls: Une approche comparée de la
France, l'Angleterre et l'Italie médiévales," *Medieval Prosopography* 6, 2 (1985), 51–77;
Louis Haas, "Social Connections between Parents and Godparents in Late Medi-
eval Yorkshire," *Medieval Prosopography* 10, 1 (Spring, 1989), 1–21. There is a full-
length treatment of god-parenting and related subjects in Joseph Lynch, *Godparents
and Kinship in Early Medieval Europe* (Princeton, N.J., 1988), though the later middle ages are not the main focal point. For another institution that yokes bonding
and social control, see Barbara A. Hanawalt, "Keepers of Lights: Late Medieval
English Parish Gilds," *Journal of Medieval and Renaissance Studies* 14 (1984), 21–37;
Caroline M. Barron, "The Parish Fraternities of Medieval London," in *The Church
in Pre-Reformation Society*, ed. Caroline M. Barron and Christopher Harper-Bill
(Woodbridge, Suffolk, 1985), pp. 13–37; Ben R. McRee, "Religious Gilds and Regulation of Behavior in Late Medieval Towns," in *People, Politics, and Community in
the Later Middle Ages*, ed. Joel T. Rosenthal and Colin F. Richmond (Gloucester,
1987), pp. 108–22.

5. Hugh R. Trevor-Roper, "Up and Down in the Country: The Paston Letters," in *Historical Essays* (New York, 1966), p. 31. Also, on the family shame for not
having built the tomb, see Colin F. Richmond, "Religion and the Fifteenth-Century English Gentleman," in *The Church, Politics, and Patronage*, ed. R. B. Dobson
(Gloucester, 1984), pp. 195–96: "yf there xulde no thyng be don for zour fadyr, yt
wolde be to gret a schame for vs alle." For a treatment that revises or debunks family
identity and filiopiety, see Michael Jones's forthcoming study of Margaret Beaufort: his paper, presented at the XXV Congress of Medieval Studies (Western Michigan University, May 1990), offered a preview of his findings, with special reference

to the Beaufort chapel at Canterbury. See also Jack R. Lander, "Family, 'Friends' and Politics in Fifteenth-Century England," in *Kings and Nobles in the Later Middle Ages*, ed. Ralph A. Griffiths and James Sherborne (New York, 1986), pp. 27–40: p. 40, "So blood relationship and marital connections did not create strong bonds of mutual interest and political support either amongst families themselves or around the throne. In fact, they were much more likely to produce hostile—often bitterly hostile—feelings as a result of disputes over inheritances and regional, territorial influences." This is a theme that Lander has stressed in numerous essays on the tangled skeins of the aristocracy.

6. Led, of course, by Peter Laslett and the Cambridge Group for the History of Population and Social Structure. Of particular interest are Peter Laslett, *The World We Have Lost*, 2nd ed., (New York, 1971); Peter Laslett and Richard Wall, *Household and Family in Past Time* (Cambridge, 1972); Richard Wall, Jean Robin, and Peter Laslett, *Family Forms in Historic Europe* (Cambridge, 1983), particularly the essay by John Hajnal, "Two Kinds of Pre-Industrial Household Formation Systems," 65–104. Herlihy, *Medieval Households*, has already been mentioned; for England, see R. G. K. A. Mertes, *The English Noble Household, 1250–1600* (Oxford, 1988), now the best discussion; see also Jacques Beauroy, "Family Patterns in Bishop's Lynn Will-Makers in the Fourteenth Century," in *The World We Have Gained*, ed. Lloyd Bonfield, Richard M. Smith, and Keith Wrightson (Oxford, 1986), pp. 32–42.

7. John Demos, *A Little Commonwealth: Family Life in Plymouth Colony* (London, 1970), and Edward Hall, *The Hidden Dimension* (New York, 1969).

8. Gies and Gies, *Marriage and Family*, 3–15; for family and primogeniture, see pp. 186–95.

9. As quoted in H. S. Bennett, *The Pastons and Their England*, 2nd ed. (Cambridge, 1932), p. 60.

10. Herbert A. L. Fisher, *A History of Europe*, rev. ed. (Boston, 1939), p. xv.

11. See Alan Macfarlane, *The Origins of English Individualism* (Oxford, 1978), for a strong if not necessarily convincing statement.

12. See Houlbrooke, *English Family*, 1–62, for a discussion that sets out definitions and the units they cover. See Laslett, *The World We Have Lost*, 1–83, for a discussion of patriarchy that explores the functional (and structural) boundaries of the institution.

13. See Steven Ozment, *When Fathers Ruled: Family Life in Reformation Europe* (Cambridge, Mass., 1983), particularly pp. 50–94 of this major study; 50: "Above all, the husband was supposed to rule." However, in many ways the book is a learned gloss on the limits of and exceptions to this norm.

14. For some quarrels within and between families, see Michael A. Hicks, "Descent, partition, and extinction: The 'Warwick inheritance'," *BIHR* 52 (1979), 116–28; R. Ian Jack, "Entail and descent: The Hastings Inheritance," *BIHR* 38 (1965), 1–17; Robin Jeffs, "The Poynings-Percy Dispute: An Example of the Interplay of Open Strife and Legal Action in the Fifteenth Century," *BIHR* 34 (1961), 148–64. Jeffs sums up these matters, p. 164: "His [Robert Poynings'] battle was not so much against King Henry as against his own niece Eleanor"; see also Lander, "Family, 'Friends' and Politics," for a survey of these matters, touching a number of families; Martin Cherry, "The Struggle for Power in Mid-Fifteenth Century

Devonshire," in *Patronage, the Crown, and the Provinces in Later Medieval England*, ed. Ralph A. Griffiths (Gloucester, 1981), pp. 123–44, on the Courtenay-Bonville hostilities; Alexander Sinclair, "The Great Berkeley Law-Suit Revisited, 1417–39," *Southern History* 9 (1987), 34–50. These references hardly cover all the recent literature, and in addition Carole Rawcliffe and Edward Powell, among others, have begun to disect instances of successful arbitration and feud-resolution.

15. Because this study concentrates on people of property and privilege, it should be clear that the sources upon which we draw so heavily not only are tilted, in terms of social and economic status, but ask questions (and seek answers) that radiate outwards from the centrality of property and succession, rather than from such other possible focal points as labor and labor values, migration, gender, or other institutions and forms of social organization. For inquisitions post mortem, see Josiah C. Russell, *British Medieval Population* (Albuquerque, N.M., 1948), pp. 92–117. On wills, Michael M. Sheehan, *The Will in Medieval England* (Toronto, 1963) remains basic, with useful points treated in Malcolm C. Burson, ". . . For the Sake of My Soul: Activities of a Medieval Executor," *Archives* 13, 59 (September, 1978), 131–36; see also Michael L. Zell, "Fifteenth and Sixteenth Century Wills as Historical Sources," *Archives* 14, 62 (Autumn, 1979), 67–74, and Rowena E. Archer and B. E. Ferme, "Testamentary Procedure with Special Reference to the Executrix," *Reading Medieval Studies* 15 (1989), 3–34. On proofs of age, see Sue Sheridan Walker, "Proofs of Age of Feudal Heirs in Medieval England," *Mediaeval Studies* 35 (1973), 306–23, and L. R. Poos, "Life Expectancy and 'Age of First Appearance' in Medieval Manorial Court Rolls," *Local Population Studies* 37 (Autumn 1986), 45–52.

16. Joan W. Scott, *Gender and the Politics of History* (New York, 1988).

17. See James B. Given, *Society and Homicide in Thirteenth-Century England* (Stanford, Ca., 1977), p. 45, for a table giving the incidence of activity regarding "relations with whom one committed homicide," p. 57, for a table of "victims slain by relatives," and p. 147, for a table of "killers and the relatives they killed according to sex of killer." Also, Barbara Hanawalt, *Crime and Conflict in English Communities, 1300–1348* (Cambridge, Mass., 1979), pp. 151–83.

18. The basic statement is Philippe Ariès, *Centuries of Childhood*, trans. Robert Baldick (New York, 1962), passim, and it has been endorsed by Mitterauer and Sieder, *European Family*, 60–62. But for expressions of the love of children and of grief at their deaths, see Sylvia Thrupp, *The Merchant Class of Medieval London* (Ann Arbor, Mich., 1948), pp. 200–201, on how Wycliff chided mothers who grieved against God's "gret mercy" in taking their young ones. Also, Alan Macfarlane, in *The Family Life of Ralph Josselin* (Cambridge, 1970), pp. 165–66, comments on "the poignancy" of the death of Josselyn's eight-year-old daughter Mary. She was the third child to die young of the five or so who failed to reach the age of ten. Josselin found it increasingly difficult to accept that "to the Lord I have resigned her."

19. Jean Fourastie, "From the Traditional to the 'Tertiary' Life Cycle," in *Readings in Population*, ed. William Peterson (New York, 1972), p. 33. Cf. Laslett, *The World We Have Lost*, 103: "You could not with any confidence expect to see your grand-children in the world we have lost."

20. Mitteraurer and Sieder, *European Family*, 6.

I Fathers and Sons: Patrilineage and Patriarchy

This chapter is divided into three sections. The first discusses the preservation of the patrilineage, the incidence of direct father-son links. It mainly relies upon the data of "soft" demography and quantitative analysis. The second looks at patriarchy, the ideology or value system through which fathers, both living and dead, asserted themselves over their sons. The third is a case study of one family, the lords Scrope of Bolton: we will see to what extent their tale embodies and exemplifies the larger and more general considerations of the first two sections. But before we proceed, a final word of caution. We do not claim that the ties between fathers and sons—or between the father, as the family's representative of this generation, and the son, as that of the next—were necessarily as important, in the full context of life, as we may here make them appear. We only argue that when they were important, and insofar as they were important, they fell within the boundaries of the issues as staked out in this chapter.

The Patrilineage

The Old Testament was interpreted and transmitted so as to offer the medieval world a strong model of patriarchy and of patrilineal descent. There were three basic attributes or facets of the picture that proved especially attractive to the mimetic formulation of the model family. One was the picture of the aged patriarch: of three score years and ten, or perhaps, in his strength, of four score and more. Another was the theme that emphasized the father's special son, the *real* son-and-heir. It was he who stood out amidst the larger flock of those descended from the old man's loins, and he it was upon whom the blessing, the birth right, would fall. And finally, when the end drew near, attention focused upon the picture of the patriarch as surrounded by his flock—his own fertility visibly reinforced by that of his descendents and of his lands. He had served his Lord and his lord, and was now seen to have been blessed. His stewardship had been a successful one.

These three projected aspects of the patrilineal drama present such a powerful and comprehensive model that they serve as a yardstick against which we can measure the degree of success of each historical father-figure, each would-be patriarch. If the father did live his full biblical span, and if he produced the son and heir who would in turn fill the land with grand-children, he had achieved a goodly portion of his proper earthly goals. In late medieval or renaissance Italy a number of treatises were produced in which the author dealt explicitly with the desirability of coupling the social and the biological, and such a model might then be woven into the history and genealogy of a particular family.[1] The English were less articulate about such matters than their urbanized Mediterranean contemporaries, and per-haps insular self-consciousness inhibited any temptation to wax so openly on the patrilineal and patriarchal theme. However, from what we can infer about English values, as well as what we can deduce from the empirical data about English family behavior and structure, it is not difficult to assert that similar values prevailed in England as in lineage-conscious Florence or Venice.[2] The English would have strongly, if silently, endorsed Italian sen-timents, though they might have blushed to hear themselves talking in this fashion.

This chapter examines that most critical of links in the family chain, that binding the father to his sons, especially to the son and heir. This latter bond was the main link, in terms of biological continuity (as the medieval world interpreted such a concept), as well as in terms of most forms of social relationship and continuity. Art helped define nature, just as it en-larged upon its own creation. Fathers begot sons, and sons in their turn became fathers; the passing of time and the fruits of generation fused into one of the dominant institutions of society, the patrilineal-patriarchal fam-ily. The incessant beating of nature's waves came to assume a meaningful rhythm to the socially conditioned ear. While this conditioning had no doubt begun long before a distinctive medieval culture can be identified—in some prehistoric dawn of male chauvinism and of patriarchal domina-tion—few forces were in operation in the fifteenth century to qualify or dilute its traditional if monotonous and generally oppressive cacaphony.

The oldest history that the medieval world knew, from the tale of creation of Adam and Eve onwards, was that of procreation and genealogy, coupled with their material and socio-economic manifestation—the transmission and inheritance of property (in which transmission the father's name and blessing played no small part). The book of Genesis was to a large extent an historical account of such begetting and transmitting. The genealogical aspects of the Old Testament made a vivid impression on the medieval imagination: the old law and the extra-terrestial covenants were transmitted, to no small degree, through a chain of fatherhood that was powerful and aggressive long before a separate priesthood came into being. The *Gospel of Matthew* reflects this patrilineal orientation, opening so boldly with the tally of the 42 generations between Adam and the New Law: "the book of the genealogy of Jesus Christ." In historical or chronological terms, the family-oriented gospel antedated the theology of Paul and Augustine, and it was often both more relevant and easier to grasp. The exalted earthly genealogy that made Christ "the son of David, the son of Abraham," was an important part of the explanation of the where, when, and why of the Incarnation. Patriarchal and patrilineal credentials evidently counted, in heaven, as on earth. This was heady wine for the idealogues and champions of a social structure defined in terms of male relationships and lines of descent.

Nor was the interest in and identification with patriarch and patrilineage confined to biblical or sacred history. If the earliest history of the Hebrews concentrated on the begetting of the generations, that of the Germanic peoples (and their medieval descendents) ran in a similar vein. The genealogies incorporated into the Anglo-Saxon Chronicle or preserved in the early king lists were designed to help mark the passing of time by means of a tally of regnal lives and accessions, along with or instead of the more fleeting secular years. Such "histories" usually stressed the divine origin of royal families, often fusing the Norse gods of pagan mythology with biblical champions and quasi-historical ancestors on the same patrilineal chain. By their tendency to legitimate any individual who gained the throne—by grafting him to a proper branch of the tree, regardless of his "real" paternity and descent—these mythopoiec histories offered a picture of lineal continuity that transcended history and appeared as a near-perfect version of patrilineal descent. Specious and imaginative father-son links were forged, perhaps long after the stark facts of deposition, murder, or adoption, and they were welded to the main structure so as to show few if any flaws. A critical social purpose was being achieved, regardless of such mundane realities as usurpation and regicide, and regardless of whether the putative ancestor was Woden, Noah, or Cerdic of Wessex. Names changed, historical circumstances and heroes varied, but patrilineal generation remained a fixed point in the shifting seas of demography, of political fortune, and of dynastic and internecine family feuds.

Given the importance of these links, for both internal reasons of self-image and identity and for the practical or external ones of property and social hierarchy, it is not hard to follow the trail of the fifteenth-century patrilineage, and to chart it along some straight courses and around some bends of the road. "You shall be fruitful and multiply" was a political and social injunction as well as a blessing bestowed in anticipation, a reward in realization. We know that in the many controversies affecting monarchy and royal succession, the service of history, of genealogy, and of heraldry could be ingeniously (and often disingenuously) summoned. In those disputes over the proper course of royal succession—amazingly common in England and France, given the public nature of the matter—the heavy machinery of patrilineal descent and birth right was slowly, albeit majestically, wheeled out, accompanied by a great groaning of rusty wheels and legal clamor.[3] By the fifteenth century such devices as the private or family cartulary or the coats of arms and shields emblazoned around the burial chapel could be called upon to play a part in a given family's search for a convincing tale of descent and succession. All the flamboyant products of family propaganda, created with an eye upon the earlier glories and triumphs of the line, were simultaneously presented to boost its claims for the present and the future. We can still look upon such fifteenth-century statements as the Rous Roll, an exceptionally handsome (and extant) representative of this genre.[4] Heraldry could be used for equally flamboyant assertions of lineage. The Chaucer tomb at Ewelme provides a powerful variation on this proud theme. On its four sides were displayed no fewer than 24 different shields, ranging in social grandiloquence from such pedestrian origins as Roet, or Roet impaling Burghersh of Ewelme, to France and England with John of Gaunt impaling Roet, or France and England quartered with Beaufort silver azure, or England with label silver for Brotherton and Mowbray impaling Neville.[5] The Cobham family made a similar statement about ancestry and collective bonding, literally in brass. Their church at

Cobham, Kent, boasts the "best series of coherent brasses in England," including the monuments of Thomas (d. 1367), John, III lord Cobham (d. 1408), Margaret (d. 1395), Maude (d. 1380), Margaret (d. 1375), John, II lord Cobham (d. 1354), Rauf (d. 1402), and lady Joan (d. 1433) with two of her five husbands: Sir Reginald Braybrooke (d. 1405) and Sir Nicholas Hauberk (d. 1407).[6]

The point is well if mutely made. Nor is there reason to see such hyperbolic declarations as anything other than serious, even if not wholly honest. The chain of the patrilineage had to have some flexibility, given its importance and the strains it might be called upon to bear. We are sometimes prone to focus more on the exceptions to patrilineal descent than upon its customary course with its heavy bias towards the eldest son. True, there were the unusual cases, ones wherein a determined father and/or his determined (and younger) son could "beat the system" to some extent. Such cases sometimes receive scholarly attention, perhaps out of proportion to their typicality, though such activity is really more concerned with land than with ideology.[7] The links of the traditional chain were constantly being reforged. Some adaptability could be allowed and even accepted, though most variations had to exist within the traditional parameters. The good old cause could be stymied from time to time, but rarely so openly or so boldly as to encourage antinomian aspirations from such dubious outsiders as illegitimate children and sons-in-law.

The patrilineal line, from father to son, and the way in which mores and behavior were shaped to strengthen the legal and biological foundations of this construct, is our subject. Though fifteenth-century fathers could (and often did) move to counter the simple force of primogeniture, as by means of such legal stratagems as uses and enfeoffments, the old and uncomplicated model invariably remained the normal one. It continued to govern most behavior and most ideology. And even when we look at men who acted to dilute or to counter the force of primogeniture and the normal dynamic or direction of the patrilineage, we see men who are usually responding to some excess of biological or genealogical riches, that is, men who were working to steer the birth-right toward some son other than the eldest, or perhaps to divide it among a number of sons, or to delay the moment of unitary transmission. They could play their game—and a serious game indeed—because there were sons to spare. Such men rarely engaged in their endeavors merely to ignore their sons in favor of other relatives, let alone non-relatives. The wayward behavior of such fathers is explicable as a kind of freedom they had earned because of their successful compliance with the first law of the family, that of being fruitful and of producing sons unto the next generation. Death, social custom, and worldly obligations imposed a relatively simply set of alternatives upon any actual family, and the bulk of the fifteenth-century evidence about paternal behavior argues that most men, regardless of their own birth order, accepted that the world did and would continue to move from father to eldest son. Where the transmission of property counted for so much, and where it mainly moved along pre-ordained lines, others—even favored younger sons or daughters—could rarely be more than outsiders, the next-but-one in the queue of the patrilineage.[8]

To a great extent the creation and preservation of the patrilineage was about real property, as well as about demography and fertility. The father held the patrimony, and its transmission was usually covered by primogeniture, leavened on occasion by some idiosyncratic admixture of personal disposition and preference. The continuity of the patrilineage was also a matter of authority: paternalism, revealed at times in its most traditional (and often most unpleasant) sense, as we saw above in the statement about *pater* and authority.[9] "Fathers and sons" is a phrase conveying an element of solidarity and cooperation, of inter-generational solidarity and of "us" against "them." It can also serve to convey the strains of coercion and authoritarianism, or of rebellion and of mutual antagonism and hostility. Genealogical bonds, inheritance, and social control were all too readily bound within the single institution that shaped virtually all aspects of family and personal life. The hold of the father upon the wife and the children was many-sided. It no doubt emanated from or originated in his control of property as well as in his supposed physical superiority and that authority bestowed, in many cultures, upon age and survival. In some dawn of history, in the oak forests of Tacitus's Germany, or in the nomadic gyrations of Abraham and Lot, or in the legal domination of the Roman *paterfamilias*, such forces had grown into immensely powerful ones. In fifteenth-century England there were some limits, of course, upon the momentum of patriarchy. But our argument here concerns the customary mesh of ideology, practice, and behavior that usually carried the day: we should not focus unduly upon those outermost boundaries of anti-social willfulness or of the desperate rebellion of youth against age. On the other hand there were checks and balances, though they might not have been apparent to a casual observer. Paternal control over many aspects of marriage was regulated by canon as well as by common law, and there was no Tarpeian rock, no recognized and condoned infanticide or bondage or debt-prostitution for extra daughters, or at least not as accepted social and familial institutions.[10] But on the other hand, most bourgeois aspects of marital choice, of vocational and professional inclination, and of outward behavior, were well within the aegis of paternal concern, if not necessarily of effective control. Last wills offer eloquent testimony to the weight of the conditions a father could place posthumously upon his sons and daughters. The dead father, like the prince of the medieval aphorism, could have a long arm.

To forge a successful patrilineal chain one had to begin by hammering together a sufficient number of links of direct father-son inheritance to run through a number of generations or a given span of time. By definition, a patrilineage posits fathers and sons. For our purposes we define a family chain as being of adequate length if it roughly covered the course of the fifteenth century. Such a chain usually needed between three and five men, standing to each other in direct patrilineal father-son descent. This requisite was the simplest biological factor, without which succession or transmission could not begin. Such a chain may seem like a simple one, a social fact primarily defined and governed by biological factors. In reality what we are seeing is a socially formulated entity—one that accords with the western model of a family through time, and existing long before and long after the fifteenth century—but nevertheless one that only assumed its primal position because of a social or cultural consensus arrived at and accepted over the centuries.

Our interests here do not lie with just demography and genealogy. If biological success (as socially defined) was a *sine qua non*, it was still only one segment of the patriarchal circle. Two other ingredients were often found, though in varying and generally in lesser degrees, before the tale of a genealogy could approach the length of that which opened Matthew's Gospel. The first was that vital satellite of biological success, good luck, or what we might refer to as a family's ability to hold onto or return to some share of secular fortune. It means not just having a son and heir—whether he was the only son or the first (and the preferred) of a brood of a dozen or more—but also working to ensure that the said son and heir could avoid the sort of catastrophes that might wipe out the line, or that might leave it alive but in drastically reduced circumstances. As a social institution, the patriarchal family and the patrilineage were vulnerable to perils beyond those of simple and stark mortality. To survive the rigors of infant mortality and of childhood, only to fall as an adult before a sentence of treason, forfeiture, and attainder, or on the battlefield in the company of one's brothers and sons, was hardly the high road to family continuity.[11] Sons might be forthcoming and survive, biologically, but if they allowed the family's place of honor to deteriorate from the castle to the hovel, they had hardly done their proper share. Genealogical or patrilineal continuity might not be ended by such social demotion, by the loss of a peerage or some lesser social and economic counterpart, but it was so disfigured that it could hardly hope to be received with much honor in its old haunts. A basic element of the whole concept of patriarchy—resting firmly atop the patrilineal tale—is that the flocks be not too sorely diminished, that the birth right and patrimony transmitted unto the next generation be no less than what one had originally received. The paternal blessings that bound the generations of the patriarchs of Israel make abundantly clear this economic aspect of birthright. If the patriarchy and the patrilineage were killed stone dead by sterility, they were also severely crippled by downward social mobility. Families could deliberately work to counter secular ill luck, just as they could fight to rise in the world. We will look, below, at some efforts to manipulate the tides of fortune and to erect bulkheads against some of its worst assaults and most erosive currents.

In addition to demographic luck and secular luck, there was another and more positive aspect to the deliberate human contribution that helped preserve the patrilineage. Nature could be reinforced by art, to and even beyond the point of manipulation. Fathers and their families developed and cultivated behavior, rules, and traditions that in turn fostered the very concept of ties and continuity between fathers and sons from generation to generation, between the living and the dead, between the main patrilineal trunk and the branches on which we find the siblings and collateral kin. Such institutions and practices became time-honored, family bonding mechanisms. They gave a common identity, a unity and a heritage to those within, one not shared with others, those without. They were neither secret nor particularly arcane, but within each family such a resevoir of practices—of common burial sites, of elaborate and precise prayers for dead ancestors, of traditional ecclesiastical recipients for family largesse, and of the explicit transmission of family heirlooms—also contributed towards the larger and more enduring goal. In aggregate, these social devices could create an inheritance comprising the intangible and the evocative, as well as of the temporal and the mundane. Such constructs helped place each man, each recipient of the patrimony, at some appropriate post along the course of the patrilineal chain, and they confirmed the two-way sense of direction that united those who had gone with those yet to come. The construct of family tradition added meaning to each individual life, just as it created a larger solidarity. It dignified and magnified the obligations that had to be shouldered into the future, as each generation saw itself standing between its fathers and its sons.

∗   ∗   ∗

Without the aid of benevolent nature (however that was defined by any given society) little could be accomplished: some sort of biological clay had to prefigure the brick of social artifice. What success did fifteenth-century fathers actually have in begetting those sons who would carry name, property, and projected self forward in time? Various kinds of data exist to help analyze this question. Some helpful and relevant material, covering a statistically significant universe of fathers and families, can be culled from four collections of fifteenth-century Inquisitions Post Mortem. These four sets of inquisitions are particularly useful, being available in print and each being fairly comprehensive in scope. Altogether they cover almost 1,000 men of property. The four sets cover the inquisitions of Yorkshire landholders between 1399 and 1422, of Nottinghamshire landholders between 1399 and 1485, of Lancashire landholders between 1399 and 1509, and of men collected into a centralized volume for the early years of Henry VII, 1485–1500.[12] If we exclude the Inquisitions held for widows' lands, those documents concerned with proof of age, the inquisitions which unaccountably fail to give the requisite information, and the occasional odd or miscellaneous document, we still have material covering, respectively, 107, 122, 103, and 645 men. From this considerable data base we can look for information about replacement rates and about the incidence or likelihood of direct father-son links.

The purpose of the Inquisitions Post Mortem was to establish the identity and the age of the heir of the recently deceased holder of the real property, as well as the extent of the property and the terms and feudal obligations under which it was held. Though there are some scholarly caveats regarding the value of the inquisitions, we should resist the temptation to laugh at a medieval record document that purports to convey precise information.[13] The Inquisitions have been belittled because of their formulaic phrases that report the mnemotechnic feats of the witnesses, as well as for their predilection for round numbers and for the heavy reliance upon such stock expressions as ". . . et amplius" in giving ages. But in most Inquisitions—and those under scrutiny here are typical of the entire genre—the age of the heir is usually reported with some precision when the precise determination of that age was of critical importance, as with a minor, or in the case of an heir just at the threshold of legal age. The tendency of the data to fade out in favor of vaguely reported ages was generally confined to data on heirs and heiresses who were clearly and indisputably of their majority. Consequently, while our reliance upon the tireless resort to such phrases as "21 and more," or "30 and more" is only trustworthy in a manner of degree, it seems sufficiently accurate for rough calculations. Furthermore, when the exact familial relationship between the deceased landholder and the heir or next-of-kin is a genuine issue, the jurors frequently display considerable genealogical acumen in unraveling relationships extending to such outer circles as second cousins once-removed, or to great-nieces and great-nephews. Given different conceptual approaches to precision and to the purpose of numerical accuracy, our inclination in the discussion below is to accept the ages and the relationships as given in the Inquisitions, especially when the intermediate genealogical links are worked out. After all, despite their obvious shortcomings, the jurors' returns had to satisfy the conflicting interests of heirs, of the would-be holders of wardships, of the curiosity of informed and gossip-prone neighbors, and of the scepticism of the crown officials.

When nature had been generous, the determination of a man's immediate heir was a simple enough business. As far as the transmission of real property and the fixing of socio-political responsibility went, a surviving son, or a grandson—the son of an older but now deceased son—sufficed. Failing such an heir, the next concentric circle of kinship beyond the son (and alternatively other sons and their male children), embraced daughters and daughters' children. The girls would partition the patrimonial estates: the resort to females meant the end of the patrilineage and, if there were more than one, perhaps the end of the unified patrimony. After children (of either sex) came siblings—first a brother, of course, or his son, and then the sisters and their children (of either sex). Then, in what we may consider as the fourth circle, were the other heirs, if needed and if available: aunts and uncles, nieces and nephews, and cousins of all degrees and definitions. And finally, in a fifth and most remote orbit, were the few instances of men dying without known or knowable heirs.

A series of jurors' phrases, found in the Lancashire Inquisitions but quite typical of any of the published collections, sums up the journey from the center of our solar system to its outermost and coldest orbits. For the fortunate there would just be an identification of the "filius et propinquior heres."[14] Beyond that, in at least the warmest circle of failure, was the "consanguinis et propinquior heres," which may have been the same as but kinder than "Thomas obiit sine herede de corpore suo exeunte."[15] Bleaker still, we have the deceased landholder who was "fuit bastardus et sine herede obiit."[16] And lastly, he of whom it had to be said, "de herede ignorant."[17] These alternatives, in descending order, pretty much summed up the world. *King Lear* can be seen as a poetic treatise written to warn us against these alternatives.

Such a gradation or hierarchy of relationships is little different from our own, whatever social uses it may serve today (or then). In terms of physical or biological procreation, the first two circles—those of son and of daughter(s)—are both pertinent. But in terms of patrilineage, as the basic element from which the molecules of patriarchal continuity were constructed, there is only the first circle, the world of the son and/or, if need be, his son. Table I-1 shows the identity or relationship of heirs of the deceased property holders as they were named on the four sets of Inquisitions, in addition to the stated age of the heir at the moment of death and inheritance. The son-and-heir not only represented the model family link, but he was by far the most common form of bond, the modal bond.[18] Sons succeeded their fathers in 72 percent of all the instances we can tally, and sons' sons were called upon an additional 4 percent of the time. This gives a combined replacement rate, for direct male heirs, of 76 percent. It is a very respectable figure, and it illustrates that the model of and the ideology about the patrilineal succession (and for the biological success upon which it was dependent) were not wildly unrealistic. Daughters and their children only figured in 9 percent of the instances of succession, while other male relatives were named 10 percent of the time, other females but 5 percent. Combining sons, grandsons, daughters and daughters' direct heirs, the rate of direct succession by a child or a grandchild of a deceased land-holder was 85 percent, or in about five cases of every six. This is a fairly impressive success or replacement ratio.

TABLE I-1   HEIRS AS NAMED IN THE INQUISITIONS POST MORTEM, BY AGE AND
RELATIONSHIP

Relationship	1–10	11–20	21–30	30+	Total	
		Age at succession				
Son	136	192	327	163	818	72%
Son's son	16	17	12	2	47	4%
Daughter(s) and her children	42	27	15	18	102	9%
Other male heir	3	26	24	61	114	10%
Other female heir	4	11	7	29	51	5%
Total	201	273	385	273	1132	
	18%	24%	34%	24%		

The sons who directly succeeded (along with the few grandson heirs) are our subject in this chapter, and the lesser and worsening family alternatives will be covered below. At first glance, sons seem not hard to come by. They were born, and a goodly number seem to have survived, that is, at least to have outlived their fathers. The 72 percent succession rate for direct father-son inheritance over such a large number of cases compares favorably with those reported by other studies of such phenomena. Manorial records from various points in the fourteenth and fifteenth centuries show that some other groups of male tenants were followed by sons in a comparable proportion of instances. At Thorney 38 percent of the tenants had no sons alive and able to receive their holdings, while 29 percent were childless. In another tally, of 48 men at Thorney, 26 had sons who were of or near legal age, 4 had sons who were very young, 4 were known to have had no sons, 9 had daughters, and in 5 cases the heir was unknown.[19] Nor do the replacement rates we derive from aggregating our numbers appear to hide any particularly unrepresentative or atypical results. The four separate sets of Inquisitions all hover about the aggregate mean rates. The ratios as calculated from each set of inquisitions are roughly similar. Neither does the spread across the century and across the face of the realm give any serious suggestion of changes or differences, either in time or because of regional or provincial peculiarities.

However, all is not as peaceful as might appear. Any given Inquisition Post Mortem shows us the nature of the link between two generations of a family at *one* particular moment: the data of the inquisition were diachronic. At an inquest, concern focused upon who followed whom into the property upon a given day. But we are concerned with patrilineal replacement within a specified family across a larger chronological canvas, not just on the day reported in the Inquisition, and we are interested in moving synchronically from heir to heir. As such, we have to take into account a series of chronological links in their chain. This approach, with its eye upon more data and more questions, offers a picture of family succession and continuity that is often much less sanguine than those reflected in the data of Table I-1.

Our earlier statistics tend to flatter the incidence of patrilineal continuity and to exaggerate the likelihood of succession and of transmission directly from father to son. Since the Inquisitions were only directed to identify the family link at the moment of transmission, the search properly ended with the identification of a son. Obviously there could be no future eye for what would happen to that son, in terms either of his own survival or his subsequent score in the game of parenthood. But the approach of "who was the heir on the day he died, and what was the heir's age," is of little use in terms of charting the ongoing fortunes of any particular family, or any group of patrilineages through time. The jurors who presented the material that has been incorporated into the surviving documents had no care for our patrilineal quest and for whether a given father-son link was part of a specific family's series of such links that might stretch back for several generations, a real line as we see it in the genealogical or biblical sense. A look at the fortunes enjoyed (or suffered) by some fifteenth-century aristocratic families in their efforts to forge their patrilineal chains, will show that while the odds in favor of single father-son transmission may have roughly stood at three to one, they dropped dramatically when we look at two or three or four successive points of transmission. By the time we come to the third or fourth link in the chain the gods of patrilineal fortune were apt to have lost interest; the odds now began to run strongly against *yet another* direct male of a predecessor's body. Immediate father-son succession for three or more generations became a difficult, if not an exceptional model for a given family, and only the occasional patrilineage had the luck (sometimes compounded by skill) to follow such a coveted lead.

The wide distinction between the presence of a son in one instance of a generational turn-over and his continuing presence as part of a series of such transitions becomes clearer when we look at the age of the direct male heirs named in the Inquisitions. The local jury that furnished the information at the inquest had the obligation of identifying the heir by name, of ascertaining his (or her) relationship with the deceased, and of giving the heir's age(s). Since the purpose of establishing age was to determine whether the heir was of legal age and ready to take control of the real property and its concomitant obligations, when the answer was clearly affirmative, there was less need for precise information, as we indicated above, and the formulaic statements and the rounding of ages appear but are of limited significance. *But* when the heir was a minor, with an imminent wardship, precision counted. The presence of various countervailing interests makes it likely that the length of minority (or the age of the minor heir) be stated with clarity and within the circumference of acceptable numerical accuracy. The heir's own impatience to recover the patrimony was balanced by the interest of others in retaining the land in wardship. As a result of the various compensating pushes and pulls, something near "the truth" probably emerged. And if we look at the male heirs in terms of their age at the time of succession, we get some insight into the way in which the original—and quite healthy—odds in favor of direct father-son inheritance were steadily eroded by demographic facts that we have no reason to think were anything but common, everyday ones in late medieval society.

Table I-2 and Figure I-1 give an analysis of the age distribution of sons and grandsons at the moment of their inheritance. The ages are shown here in five-year categories so as to provide a more detailed analysis than in Table I-1.

TABLE I-2   SUCCESSION BY DIRECT MALE HEIRS BY AGE OF HEIR, BY SETS OF INQUISITIONS

| | Age at succession | | | | | | |
	1–5	6–10	11–15	16–20	21–29	30+	Total
By a son							
Yorkshire	8	13	10	12	14	10	67
Nottingham	9	11	14	6	23	17	80
Lancashire	4	7	13	3	23	27	77
Chancery	40	44	62	72	104	109	431
Totals	61	75	99	93	164	163	655
By a grandson							
Yorkshire	—	—	1	1	1	—	3
Nottingham	—	—	—	—	2	—	2
Lancashire	—	—	2	2	2	1	7
Chancery	2	14	4	7	7	1	35
Totals	2	14	7	10	12	2	47

FIGURE I-1 AGES OF SONS AT SUCCESSION, BY SETS OF INQUISITIONS[a]

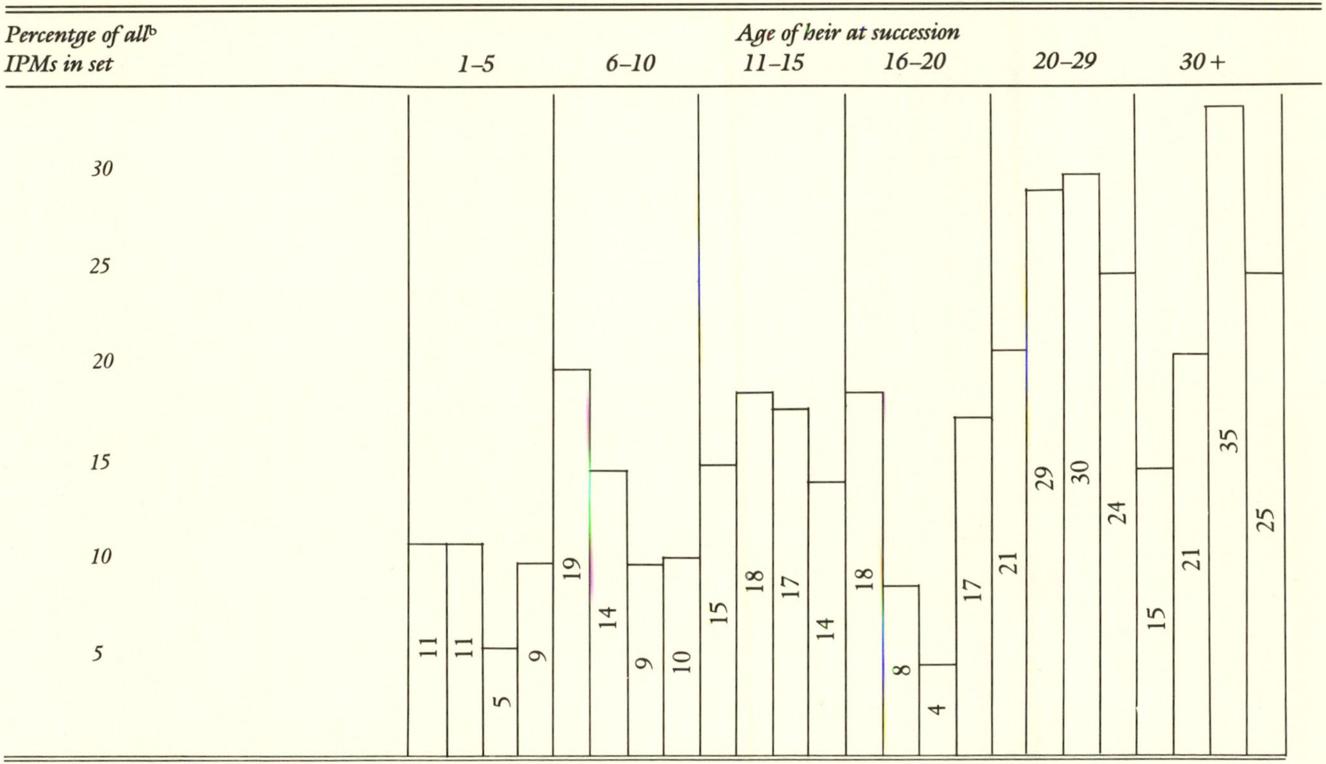

[a] The respective order of the sets of Inquisitions is Yorkshire, Nottinghamshire, Lancashire, and Chancery.
[b] Totals of percentages, because of rounding, do not always equal 100%.

It seems reasonable to argue that the younger the heir at the moment of inheritance, the less likely he himself would eventually be to survive to father, in turn, his own children, the children who hopefully would be of legal age when he himself died. And conversely, the older the heir the more likely he already was, at the point of entry into the inheritance, to be or soon to become the middle link of a successful and ongoing, three-generation patrilineal chain. Table I-2 shows that half the sons named as heirs were not yet of legal age: 328 of the 655, or precisely 50 percent, were named in the Inquisition as being less than 21. And of this pool of 328 minor heirs, a large fraction (136 of 328, or 41 percent) were identified in the Inquistion as being aged 10 or less, 59 percent (192 of 328)as being between ages 11 and 20. Research into individual families reveals that many of these minors did indeed grow up to live full lives (at least in a quantitative sense) and to produce sons who would survive to succeed them.[20] However, in aggregate, the chances are that we are left with a next generation comprised of many young heirs who would die young and be without (male) heirs of their own bodies when their time came. Perhaps the ratio of successful links, for the 328 minor heirs named in the Inquisitions, was again in the neighborhood of two-thirds, just as our full complement of 964 men of property had surviving sons in roughly two instances of every three. So youth, as a factor, entered the tale of patrilineal succession in some indeterminate fashion, but pretty surely to dilute or to qualify the ratio of successful father-son transmissions that had seemed so impressive at first glance. The age of the fathers themselves is of little direct concern nor was it given—except by inference—in the Inquisitions. However, we can assume that most of the men who died with minor heirs—whether such heirs were sons, daughters, or brothers—were apt to have been in their mid-40s, at the most, while many must have barely been of legal age at their death. Given the early age of marriage and for the beginning of procreation, especially among the sons and daughters of the propertied classes, the logic of this conclusion can be refuted in many individual cases, no doubt, but it gains momentum when we deal with hundreds and hundreds of instances, as we are doing here.

There was some variation among the different sets of Inquisitions regarding heirs' ages (as shown in Figure I-1). In the Yorkshire material, heirs under age 10 represented 30 percent of the total group, and all sons under legal majority amounted to a full 64 percent (43 of 67 heirs). This was the highest proportion of minor-age heirs we encounter. For the Inquisitions from Nottinghamshire, Lancashire, and those calendared in the Chancery records, the percentages for age categories 1–10 and 11–20 were 25 and 26 percent, 14 and 21 percent, and 19 and 31 percent respectively. In aggregate, sons aged 1–5 inherited 9 percent of the time, sons aged 6–10 12 percent, those of 11–15 14 percent, and those aged 16–20 13 percent. Youth was more than served: It was offered golden opportunities, much more frequently than either family continuity, the administrative and fiscal health of the estates, or the family's political place in the sun could wish for. While most of those heirs who came into their inheritance when aged between 16 and 20 probably lived to marry and to have at least a good chance of father-hood, what obstacles must have awaited those boys named as heirs in the inquisitions with such identifications as being one-half year and more, or "20 weeks and 4 days and more," or "either 32 weeks or 35 weeks."[21] When these considerations are put alongside the 261 daughters and other heirs shown in Table I-1 (27 percent of the grand total), our sanguine views about high father-son replacement rates and patrilineal success fade a bit. If the odds were always that a given father would be followed by a son (or a son's son), probability stopped well short of a guarantee. Moreover, success at the moment of transmission was hardly, by itself, an assurance of lineal continuity.

In half the cases of father-son succession, the son was a minor. Grand-sons, by whom we only mean the son of the now-deceased eldest son (for children of daughters are a sub-set contained within the category of daughter-heiresses), were minors in 70 percent of the relatively few cases where they figure: 33 of 47, and under age 10 in 16 of these instances. Where daughters or their children were the heirs—in 92 cases (10 percent of the total universe of the four sets of Inquisitions Post Mortem)—they too were usually minors. So the overall conclusion seems to be that biology—always as defined by society, rather than by remote or abstract laws of nature—gave patriarchy and the patrilineage enough momentum so that the social model was a difficult but, with some luck, a not wholly unrealistic aspira-tion. Families could expect to see the son succeed the father *most* of the time. That the son was equally likely to be below full age as he was to be above was a problem that only time and future circumstances (or good fortune) could unravel. But at least the societal and biblical model, if not invariably or readily achieved, was well this side of a utopian standard of virility and survival. A longer chain was perhaps a real if distant possibility. After all, fathers did frequently beget sons.

The genealogies and the king lists of barbarian Europe were written after the fact, and edited to emphasize (or to fantasize) continuity and patrilineal success. They often fabricated legitimacy and longevity, and to realize their political ends they were so woven as to accommodate outsiders and collateral kin within their lists and branches. Where information is available, we can sometimes decipher this policy of inclusive obfuscation. For the aristocracy of the fifteenth-century—relatively well recorded and well studied—we have much more detailed information regarding vital statistics, identities, and succession. We can also look at a fairly large number of families. Data on the fifteenth-century peerage permit a close analysis of the patrilineal success (or failure) rate of each line "begun" by a peer, counting from his first summons to the House of Lords after the accession of Henry IV in 1399 (regardless whether he was actually the first man in terms of his own family's prior chain). How many of these peers were able to transmit title and patrimony directly from father to son through the course of the century? Even this basic question admits of some complications. To tally father-son-grandson succession, in a direct line, is obviously the simplest and most successful or desirable route. But even seemingly successful families sometimes had to deviate. If a man died without children and his brother succeeded him, this would represent the end of the first man's direct line. But, as we can see by hindsight, this was not the case for his (dead) father's line. *That* chain of patrilineage was now being preserved and continued by a younger son (and perhaps by that son's own line). And after this wrinkle, what about those instances in which the next heir was a male first cousin? The line of the common grandfather was still intact, though some shorter ones had come and gone. No wonder early medieval chroniclers and annalists just slipped Anglo-Saxon kings into the record as sons, whatever the lost or unspoken genealogical verities might have been. Figure I-2a,b,c offer some case studies of the three obvious permutations. Figure I-2a gives a schematic example of a patrilineal chain that endured through our years without problems (as exemplified by the Percies), Figure I-2b of the next-best-alternative route (with the Fitzalan earls of Arundel as the example), while Figure I-2c displays failure and eventual termination (as in the case of Beauchamp earls of Warwick). And since we have been talking in grim tones, the indirectly linked patrilineage (as in Figure I-2b) must count as failure, just as surely as the total termination of the male line (as in Figure I-2c).

In explanatory terms, simplest is best. Did families survive, and were successful patrilineal chains common—in contrast to separate instances of successful father-son transmission? When he surveyed the data on the survival of late medieval aristocratic families in this period, Bruce McFarlane

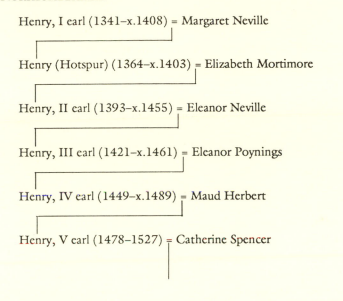

Henry, I earl (1341–x.1408) = Margaret Neville

Henry (Hotspur) (1364–x.1403) = Elizabeth Mortimore

Henry, II earl (1393–x.1455) = Eleanor Neville

Henry, III earl (1421–x.1461) = Eleanor Poynings

Henry, IV earl (1449–x.1489) = Maud Herbert

Henry, V earl (1478–1527) = Catherine Spencer

[a] Here and below, x. = died by violence.

FIGURE I-2B COLLATERAL SUCCESSION—THE FITZALAN EARLS OF ARUNDEL

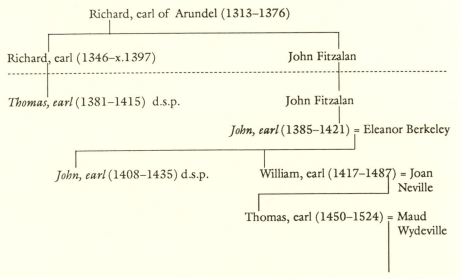

Richard, earl of Arundel (1313–1376)

Richard, earl (1346–x.1397)   John Fitzalan

Thomas, earl (1381–1415) d.s.p.   John Fitzalan

John, earl (1385–1421) = Eleanor Berkeley

John, earl (1408–1435) d.s.p.   William, earl (1417–1487) = Joan Neville

Thomas, earl (1450–1524) = Maud Wydeville

FIGURE I-2c THE END OF MALE SUCCESSION—THE BEAUCHAMP EARLS OF
WARWICK

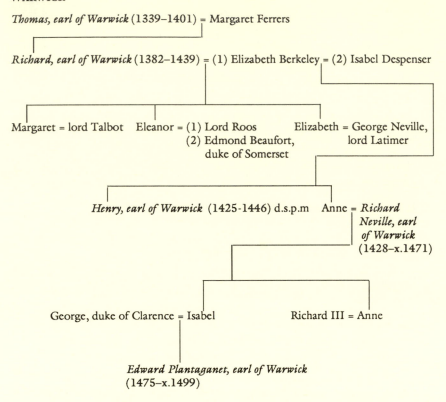

remarked on "the transitoriness of male lines," and his analysis goes into
the matter in some detail: "On the average during the period 1300–1500, a
quarter of the [aristocratic] families . . . became extinct in the direct male
line every twenty-five years; in fact just over 27 percent."[22] Though this is a
rather awkward way of expressing the conclusion, since it tallies the patrilineage in terms of chronological divisions rather than by personal or intergenerational milestones, it can stand as our most considered conclusion.
While some families lasted and lasted, others entered, played a short scene
or two (perhaps with but a single actor, as we shall see), and then left the
stage, never to return. New figures (and new families) were always ready
to make an entrance. *De novo* peerages meant the introduction of men,

sometimes the younger sons and brothers of older or existing peers, with new claims. There were also those newcomers whose legal claims rested on marriages to the heiresses—the daughters (and their children) who were called forward in 10 percent of the instances of transmission shown in the Inquisitions—because of the continuous and constant termination of the direct male lines. The mortality here was of patrilineal lines, of male-linked families, not just of individuals. When a man died without male children, there may have been strong political and economic considerations in favor of keeping the peerage alive and militating for its transmission to (and then via) a daughter. Very often in this century her husband and ultimately her children were named as her father's successors in the peerage and to the patrimony.[23] But, as we said in discussing the Inquisitions Post Mortem, while this second-best alternative served some important political and economic purposes, it had nothing to do with patrilineal reckoning and the preservation of the patriarchy. If there were no sons, then there were no sons: The tale was over. The would-be father of male children had failed. He had failed himself, and he had failed his own father. In addition, he had betrayed those more distant progenitors who had begotten him.

There is little reason to think the fifteenth-century peers were any less fertile than other groups of the day. Sporadic scholarly comments about aristocratic sterility, due to systematic in-breeding and the degeneration of the stock, remain unconvincing (if not politically offensive). We need stronger evidence, based on firmer data than are likely to turn up, before we accept that the nobility of late medieval England "inherited a greater disposition toward sterility than the population as a whole."[24]

There was also the possibility that the Wars of the Roses, with their effusive blood shedding, led to a mass extinction of aristocratic lines. This interpretation is now generally discarded and discredited, though we caution against total dismissal, at least pending a further discussion below.[25] For the time being we will ignore the political causes and ramifications of family mortality, and simply look at the record of patrilineal continuity displayed by these aristocratic families. They offer us a well-documented group—one for whom succession and inheritance were critical and therefore apt to be well recorded, their disputed cases and claims well aired.

Our examination certainly reveals the rapacious nature of late medieval mortality statistics, when they are calculated from the perspective of specific families and their continuity. The picture is considerably worse than the calculation of replacement rates, based solely on the Inquisitions

Post Mortem. Of the families (or patrilineal chains) comprising the fifteenth-century peerage—beginning our count for each line with the first male summoned after Henry IV's accession—very few lasted in a direct father-son chain to or beyond 1500. This is the case for numerous men (and lines) who were only summoned for the first time at some point well after 1399: Even the shorter run was beyond many of them. Most lines and families who got through at all to 1500 had to resort to at least one use of a collateral male line, a device that ended the patrilineal chain as we have defined it, by the Procrustean criteria that only accepted the model of Figure I-2a and rejected the alternative of Figure I-2b. Straight father-to-son succession for a full century was rare. Many more of our lines came to a dead end, in terms of male continuity and transmission, than were able to thrust themselves forward.

Demographic fortune and secular luck were perhaps especially necessary for the peers, and for those near them, atop the social pyramid. High rank carried certain dangers from which lesser men and lesser families were apt to be sheltered. The incidence of death in battle and of death from political execution hardly made it easier for the peers to raise those sons who in turn would live to repeat their performance unto the next generation. Of the peerage families, that is, of the patrilineal lines represented by the men summoned to the House of Lords at Henry IV's accession parliament of September, 1399, only some dozen or so went all the way through to 1500 by dint of a direct chain of father-son links. Some of the families had a fairly easy time of it: the Greys of Wilton, with three men, just about sufficed, running from Richard, VI lord (1393–1442), through his grandson George (c. 1450–1499). The earls of Shrewsbury had little trouble, despite the death of the first Talbot earl in France in 1453, and four males in direct succession sufficed to span the years between the earl's first summons (as lord Furnival, because of marriage to the Furnival heiress) in 1409 and his great grandson's death in 1537. Some of those families who went the distance got through by virtue of a resort to a grandfather-grandson succession, falling back on that (acceptable) alternative when an intermediate son had predeceased his father. When Reynold, III lord Grey of Ruthyn, died in 1440, his son and heir John was already dead. But John's son Edmund was already aged 25 and quite ready to step in. Edmund lived a long life, and at his death in 1490 his second son and heir was available, by now long of legal age and in service until his own death in 1503.

Table I-3   Families with Father-Son Succession Through the Fifteenth Century

Family	Men in the chain (total life years)	First birth–Last death	Ages	Average age	Number of violent deaths
Audley	5 (126)	1371–1497[a]	37, 61, 70, 37	51	2, 4
Beaumont	3 (127)	1380–1507	23, 51, 69	48	2
Clifford	4 (135)	1388–1523	34, 41, 26, 69	43	1, 2
Fitzhugh	5 (155)	1358–1513	67, 53, 45, 29, 27	44	—
Grey of Ruthin	3 (141)	1362–1503	78, 75, 40[b]	64	—
Grey of Wilton	3 (106)	1393–1499[a]	49, 73, 39	54	—
Percy	5 (186)[c]	1341–1527	67, 62, 40, 40, 49[b]	52	1, 2, 3
De Vere	4 (173)	1340–1513	60, 32, 54, 71	54	3
Scrope of Bolton	6 (179)	1327–1506	76, 33, 26, 41, 60, 38	46	—
Talbot	4 (154)	1384–1538	69, 47, 25, 70	53	1, 2
Stafford	4 (143)	1378–1521	25, 58, 28, 43	39	1, 2, 3
Zouche	4 (153)	1373–1526	42, 59, 36, 67	51	—

[a] These lines ended so close to 1500 that we have taken a slight liberty.

[b] These lines resorted to one instance of a grandfather-grandson transmission.

[c] This does not include Hotspur (x 1403), the link between the first and the second men shown in the table.

Thanks to some impressive longevity and to good luck, three families spanned the century with but three men: father, son, and grandson. Counting from the birth of the grandfather through the death of the grandson, the three Beaumont lords lasted 127 years, three earls of Oxford 128. The Greys of Ruthin needed three men to cover the four generations, as we have seen, and the four together spanned 106 years between Reynold's birth in 1362 and his great grandson's death in 1503. Most of the successful family chains had four men, and some of the four-man lines ran a good bit longer in chronological terms than did those with but three links. The Talbots lived to cover 154 years, the Staffords 143, the lords Zouche 153. The lords Fitzhugh needed five men to get through the century in a direct series of father-son steps, as did the Percies of Northumberland (who also had a sixth man, Hotspur, as the link between the I and the II earl): the Fitzhugh men covered 155 years from the first birth to the last death, the Percies 186. The Scropes of Bolton needed six men, though the long fourteenth-century span of the first lord (1327–1403) stretched out their total years to 179. Many of these families also had some considerable share of secular luck atop their demographic fortune: a number of violent deaths, accompanied in some instances by sentences of treason, attainder, and forfeiture, but all eventually straightened out by an heir who was able to catch the king's eye and to regain his "rightful place."[26] Though the Staffords had to weather four violent deaths they still survived into the reign of Henry VIII without a break in their direct male succession. The Percies also had four such deaths among the fathers (plus that of Hotspur, in 1403), the Cliffords three such deaths in immediate succession (coming in 1422, 1455, and 1461), the Talbots two.

Longevity of the individual members of the line apparently had but little to do with the family's collective grip on continuity. For the peers, at least, with marriage usually around if not before the point of legal age, fatherhood was probably coeval with or antecedent to political maturity and independence. Thus even the younger men included in the lists of Table I-3 had sufficient chronological and marital opportunity to do their patrilineal duty: had they not, they would not figure here. Death in the mid-20s could put the patrilineage in jeopardy, but the Beaumonts, the Cliffords, and the Scropes of Bolton were but some of those lines that survived such storms. The relatively low correlation between longevity and patrilineal continuity comes into clear focus when we look at the "average age" or life span of the men in the chain. For the fifteenth-century peers as a group, the average life expectancy for a universe of about 450 men was probably a bit over 50.[27] Only 6 of the 11 families shown in Table I-3 could boast of a mean much beyond 50 years for its men, and only the Greys of Ruthyn were significantly beyond the half-century figure. Within most families there was a considerable fluctuation. The Scropes of Bolton are a good example: one peer who lived into his mid-70s can be set against three who failed to reach 40. The Fitzhughs had two men (of five) live beyond 50, the Greys of Ruthin, two of three; the Percies, two of five; the de Veres, three of four; the Scropes of Bolton, two of six; the Talbots, two of four; the Staffords, only one of four; the Zouches, two of four. *In toto*, for these families, there were 45 men in the successful chains covered in Table I-3, and only 18 of the 45 who lived past 50 (or but 40 percent of the total). Nor was violent death by itself such a threat, especially since so many peers died violent deaths when already at a fairly advanced age. The Percies lost four successive males (plus Hotspur, a connecting link between his father and his son), but every one of them lived to at least 40, the first two of the four to about 60. So not only were there sons, but the heirs of the next generation were often of full age. When this was the case it certainly may have helped cushion the family against a wardship and the risks of further economic and political spoliation. Even a short and unlucky life could be sufficient to ensure the continuity of the patrilineage, thanks to early marriage and early fatherhood.

If we look at how some families grasped at lesser forms of male succession through the course of the century, we appreciate the good fortune of the successful few. Many lines wound up being preserved and transmitted by a resort to some route other than the straight path of the patrilineal stepping stones. Examples and alternative solutions abound. The Fitzalan earls of Arundel got through the years between 1399 and 1500 by resorting once to a brother, and later to an uncle in their quest for the next of kin (as reckoned, for peerage purposes, by male descent and inheritance). This was certainly better for the family fortune and the patrimony, of course, than having the line die out or be subsumed, via female descent, into some other patrilineage. But it ended what we have defined as patrilineal continuity, and families often suffered a real loss of status and power when they had to shift to collateral lines, just as they did when a long minority (or a series of minorities) befell them. The lords Berkeley got through the century because a nephew and then a brother were available, the Courtenay earls of Devon because of younger sons and brothers, and several other families because a childless peer was immediately succeeded by a brother or a brother's son. In these cases the descent from the original patriarch who had been enthroned in 1399 (or at some earlier date) may have been direct in terms of each separate heir, but the string of fifteenth-century men was not arranged in the proper order. These families' attempts at patrilineage had proved abortive. The examples of what we can call indirect continuity already referred to, as well as similar cases provided by such families as the lords Roos, the Stourtons, the de la Pole earls of Suffolk, the Neville earls of Westmorland, and the Butler earls of Ormond, all fail to meet our constricted definition of a patrilineage. Such family lines (or clans?) do offer a variety of next-best alternatives, the playing out of a series of decent but ultimately losing hands.

The data that we have extracted from the Inquisitions flattered the record of father-son succession. So does an emphasis upon those families that succeeded (or that almost succeeded). Such families were unusual, their success exceptional. The commonest fate for the aristocratic patrilineages (as probably for all others) was termination: the end of the direct road of male succession. Sooner or later, a son would have no son, nor would any of his brothers. The peerage title might be continued through a daughter or a sister, and the estates either transmitted with her or divided and scattered among various heirs. Regardless, the stately hopes and claims of the patriarchy lay forgotten in the dust. The great Warwick earldom and the patrimony of the Beauchamps may have been preserved, via a marriage with the Nevilles and then, temporarily, through the marriages of the earl's two daughters. But the Beauchamp line as a patrilineage—for all its mythical links with Guy of Warwick and its fabulous and carefully cultivated pretensions to a pre-Norman past—ended when duke Henry died in 1446, leaving only a daughter.[28] The Abergavenny title also passed from the Beauchamps to the Nevilles when II lord Richard died without male children in 1422 and left a daughter, the wife of Edward Neville, eventually summoned to the peerage as III lord Abergavenny. This was the common fate, the human condition, and the century saw such families as the Mowbrays, the lords de la Warre, the Dacres of Gilsland, the lords Furnival, the lords St. Amand, and the Scropes of Masham, among others at the upper rungs of the ladder, lose their male identities as daughters' husbands and then daughters' sons stepped into the maternal grandfather's place. Political convenience and economic opportunity made the daughter-heiress an attractive commodity on the marriage market, and her ability to transmit her father's title (and lands) was hardly the least of her charms. But from the view of the male lineage, it was sad ending, a very weak, second-best alternative that might keep the parliamentary title but not the male line alive.

More lines came to an end than were continued by means of a daughter's marriage. Death without children, or without surviving male children, or without legitimate male children, was—if not quite a biological and social constant—at least a familiar phenomenon in the halls of the mighty, as it no doubt was among the lesser and the less-documented of the land. Exalted examples are easy to come by, and the tale of frequent and abrupt termination is probably a typical one at all levels, pertaining to all sorts of men and all ranks of families. At any single point of transition, as recorded by the Inquisitions, about one quarter of any largish group of landholders lacked the requisite direct male replacement. Sometimes we can see a whole series of fell turns of fortune's wheel. The various fifteenth-century dukes of Bedford elucidate this point. The dukedom of Bedford was a peerage reserved for men in or close to the royal family. Between 1435 and 1495 three successive dukes were created, *de novo*, and each in turn died without any surviving legitimate children, male or female. Since each duke had not been his father's heir (as each was a younger son), each man looked to represent the beginnings of a new patrilineage. Henry V's brother John died at age 46, in 1435, leaving no legitimate surviving children. George Neville, son of John, earl of Northumberland, died, unmarried, at age 26, in 1483. Jasper Tudor died at age 65, in 1495, leaving only an illegitimate daughter (who became the mother of Stephen Gardiner, bishop of Winchester). The royal dukedom of Gloucester was held by men who suffered a similar fate: Henry V's brother, duke Humphrey, left only bastards upon his death in 1447, and Richard III had outlived his only legitimate child by the time of his death at Bosworth in 1485. No wonder earlier generations of historians commented adversely on the unimpressive blood stock of the upper classes.

These royal dukes of Bedford and of Gloucester had each been the recipient of an individual peerage creation. But if we think of the century as a chronological cross section, cut at right angles across the grain of both older and newer family lines, we find more established lines equally susceptible to an abrupt terminations, to sentences from which there was no appeal. Many an old patrilineal chain just wound its way to the point of the next transition and then snapped. Thomas Bardolf was the fifth lord of his family, all in direct father-son succession, when he died, without male heirs, in 1408, William Botreaux the third in a direct father-son linkage at his death in 1462, when he was only survived by a daughter, Hugh Burnell the third consecutive direct male heir of his family at his death in 1420, and he was succeeded by three granddaughters, the children of a son—a casualty at Agincourt—who had pre-deceased him by five years. John Charleton of Powis was his family's fourth successive peer upon his demise in 1401, his heir—his brother Edward—was the fifth and last lord upon his death in 1421 (when two daughters received and divided the inheritance). In some cases the end was long foreseeable, if unavoidable. In others, the death of other children and even of grandchildren put quit to what had seemed another successful bridging operation. Many families had apparently been well along the road to a sustained father-son chain when the luck turned and no sons were forthcoming: the Darcies, the Greystokes, the Harringtons, and the Scropes of Masham were among those upon whom such ill fortune fell. The past provided no collateral for the future. There were also those peers, from newer lines, whose hopes of a patriarchal old age were blasted almost from the start by colder winds. Lord Bonville had first received a summons to the peerage in 1449, and by his death in 1461 there was only a great-granddaughter left to succeed him. Lord Wenlock was probably about 60 when he was first summoned to Lords in 1461, and at his death (killed at Towton in 1470) there was a widow but no sign of any children or their heirs. Thomas, II lord Camoys, had had a son-and-heir in his own right, but on his death in 1421 the son was already dead and a young grandson was his heir. The boy, in a fashion probably all too

common among the huge pool of under-age heirs we looked at in the Inquisitions, succeeded at age seven and died, unmarried and childless, at age
12, in 1426. There were no further heirs of the Camoys men, no further
summonses: the peerage and the patrilineage were gone.

The specter of the family's extermination was always present, just as
was that of individual death. Uncertainty was a part of life, and some of
the family lines that did get through the course of the fifteenth century
played out early in the next. The Beaumonts, peers since the early fourteenth century and bridging the entire span of the fifteenth-century with
but three men, saw the line end when William, VII lord Beaumont, died
childless in 1507, aged around 68 or 69. The lords Fitzhugh, first summoned
to the peerage in 1321, had a similar fate befall them when George, VII lord,
died in 1513. The de Vere earls of Oxford had to resort to a collateral line in
1513. They had come all the way down from 1331 with only one such dodge
(in 1392, when the IX earl died and his heir was his uncle, his father's
younger brother). If we leave the arbitrary convention of a century as a
unit of measure and look rather at the successive generations within a family, we encounter much the same story in slightly different garb. The patrilineage, through time, demanded an unbroken run of males, with each one
in turn socialized to see his role in an ongoing dynastic saga. The wreckage
of unsuccessful patrilineal launchings littered the genealogical and social
landscape. The laconic records of the day rarely reveal men's feelings about
their lack of heirs: bitterness, frustration, and envy were usually cloaked by
their reticence and by our loss of pertinent sources. We can learn much
more about contemporary interest in arranging a marriage than about the
disillusionment of having done so to no avail. But if we look at the Berkeleys, we have the family's seventeenth-century chronicler, almost too eager
to reflect upon a moral tale that he draws from the hostility between William, I viscount and marquis (d.s.p. 1492), and his brother-and-heir, Maurice (d. 1506). As Smyth tells the tale, much of the family's fate and fortune
was determined by William's personal animosity, an animosity created to a
considerable extent by his unhappiness over his own lack of direct heirs
and by his brother's more successful spin of the wheel. The marquis bar-
tered away some of the patrimony in return for his new title, thereby an-
gering his brother and heir.[29] Then, to compound matters, he entered into
three marriages, and in each case his relations with his wives lacked the
customary (and pragmatic) equilibrium: "The first hee loved not, nor shee
him: the second hee loved entirely both living and dead, and shee him: the
third hee loved, and shee over-ruled him for her own ends, to the advancement of her selfe and her kindred."[30] Finally, in a will that slighted the

brother, the marquis gave full vent to a life of frustration and bitterness, to the horror of the family's historiographer: "I feared that at the making of this will sickness had bereaved this Lord of understanding. . . . This man was born for himself and intended his house and family should end in himself, a position that the heathen abhored."[31] The Berkeley divisions may have been extreme, and we learn of them from a source that does dramatize the family tension, but the letters of the Pastons certainly convey the uneasiness of parents when their grown sons had yet to wed and produce the necessary heirs.[32]

The reflections here concerning the odds against any given father begetting a long chain of direct male successors were probably applicable to most of medieval society, not just to the aristocracy. Studies of the upper class landholding families in the fourteenth century offer a picture of much the same kind of swinging pendulum, with family terminations and inheritances via daughters balancing the greatly preferred arc of male continuity.[33] Professor Thrupp's examination of the London bourgeoisie presents a very similar tale in a different social milieu, but in one no less concerned with continuity, no more successful in manipulating the results.[34] If the English monarchy itself was able to avoid the need for and resort to a collateral transmission from the accession of John through the death of the childless Richard II, few other upper class families were so fortunate for so long. The royal chain of patrilineage can be seen as running from John's birth in 1167 through Richard II's deposition in 1399: the six kings had an average life span of 55 years (their respective longevity being 49, 65, 68, 43, 65, and 33). We can see that John, as a younger son, began a new line, as we have been counting the matter, and within that line there was only once a resort to a grandfather-grandson link during the years of continuity (that between Edward III and Richard II). This is a record quite comparable to the fortunes of some of the successful families we looked at in Table I-3, for example, the Percies or the Fitzhughs or the Scropes of Bolton.

But the royal family was luckier than most. The fate of the English baronage in the generations following the Norman conquest shows that the fifteenth century picture was roughly what it had been 300 years earlier. Norman and early Plantagenet analogues for the fifteenth-century are readily available.[35] When Henry I granted the barony of Bourn to one of his familiars, Payn Peverall, in 1122, he may have been fairly confident that no great hereditary power block was being created before his very eyes. Payn was dead, without children, by 1133, to be succeeded by a nephew, William Peverall. William died on the Crusade of 1147, leaving four sisters, but neither sons nor surviving brothers. Of the sisters, Maud married Hugh de

Dover and they both died childless, Alice married and her lands went to her husband's family, Asceline left a son, who in his time died childless, and a daughter who left direct descendents. Hardly a very productive brood or much of a patrilineal breeding ground. And the genealogies of Payn's contemporaries offer many similar tales. For a bit more success we can turn, in these years, to the earls of Chester. They managed a direct father-son string from Ranulph I, who died c. 1129, through his son Ranulph II (d. 1153) to Ranulph II's son Hugh (d. 1181) and on to Ranulph III, who finally died childless in 1232, leaving three sisters and a nephew. Of the sisters, Maud left a son who died childless in 1237. The second sister died childless in 1246, and only the youngest had children. Hugh, son of the sister who had pre-deceased Randulph III, himself died childless in 1243. A look at the descent of the Anglo-Norman barony of Irthington (c. 1150–1270) is another such story: they are fairly typical in their brevity. Hubert I received the barony and he had an eldest son, Robert, who inherited but who in turn died childless. Robert's brother Ranulph then inherited, and he left a son, Robert II. Robert II's son was Hubert II, who represented the end of this effort at a male line: "for his heir was his daughter Maud."[36] The Jesse tree came down more easily than it grew: indifferent nature might hold its hand for two or three or even four generations, but sooner or later it invariably turned hostile.

*   *   *

A larger consideration of the social institution of patriarchy embraces more than just genealogy and demography. Patriarchal ideology turned the phenomenon of lineal continuity into a powerful social artifact. We have already referred to the way in which a social consensus about birth order and the priority of the male heir came to be seen as part of a "law of nature," rather than as constructs pragmatically or arbitrarily imposed by society as part of its interpretation of the process of procreation. Patriarchal ideology emerged as both a cause and an effect of this interpretation. As such, the efforts of a family to hold onto its luck became of some importance. Such good fortune meant the ability, if not to avoid, at least to ride out some of the malevolent fates that lurked at the edges of the simple failure to produce male heirs. For the upper classes there were peculiar political risks, and they remind us of how survival itself could be a feat, upward social mobility a considerable *tour de force*. At the top of the pyramid, fifteenth-century life—for individuals and for their lines—could be extremely dangerous. The plots and rebellions that sprang from the dynastic coup of 1399, the interminable wars in France, and the baronial struggles that ran intermittently from the 1450s into the 1490s were all sanguinary affairs. The upper class paid a high price for its place in the sun, and the human losses can be plotted with some detail, chronicling both the fall of individuals and the ways in which family and patrilineal fortunes could come tumbling down with them. If we look at peerage mortality, mainly as a result of the waves of political and military crises that had to be breasted, we see both high death tolls and their direct if adverse effect on family continuity. In fact, if we are not about to go back to the idea that the Wars of the Roses killed off the nobility, we at least want to assert that such episodes as Towton, Barnet, Tewkesbury, and Bosworth were more than normal episodes in the turn-over of the generations. Patrilineal lines, as well as individual lives, were terminated. While some victims of violence died long after their likely years of parenthood (whether realized or not), others were cut down in their prime, their obligation to the patrilineage as yet unfulfilled. We have remarked that longevity had but a limited correlation with fatherhood. On the other hand, we have also discussed the way in which the odds against family survival and continuity lengthened as men ran risk after risk, and as minor heir after minor heir was pushed forward before his proper time.

Table I-4 shows how uncertain, as well as how violent, aristocratic life was in the fifteenth century. Death by unnatural means claimed 76 men in the course of the century, or almost one-quarter of the entire peerage.

TABLE I-4   VIOLENT DEATH AND SUCCESSION BY SONS

Died during	20–29	Age at death 30–49	50 +	Total
Reign of Henry IV				
succeeded by a son	2	4	1	7
died without male heir	2	3	1	6
French Wars				
succeeded by a son	2	2	1	5
died without male heir	4	4	—	8
Wars of the Roses				
succeeded by a son	3	17	13	33
died without male heir	4	11	2	17
Total	17 (7/10)[a]	41 (23/18)[a]	18 (15/3)[a]	76 (45/31)[a]

[a] Figures in parentheses show first the number within each age group succeeded by a son, and second the number who died without male heir.

How different was violent death in terms of its effect upon the family from other (or all) forms of death? The Inquisitions showed us that about 65–70 percent of the deceased landholders were likely to be directly succeeded by a son. The universe of the 1,000 men covered by the four sets of Inquisitions included some men who were killed, including some of the peers, but violent death was present in nothing like the proportion found when we just consider the aristocracy.

The data of Table I-4 indicate that violent death, at least when considered in this sort of statistical aggregation, really did undercut the construction of patrilineal chains at the top of society. It not only claimed over one-quarter of the universe of fifteenth-century peers, but it fell most heavily upon young men (that is, upon men who died somewhere between ages 20 and 29) and it claimed a large number of men who died without a son or a grandson. If we look at the men in terms of their age at death, it seems that early (and violent) death did indeed have an adverse effect upon the continuity (and hence, the existence) of the family (let alone the patrilineal) chain. Only 7 of 17 men (41 percent) killed before they reached 30 left a son as their heir. If we think of 72 percent as the rough norm of direct father-son replacement for any large group, we see how far below the standard we fall here. In contrast, more than one-half of those killed after they reached middle age (that is, between ages 30 and 49: 23 of 41 men, or 56 percent) had sons, and an impressive 83 percent of those killed when 50 or more (15 of 18) had a son. A longer life span—at least longer than the third decade—did help preserve the chain: it was positively correlated with the likelihood of a male heir. Longevity, not the cause of death *per se*, is the critical variable, except that it was violent death that was working against longevity, and so, by extension, against fatherhood. This conclusion may seem a bit at odds with what we said above about the links between longevity and patrilineal success. However, different data seem to reveal different facets of the picture. Violent death—to a striking degree for the youthful and to a fairly strong degree for the middle aged—ended the patrilineage we have been defining and searching for. If the Wars of the Roses did not end that many families, as judged by some more flexible or comprehensive definition than the one we are applying, violent death certainly worked towards that end with a considerable appetite. In all, 45 men died by violence and left sons (or grandsons), 31 so died and failed to do so. This gives a father-son replacement rate of 60 percent for this universe, some 13 percent below that reflected in the larger universe covered by the Inquisitions Post Mortem. Since the Inquisitions do not give the dead father's final age, but only that of the heir, a more precise comparison for the larger universe regarding the death of young men and the survival of their heirs is not possible. Military and political danger was indisputably hard on direct father-son links, and families with a tradition of service in the French campaigns or families that regularly answered the summonses of such great regional lords as the Nevilles or the Percies may have run an appreciably higher risk than most. Military careers were rarely conducive to family health, whatever they may have meant in terms of prestige and economic opportunities.

Violent death beat against the walls of family continuity. It cut off would-be patriarchs in their youth or in middle age, and it denied them the glory of their full years and their white heads. Of the 76 who died by violence, 54 percent fell while in their middle years, only 22 percent in youth, and 24 percent in old age. Violent death for the aristocrats was frequently the direct result of a flawed political decision, an ultimate form of bad luck. In such cases there could be not just death, but—for the heir and the surviving family—attendant dishonor that carried socio-economic demotion. While the list of those who died by violence does include a few revered and non-partisan victims of the French wars, the list is mainly a miniature census of the politically mistaken, the "traitors" who guessed wrong in a dangerous age of many guesses. Family honor and patriarchal legitimacy might be posthumously reasserted, as in the lavish funeral and reinterment given to such revindicated father-martyrs as the duke of York and the earl of Salisbury when their sons had once again been able to claim center stage.[37] But against this sort of *ex post facto* vindication, we should remember a series of grisly deaths and executions for traitors, with the heads and quarters of such mistaken gamblers as the earl of Kent or lord Bardolf gracing city gates for some months after their execution.

Men who guessed wrong could look forward to the loss of honor, of worldly goods, and of their lives. But when the sentence of forfeiture and attainder was dressed in the full regalia of legal and parliamentary robes, it fell upon their descendents and heirs as well. It snipped the patrilineal thread, as surely as it made sport with the patrimony. As Jack Lander says, "Attainder for treason was followed not only by the most savage and brutal corporal penalties and the forfeiture of all possessions, but in addition by the corruption of blood passing to all direct descendents, in other words by the legal death of the family."[38] In practice, of course, such sentences were not infrequently reversed or lifted, the heirs (eventually and gradually) allowed to recover that which had once been theirs. The process of

recovery could be very long, and the chances of each successive step forwards made dependent upon the degree of loyalty demonstrated at the
previous plateau of advancement. The Percies offer a good example of a
family that climbed back to great prominence: luck and favor eventually
served to reunite patrimony and patrilineage. But their climb took a very
long time, and encompassed many steps forwards and many long halts
along the way. A detailed study of the Percy family catches the insecurity
that accompanied two generations of slow ascent and reacquisition. At
each successive stage of the recovery, "the onus of proving his claims" fell
upon the earl, though in this case the quest was generally successful.[39]

Other families also worked their way back from disgrace. Sometimes
the swing of fortune's wheel was enough to change the face of things.
Some of those attainted by Edward IV were restored, as a matter of course,
by Henry VII, if not by Edward IV himself when in a conciliatory mood,
perhaps after some years had passed.[40] Randolf Dacre was first killed at
Towton (29 March, 1461) and then attainted in Edward's first parliament.
His brother Humphrey craved forgiveness and received a general pardon
in June, 1468, "as the seid Humfrey is as repentaunt and sorrowful as eny
creature may be, of all that which the said Randolf or he may have doon
or committed."[41] Lionel, lord Welles, also fell at Towton and was posthumously attainted on 21 December, 1461. His son and heir Richard, though
pardoned on 5 February, 1462, did not recover his goods and property until
11 July, 1465. Full restoration was only decreed by Parliament, covering his
blood (inheritance) and honors, in June, 1467. But even with all these
twists, the family course was not about to straighten out. Welles's son re-
belled and was killed in March, 1470. His attainder only came in January,
1475, its reversal in the parliament of 1 Henry VII.[42]

So for some the light shone again. These men and their families rode
the tides of change, and their secular luck brought them, once again, to the
top. They had a further factor working for their recovery: the hierarchical
and patriarchal social structure. Too much downward mobility could set
an unhealthy climate regarding the entire cosmos of privilege and patriarchy. Some went down to illustrate a lesson about obedience and social
control. Some were demoted because their danger was too sharp or their
status too questionable. Nor was every family that was pushed down necessarily helped up again. Just as lines reached the end because of death, so
others sank almost as low because of socio-political demotion. Historians
talk more of upward than of downward mobility.[43] But we should also
spare a moment for those unfortunate families who waited in vain for the

further summons to Lords, for the letter of pardon and restoration, for the indication that the groveling petition that assured future loyalty would be well received. Those who waited for such news—and especially those who waited in vain—kept their vigil for themselves, for their descendents, born and unborn, and even for their ancestors. The call of the patriarchal trumpet could echo through the hills and valleys for several generations before, like Roland's horn, it fell silent at last.

The Strength and Limits of the Bond of Patriarchy

So far we have talked more about vital statistics and demographic data than about the ideology of the family and the link between ideology and behavior. The patrilineage, we have argued, was an objective albeit a socially defined "fact," and we have been examining various kinds of data to see what they say about the coincidence of demographic resources and social continuity. Patriarchy was an idea, an ideal type that crystallized into a major component of the social system, with a set of values created to explain, control, and perpetuate the hierarchical pyramid. Its worth was exalted to the point where it largely governed the definition of the family, and thence it controlled function and interaction. Each person's role within the patrilineal and the patriarchal drama also became a critical factor in the molding of his or her individual conception of self—of what we refer to as ego identity. Individual and collective behavior, internal and external expectations, and social norms were created or modified to fit the patriarchal model. Institutions were evaluated and embraced in terms of whether they contributed to or detracted from its realization. By the fifteenth century there was—or was still—a wide variety of social constructs and practices designed to emphasize the merits of patriarchal descent and of the attendant patriarchal values. Nor were these constructs mere ornaments, loosely attached to the facade of the genealogical and biological carriage as it creaked its way through this world. They were integral to the planning and the engineering of the nuclear family and the extended one. Within the former, the father-son relationship was the critical one. It pretty much called the tune heard through the many chambers and corridors of the horizontal family as the other kin stood back, awaiting what fate and affection might bring them, if anything. The values and institutions of patriarchy played—as long as there were direct male heirs and no irreversible social demotion—a vital part in legitimating and explaining the ongoing model. They did much to define and focus collective loyalty and identity.[44]

We saw above, in the shields on the tomb at Ewelme, an example of acquisitive patriarchy, of the way in which a man or a lineage could assert itself as the point of convergence of many lineages, the heir of many lines. Ancestors could be numbered amongst one's "collectibles," and the Ewelme tomb was unusual and extreme in its comprehensive flamboyance, with its 24 badges pushing so many varied claims, some extremely tenuous. But it was hardly peculiar in the thrust of its ideological statement. Many men, and many families, made similar claims. Lord Darcy's tomb bore the shields of his many ancestral chains: Darcy, Meinell, Grey of Heton, Grey of Wilton, Fitzhugh, Ufford quartering Willoughby.[45] Some of these quarterings were claimed by dint of male descent, but many others had come by way of marriage and female inheritance. In the ideological presentation that was being made, the male just swallowed the lineage of his female progenitors. Unlike the lean kine of Pharoah's dream, eating the fat kine and showing no sign of their greed, the devouring patriarchal line was only too willing to display the results of his appetite: status grew as the lineage was seen to have consumed. In such symbols as the shields, with their ever-more complicated quarterings, lay not just the claim to land and to the patrimony now being subsumed, but also to a more mystical claim. The birth right, the manna of each line and the virility of its lineal, patronymic founder, were being ingested. When Sir Roger Kynaston slew lord Audley at Blore Heath in September, 1459, he appropriated the dead man's coat of arms as his own, and ever afterwards it was the Kynastons who bore "ermine with a chevron gules," in honor of their ancestor's great feat.[46] What Sir Roger was claiming was perhaps a bit ambiguous, but there was a touch of the triumphant David, swinging the giant's head, or perhaps the putative cannibal who eats his enemy's heart to absorb his bravery.[47]

The patrilineal chain was a vertical one, by definition, and the hierarchical values of patriarchy ran, for the most part, along this path. Each patriarch in turn staked a claim to his allotted segment of the diachronic chain. He came immediately after the father (or, occasionally, the grandfather) who had preceded him, immediately before the son who might be eagerly stepping on his heels. Benefaction, chantries, and other such devices and strategies, catching both the eye and ear, emphasized the strength and reality of the supposedly endless queue made up of those still of this world and of those now in the next. Ancestors and parents were singled

out for mention when there was occasion to reflect upon the relation between the individual and the lineage. Chantry prayers, of course, were usually said either for those now alive or for those already dead: "to pray for
the saules of me, my fadir, my modir, my graunte-sires, my graunte-
moderis, and alle christen saules," as a donor might spell it out.[48] But the
prayers could move forward with time's arrow, if one so chose. The duke
of Warwick founded a chantry with an eye upon the future: "that God
wold send him eyres male."[49]

Men could proclaim their position on the family chain, making genealogical "facts" into a source of both pride and identity. John Stourton
began his will by stating that he was the elder son of John Stourton, formerly Lord of Stourton, brother of William Stourton, son and heir of the
said John Stourton of Stourton. The tomb was to be "throughout honestly
paved with 'tyle' of my arms and the arms of my mother."[50] A man of lesser
rank, or a newcomer, might strive for the same end by talking more of his
social climbing: Sir Edmund Mountforde wanted a tomb, with "my armes
sett therupon with a scripture—Here lieth Syr Edmunde Mounteforde,
knyght, somtyme Councelour and kerver with the most blessed Kyng
Henry the vith and after Chambyrlayne the high and myghty Prynce Jasper
duke of Bedford, brother to the seid Prince the seid kyng."[51]

Consonant with this public declaration of family rank and membership, men took pride in displaying their detailed knowledge of descent and
kinship tables. Such matters had ancient and most honorable pedigrees. As
Thomas Gate wrote to Thomas Stonor, "it is resonable a gentilman to
know his pedegre and his possibilyte: seynt Poule foryete nat to write to
the Romayns of what lynage he was descended, Ad Romanos xj." Then
Gate moved from an expression of the general to the specific, and he elu-
cidated his claim to the patrimony of the common ancestors: "Our faders,
of whos sowlez God have mercy . . . their moders weren cosyns germaynex
descended of Sir Milys Beauchampt, knyght . . . which Milys had issu Robert Beauchamp, Bessayle of your kynnesman aforeseid, and dame Elizabeth, my Bealaylez, maried to John du Brutewell, myn auncestor."[52]

This interest in and ability to trace the line seems to have been fairly
common. The desire to see a pedigree, as part of the negotiations of marital
diplomacy, was not obtrusive. Margaret Paston asked John, "I pray you
sende me a copy of hys petygre, that I may schew to hyr how worchelppfull
it is . . . He is more worcheppfull in berthe and in lyuelode ther-to than
they or ony odyr can preue."[53] Of course, the same obsession with such ties
and links could make people susceptible to chicanery regarding false family

connections and bogus claims upon the patrimony. Edward Sely and Davy Sely brought a claim against one Rauf Marche, who "hath lobored to disherite Simon Sely of London in name of the seid Edward by untrewe meanes, seiying that Edward's fader shulde be son and heire unto John Sely late of Chesilden, and not John Sely late of London fader unto Symond, and that Edward shulde be cosyn and heire unto Laurence Sely late of London and not Symond."[54] We can label this as pure and deliberate fabrication, centering around the existence of two or three illegitimate sons and taking advantage of the frequent coincidence of Christian names, a minority, and the concomitant opportunities for confusion and enrichment. Where there is a game, there is apt to be cheating.

In sum, we should not grow too sentimental over these proclamations of father-son continuity, nor over the propagandistic efforts made to reinforce and preserve them. Ancestors could be useful credentials, produced when most needed. It is salutary, however, to remember the gulf of misunderstanding that *also* characterized Turgenev's *Fathers and Sons*. Just because fathers and sons were engaged in a common enterprise is no compelling argument for sustained interpersonal cooperation. While the common goal may have been implicitly endorsed, the enterprise neither needed nor necessarily received complete harmony between the participants. Common endeavors and personal sympathy are readily separable. There is evidence aplenty of coercion, of social control of the crudest sort, and of ambivalence if not of open hostility. Families were "about" authority as well as about lineal continuity and collective enterprise. Even when the relationships were close (in proximity, if not in sentiment), the idiom of fifteenth-century hierarchy and personal intercourse was such that "children were brought up to regard their parents, and especially their fathers, with such awe that familiarities became unthinkable."[55]

The father, we are regularly told, was the unquestioned lord and master. He had any number of ways in which he could assert himself, impose his will upon his principal heir (not to mention upon his lesser children). But here, too, there was an element of reciprocity, of mutuality. In many ways the father needed his son and heir, and some sort of two-way dynamic often existed.[56] In return for what the authoritarian figure of the father imposed upon the son, it was the very fact of the son's existence and survival that guaranteed the father's full self-realization and fulfillment as an intermediary in the lineage. In the case of the eldest son the two-way arrangement was probably closer to an equitable exchange, certainly closer than it was likely to be for the younger sons/brothers. On the other hand, we would be idealistic (or foolish) to suggest that it was ever likely to be an egalitarian relationship in any developed sense. All sons, and particularly younger sons, suffered more impositions and denials than they were likely to realize—let alone be able to impose—by way of compensation. After all, no society, let alone such an hierarchical and patriarchal one, aims to be completely fair, certainly not to all the troops. The late medieval family is an unlikely battleground on which to fight the good fight for equality of inheritance between sons, let alone for the larger context of parity between the generations or the sexes.

The authoritarian aspects of patriarchy were very real.[57] Some of these justifications of patriarchal power lay in the economic and military spheres, while others rested upon the father's role as the household or family spokesman for such social and political obligations as taxes, the tithe, and frankpledge. But his authority was also exercised for less practical and obvious or external reasons. He was a trustee of sorts, in his own generation, for the longer enterprise through the *longue durée*. As the vicegerent or lieutenant he would have to answer to the ancestors for the quality of his stewardship, one that covered the family's material resources and its arcana and regalia. There was little quarrel with the view that social institutions were transmitted and perpetuated through the replication of mores across the generations. Authority could wear a sharp mien, and the father's patriarchal guise was doubtlessly judged by his own children, in most instances, to be well short of the benevolent.

Medieval writers did not state the case for patriarchy as baldly as did Sir Robert Filmer in his *Patriarcha*, in the seventeenth century, wherein he depicted the father as king, in miniature, but a petty king well supported by the full panoply of divine right. "Creation made man Prince of his posterity. And indeed not only Adam, but the succeeding Patriarchs had, by right of fatherhood, royal authority over their children." Moreover, little in our review of the fifteenth-century evidence leads us to suppose that fathers of the earlier day would have taken offense at such a strong formulation of the relationship. They would have been happy to endorse the idea that "in the Decalogue . . . the law which enjoins obedience to Kings is delivered in terms of 'Honour thy Father', as if all power were originally in the Father."[58] Though the ideology of Reformation and of two centuries of state-building lay between our families and those to whom Filmer spoke, had expectations changed all that much? As a recent student summed it up: "What late medieval English people asked of authority above all was political tranquility and loyalty, government that would do right to all equally, family solidarity with obedience to parents, the protection of the local lord and his courts, and a happy homelife."[59]

It is hard to gauge the totalitarian streak that ran through family history. There are few explicit discussions from late medieval England on the relationship of family "theory" to behavior and to individual interpretation. Nor is either "theory" or literary presentation of human interaction a wholly reliable map for a journey into "real life." The de facto formulations or compromises that probably helped make many precise historical situations tolerable for the various parties usually remained below the level of public utterance or scrutiny. That parents—and in the eyes of the law that meant the father—could arrange children's lives and push them into arranged marriages is but a truism. On the other hand, even a cursory look at the marriages of the Paston children reminds us of how many barriers stood between the accepted dogma regarding patriarchal fiat and the actual event.[60] Even the most unyielding of would-be autocrats had to be content, perhaps on any number of occasions, with his children's opposition and dilatoriness, let alone with the toils of the ecclesiastical insistence upon some element of personal choice. Restrictions to marriage based on contemporary definitions of consanguinity and affinity could bedevil parental lotteries. Moreover, while the church did not say that children *should* marry whom they chose, it was firm in upholding the line that if they somehow did so the validity of the union was generally to be upheld. Nor, in recent scholarly studies that embrace a wider data bank, does coercive parental pressure seem to have been a major factor in bringing unwilling boys and girls together.[61] So while Paston parents might know whom they wanted their children to wed and whom they did not, such deliberations could be a long step from a consummated union. The success of the Paston parents in arranging the chosen marriages was really quite limited and unspectacular. Personal conflict and pertinent external factors were likely to be of sufficient strength to dilute the wishes of many an authoritarian father. Such realities did not weaken his hold, in theory, and he was usually free to try again. Parents, as well as their children, could be resourceful and resilient.

The authority of fathers over sons and the prescribed deference of sons to fathers were constants. But beyond such a generalization it is not difficult to find considerable variation in the relationship when we look at behavior and interaction. Young sons, in the most obedient and respectful guise, might present themselves for patriarchal approval, as in a letter we have from the earls of March and Rutland, aged 13 and 6 respectively. They addressed the duke of York in terms mainly of interest to us for their slavish conformity to the patriarchal models of expression: "Ryght hiegh and myghty Prince our most worschipfull and gretely redoubted Lorde and Fader in as lowely wyse as any sonnes can or may be recomaunde us un to your good Lordschip."[62] And since they were answering a letter from the duke in which he presumably had told them that he had been named protector of the realm, their political good wishes were but pieties: "We thanke almyght God of his yest Besechyng hym hertely to geve yowe that grace & cotidian fortune here aftur to knowe your enemyse & to have the victory of them." The conclusion was in the same vein: "We besche Almyghty God geve yowe as good lyfe and long as your owne Princely hert con best desire." Though this letter was to a considerable extent a classroom exercise, it is probably a good reflection of how sons were *supposed* to communicate.

But affection and sentiment could peep from behind the lowering clouds. Nor were the vectors necessarily just from the children to the father. When parliament turned in 1450 upon the king's favorite, the duke of Suffolk, he was forced to abjure the realm. His preparations for departure included a moving letter to his young son; "My dere and only welbeloved sone, I besche oure Lord . . . to blesse you, and to sende you euer grace to love hym."[63] The boy was to follow his father's staunchly Lancastrian footsteps and to be loyal to the king: "chargyng you, as fader can and may, rather to die than to be the contrary . . . as hertily and as lovyngly as ever fader blessed his child in erthe . . . and that youre blood may by his grace from kyndrede to kyndrede multeplye in this erthe to hys service." Though we may now see private or personal medieval letters as containing an element of public literary exercise, Suffolk's particularly personal expression is unusual, and the rhetorical aspects of the letter do not seem to be modifiers of his sincerity. Like the advice given by the Goodman of Paris to his young wife—given lest a future husband think he had not trained her properly—Suffolk's farewell address perhaps stands somewhere between a private dialogue and a treatise on manners. But it also shows us that it could be considered as quite seemly for a father, at least when facing a moment of ultimate reflection, to display deep paternal affection. You could, on occasion, admit that you cared.[64]

Sons, of course, were invariably expected to address their fathers with an old fashioned courtesy and respect, as York's sons had done. After all, if there ever was such a time, the later middle ages would qualify as part of "the good old days." In the extant family correspondence deferential phraseology is a common and familiar feature. If anything, the accustomed phrases of hierarchy were apt to become accentuated or exaggerated when the substance of father-son relations was somewhat short of harmonious. When the Paston sons were communicating with their father, without undue passion or tension, they might use the language of traditional respect and formality: "Most reverent and worschepfull fadyr, I rekomawnd me hertyly, and submytt me lowlely to your good faderhood, besechyng yow for cheryte of yowr dayly blyssyng."[65] An appeal for money was no less respectful, as we might imagine: "Aftyr all humbyll and most due recomendacion, as lowly as I can, I beseche yow of your blyssyng."[66]

Such one-sided and respectful address was but part of the normal run. It offers only limited insight into the tension that might exist between the father, wishing for domination, and a son, longing for independence. When the son had sorely alienated his father, the mother might be called upon to act as an intermediary. But even as powerful a woman (and matriarch) as Margaret Paston expressed herself with circumspection. As she said to her son: "I hope he wolle be your good fader hereafter, yf ye demene you well, and as ye owe to do to hym . . ."[67] But at least she did try to sooth the troubled waters and to calm the patriarchal wrath. She wrote to her spouse concerning their troublesome offspring: "I understand . . . that ye wolle not that your sone be take in to your hows, nor holpe he you, tylle suche tyme of yere as he was put owt therof. For gods sake, sir, a pety on hym."[68] And she too had to tread warily and make clear that if she had to choose, it was not in favor of the younger generation, against her own: "I pray you thynk not in me that I wyll supporte hym ne favour hym in no lewdnesse, for I wyll not. As I fynd hym hereafter, soo I wyll lete you have knowlych."[69]

There is no question but that epistolary conventions are apt to be conservative. It may be risky to build a whole edifice of father-son interactions and relations on a few phrases from such formulaic documents. But on the other hand there is nothing in these examples that seems atypical, judging by what we learn from other sources that emanated from the propertied (and literate) classes. The few aristocratic exchanges that we have carry much the same tone as those recorded for great gentry, like the Pastons, or for those people of the commercial world, for example, the Celys, quite concerned to ape their landed superiors. Titles and modes of address, beyond the family as well as within, can be read as an important barometer of hierarchy and deference. Like manners, they both regulate and reflect social relations and self-perception. It was when the Paston sons were not dutiful and obedient that it was especially important not to permit language to slip from the expected standard or perhaps to raise the customary standard. As a father, Richard Cely might express great solicitude for a son during or immediately after the boy's illness, but a son well knew that he had to move with care if he wished to remain in the sun. The father could voice his worry, when he so chose: "I grete you wyll, desyryng for to here of youre reqvreng, for I understande . . . ye were sore seke at Bregys, were-for youre moder and bothe youre breon and Wyll Maryon and I were sory and hevy for you . . . and I tryste to God ye be reqvrede and wyll amen-dyd."[70] In return, the admission of such tender sentiments, let alone their open expression, made it all the more incumbent upon the son to be circumspect in dealing with the father who had declared his deep concern. Deference, and perhaps even fear, can be heard in the words of one Cely brother to another: "Brothyr, owr ffathyr ys now at Calles, and ys whor-shyppffull, and so takyn, and ffor owr honesteys latt vs se that all thyng anbowt hym be honest and clenly. He ys nott now at Allay, and the mor whorshyppffull as he ys at Calles, the better belowyd shall whe be, and the mor sett by thys actys the world / Brothyr, Y vnderstonde he hathe no mo to whaytt vppon hym but yow, Do yowr dewte, and at my comyng to Calles I shall do myne."[71] This was not casual chit-chat, nor is there any impression that brothers on the edges of disfavor could afford to band together against the old autocrat.

Had we more evidence, we would perhaps find almost as many versions of father-son relationships as we had fathers and sons. We all know the tales of the strained sympathy between the grim Henry IV and the feckless Prince Hal.[72] Such legends are a compelling chapter in the mythic history of the age, and the dramatic possibilities of the tale have been enlarged by a multitude of authors and of literary talents. On the other hand we should remember that the link between Henry Bolingbroke and his first son—whatever its emotive timbre—is the only father-son royal relationship between two adults in the entire course of the fifteenth century. The story readily serves as a moral tale for such themes as paternal concern, the transmission of the birth right, and the assumption of resonsibility; it has the proper ending, sad but ennobling. Other historical legends about lesser fathers and their sons were likewise woven to illustrate how love could outshine and triumph over misunderstandings, confusions, and tragedies. When the earl of Shrewsbury died at Chatillon, in 1453, he fell alongside his younger son, lord Lisle. The earl, now in his mid-60s, was the veteran of a generation of French warfare, while the son was a virtual neophyte and was only about aged 26 or 27. In Aenius Sylvius' history of his times the details of the two Talbot deaths were reported as a chapter in the tale of family drama. The father turns to the fledgling son and urges him to leave the fatal field: "I cannot die without glory nor fly without same, seeing the number of brilliant exploits I have to my credit, but you, my son, are just beginning your career as a soldier, and flight will not disgrace you nor death make you famous."[73] The son, naturally, proves honorable if disobedient, and he fights and dies with his father. But in terms of the Talbot patrilineage, there was also a pedestrian side to the tale. Another son was far from the battlefield, and he was about to inherit the titles and estates, and live until he fell, a few years later, in the Wars of the Roses.

When a whole string of Clifford family males died in battle a legend grew up to emphasize their patrilineal bonding. At the battle of Wakefield lord Clifford stepped up to kill the earl of Rutland, the duke of York's second son. "Save him," the chaplain said, "for he is a prince's son, and peradventure may do you good hereafter." But Clifford responded to an even more elemental call, and he answered, "By Gods blode, Thy father slew myne, and so wil I do the and all thy kyn." And he was as good as his word, for then he "strucke the erle to the hart with his dagger."[74] This has all the earmarks of the classic bloodfeud of the early middle ages, with its need to announce that family honor had been served.[75]

Such forms of expression and behavior shaped the framework within which people chose to conceptualize the family and to compress the large and unwieldy threads of tortuous father-son relationships into a patterned tapestry. What was "really" said was of little interest when set against an account of what "should have been" said, along with a concern for "how" it was said. And it was from this body of prescribed phraseology that the family myth was cut, the idiom through which people expressed themselves shaped and displayed. Thomas Stonor spoke as a dutiful representative of the next generation when he reported the deaths of his mother and stepfather: "Like you to wyt that my ffadyr is gone to god also . . . and my modyr on Saterday by the morne, and my ffadyr on munday by dayrove."[76]

*　*　*

It was in death as it had been in life: fathers often sought to control their sons. Through the last will and testament the father could continue to impose conditions upon the sons, seek to shape their lives from beyond the grave. The conditions could be benevolent, clearly laden with strong, positive feeling, or they could range towards colder and more oppressive commandments. Regardless of tone, most wills from fathers contained clauses revealing a posthumous clutch upon the child's future freedom of action. Furthermore, there are frequently conditions above and beyond those needed merely to regulate the transmission of property and the disposal of personal goods. They relate to peculiar but important variations of parent-child relationships. Some of the forms of testamentary clauses that concern us represent the more bold-faced forms of paternal dictation, of social control, expressed to shape or to limit the alternatives that now lay before the (often full grown) child. Some of the parental conditions were political and economic, coupling family business endeavors to public life, as when they sought to direct marriage alliances towards predetermined social and economic ends. Others concerned intra-familial relations, the shared burdens of siblings or of the children towards the widow, or of one particular child towards younger brothers and sisters. Clauses covering the disposition or transmission of goods reveal sentimental and personal impulses as well as a concern for the business being transacted.

The burden of complying with the father's wishes was part of the son's repayment for the birth right, and parental blessings did not necessarily come at bargain rates. The heavy if loving hand of the father could be felt as he might seek to push his descendents towards an enterprise of which he had been the path finder and prime mover. The course he had charted was not to be abandoned just because he was gone, nor was the heir to be encouraged to think about changing directions. Or, so we speculate, many a father argued, first to himself and then, in his will, to others. The contemporary value system generally gave full support to such views, whatever we think of the "truth" they contained. Relevant testamentary clauses, along with the burdens they carried and imposed, became elaborate sets of rules by which the sons had to play, perhaps for many years after the father's death. And like most rules governing games, they became formalized and rich with symbolic value.

In the behavior of their members, the strata of medieval society mirrored each other with appropriate gradations for wealth and dignity. The royal family possessed such personal goods as the regalia of the realm, such convenient burial chapels as Westminster Abbey, the cathedral church at Canterbury, and the chapel of St. George at Windsor. Lesser families had their equivalent heirloom treasures and traditions, of whatever worth and antiquity, though the best of these—like that of England itself for the Prince of Wales—were usually reserved for each family's eldest son. But like the patriarchs of Israel, an individual father could occasionally intervene in the semi-automatic process to complicate the transmission between generations. He might act to transfer the birth right to a younger but preferred son. Such idiosyncratic behavior might be inadvertent or even the result of chicanery, as it had been with the blessing that Isaac bestowed upon Jacob, or it might express some peculiar preference or idiosyncrasy, as with Jacob and the blessing he gave to Joseph's sons. It could relate to personal items or perhaps—through uses and enfeoffments and such legal devices—encompass the bulk of the patrimony.

Usually, being the eldest son was most of the story, though on occasion even he could come up short. Sometimes one had to be the eldest son and *still* have to obtain the explicit endorsement of the father. This could be specifically stated, as in the stipulations and terminology of the will, or implicitly, marked simply by the absence of competing bequests or enfeoffments that would divert the patrimony to younger brothers. In most instances, among the propertied classes, the father simply held back and the law operated, more or less mechanically, to transmit the bulk of land, along with the patriarchal identity, to the eldest son. Fathers were sometimes moved to speak in positive terms about the heir, perhaps to emphasize that inheritance was a responsibility and a privilege, not just a mechanistic channel for the transmission of tangible and dumb objects. A father might leave his son his goods, and then towards the end of the will ask that a special task be performed, as a favor: "supplico filio meo quatinus super benedictione mea."[77]

But the widest window into the world of father-son relationships comes from examining the testamentary clauses that set out conditions, blessings, and hopes between the fathers and their survivors. There were two main types of such conditional clauses through which fathers sought to involve themselves posthumously in sons' lives. One category covers what we can characterize as demographic or patrilineal contingencies, while the other was concerned with the control of behavior. The two types of conditional clauses were not mutually exclusive, nor were they necessarily at odds with positive paternal feelings.

The father's first concern was that he have a son and heir, and that the son in turn continue the chain. Personal goods, land covered by enfeoffment—as so much land was by the fifteenth century—and the birth-right of the patriarchal blessing had to be steered accordingly. But what if the son and heir died without heirs? We know, from our statistical examination of heirs and replacement rates, that such prospects were more than mere phantoms of a dark genealogical night. If the son failed the father, the father might make certain that that son in turn was made to pay a price. The blessing and the riches would be transferred from the first-born to his brother(s), usually in a descending order of age. Such an obvious and necessary strategy can also be seen as the father's posthumous revenge upon the sterile son, a withdrawal of allegiance or status that moved the transgressor out of the chain of the birth-right. And if there were no brothers to take his place, or no brothers with children, the patrimony with its attendant blessing could even be moved beyond the pale of patriarchy: to heiresses or to nephews or male cousins, or even, alas, to the bloodless world of charitable and spiritual uses.

We can see in some detail how these various testamentary practices or options operated. In a will of 1415, Thomas Walwyn of Much Marcle, Herefordshire, left land to his wife, "to holde hit to terme of here lyve."[78] Then in the proper course of time the land would go to "Richard my son and to hers of his body frelych be-gotun for euermore." But what if transmission by way of his first choice—this best of all alternatives—was not possible? What if Richard had no such heirs, "be-gotun for euermore"? Such possibilities, unfortunately, were only too likely and had to be kept constantly in mind. If, "pour defaut of issu," Richard's line failed, there was next a nephew Thomas. And then, if Thomas and "the hers of the body of the forsaide Thomas Walwayn be-getun" were not forthcoming, there was William, brother of the forsaid Thomas. And if William could not produce "Heirs of his body frelych be-gotun for euermore," then the search went on and on, until finally old Thomas' interest seems to have been exhausted and the supply of names began to fail. In this particular case, for one block of the land, two nephews were interposed between the first son and what seem to be some younger sons, assuming that old Thomas's kinship terminology was literal rather than figurative. Perhaps age, administrative convenience, or some personal arguments entered in but were left unstated. For some of Thomas's other lands the transmission would simply be from son to son; we are not witnessing an instance of systematic disinheritance of younger sons in favor of their male cousins. But we are witnessing an almost frantic search for the recreation of a patrilineage. The whole process shows the keen edge of the old man's need for sons. Without them, and then without their subsequent progeny, the glass was dark. The grim sentence of "for de-faut of issu" was one from which there was no appeal.

Lord Lovel worried about the entail of his lands, to the point where his will became a series of "if . . . then" conditional clauses pertaining to both survival *and* obedience. He tried to drive his supervision home, to the last: "If the same William my sone or eny of the heires male of his body begenten do or suffre anything to be doo . . . thanne . . . the said astate tayled vtterly to be voyde." And worries about survival are expressed in a similar style: "in case the said Robert dye withoe issue male of his body begeten . . . And if the said William die, withoe Issue male . . . and in case the said henry die withoe suche issue. . . ."[79]

However, we have seen that sons were usually available, and we should not overdramatize the father's dilemma. When there was a son as the next full partner, he almost always figured in the father's will. He was his father's alter-ego, the replication of self unto the next generation. The bond between the male stepping stones was often revealed as stronger and tighter than one merely needed for the transmission of property. There were lineal success stories, examples of which men turned to with pride and confidence. Some men, in their wills, still saw themselves as their own long-dead father's son, and their identities were still being defined and expressed in the idiom of the patrilineage, as when Edward, II lord Hastings, asked for burial "nyghe to the tombe of my lord my fader whose soule god pardon."[80] Given that the father had been executed in 1483 and the son lasted until 1506, this was filiopiety with a good memory. John Bourgchier not only wanted burial "next my lord my fader and my lady my moder," but he (still) identified himself as "I, John Bourgchier, knyght one of the sonnes of Sir Herry Bourgchier late Erle of Essex."[81] Richard Poynings, of another minor aristocratic family, followed much the same path. He said, "Y Sire Richard Ponynges knyght eldeys sone of my most worthy lord and fader lord of Poynynges . . ." when he expanded upon his last wishes.[82]

Other fathers might list their male children in a rank order, going through the birth order in a fashion reminiscent of an Old Testament patriarch. An alderman of York, at the end of the century, distinguished between "filio meo primogenito et heredes," the "filiis meis junioribus" and then George and Guy, "filiis meis bastardis."[83] Nor was he about to relax his hold. Though all five sons were named as executors, the trust was not without qualifications: "chargeyng them as they wyll aunswere to me at the day of dome that they ful fyll my mynd." John Cokayn of Bury Hatley, Bedfordshire, left goods to his "heir apparent and to his heirs," and then other goods to a second son, a third son, and a fourth son.[84] The sons were certainly left in no doubt about their place in line when they were singled out in such a fashion: "Thomae . . . primogenito meo," and then "Edmundo, filio meo secundo genito," and then "Ricardo, filio meo tertio genito," and, finally, "Edward . . . filio meo quarto genito."[85]

These were clauses that reflect worries about survival and the relationship between the heir's age and his chances of lasting long enough to enjoy his preferred status. The other type of conditional testamentary clause between father and son is that through which the former sought to govern the behavior of the latter. Social control did not end at the grave, and in a world with such strong patriarchal values, no one seems to have taken any principled exception to the existence of such clauses, not even, it would seem, the heavily bridled and discontented sons. Obviously, specific clauses could be irksome, and no doubt even many a dutiful son cut some corners when the opportunity arose. But that the inclusion of the clauses of social control and restriction was part of the patriarchal prerogative does not seem to have been in dispute. Within the fairly wide perimeters of the common law governing inheritance (and disinheritance), the father could be sovereign if he chose to turn his wishes in that direction.

Conflict between fathers and sons is a real theme, if not always the major one, in plotting these relationships. The "for de-faut of issu" clauses that we saw sprinkled so liberally in Thomas Walwyn's will reflect both a realistic appreciation of demography and a fear that sons would fail to do their basic duty. The next generation might not, in A. E. Housman's words, "get you the sons your fathers got." So in a similar fashion, clauses seeking to impose control reveal a last chance for manipulation, a final opportunity—permitted by law and encouraged by custom—for domination. But the clauses sometimes reflect a more benign side to the world of parenthood: a concern lest the son go astray and, in his wanderings, reflect adversely upon the father. And if in his wayward course he also squandered the patrimony, then shame, dishonor, and even poverty might fall upon the line. Thus the motives and purposes of the many testmentary clauses and of their imposed conditions are at least mixed ones, well short of or more complex than a simple social control model. Family interactions perhaps had little trouble accommodating a wide range of affection and hostility, of creative or productive tension, and of destructive and emotionally taxing conflict.

Roger Flore of London and Oakham had high hopes for his son Thomas when Roger came towards his end in 1424 or 1425. His will contains the contingency plans we saw above in the will of Thomas Wal-wyn, but it puts much faith in the immediate son and heir. It also contains some of the "bonding" devices that served, beyond the mere transmission of tangible goods, to turn each set of intergenerational contacts into links on a longer chain. Firstly, the son-and-heir Thomas received many personal items from his father. They were described with that almost sensual detail that reminds us of how people in a visually and orally oriented age could mentally inventory their personal goods. Personal possessions that were handed from generation to generation often carried some special sentimental value: perhaps a more appropriate term for their role, in this context, is a patriarchal value. Roger's eldest son, his heir, was to receive, *inter alia*, "my maser of a vine rote, the which was my faders."[86] But a bequest was not a free gift, and when the heir received such an item he assumed a responsibility—perhaps one he would not be able to meet. In addition to the "maser of a vine rote," there was "my grete maser the which I calle sele, for the terme of his life, and so from heir to heyr lome." Nor were these gifts, nor any others in the father's power to bestow, an inordinate bequest, and no amount of paternal generosity could check the tides of time. Roger wanted to be sure that "no man merueil thogh I do well to him, for when almyghty god list to take me oute of this wreched world to his mercy, than shall he be left faderless and moderles, grauntfaderless and grauntmoderles."

But this father too knew that all was uncertain. Though he might leave bequests and shares to all his children, whether mentioned in the will or handled as *inter vivos* settlements, he was under no illusions about his ability to control the future. The long night of uncertainty was too dark. The oldest son might not live long, and there might be no sons of his body. "And yf hit so befell that he died, leuyng me, than wull I that myn eldest sone that ouereleueth me haue hit I haue be-qweythen my sayd sone Thomas." The grim game of pass-along had to be envisioned, just in case. At least Roger Flore had done his own job well, for he could refer in the will, after son-and-heir Thomas, to "Robert my son," then to "Iames my son," and finally to "Iohn my son." Nor were the younger boys only for contingency plans. They did receive some choice items: a "flat pece of the suit that were my faders (of whos soule god haue mercye) . . . the keuered pece of syluer the which was mayster Robertis Stoneham . . . six seluere spones ouer the other keuered pece, the which my lord Le Ware gaf him whan he was cristned." Even the two daughters were well remembered: Anne's bequests included a "standing pece that was my faders," and Joan

was left a "keuered pece of siluer, the which the provost of Coderstoke gaf
me." But even within this family, where the phraseology of the father's will
suggests much warmth and affection for all the children, the eldest was
special. The father's blessing upon the eldest son is exceptionally powerful
and personal: Roger Flore said, "More-ouer I wull that Thomas my son
haue my portoos, charging him, on my blessing, that he kepe hit, terme of
his life, so that god wull her-after sende him deuocion to sey his seruice
ther-on, and I haue done, that thenne he may haue such a good honest
boke of his owne."[87] Within this particular family web the theme of control
was a muted theme, and one has to listen closely to catch it. It was heavily
overladen by affection. But how many contigencies could one cover, how
many conditional clauses could one introduce? John Goldwell stipulated
that "if it happe any of my seid children to decesse without issue of their
bodies lawfully begoten, I wole that eche of theim the others heire."[88]

Other affectionate fathers might be less restrained regarding the use
of their powers. They saw their sons as junior partners, ready to be used
for the consummation of all sorts of unfinished business. Thomas Colpeper
wanted his son Nicholas to make a pilgrimage on his behalf to Norwich.
Though he was to go in person ("en as propre persone ferra un pilgrimage"), he was to be reimbursed from his father's estate for his pains ("qil
avera ses costes et expenses pour mesme de mes biens et chatieus").[89] Another father felt that his son and heir was the appropriate guardian of a
younger brother, a logical arrangment that was used far less often than we
might expect.[90] But a son could also be remembered as the product of the
union of two bodies and two family lines. It is comforting to speculate that
William Kayleway had this in mind when he left his son William "one silver
cup which I had of the gift of Joan, mother of Joan, late my wife."[91]

Sometimes a father was not inclined to mince words: The imposition
of conditions was a part of his patriarchal sway, and he had little reluctance
to exercise it. John Dicker said that if his son Robert "behaves himself well
and kindly towards . . . [his mother], with all the other things I promised
him," then the bequest would run his way. "But if by chance the said Robert
ert shall do otherwise in anything he has promised to do, or shall behave
himself otherwise than he has promised . . . I will then that he shall have
none of the said things named in my will."[92] This was tough, and much less
ambiguous than the phrasing of William Balam, who just referred to "William my son to have all such promises as I promised hym at the day of his
marriage."[93] Perhaps the longest arm of all was that stretched out by
Richard Chamberlayne, who in 1496 talked of "when my sonne William

commyth to the age of twenty-six yeris thenne I wil that he do take and preceyve his part [of the property] . . . so that he be reuled by his moder tylle he come to the saide age of twenty six yeares . . . And yf any of my said three sonnes be not ruled and goverend by there said moder in fourme aforesaid, thenne I wil that he or they . . . shall take no part of the issues of the said maners."⁹⁴ William Manyngham of Bedford was in the midst of an even hotter conflict, rudely interrupted but hardly ended or healed by his death. His references to his son were virtually a malediction: "For he hath ben unto me bothe yong and olde an Innaturall and unkynde sone conspiring my deth he and his moder togiders in my grete trowble after barnet feld whan I had made my peas with Kyng Edward then they empeched me of newe, which cost me grete goods. Also he hath disceyved me oftentymes and ylle diffamed my by unkynde and Innaturall Wordes . . . he hath gaped after my deth with moche unkynde language . . . [and meanwhile] I have delte with hym as a naturall fader and so entended to have contynued Save only for his manyfold deservinges."⁹⁵

So if affection was not always the strongest link—at least not as expressed in or reflected by terms we readily recognize—it paired with the parental obligation to help sons along in this world. Edward Cheyne left money for "my soule and for my fadir soules," as well as money for each of his two sons, "to fynde hym to scole."⁹⁶ This three-generational link was reinforced when son Edward received a "grene bed" with "The armes of John Cheyne" (the grandfather) thereupon. Old Edward also left £10 to "be paied for my fader old dettes and wronges that my fader and y have don to ony man which may be lawfullich yproved." The eldest son also received a set of third generation heirlooms, transmitted according to a long clause in Edward's father's will. The clause from the older will is quoted—an unusual touch in a fifteenth-century will—and the operative phrase was that the goods were to go, in "turne to my next heir malis that beren the surname of Cheyne . . . fro eir male to eir male." This is as graphic as a genealogical table or a Jesse tree. The vertical, patrilineal chain was being held up with a flourish.

Such signs of the patriarchy as an enterprise are not hard to find. In many a will the father faced death with the wife still pregnant, the son-and-heir as yet unborn. Prayers for her safe confinement and for the baby's (male) sex and future health and proper upbringing were about all one could do in such circumstances, as many a father was driven to accept. Medieval couples, like all too many modern ones, could be uncertain about the early days of pregnancy: "If Alice his wife prove to be enceinte within half a year after his decease."[97] When things were better defined, clearer arrangements could be made, as when John Olneye of London left the remainders from his tenements "to his infant en ventree sa mere."[98] John Choke of Long Ashton, Somerset, hedged his future commitments: if the child "now being in my wyfy's bely" be a girl, she is to receive 100 marks, and "if it be a sonne," then a full share of the enfeoffed lands.[99] Because a daughter came under her husband's control upon marriage, she could be entrusted to receive her share of the property when a good bit younger than her brother. Thus even children still *in utero* could be singled out for separate treatment. John Danby thought ahead, beyond his wife's coming confinement, and into the teens of the unborn child: "my wiffe to have ye guydynge of him unto he be xviij. If it happyn to be a doghter, she to have ye kepyng of her unto she come to xiiij."[100] But fear about survival was uppermost, perhaps even stronger than the love of domination: "I bequethe to the child in my wife's wombe, if god fortune hit to have cristendome and live, 5 marc."[101]

That children were placed, by a dying father, under their mother's control was but a commonplace. She—now perhaps a person of import and of independent judgment, by virtue of his death—could command the boy's obedience. He might stand to lose his inheritance if he cross her, as we saw above. Good behavior was essential, and social control in this area could be levied with virtually no court of appeal: "Yf any of my saide three sonnes be not ruled and governed by there said moder, in fourme aforesaid, thenne I wil that he or they . . . shall take no part of the issues of the said maners."[102]

An eldest son could also be called upon to assume responsibility for others, farther back, in the family. John Wardham asked his son-and-heir to distribute L2 to each of his two other sons and to four daughters, all within a year of the father's decease.[103] John Pilkington expected his heir, Edward, to turn Grenehirst manor over to Robert, "my bastard sone," when the heir "be of age of xxiiij yere."[104] The earl of Northumberland worked in the other direction. His younger son William received land to "the intent he shall serve his brother Henry, myne heire apparent, till he come to the age of eighteen years."[105]

But behind all the instructions, the bullying, and the manipulation lay those realities that were scarcely touched by parental worry and parental fear. These existed in many forms, many guises. There was the fear that there would be no children at all, or that they would all die young. As one uneasy, dying parent put the matter: "Iff alle my children dye, as God forbede," or else "as god defend."[106] There was the fear that the son would misbehave. Though this was rarely reflected in the sources with total frankness, it was a constant worry, as it has been for the earl of Northumberland. We might think of the generations as bound together by the long string of "ifs." "*If* the said Robert behave himself . . . [but] *if* by chance the said Robert shall otherwise."[107] And even more starkly, on the negative side: "if the said Thomas or anyone in his name in any way vex or impede my executors, then the said legacies . . . shall be void."[108] There was also the fear that the son would fail to have the sons to whom he in turn could transmit the family heirlooms and traditions. We can reflect on the provisions of William Kayleway of Shirborne. In 1469 he left land to John, son of his son-and-heir William, and then to John's male heir, "of his body lawfully begotten for ever." In default of such heirs, then John's brother William, and then their father and his other heirs. And if there were no males at the end of this chain, then William's own heirs stood in line. Were they apt to be the daughters of son William, Agnes and Alice (referred to as the "altero" [other] daughter)?[109]

In addition there was the fear that the souls of the departed would not be remembered. We know that the Pastons never quite got around to endowing the family chantry, and they were probably far from unique in their dereliction. Nicholas Blackburn fairly pleaded that his wishes suffer no such fate.[110] There was the fear that the blessing itself, as well as the accompanying material goods, would be squandered. A Buckinghamshire man wanted the widow and the son to keep a common household, "on to the tyme that John my son be maried or sette vpp household," and if they could cooperate longer, so much the better: "if they can longer acorde to be at theire will." Such harmony was worth heavenly points, both for the dead father who had kept his stewardship, and for his survivors: "That blessing that god gave to alle chidryn fulfilling their fadere and moders will and my blessing as ferre as god will geve me leve I geve hym."[111] If only it were so easily arranged in practice.

And lastly there was always the fear that the ways of the world would prove to be too much. The duke of Suffolk may have urged his son to adhere to the House of Lancaster, from king to king. But other peers may well have looked at Suffolk's fate—death by beheading on Dover sands shortly after his pious epistle and his attempt at flight—and draw a different conclusion about the perils that would soon confront their fatherless sons as denizens of the earthly city: "to leve right wisely and never to take the state of Baron upon them if they may leye it from them nor to desire to be grete about princes, for it is doungeros."[112]

Fathers could worry, and fathers could endeavor to reach out from the grave. Their efforts are a vivid testimonial to the power of the patriarchal ideology: The father was free to try and control and direct his children in almost any way he could. Fathers' success after death—even more, no doubt, than in life—was but qualified. Dutiful and obedient sons followed the lead in large part because it was mutually advantageous, and because they had been socialized to go in that direction, not just because a spur of coercion was apt to dig into them if they tried to relax in the saddle. And sometimes, the final peace between father and son only came when all further dialogue was beyond amendment, as when William Balam said that *now* "William my son [is] to have all such promises as I promised hym at the day of his marriage."[113]

A Case Study of the Scropes of Bolton

Individual families can offer detailed case studies of father-son and patriarchal relationships to illuminate the themes we have discussed above. The case study approach cannot be a random one, for both a high level of contemporary record keeping and of extant biographical and demographic material are prerequisites. Such desiderata make a noble or an eminent bourgeois family the obvious subject of the studies, and the lords Scrope of Bolton lend themselves with particular felicity.[114] The Scropes of Bolton were the dominant family of Wenslydale in Yorkshire from the late fourteenth through the end of the fifteenth century. As a patrilineage, they had the demographic fortune to survive, via direct father-son links, through the full course of the years. They had enough secular luck, aided and abetted by cultivated self-interest and some shrewd flexibility, to withstand several bad patches and to ensure that when they did sink—as they did from time to time—it was but a temporary demotion. They never descended too far to be able to rise again. Furthermore, they fostered family traditions and customs, and bound themselves tightly into the social world of the Yorkshire dales. Strong local loyalties were a useful hedge against too much dependence upon the king and too much reliance on currents that washed against the uncertain shore lines of far-distant London and Westminster. Ties of marriage, of friendship, and of joint activity with other noble families were of great value, but—as with royal service—there was always the chance that bonds fastened to a rising star could not be undone in time if it became a falling one. The road to fame and fortune was lined with cousins' heads, and those who were clever were also careful.

The family tale of the Scropes through the course of the century reinforces an important lesson about social mobility in a hierarchical society: no matter how hard it had been to rise in the first place, it was usually much easier to stay near the top once one had arrived. The Scropes owed most of their fifteenth-century eminence to the great record of their first peer, I lord Richard (1327–1403), compiled in the second half of the fourteenth century. Richard had made a mark in the royal service (as a soldier and a political civil servant), in John of Gaunt's service in England and on the continent, and in the French campaigns. His had been a model career, in terms of length, honor, and rewards. T. F. Tout characterized him as one of the new breed of courtier-servants, a combination of soldier and royal servant who was also—especially through his marriage with a de la Pole daughter—tied to the nascent capitalist interests that stood behind so much government policy by his time.[115] Though his prestige and public role were never again matched, or even seriously approached, by any of his direct descendents, he left a direct line of male heirs who were, for the most part, able to emulate enough of the essential features of his upward climb to survive as a patrilineage near the top of the social pyramid.[116]

The chronological chart and the genealogical table (Figure I-3a,b) show that even demographic good fortune was, in part, a human construct. Procreation and survival assume an importance for the historian within the framework of social institutions; biological processes and events were regulated and structured to provide the maximum social and familial benefits. In terms of simple longevity, the family record was hardly impressive. Of the seven male heads of the family, from Richard (1327–1403) through the VII lord Henry (1480–1533), only the founder lived to be over 60, and of the rest V lord John was the only one even to get near that plateau. The mean longevity of the seven peers was 48 years, their median life span but 43. These figures are actually below average for the men of this century, and if we compare them with those of other successful patrilineal chains (Table I-3), we can see them as arguing to the Scropes' disadvantage. They are all the more striking for a family that wholly avoided violent death (except for the earl of Wiltshire, of little importance for our considerations) and for one that never had to resort to a grandfather-grandson transmission. The life spans—long or short—sufficed to enable each lord to beget the son who would follow him. Age at marriage was a

FIGURE I-3A   LIFE SPANS AND OVERLAP OF THE LORDS SCROPE OF BOLTON

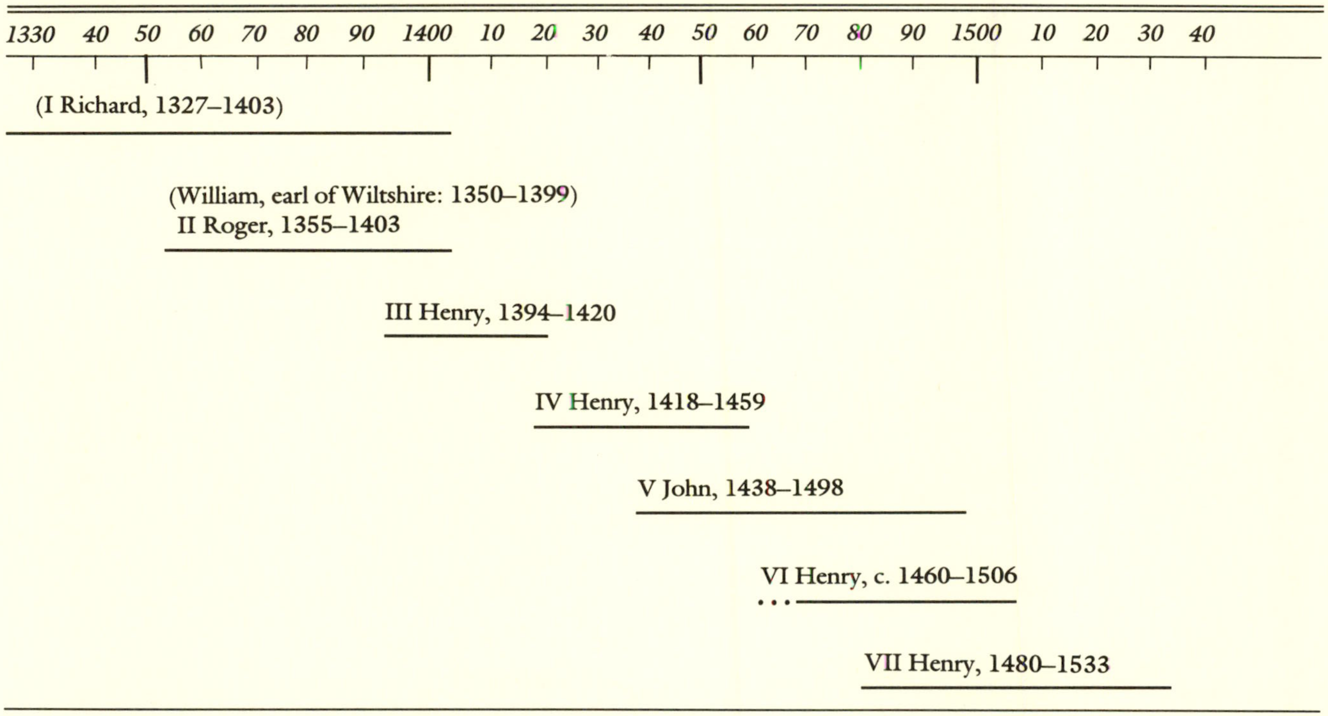

1330 40 50 60 70 80 90 1400 10 20 30 40 50 60 70 80 90 1500 10 20 30 40

(I Richard, 1327–1403)

(William, earl of Wiltshire: 1350–1399)
II Roger, 1355–1403

III Henry, 1394–1420

IV Henry, 1418–1459

V John, 1438–1498

VI Henry, c. 1460–1506

VII Henry, 1480–1533

FIGURE I-3B THE SCROPES OF BOLTON

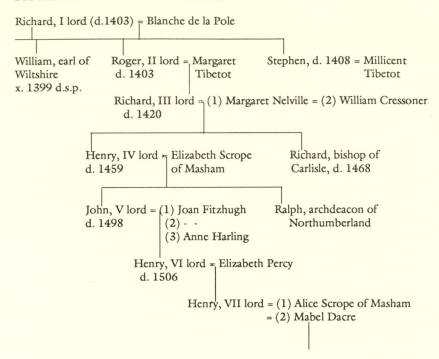

moveable feast, and the Scropes always seemed to have made sure it came early enough to protect and to help preserve the line against whatever the fates might have in store. Even when sons came late, luck ran their way. The heirs of the first two peers were not born until their fathers were at least well into their 20s: III lord Richard's son when the father was about 24, IV Henry's son and heir when he was 20, V lord John's when he was nearly 30, and VI lord Henry's when he was very young. But except for this last Henry, none of the fathers was really young, that is, still in his teens. In some families early death made any delay in fathering the next generation a fatal hurdle, but not here. Such risks were partially countered by the fact that all the heirs, except for II lord Roger, were eldest sons— another touch of luck. As we said above, sons who survived childhood usually survived long enough to become fathers, and it was not early death (that is, in early adulthood) that ended family lines, but rather the absolute failure of male heirs, or their total pre-decease. In chronological terms, the

Scropes had but two grandfather-grandson overlaps, and they never had to resort to these links to bridge the gap between heirs.

The Scrope men married at reasonable ages. The family was also fortunate in finding brides who proved to be fertile. Only VII lord Henry's first wife failed to produce at least the requisite male heir. Since she and Henry had been married for about 15 years, her failure was probably irremediable and the situation perhaps growing grave when she left the family fold; thoughts of Henry VIII and the aging Katherine of Aragon come to mind. A second marriage soon did the trick, and we are not surprised to discover, once again, that widowed peers had little trouble finding young wives, with good prospects for both dowry and fertility. Because few of the Scrope men lived to great ages, their wives generally outlived them, and later we will look as their collectives fates as the family's widows. Of the seven Scropes in the patrilineal chain, only two married more than once: V lord John three times, VII lord Henry twice. The short lives of the men militated against more than one marriage.

In fortunate families, one son was enough for each generation, though it might be useful to have some extras in reserve. The mere existence of younger children can be hard to ascertain, especially when the first-born was alive, of sound mind, and ready to step into his proper place. The I lord Richard had at least two sons beyond his eldest, William, Richard II's earl of Wiltshire: the II lord, Roger, and a younger son, Stephen, who will crop up from time to time below. The III lord Richard had at least one son beside his heir, IV lord Henry, VI lord Henry had at least two sons, and VII lord Henry had the heir and at least two more. There is no conclusive evidence regarding II lord Roger or V lord John. The impression of the family, based on their wills and our knowledge of their political history, is one of a nuclear flock of limited size, and then of involvement in larger networks of in-laws and collateral kin groups. But again, from the perspective of the patrilineage, it is not the quantity of the relations and relationships that is vital, but rather the quality of the one particular link between the generations. Here the Scropes were always able to do their duty, and they always managed to coax a sometimes-reluctant nature into giving them sufficient stock to maintain the house.

Secular luck was also needed at times. For a family that never rose above the middling ranks of the nobility, they had good fortune in finding well born wives for their sons. Such women may not have been much protection against adversity when things were really bad, but they (and their male relatives) could help in many of the lesser situations when a slight nod helped elevate one man or family from the run of the pack. The market value of the male heirs to the Scrope peerage was based in part on their importance in Wenslydale, a site that gave them a role in linking Yorkshire communication and trade routes, as well as a compact if moderate estate.[117] Their visibility in royal service, in local affairs, and in military matters made them a reasonable catch for an important family looking for useful if lesser allies or satellites. Consequently, from I lord Richard onwards the male head of the family married (or was married to) and produced the next heir by a wife who linked the Scropes with important families, more often than not their social and political superiors: the de la Poles, the Tibetots (Tip-tofts), the Nevilles, the Scropes of Masham, the Fitzhughs, the Percies, and the Dacres. In respective chronological order these wife-mothers were an earl's sister; a coheiress to her family lands (sharing the Tibetot estates with two sisters, one of whom married her husband's younger brother); an earl's daughter; a Yorkshire cousin of equally distinguished if somewhat tarnished family; the daughter of a peer and, through her grandmother, daughter of a second peer; an earl's third daughter; the seventh a peer's daughter and granddaughter. The second and third wives of V lord John were not of noble families, nor did they bear him children, and VII lord Henry's first wife was an heiress (though of no use, it transpired, when it came to bearing male children). Marriage into higher families carried some danger but many opportunities, and in no case was the marriage of the Scrope son and heir contracted at less than an equal social level. If they were not important enough to catch any major heiresses, I lord Richard's royal service had brought him the wardship and marriage of the three Ti-betot girls in the 1370s, and later the Scrope of Masham heiress was deliv-ered into the family's care.[118] Well born wives brought no guarantee of fecundity, but they could be a valuable hedge against social demotion. In the political troubles surrounding the accession of Henry IV, as during those of V lord John's difficult days in the 1480s, and during the two long minorities the family had to weather, the existence of powerful in-laws (and guardians) was a useful asset.

Scrope males tended to be youngish when they followed their fathers to the peerage, since the fathers had frequently failed to reach the average aristocratic life span of the early or mid 50s. After the first two lords, the heirs upon succession were 9, 2, 21, 30, and 26: an average age of not quite 18, with two minorities in but five instances of succession. The two minors had long minorities, and their fortunes in surviving and succeeding offer another instance of the family's persistent good luck in escaping the travails that could accompany a rapacious wardship or a disparaging marriage. III lord Richard spent his early years of minority in the custody of Queen Joan of Navarre.[119] Then his wardship was turned over to Ralph Neville, I earl of Westmorland, around 1413, and he proceeded within the next few years to marry the earl's sixth daughter.[120] She produced an heir, IV lord Henry, who was but two years old when his father died. But young Henry was now under the protection of his powerful maternal kin: first his grandfather, the earl, until the old man died in 1425, and then his uncle, Sir Richard Neville.[121] He grew up to marry Elizabeth Scrope, fourth daughter of John, lord Scrope of Masham, when in his mid-teens. Previously his mother had given £1,000 as a recognizance, in 1420, in order to be able to keep him and his brother Richard, future bishop of Carlisle, under her authority and unmarried.[122] This was a good investment, as it kept control of the heir in family (and Neville) hands. Henry was at Rhodes with his father-in-law, lord Scrope of Masham, when he first sued for his lands in 1435, and he did not recover full livery until 1440.

There were other kinds of luck, just as there were other situations that called for it. The Scropes opened our period in a precarious position. Though I lord Richard's good service had pleased various masters for many years, the tyranny of Richard II had forced difficult choices and dilemmas upon this family, as it did for many others in the baronage.[123] I lord Richard, having put in a good lifetime of service, seemed to have used his age as an excuse for withdrawal that was *de facto* retirement from Richard II's government when the tenor of political and court life became unpalatable. However, his eldest son, William, was very much part of the royal circle.[124] Father and son seem to have drifted away from or to have broken with each other by the time the son was elevated in 1397 to the earldom of Wiltshire. This meant, in effect, that at the deposition crisis of 1399 the family had a foot in each camp. When Henry returned to lay hands upon the crown, William Scrope was one of the few to die for an accumulation of crimes, errors, and stupidities. Nor did this blood-letting necessarily clear the way for a return to favor by the late earl's father and family. Old Richard—now approaching three-quarters of a century in age—had to humbly petition the king, asking that his years of good service be considered ample guarantee of loyalty to the new dynasty as well as collateral for the return of confiscated or jeopardized estates. Though it is possible that there was an element of play-acting in old Richard's abject apology and pleading—stage-managed to illustrate Henry IV's clemency and power and perhaps done to emphasize ties that went back to John of Gaunt—it seems wise to take the record as the sober narration of a dangerous passage. Richard and his second son and now heir, Roger, were accepted by the Lancastrian dynasty: the lands were restored, the family position no longer considered questionable, and lord Richard's eldest remaining son recognized as the heir-apparent to the patrimony and the parliamentary title.[125] A third son, Stephen, had been associated with his eldest brother and Richard II, especially in their Irish ventures. He ran some considerable risk before the penumbra of royal forgiveness was expanded to accept his *mea culpa* and to reaccept him as fit and trustworthy for royal service. By the time his father died in 1403 he too was back in favor, serving once more in Ireland.[126]

Nor were these scrapes at the beginning of the century the family's only brush with political and social demotion (if not worse). In the 1470s and 1480s V lord John ran a dangerous course. His Yorkist loyalties wavered sufficiently to bring him into Edward IV's disfavor, and then they resolidified to the extent that they were hardly to be seen as commendable virtues by Henry VII. John was an active solider as well as a northern political leader: he had been with Edward IV at Northampton in 1460, and came away from the battle of Towton (March, 1461) "sore hurt." He fought for the ruling house at Hexham in 1464 and was on the wrong side of the Richmondshire rising of 1470, though his submission was accepted and he received a pardon. He worked for Richard III and after Bosworth was still sufficiently disaffected with the new ruling house to be involved in an attack upon York on behalf of Lambert Simnel, in June, 1487. He again received a royal pardon, in February, 1488, and finally straightened out the course of his life. After that, his service to Henry VII was proper and appropriate for one of his status.[127]

There had also been some physical dangers, over the century, posing further threats to a dynastic thread that was rarely much more than one strand thick. III lord Richard had a fairly distinguished military career with Henry V. He led 15 men-at-arms and 45 archers at Agincourt, and in 1418 he commanded four barques and four balinques for the king's fleet. He was with Henry V at the siege of Rouen in 1418–19. The dynasty must have shaken every time he rode onto the field, for his son and heir was only born in 1418. His uncles and his father had all died within the past decade, and there was no knowing if their rather indifferent longevity pattern, rather than that of his aged grandfather, was going to set the tone.

Minorities were also critical "events" for a family that hoped to survive, let alone to prosper. The two Scrope heirs who inherited while under age were ultimately fated for short but adequate lives. Neither was ever summoned to the House of Lords. While I lord Richard had been a regular member of the upper house between 1371 and 1402, his grandson, III lord Richard, only lived to be 26 and was never called, especially since he spent most of his short adult life on the French campaigns. His youthful accession and early death left the family at the precipice of social demotion. Young Richard's son, IV lord Henry, was but 23 when first summoned in 1441, and yet he continued to be called regularly until September, 1455. But Henry's grandson, 30 when his father died (in 1498) and 38 upon his own death in 1506, was never summoned; his son only came into the parliamentary peerage in 1514, when he was in his 30s. So a minority and a young nobleman served to lower or weaken one's inherited status, though in these cases not to bring it to an end. The recovery from this kind of *de facto* social demotion might require a period of apprenticeship in public life. But the Scropes managed to escape such dangers, as they did others. Eventually, VII lord Henry rose to become a regular if not a vital cog in early Tudor legal and political affairs. He was summoned to Lords from 1514 through 1529, just a few years before his death.[128] His surviving son and heir (VIII lord John, the third but eldest surviving son) was summoned through most of his life, despite his participation in the Pilgrimage of Grace in 1536.

So the family generally managed at least to hang on. Given the shifting fortunes of this world, that was not only a reasonably happy fate, but rather unusual one. Sufficient fertility, sufficient survival, and sufficient luck to overcome some serious obstacles and setbacks were the characteristics of the family. They came through the years between Richard II's fall and Henry VIII's accession with some close shaves. But the patrilineal chain held, and within its protective arms all else could be accomplished and preserved with adequate success if not always with glory. In one sense we are arguing that when the chain held it could serve to cover innumerable problems: the risks of rebellion and even of treason and forfeiture, of minorities, and of weak and indifferent patriarchs. It was a force of such magnitude that it was rarely denied or contradicted. But, within a complex and hierarchical society, we can see how open ended and ambiguous questions of public policy and political fortune were resolved in favor of patrilineage and patriarchal continuity because it was in society's larger interests to accept their primacy if such a solution was biologically and politically possible. Therefore, we argue, family continuity and the patriarchal value system were both cause and effect of family fortune.

*   *   *

Nor was the whole secret just one of birth, copulation, and death. In the testamentary benefactions of the men of the Scrope family, we can identify two threads that illustrate their patriarchal approach and show how selected forms of behavior could enhance this image. One of these is contained in the series of bequests that run from each father to his son and heir (and to his other sons and other relatives). Such bequests governed the transmission of worldly goods and as such have an obvious practical, economic, and tangible role. They also serve as bonding mechanisms between the generations, between the links of the family chain. As such they have a powerful intangible and spiritual significance. They are an integral part of the ritual bonding between the males of the patrilineage. The other thread in the wills concerns the practice and use of local benefaction. The Scropes of Bolton worked, with some considerable dedication (and at some expense), to tie themselves to the ecclesiastical and eleemosynary institutions of their native region. Aided by a good run of extant family wills, we can follow their footsteps. In the wills we find a number of customs or strategies for reinforcing the concept of patriarchy and of the patrilineage.

When I lord Richard made his will, in early August, 1400, he was an old man who had just lost his eldest son and had just managed to hang on to his own and the family's privileged status and estates. But the good news was that his (second) son and heir Roger was already a father; the continuity of the male line was assured. As such, Richard's will is almost a case study in patriarchal ideology and benefaction. To Roger, "filio meo precarissimo et heredi," came goods and wealth.[129] But of special interest to us are those bequests that symbolize the patrilineage, for example, "unum par de paternosters de corale cum monili arueo, quae quondam fuerunt domini patris mei." As the son and heir, Roger would keep state at Bolton in a worthy fashion, and household and domestic items were given for appropriate rooms: ". . . pro capell de Bolton in castro . . . pro principali camera . . . pro aula ibidem." More heirlooms, naturally, for the next in line, items whose aristocratic provenance and descent were a matter of pride and well worth some explication: "j compam cum aquario predicto habui ex dono domini Comitis Arundell, ij discos pro elemosina de argento cum armis meis et armis Comitis Suffolciensis, quos habui ex lagacione predicti Comitis, sub tali condicione quod semper remaneant rectis heredibus meis in memoriale Comitum predictorum."[130] It is easy to forget that these patriarchs were also soldiers, and we see the bequest of "meliorem gladium meum sum omnibus armaturis meis."[131] The whole collection of bequests, covering the material and the immaterial, together comprise the testamentary birth right, the special set of bonds between father and first (surviving) son.

There was another son, and he received his share of consolation prizes. The bequests to Stephen show both sides of paternal ties towards a younger son: "filio meo secundum gladium meum, cum benedictione mea," among numerous goods. Other kin were also remembered: "Isabellae, karissimae filiae meae," "Margaretae filiae meae, uxori Rogeri Lescrop filii mei," "Milicentae karissimae filiae mae," "domino Stephano Lescrop, consanguineo meo," "Domino Archiepiscopo Ebor, carissimo patri et filio meo," "Domino Johanni Lescrop, consanguineo meo," "Domino Henrico Lescrop, consanguineo meo," and "Henrico fitz Hugh, consanguineo meo." And when Richard came to the end of his will, he named his sons as his executors. Here again he was concerned to spell things out, a matter of pride as well as a need for clarity: "ordino et constituo executores meos, pro magna gratitudinis affectione, Rogeram Lescrop filium meum et heredem, et Stephanum Lescrop filium meum, et fratrem ejusdem Rogeri, sub benedictione mea." Understatement was not his style, and the events of his last decade must have shaken and reminded him of the insecurity of all earthly things.

The will of II lord Roger was written only some 37 months after that of his father. This time the son and heir, III lord Richard, was still a minor, and the father had to face a different sort of patriarchal situation. He spoke of young Richard much as his own father had but recently spoken of him: "prekarissimo et heredi."[132] The chain of transmission for worldy goods was also made explicit in a similar fashion, and we again encounter the coral *pater noster* that he had recently inherited: "quae quondam fuerunt domini patris mei." In a similar vein there were the *portiforium* and the missal, to go to the son and then from Scrope heir to heir in line. We see the same pride in the tale of acquisition and provenance: items which had belonged to lord Arundel, a silver cup with Scrope and Westmorland arms, dishes with Suffolk arms ("quos dominus pater meus habuit ex legacione Comitum . . . quod semper remaneant rectis heredibus meis in memoriale Comitum"). Again, we see the urge to discuss the way in which household furnishings were to be arranged: "pro principali camera . . . pro aula ibidem," and so forth.

Roger's son and heir, III lord Richard, died young. He was about 26 when he made his will in 1420. He left two very young sons, IV lord Henry and Richard, who became bishop of Carlisle.[133] The gifts to the children were perfunctory; the problems of the imminent minority, plus the peer's death in France rather than at home, may have made the usual detailed mental inventory of Bolton Castle's rooms and goods seem superfluous. Richard simply said "Y wyll that the eldest sone that y have by here have xx li. of gold. And y wyll that the yonger sone that y have by here have xx li. And y wyll that they be governed by myn exectours."

In this instance there were few details regarding father son transmission and more concerned with assuring that the executors would play squarely and honestly in carrying out their duties. In fact, cousin Marmaduke Lumley was to receive one of the family's precious heirlooms, the "cuppe of sylver ys jcalled the Constable bolle," perhaps to bind his faith to his more onerous duties as executor.[134] Richard died while on service in France, and the whole tenor of the will is different. It is not only much briefer than those of his father and grandfather, but it carries little of the tone of the Old Testament patriarch, surrounded by relatives, family possessions, and *his* lands and dwellings. There are no elaborate lists of personal possessions, no comments about where to shelve and arrange furnishings and knickknacks. A youthful, foreign death generated a will with a different psychological tone.

We have no extant will from Richard's son and heir, IV lord Henry, but we do from his own successor, V lord John. He was about 60 when he wrote his will in July, 1491, still "hole of mynde and in competent heale of body," as he tells us.[135] He was speaking, as a patriarch, to a son of about 30. First comes the most explicit statement about the transmission of birth right that we have in any of the Scrope wills: "To my sone and heire Hnery Scrop Goddes blessyng and myn, and all my stuffe that I have in my castell and place at Bolton." In a codicil of August, 1498 (some 3 months before the will was probated), John added to Henry's share, "all my parlement robys." Like his great grandfather at the beginning of the century, he singled out some other male relatives for bequests: his brother Ralf ("my lityll Bibyll that is at Bolton") and his brother Robert ("my chaemlett gowne").

There are no great surprises in these wills. The ties between fathers and sons offer strong examples of the bonds and relationships we have been discussing. The ties are illustrations of positive links. Other males of the family, out of the direct patrilineage line of succession, played the same game to a lesser extent. Stephen, I lord Richard's younger son, died in 1409, perhaps of the plague while on Irish service. He left a young boy, Stephen, and the father turned to the heir with sentiments comparable to those of his own father and his older brother Roger: "lego Stephano, filio meo praecarissimo et haeredi . . . cum benedictione mea, Beatae Mariae, Omnium Sanctorum et Sanctarum Dei: et unum gladium longum, quondam Edwardi regis Angliae, et mihi legatum per patrem meum."[136]

Beyond the bequests we encounter in the wills, the other device the family used to assert its continuity and prestige was local ecclesiastical patronage and benefaction. This was the common practice, and we hardly wish to imply that the Scropes had devious or manipulative ends in mind in their behavior, nor that they differed from others of their position and level of affluence. They did what was natural to and expected of wealthy families: They patronized the institutions of their corner of the world, and they obviously chose to enrich those houses within which many of them would rest until the second coming. But the end result was the development of a family tradition and a cumulative visible display of family munificence as heir after heir played his role. Local patronage and patriarchy went hand in hand.

In his will of 1400, I lord Richard asked for burial in the abbey church of St. Agatha, Richmond. This house was the family's perennial favorite, and its protection and support were probably accepted as part and parcel of Richmondshire Wenslydale "good lordship." In addition to his mortal remains (with their accompanying payments and fees), there were gifts of vestments, ecclesiastical goods of some splendor, a handsome cash bequest to the abbot, and lesser sums to each canon. Nor were other regional establishments neglected: regular, collegiate, and secular establishments at Egglestone, Meredge, Ellerton on Swale, Bradley, Jerveaux, Coverham, York, and all parish churches within Richmondshire, the Franciscans at Richmond, the hospital of St. Nicholas at Richmond, and many, many more houses benefited from the old man's generosity. Nor did Richard neglect his patriarchal distributions to a lesser flock: "cuilibet tenenti meo infra Richemondeshire ad jobitum meum existenti, claudum, secum, [caecum], vel impotentem, in cubiculo jacentem xiijs. iiijd. Item cuilibet ceco infra Richmondshir quibuscunque villis iijs.iiijd. qui mendicus vel pauper fuerit. Item xxl. ad distribuendum inter pauperculos tenentes meos . . . ab obitum meum existentes."

If the provisions of Richard's will were implemented to the full extent, we have before us an extensive local network of charity and subsidized prayers. They contributed to the perpetuation of family identity. Roger followed his father's lead, with burial at St. Agatha and numerous gifts to the house and to its separate personnel, £40 to the abbot and smaller sums to each canon. III lord Richard, though dying at Rouen, also followed suit: "my body to be byryed atte the abbe of Seynt Agase in Richemon-schyre." He followed his grandfather's lead in distributing largesse to other Yorkshire institutions as well: £10 to the fabric of York cathedral, money ("as myn executours thenke godly") to the four orders of friars in York, and cash to the friary at Richmond. He also left provisions for the creation of a college—a largish establishment that was probably never built—of five priests, five clerks, and three "pouer men." The endowment was meant to be sufficient to support a handsome life style, but this project was probably another casualty of the minority and wardship of his son and heir.

Some 70 years later lord John was still in the beaten path: burial at St. Agatha "yf it fortune me to deceasse wtynne the forsaid shyre," plus gifts of cash and vestments, and "my Bybill inprented, and my book, also in-prented, called Cronica Cronicarum." There were small distributions to some other local institutions: the college at Rushworth, and to the parish priests of Weston and of Barhambourne. II lord Roger's brother Stephen also asked for a burial at St. Agatha, and he too gave money to individuals within the house. As we saw in his patriarchal bequests, he was quite as-sertive about his place on the chain. He, with his father and his brother Roger, had come through some difficult times, and he knew that he was but one neck away from the main line of succession. Burial was to be "in ecclesia abbatiae Sanctae Agatae juxta Richmund, juxta tumbam domini Ricardi, patris mei, ibidem." He must have had suppressed patriarchal in-clinations, for he too distributed considerable largesse to the individual brothers of the house, to other Richmondshire and Yorkshire institutions, and to the poor—tenants and otherwise—of the neighborhood. He was seemingly pious, generous, and perhaps inclined to fill some of the role that his brother Roger has only lived to fill for about five years after their father had died.

The wills of the men of the family confirm and reinforce the lessons we drew from a study of their demographic fortunes and political lives. There is every reason to believe that they, collectively, had a keen and sus-tained (and self-sustaining) view of family continuity. They not only worked to survive, but they worked to keep their traditions, their intergen-erational links, and their local role alive and highly visible. There are many indications of danger, of miscalculation, and perhaps of frustration at their inability to rise still higher in the councils of the realm. On the other hand, there are numerous indications that the Scropes recognized the nature and limits of the resources on which their position and role depended, and that they fully enjoyed their long run in the drama of patriarchy. For all their problems and periodic slips from grace, they have to be classified as a successful family and a model for the themes on which we have enlarged at such length.

Notes

1. For some family treatises of medieval and renaissance Italy, see *Leon Battista Alberti, Della Famiolia*, trans. A. Guarino (Lewisburg, Pa., 1971); see also Gene Brucker, ed., *Two Memoirs of Renaissance Florence: The Diaries of Buonaccorso Pitti and Gregorio Deti*, trans. Julia Martines (New York, 1967).

2. Francis W. Kent, *Household and Lineage in Renaissance Florence* (Princeton, N.J., 1977), is a model study for a structural approach. Kent too worries about the problems of circular reasoning and tautology that can accompany a study of kinship that begins by examining society "through kinship-colored glass" (p. viii). Kent's notes offer a good guide to current work on the family in renaissance Italy, up to the time of writing. See also, Diane Owen Hughes, "Urban Growth and Family Structure in Medieval Genoa," *Past and Present* 66 (1975), 3–28, and David Herlihy and Christiane Klapisch-Zuber, *Tuscans and Their Families* (New Haven, Conn. and London, 1985).

3. John W. McKenna, "Henry VI of England and the Dual Monarchy: Aspects of Royal Political Propaganda," *Journal of the Warburg and Courtauld Institute* 28 (1965), 145–62, and "Piety and Propaganda: The Cult of Henry VI," in *Chaucer and Middle English Studies in Honour of Rossell Hope Robbins*, ed. Beryl Rowland (London, 1974), pp. 72–88; Ralph A. Griffiths, "The Sense of Dynasty in the Reign of Henry VI," in *Patronage, Pedigree, and Power in Late Medieval England*, ed. Charles Ross (Gloucester, 1979), pp. 13–36.

4. John Rous, *The Rous Roll*, historical intro. Charles Ross (London, 1980), pp. v-xviii. For cartularies, see Godfrey R. C. Davis, *Medieval Cartularies of Great Britain: A Short Catalogue* (London, 1958), pp. 140–56, covering secular and family cartularies; Viscount Dillon and W. H. St. John Hope, eds., *Pageant of the Birth, Life, and Death of Richard Beauchamp, Earl of Warwick* (London, 1914); Anthony R. Wagner, *Pedigree and Progress* (London and Chichester, 1975). On the development of what we recognize as self-consciousness in late medieval Europe, see Georges Duby and Philippe Braunstein, "The Emergence of the Individual," in *A History of Private Life: II. Revelation of the Medieval World*, ed., Georges Duby, trans. Arthur Goldhammer (Cambridge, Mass., 1988), pp. 549–57.

5. E. A. G. Lamborn, "The Arms on the Chaucer Tomb at Ewelme," *Oxoniensia* 5 (1940), 78–93; "On the Heraldry at South Kilrington," *Yorkshire Archaeological*

Journal 22 (1913), 226–30; "Enumeration and Explanation of Devices . . . of the House of York," *Archaeologia* 17 (1814), 226–27; see Nigel Saul, *Scenes from Provincial Life: Knightly Families in Sussex, 1280–1400* (Oxford, 1986), pp. 140–60, on the building and decoration of Etchingham church and p. 151, on the play element in the use of coats of arms.

6. J. Newman, *The Buildings of England: West Kent and the Weald* (Harmondsworth, 1969), pp. 219–21; Peter W. Fleming, "Charity, Faith, and the Gentry of Kent, 1422–1529," in *Property and Politics: Essays in Later Medieval English History*, ed. Anthony J. Pollard (Gloucester, 1984), pp. 36–58; Michael A. Hicks, "Piety and Lineage in the Wars of the Roses: The Hungerford Experience," in *Kings and Nobles in the Later Middle Ages*, ed. Ralph A. Griffiths and James Sherborne (Gloucester, 1986), pp. 90–108. On the propaganda of burial, see Elizabeth A. R. Brown, *The Oxford Collection of the Drawings of Roger de Gaignières and the Royal Tombs of Saint-Denis*, Transactions of the American Philosophical Society 78, pt. 5 (Philadelphia, 1988), and full notes and bibliography.

7. Kenneth Bruce McFarlane, *The Nobility of Later Medieval England* (Oxford, 1973), pp. 61–82. For an interesting if unconvincing exposition, see Alan Macfarlane, *The Origins of English Individualism* (Oxford, 1978), especially chapters 4 and 5, on land ownership, 1200 to 1750; J. M. W. Bean, *The Decline of English Feudalism, 1215–1540* (Manchester, 1968), pp. 104–79, on uses; and see Michael A. Hicks, "The Beauchamp Trust, 1439–87," *BIHR* 54 (1981), 135–49: p. 137, on "the use as a flexible device extending the current tenant's control at the expense of the heir," and p. 148, for various strategies that did not divert the path of primogenitary inheritance, but that "deferred the inheritance of the main line." See J. L. Barton, "The Medieval Use," *Law Quarterly Review* 81 (1965), 562–77: p. 570, "The heir represented his ancestor much more fully than the feoffee represented his feoffar," a point that medieval fathers—if not always modern students—had little trouble remembering. See also Stroud F. C. Milsom, *The Legal Framework of English Feudalism* (Cambridge, 1976).

8. R. G. K. A. Mertes, *The English Noble Household, 1250–1600* (Oxford, 1988), pp. 161–69; Susan D. Amussen, *An Ordered Society: Gender and Class in Early Modern England* (Oxford, 1988), pp. 36–66, on patriarchy and husband-wife relationships; p. 36, "The family was a social, public instituion, not a private one that could be left to its own devices. On that everyone was in agreement."

9. Michael Mitterauer and Reinhard Seider, *The European Family*, trans. Karla Oosterveen and Manfred Hurzinger (Oxford, 1982), p. 6. For a discussion that tries to balance various values and approaches, see David Bakan, *And They Took Themselves Wives: The Emergence of Patriarchy in Western Civilization* (New York, 1979), p. 12, with a useful emphasis on "the basic relationship between men and their women's children, as the key to the social reality of the family."

10. Michael M. Sheehan, "The Formation and Stability of Marriage in the Fourteenth Century: Evidence of an Ely Register," *Mediaeval Studies* 33 (1971), 228–64, and "Choice of Marriage Partner in the Middle Ages: Development and Mode of Application to a Theory of Marriage," *Studies in Medieval and Renaissance History* n.s. 1 (1978), 1–33. For the legal approach, see Richard H. Helmholz, *Marriage Litigation in Medieval England* (Cambridge, 1974), and see James A. Brundage, *Law,*

Sex, and Christian Society in Medieval Europe (Chicago, 1987), for canon law and a rich collection of material on virtually all aspects of marriage and sexual relations. From a different direction, Richard H. Helmholz, "Infanticide in the Province of Canterbury During the Fifteenth Century," *History of Childhood Quarterly* 2 (1975), 379–90.

11. James H. Ramsay, *Lancaster and York* (Oxford, 1892), II, 114. A grim family tale: the father (Michael, VII earl of Suffolk) died at the siege of Harfleur, the eldest brother among his surviving children (Michael, VIII earl) was killed at Agincourt, two younger brothers fell in the same day at Jargeau, and the brother who had become the earl was taken prisoner and subsequently exchanged for a younger brother, who died in "ennemyes handes."

12. Full references to the four sets of Inquisitions analyzed here are given in the list of abbreviations following the preface.

13. Roy H. Hunnisett, "The Reliability of Inquisitions as Historical Evidence," in *The Study of Medieval Records: Essays in Honour of Kathleen Major* ed. D. A. Bullough and Robin L. Storey (Oxford, 1971), pp. 206–37. Most of the material discussed by Hunnisett in arguing against reliability focuses on the formulaic nature of the proofs of age and the ready use of rounded figures, rather than on detectable errors of either identification or minority-majority questions. See also E. R. Stevenson, "The Escheator," in *The English Government at Work, 1327–36. Vol. II: Fiscal Administration*, ed. W. A. Morris and J. R. Strayer (Cambridge, Mass., 1947), pp. 109–67; See also, Josiah C. Russell, *British Medieval Population* (Albuquerque, N.M., 1948), pp. 93–95, 102–14, for a more sanguine view of the value and reliability of inquisitions and proofs of age than that of most critics.

14. *Lancashire*, I, 77.

15. *Lancashire*, I, 76. Also II, 19, 81, "obiit sine herede."

16. *Lancashire*, I, 92.

17. *Lancashire*, II, 54.

18. Alan Macfarlane, *The Family Life of Ralph Josselin* (Cambridge, 1970), p. 156, a circle graph of friends/neighbors, and p. 157, one of "intimate, effective and peripheral kin," constructed to show relative proximity to ego.

19. Ada E. Levett, *Studies in Manorial History*, ed. Helen Maude Cam, M. Corte, and L. Sutherland (Oxford, 1938; repr. New York, 1963), pp. 256, 285 ff. In the accounts of six manors, of a total of 358 tenants 118 were succeeded by sons (of whom 70 were of age, 48 minors), 51 by daughters (24 of age, 27 minors), 103 by other relatives (75 of age, 28 minors), and 86 by miscellaneous or unknown heirs or by no heir at all. See also, on replacement rates, Sylvia Thrupp, "The Problem of Replacement Rates in Late Medieval England," *Economic History Review*, 2nd series 18 (1965), 101–19; Zvi Razi, "Family, Land, and the Village Community in Later Medieval England," *Past and Present* 93 (1981), 3–36: p. 27, "As far as land was concerned, distant relatives were more important to a villager living in 1400 than to one living in 1300." See also Russell, *British Medieval Population*, chapters 7–10.

20. See Joel T. Rosenthal, "Heirs' Ages and Family Succession in Yorkshire, 1399–1422," *Yorkshire Archaeological Journal* 56 (1984), 87–94, for a more detailed analysis of the material printed in *Yorkshire*; see also Sue Sheridan Walker, "Free

Consent and Marriage of Feudal Wards in Medieval England," *Journal of Medieval History* 8 (1982), 123–34.

21. For some long minorities, as reported in the Inquisitions, see *Nottinghamshire*, I, 154, and II, 8; see also *Yorkshire*, 9. For a precise dating of the age of minor heirs—impressive for their precision if not necessarily for accuracy—see *Lancashire*, I, 86, 112.

22. McFarlane, *Nobility of Later Medieval England*, 147. The issue is treated in detail, pp. 136–76, with tables (pp. 173–76) on the incidence of survival, by quarter-century intervals. Also see Jack R. Lander, *Conflict and Stability in Fifteenth-Century England* (London, 1969), pp. 174–75; *CP*, V, app. H ("Earldoms and Baronies in History and Law and the Doctrine of Abeyance"), pp. 649–79 on peerages to which no successor was summoned.

23. Lander, *Conflict and Stability*, 174–75.

24. McFarlane, *Nobility of Later Medieval England*, 144. For an older statement on the effeminate condition of the nobility, see William Denton, *England in the Fifteenth Century* (London, 1888), pp. 260–61: ". . . the physical vigor of the members of the baronage was but slight. The barons . . . were for the most part low in stature and feeble in frame." Denton expatiates on "The physical degeneration of many of the peers." Much was also made in the older literature of the way in which the towering and vigorous Edward IV was so soon worn out by "excess."

25. The current view, which is against extensive decimation, is summarized by Kenneth B. McFarlane, "The Wars of the Roses," reprinted in *England in the Fifteenth Century* (London, 1981), pp. 231–67. This is the "Raleigh Lecture" of 1964; pp. 257–59 are most relevant. McFarlane says the matter would have been sorted out long ago, had we but followed the enlightened lead of T. L. Kington Oliphant, "Was the Old English Aristocracy Destroyed by the Wars of the Roses?" *TRHS* I (1872), 351–56. This issue is a fairly standard one for discussion: Charles D. Ross, *The Wars of the Roses* (London, 1976), pp. 151–62; Anthony Goodman, *The Wars of the Roses: Military Activity and English Society, 1452–97* (London, 1981), pp. 209–12; Thomas B. Pugh, "The Magnates, Knights, and Gentry," in *Fifteenth-Century England*, ed. S. B. Chrimes, Charles D. Ross, and Ralph A. Griffiths (Manchester, 1972), pp. 86–128; J. R. Lander, *Crown and Nobility, 1450–1509* (London, 1976), appendices, pp. 301–08, 321; C. F. Richmond, "The Nobility and the Wars of the Roses, 1459–61," *Nottingham Medieval Studies* 21 (1977), 71–86.

26. There are still but a limited number of monographic treatments. For the fall and subsequent rise of the Percies, see J. M. W. Bean, *The Estates of the Percy Family, 1416–1537* (Oxford, 1958); for comparable problems, as suffered and partially overcome by the Staffords, see Carole Rawcliffe, *The Staffords, Earls of Stafford, and Dukes of Buckingham, 1394–1521* (Cambridge, 1978).

27. On the demography of the peerage, see Thomas H. Hollingsworth, *The Demography of the British Peerage, Population Studies*, suppl. vol. 18, 2 (1964); Joel T. Rosenthal, "Mediaeval Longevity and the Secular Peerage, 1350–1500," *Population Studies* 27 (1973), 287–93; as a corrective to Rosenthal's calculations, Thomas H. Hollingsworth, "A Note on the Mediaeval Longevity of the Secular Peerage, 1350–1500," *Population Studies* 29 (1975), 155–59. From the other end—fertility and infertility—useful comments in Thomas H. Hollingsworth, *Historical Demography*

(London, 1969), pp. 206–10, and Edward Anthony Wrigley, *Population and History* (New York, 1969), pp. 62–67.

28. Hicks, "The Beauchamp Trust," 135–49.

29. For the bitterness of a childless peer and the decline of the Berkeleys, see John Smyth of Nibley, *The Lives of the Berkeleys*, ed. J. Maclean, Bristol and Gloucester Archaeological Society (1883), passim. See also McFarlane, *Nobility of Later Medieval England*, 55: "Almost always when a man is found dispersing his inheritance, it turns out that he was childless or without male issue."

30. McFarlane, Nobility of Later Medieval England, 138.

31. McFarlane, Nobility of Later Medieval England, 147.

32. Colin F. Richmond, "The Pastons Revisited: Marriage and the Family in Fifteenth-Century England," *BIHR* 58 (1985), 28–31; Ann S. Haskell, "The Paston Women on Marriage in Fifteenth-Century England," *Viator* 4 (1973), 459–71; Philippa Madden, "Honour Among the Pastons: Gender and Integrity in Fifteenth-Century English Provincial Life," *Journal of Medieval History* 14 (1988), 357–71.

33. George A. Holmes, *The Estates of the Higher Nobility in Fourteenth-Century England* (Cambridge, 1957), pp. 7–40 ("The Inheritance") and pp. 41–57 ("The Tenure of the Inheritance"): p. 40, ". . . a natural emptying and replenishing of the ranks of noble society by the extinction of old families and the elevation of new ones, there was also a definite tendency for inheritances which survived to grow larger." Noel Denholm-Young, *The Country Gentry in the Fourteenth Century* (Oxford, 1969).

34. Sylvia Thrupp, *The Merchant Class of Medieval London* (Ann Arbor, Mich. 1948), pp. 222–33, on "the fluidity of the merchant class;" p. 200, for a table of testators' heirs, showing that of 805 cases between 1288 and 1527, 286 were lacking heirs in the male line; p. 222, for the reminder that "heavy odds against the survival of male heirs do not preclude the chance favoring of individual families for successive generations." And in Italy, Kent, *Household and Lineage*, 252: ". . . a vision which defined the family both as a living continuum of 'ancestors, and of the living, and of those who by grace are to come.' 'Men desire sons, grandsons, and descendants' . . ."

35. For the barony of Bourne, Ivor J. Sanders, *English Baronies: A Study of their Origins and Descent, 1086–1327* (Oxford, 1960), pp. 19–20.

36. On the barony of Irthingon, Sanders, *English Baronies*, 124.

37. The description of the Earl of Salisbury's reburial, at Bisham, is in Edith Rickert, *Chaucer's World* (New York, 1948), pp. 107–10: taken from *A Collection of Ordinances and Regulations for the Governance of the Royal Household*. On the way in which hearts hardened, as did the lines of partisanship, see Margaret Kekewich, "The Attainder of the Yorkists in 1459: Two Contemporary Accounts," *BIHR* 55 (1982), 25–34. "The transition was from clemency to political propaganda . . . unprecedented for its vicious clarity . . . [and ultimately] to bloodshed."

38. Jack R. Lander, *Crown and Nobility, 1450–1509* (London, 1976), p. 127. The issue is treated, pp. 127–57, 307–08 (for a table that gives data on attainders and their reversals, 1453–1509: also, pp. 267–300, on Henry VII's use of bonds and recognizances as a form of social control and political coercion.

39. Bean, *Estates of the Percy Family*, 69.

40. Michael A. Hicks, "Attainder, Resumption, and Coercion, 1461–1529," *Parliamentary History* 3 (1984), 15–31. Edward IV revoked 42 of 140 acts of attainder, Henry VII 46 of 138. However, the revocations were due more to political vicissitudes than to royal clemency: "The politics of attainder may be described as a rather complex game in which the king wrote the rules *and* cast the dice" (p. 23).

41. As quoted in *CP*, from *RP*, VI, 43–45.

42. Lord Welles petition, *RP*, V, 617–18: "He is left so bare of lyvelode that he may not do to youre Highnes so good service as his hert specially desireth to doo, nor like accordyng to the degre that he is called to."

43. See Joel T. Rosenthal, "Down the Up Staircase:Quondam Peers and Downward Mobility in Late Medieval England," *Medaevalia* (forthcoming).

44. See Georges Duby, *The Knight, the Lady, and the Priest: The Making of Marriage in Medieval France*, trans. Barbara Bray (Harmondsworth, 1985), pp. 87–106, for some suggestive parallels. Despite its value regarding the structure of authority, there is no index reference to "patriarchy" in Marc Bloch, *Feudal Society*, trans. L. A. Manyon (Chicago, 1961). In addition, there is no citation for this topic in the *Dictionary of the Middle Ages* or *The Encyclopedia of the Social Sciences*.

45. For Darcy, see *CP*, IV, 63; See also Barry Coward, *The Stanleys, Lords Stanley, and Earls of Derby, 1385–1672*, Chetham Society, 3rd series 30 (1983), 2–4. An early seventeenth-century coat of Stanley arms gave them nine quarterings—Stanley, Bamville, Latham, Man, Harrington, Goushill, Strange, Montalt, and Brandon—and seven of these claims were through marriages with heiresses. For the dukes of York and the display of their assertions at Fotheringay, see *VCH Northampton*, II, 242–43.

46. For Audley and Kynaston, see *CP*, I, 341.

47. *CP*, I, 24. In the late fourteenth century the childless earl of Pembroke told lord Abergavenny that he could be his heir if "he bore the earl's arms undifferenced." Along this same line, see Thomas Fuller, *A History of the Worthies of England*, ed. P. A. Nuttall (Cambridge, 1840; repr. New York, 1965), I, 348: "when she [Maud Lucy, wife of the earl of Northumberland] saw that she should die without issue, [she] gave to earl Henry her husband the castle and honour of Cockermouth, with many other manors in Cumberland and Westmorland, with condition that his issue should bear the arms of the Lucies quartered, with their own arms of the Percies."

48. *TE*, III, 305.

49. Hicks, "The Beauchamp Trust," 137.

50. *SMW*, I, 143–44.

51. *Oxfordshire*, 48. For a different strategy or a different route, in the quest for immortality, there is the supplication of Robert Hylle,that the burial church "insert our names Robert and Isabelle in their mortiloge, and every year on the days of our deaths and of our anniversaries our names shall be read" (*SMW*, I, 403).

52. Charles L. Kingsford, ed., *The Stonor Letters and Papers, 1290–1483*, Camden Society, 3rd series 29 (1919), 136–37.

53. Norman Davis, ed., *Paston Letters and Papers of the Fifteenth Century* (Oxford, 1971), I, 256–57. See also McFarlane, *Nobility of Later Medieval England*, 113–14, quoting from the Stonor letters: "It is reasonable [for] a gentilman to know his

pedegre and his possibilyte." Hugh Paget, "The Youth of Anne Boleyn," *BIHR* 54 (1981), 162, quoting Cavendish's *Life of Wolsey*, where the earl of Northumberland says of Anne that her "state of descent is equivalent to mine when I shall be in most dignity."

54. *CCR 1454–1461*, 355–57. Family feeling led to such sentiments as, "I hadde lever that John and John thy brethern bastardes receive the same than any other straunge persons."

55. Henry S. Bennett, *The Pastons and Their England*, 2nd ed. (Cambridge, 1932), p. 71, where there are more references to literary and didactic texts that elaborate the theme of "reuerence to thy parents deare." But no behavioral pattern or value system is without its qualifying instances, and when William I's wife aided their son Robert in a rebellion against his father, she said, "O my lord, do not wonder that I love my first-born child with tender affection. By the power of the Most High, if my son Robert were dead and buried seven feet in the earth . . . and I could bring him back to life with my own blood, I would shed my life-blood for him" (*Orderic Vitalis*, 3, 102–4): quoted, Ralph V. Turner, "Children of the Anglo-Norman Royalty and Their Upbringing," *Medieval Prosopography* 11/2 (1990), 36.

56. On the strength of the two-way pull, see Colin Richmond, *John Hopton, A Fifteenth-Century Suffolk Gentleman* (Cambridge, 1981), pp. 136–42; Hans Medick and David Warren Sabean, "Interest and Emotion in Family and Kinship Studies: A Critique of Social History and Anthropology," in *Interest and Emotion: Essays in the Study of Family and Kinship*, ed. Hans Medick and David Warren Sabean (Cambridge, 1984), pp. 9–27.

57. Medick and Sabean, "Interest and Emotion," pp. 75–79. For instances of hard feelings between fathers and sons in an earlier century, George C. Homans, *English Villagers of the Thirteenth Century* (Cambridge, Mass., 1941), pp. 154–58. Some continental examples are presented, Jane K. Breitscher, "As the Twig is Bent: Children and Their Parents in an Aristocratic Society," *Journal of Medieval History* 2 (1976), 181–91.

58. Robert Filmer, *Patriarchia and Other Political Writings*, ed. Peter Laslett (Oxford, 1949), pp. 57, 62. For a discussion of Filmer and the evolution of his ideas, Gordon J. Schochet, *Patriarchalism in Political Thought* (Oxford, 1975). For the grain of salt with which Filmer and his followers should be read, see Miriam Slater, *Family Life in the Seventeenth Century: The Verneys of Claydon House* (London, 1984), p. 75: "He was an ardent Royalist, given to employing the typical 'head and members' metaphor—a choice of imagery much utilized by the political and social conservatives of his time." On a more elementary level, for manifestations of the hierarchical approach that is a concomitent of patriarchy, see William Nelson, ed. *A Fifteenth Century School Book* (Oxford, 1956), pp. 13–18, 66–67, on dutiful obedience and related themes; p. 15: "I love my father and my mother best of all the worlede. Howbeit: thei be not all the kyndest to me." So it goes.

59. Francis R. H. DuBoulay, *An Age of Ambition* (London, 1970), p. 141.

60. Colin Richmond, "The Pastons Revisited," 25–36. On marriage, there is still interesting material in Frederick J. Furnivall *Child Marriages, Divorce, and Ratification . . . 1561–66* Early English Text Society, 108 (London, 1897).

61. See Michael Sheehan, "The Formation and Stability of Marriage" and

"Choice of Marriage Partner." See also Joel T. Rosenthal, "Aristocratic Marriage and the English Peerage, 1350–1500: Social Institution and Personal Bond," *Journal of Medieval History* 10 (1984), 181–94.

62. Samuel Bentley, *Excerpta Historica* (London, 1833), pp. 8–9.

63. James Gairdner, ed., *The Paston Letters* (London, 1895), I, 121–22. See Charles L. Kingsford, *Prejudice and Promise in Fifteenth Century England* (Oxford, 1925; repr. London, 1962), p. 172: "Can one without prejudice see in it [Suffolk's letter] anything but the unaffected statement of the principles which had inspired the writer himself throughout his public and private life?"

64. On Suffolk as an author, see Kingsford, *Prejudice and Promise*, 171–76. On letters and letter writing, see Norman Davis, "The *Litera Troili* and English Letters," *Review of English Studies* n.s. 15 (1965), 233–44; on the "courtesies of intercourse," see Alison Hanham, *The Celys and Their World: An English Merchant Family of the Fifteenth Century* (Cambridge, 1985), p. 12. See Eileen Power, ed. and trans., *The Goodman of Paris* (London, 1928), pp. 42–43, "I would that you know how to give good will and honour and service in great measure and abundance more than is fit for me, either to serve another husband, if you have one, after me, or to teach greater wisdom to your daughters, friends, or others, if you list and have such need."

65. Gairdner, *Paston Letters*, II, 39.

66. Gairdner, *Paston Letters*, 39, and II, 92–93.

67. Gairdner, *Paston Letters*, II, 142: The letter continues in this vein: "I charge you upon my blyssyng that in any thyng towchyng your fader that shuld be hys worchep, profyte, or avayle, that ye do your devoyr and dylygent labor to the fortherans therin, as ye wulle have my good will, and that shall cause your fader to be better fader to you."

68. Gairdner, *Paston Letters*, II, 175–77.

69. Gairdner, *Paston Letters*, II, 178–79.

70. Alison Hanham, ed., *The Cely Letters, 1472–1488*, Early English Text Society, 273 (1975), letter 67.

71. Hanham, *Cely Letters*, letter 4.

72. Antonia Gransden, *Historical Writing in England: vol. II, C. 1307 to the Early Sixteenth Century* (Ithaca, N.Y., 1982), pp. 194–219: p. 195, on how Shakespeare "created his Henry V from pre-existing legend."

73. *CP*, VIII, 27.

74. As quoted in *CP*, III, 293.

75. John M. Wallace Hadrill, "The Blood Feud of the Franks," in his *The Long-Haired Kings* (London, 1962), pp. 121–47: p. 141, ". . . the requirements of the feud that the outcome of vengeance should be publicly displayed and not hidden."

76. Kingsford, *The Stonor Letters*, letter 91.

77. *Chichele*, 79.

78. *Fifty*, 22–26.

79. *Lincoln*, 82.

80. PCC, 37 Bennett.

81. PCC, 27 Vox.

82. *Collectanea Topographica et Genealogica* (London, 1834–43), III, 259.

83. *TE*, IV, 135–36; *TE*, III, 246–48, for a reference to "primogenito meo . . . meo secundo genito . . . meo tertio genito . . . meo quarto genito . . ."

84. *Bedford*, 8–9. In *Buckinghamshire*, 52–53, the testator refers to "Johanni Donyngton seniori filio Johannis filii mei nuper defuncti . . . [et] Roberto Donyngton junior filio dicti Johannis."

85. *TE*, III, 247–48.

86. *Fifty*, 55–64.

87. *Fifty*, 59.

88. *Oxford*, 28–29.

89. *Chichele*, 385: The father was on to a good thing: "Jeo lise et ordeigne que mesme Nicholas ferra autre pilgrimage a le shryne Seint Thomas de Chauntirbury en sa propre persone et la offrer un rolle door et avera pour mesme ses costes et expenses."

90. *Chichele*, 36; *SMW*, I, 218–19.

91. *SMW*, II, 58–59.

92. *SMW*, I, 218.

93. *SMW*, II, 38.

94. *Oxfordshire*, 55.

95. *Bedford*, 46: Manyngham senior was determined—unlike so many of the rest of us—to have the last word in a family quarrel. He said that he was driven to act in such an extreme fashion because of his son's "Innaturall and unkynde dealyng caused me to doo as I have done."

96. *Chichele*, 48: If the son-and-heir carried out the provisions of his father's will, the son would receive "a short sword garnizsed with gold, a bible in frenssh of ij volom and sauter glosid of Richard Ermyth, a cuppe with the covercle of silver called John of thrumm."

97. *Sharpe*, I, 354.

98. *Sharpe*, I, 606–7.

99. *SMW*, I, 273–75.

100. *TE*, IV, 273.

101. *SMW*, I, 221.

102. *Oxfordshire*, 55; also, *SMW*, II, 59: ". . . if by chance the said Robert shall do otherwise in anything that he promised to do . . ."

103. *SMW*, I, 225–26. See *Chichele*, 519, where an older brother is to have custody of a younger, and a grandfather is to look after some children not yet of age.

104. *TE*, III, 240; also, *TE*, IV, 40.

105. *Collectanea*, II, 65.

106. *Oxfordshire*, 47. This father was obviously worried, for he wished them "Godes blessing and myn." For another example of someone facing this dilemma, 74: "And if it happen . . . my sonnes, to departe to god within age."

107. *SMW*, II, 58–59.

108. *Oxfordshire*, 34.

109. *SMW*, I, 218–19.

110. *TE*, II, 19–20. He named the members of the family, and then added, "and all the saules of tham, that I have hadd any thyng in this world undeserved."

111. *Buckinghamshire*, 201.

112. PCC, 27 Logge.

113. *SMW*, II, 38.

114. Bridget Vale is preparing a full length study of the Scropes, drawing from her University of York dissertation.

115. Thomas Frederick Tout, *Chapters in the Administrative History of Medieval England* (Manchester, 1920–37), III, 277. For service with John of Gaunt, see Sydney Armitage Smith, ed., *John of Gaunt's Register*, Camden Society, 3rd series, vols. 20–21 (1911), and Gaunt's will, *TE*, I, 229. I lord Richard is covered by the *DNB* and *CP*, XI, 531–39.

116. Charles D. Ross, "The Yorkshire Baronage, 1399–1435," D. Phil. thesis, Oxford University, 1951), p. 188. Much biographical material was collected by Nicholas Harris Nicolas, ed., *The Controversy Between Sir Richard Scrope and Sir Robert Grosvenor* (London, 1832), vol. II, passim.

117. See Ross, "Yorkshire Baronage," pp. 187–206, for the Scrope estates and finances.

118. For the wardship and marriage of the Tibetot heiress, see *CPR*, 1377–81, 539: Richard Scrope paid 230 marks for the custody of the three girls and their lands. See *CCR*, 1385–89, 27, for the partition of Tibetot land between the heiresses and their husbands, Roger Scrope, Stephen Scrope, and Philip Despenser. See also, *CFR*, VII, 215; *CFR*, VIII, 179–80, where £227. 7s. 3¼d. was to be paid for custody of the land, and 1000 marks for the marriages: British Library, Additional Manuscript 28,209, 6b; *CPR*, 1369–74, 396–97, 468–69. Richard, III lord Tibetot, died, s.p.m., 13 April 1372, aged about 31. All three of his daughters bore male heirs.

119. *CPR*, 1401–05, 362.

120. *CP*, XI, 542–3.

121. Ibid.

122. *CCR*, 1419–22, 128, 208. Bishop Richard's will, of little value for our purposes, is printed in *TE*, III, 169.

123. I lord Richard received various favors and grants from the king: *CCR*, 1392–96, 94, 221–22, 225, 373; *CFR*, VII, 249–50; *CFR*, IX, 49, 88; *CFR*, XI, 10, 195–96.

124. For William Scrope, earl of Wiltshire, *CP*, XII, ii, 730. Though Scrope was childless at his death, his widow married three more times and had children in at least two of these marriages.

125. Ramsay, *Lancaster and York*, I, 15. See also, Nicolas, *The Controversy between Sir Richard Scrope* II, 29–30; *RP*, III, 453. British Library, Add. Ms. 28,209, f. 13: Lord Richard said, "he would alwayes be loyall and true to his majesty, but never bear any office under him againe."

126. The *DNB* entry for I lord Richard also carries some brief biographical information for Stephen.

127. For John, see *DNB* and *CP*, XI, 544–45. For recent accounts of some of his activities, particularly on behalf of Richard III, Charles D. Ross, *Richard III* (London, 1981), pp. 49, 118, 120–21, 160, 182, 197, 206: all these references build a picture of Scrope as being one of the northerners whom Richard III used, in the south and southwest, to control unfamiliar areas through a reliance upon old (and transplanted) friends. See also, Michael Bennett, *The Battle of Bosworth* (Gloucester,

1985), passim. For Henry VII's relations with John, see *CPR*, 1485–94, 190, 199, 216, 273, and William Campbell, ed., *Materials for a History of the Reign of Henry VII*, Rolls Series, 60 (2 vols., London, 1873–77) II, 235, 448. In February 1488, John received a license to go anywhere in England, "not more than twenty-two miles distant from London." He had to post a bond of £2,000 for good behavior: in July 1489 the leash was loosened, or at least extended, and he was allowed to go anywhere south of the Trent.

128. For Henry, VII lord Srope, *CP*, XI, 546.

129. *TE*, I, 272–78: the manuscript is Lambeth Palace Archepiscopal Registers, Arundel's Register, 201b–203b.

130. Naming the provenance of special items was a common practice among all levels of propertied folk. Hugh Willoughby left his son a chalice, "somtyme Ladie Bardolf," and a ewer that had been "somtyme Lady Bassett" (*TE*, II, 130–31).

131. Richard had seen combat at Winchelsea, Berwick, Paris, Calais, and Najera, to name only some of the more prominent engagements in which he had participated.

132. *TE*, I, 328–31: the manuscript is Lambeth Palace, Arundel's Register, 204a–205b.

133. *TE*, IV, 1–3: the manuscript is PCC 49 Marche.

134. The Lumleys, the Scropes of Bolton, and the Nevilles were intertwined for several generations. For the Lumleys, *CP*, VIII, 269–73, and Edith Milner, *The Lumleys of Lumley Castle* (London, 1904).

135. *TE*, IV, 94–97; the manuscript is PCC 26 Horne.

136. *TE*, III, 38–40; the manuscript is Lambeth Palace, Arundel's Register, II, 40b–41a.

II Networks: The Horizontal and Collateral Family

As the Winds of Law Blow

These essays, as we stated above, are designed to present a brief for the simultaneous existence of various forms and permutations of family structure. Individuals lived lives that were cast into and contained within a number of societal molds, and family was but one of them. And then, within that mold labeled family, there existed variations of form, along with variations through time. We have looked at some of the aspects of the father-son relationship in the previous essay. Though most men were fathers, and all men were (or had been) sons, even that particular and critical relationship was by no means the only one that linked those whom society defined as kin. Nor was it always as important for the concerned parties as we have perhaps made it seem by our close inspection.

In this chapter we move outwards, away from the short and relatively inflexible bond between fathers and sons. Our attention turns from the vertical axis that defined and linked the patrilineage (through time) and that reinforced the values of the patriarchate, and we look now along horizontal planes, towards the more flexible bonds and relationships between siblings, cousins, and the other cognatic and agnatic kin who often lived, worked, schemed, and fought together. The interactions of these horizontal kin may actually represent only a small fraction of the sum of significant social interaction that comprised each individual's private and public life, a small proportion of the total number of the bonds, links, and relationships of the full biography. The sum of the instances of interrelationships between kin can take on its own existence, whether we study lives or families. That sum becomes the social entity that we identify—and the danger is that we reify—as the history of a family, and the moments or instances of interaction become the "events" of family history, as surely as those contacts and clashes of armies are the most significant events of military history.

Some fathers were closely involved with their sons, others less so. Not even the high walls of patriarchy shaded all living spaces in an identical fashion. Regardless of the level or the temperature of the affect, this was the most inescapable tie of all, and the chances are that few among the propertied classes ever forgot the father-son bond for very long. However, as we move outwards, away from the center and into and through the successive concentric circles and rings of relatives and relationships, we move into a world wherein a greater element of volition becomes a more and more familiar ingredient in the drama of social life. In a structural sense, in the late medieval as in the modern family nexus, a cousin is a cousin, a great-nephew a great-nephew, and so forth. In definition, fifteenth-century English families were bilateral: one was equally related to those on the mother's as on the father's side, to female cousins as to male cousins, to nieces and to nephews. Moreover, the bonds established through marriage with the in-law kingroup were a genuine category of relationships, fully embraced by the definition of consanguinity and affinity, and a source of endless problems and negotiations over marriage and remarriage. The strength of such links was reinforced both by ecclesiastical definitions and, to some extent, by the accepted customs of the day. But a different perspective is also possible when we deal with these "other" relationships. Except for the instance of inheritance by and the legal determination of "the next of kin," in the absence of closer and more obvious relatives, one had some degree of freedom to take or to leave such relatives. Personal choice did not determine the members within one's circles of kin, but personal choice did help determine the quality and the quantity of interaction between ego and those folk. In the horizontal family network, choice did play some role: one could, in part, pick and choose one's effective relatives.

To some considerable extent, in historical inquiry, we are likely to find that for which we search. It is not hard to come up with many forms of social interaction that emphasize the importance of family networks, and we shall do this below. But on the other hand it is equally possible to offer examples and forms of social relations that had little to do with ties between relatives, little dependence upon family networks. We have referred to the way in which historians have made the comparison or dichotomy between the nuclear and the extended family into an idol of family studies. Other polarities, we have tried to show, are more useful for our overview of fifteenth-century society, and there is little reason to think that young men and women had to choose between mutually exclusive models before they could set up housekeeping or look for prospective godparents for a christening. The examination of the household in time past has generally revealed, where a largish number of people are included, a familiar admixture of some who were related by blood or marriage, of some who were unrelated, and of some who were as yet unrelated. Where data are lacking we can do little with such material except acknowledge its reasonable guise and its probable relevance to our people. In our introduction we alluded to studies of other forms of social bonding. Studies of christening and of god parenting practices present a picture in which important supportive roles are played by relatives and by non-relatives alike. Grandparents and brothers and sisters might sponsor the child and choose his or her name, but so might friends, neighbors, and associates connected through commercial or public links. Godparents might be relatives, but no matter how linked, they also had to be chosen—through some act of volition—by the natural parents. Virtually any dip into the modern scholarship on the biographies or the prosopography of such men as those who sat in the late medieval House of Commons—to choose a group of moderately prominent men for whom we have reasonable data—reveals how such men were apt to spend their lives wandering in and out of the world of kin-oriented and kin-heavy networks.[1] A cursory examination of the Cannings-Young network in the Bristol area, or of those in which many of the speakers of the House of Commons moved, quickly brings this home.[2] What was true for the personnel of the House of Commons was no doubt true for that of the world of manorial courts, of county commissions, and innumerable commercial ventures—legal and not-so-legal—that took place at the edges of the historical record.[3]

The horizontal family network was more elastic, more subject to individual definition and choice, than was the vertical patriarchal network binding father and son. It can be thought of as a broad stage with an ongoing morality play. Upon it some men performed for long periods of time, others hardly at all. While on stage one man might exert himself with great zeal for a while, and then perhaps choose to withdraw, perchance to absent himself permanently, while another could offer a substantial but less enthusiastic performance. In tracking its vicissitudes, its varieties of embrace, and its degrees of comfort or discomfort, we will proceed to examine the horizontal family network much as we did the patrilineal tie: first we will look at some "soft" demographic material, then at some affective and qualitative material, and then the case study approach. Nor was the cast list limited to men, and if men usually set the tone we do not wish to imply that women were invariably the silent partners and "objects" in the relationships.

There is no way to determine "how many" relatives an individual had. Too many ambiguities and definitional hurdles stand in the way of a clear view of the finish line. Where genealogical information was sufficiently known, how distantly related could a relative be? And where did the links from a common ancestor cease to have meaning? Probably, we assume, where ecclesiastical definitions of consanguinity ended: those whom one could marry were not one's relatives, and vice versa.[4] But more realistically, for what proportion of the populace was such material ascertainable? Tracing and identifying third and fourth cousins was a reckoning not beyond the cunning of local and ecclesiastical records, whether written or in the folk memory, when such information (or pseudo-information) was needed. We see this in the Inquisitions returned for men who were without obvious or near heirs. But did the shifting sands of geographical mobility, as well as of illiteracy and ambiguity, view such data as exotic information, perhaps rarely used and rarely of much impact upon the world of affective kinship? What about those vast legions created by affinal and spiritual ties, those great circles of personnel that could ripple outwards indefinitely as one's kin married and remarried, stood sponsors at successive baptisms, bore children and raised stepchildren. And by way of contrast to this exponential growth, as we shall see, there were the members of families with whom one actually participated in common action. How much smaller were the latter circles than the former? How readily could the individual in the center control its contractions and expansions? And how often was potential power tested or exercised?

There are no simple answers to these questions. Nor, we suggest, is there the same answer even for a given person at different times through the life cycle and the rhythms of life experience. There were varying responses at different points along the biographical line and in different contexts and circumstances. Any inquiry into social and family history is, to some degree, a search for a method as well as a presentation of the data and the conclusions thence derived. Acordingly, we will look here at some of the odd corners and angles of the polygon, even if we are judiciously reluctant to be definitive regarding either its area or its precise shape.

When we analyzed the four collections of Inquisitions Post Mortem we found that in about 80 percent of the instances of succession, a son (or a son's son) or a daughter was named as the next of kin and as the heir of the deceased property-holder. Now we will look at that other 20 percent.

Who was the next best alternative, as such alternatives were defined by local custom and the common law? The information is of real albeit of limited value. It takes us, usually without equivocation, one clear step sideways, away from the direct patrilineal stairway. But it only takes us that *one* step, or at least one step at a time, since once *the* heir (or possibly the collection of heiresses) was named, there was no interest in identifying any further members of the supporting cast, the understudies to *the* understudy. Once a man was named as his brother's closest kin and now as his heir, the information sufficed to end the inquiry. Whether this particular brother was the only such relative on the horizon, or whether he was simply the senior, and thereby the primary member, of a team of a dozen siblings, a dozen uncles and aunts and nephews and nieces, and of uncounted first cousins, is beyond our ken (unless we have considerable extra information). The judicial or inquisitorial proceeding that ultimately produced an Inquisition Post Mortem was one with a precise but a limited and predetermined curiosity. Once the inquisition arrived at a satisfactory answer to its specific queries—whatever that answer was—it quit. Unpaid service has a limited attention span.

Nevertheless, we get some interesting data on nearest relationships and survival from an analysis of the heirs named for the unfortunate 20 percent who did not have direct heirs of their bodies.[5]

TABLE II-1   SUCCESSION BY "OTHER" RELATIVES THAN A SON

	Age at succession				
	0–10	11–20	21–30	31 +	Total
Relationship to deceased landholders					
daughter	36	24	14	15	89
brother	1	12	13	29	55
sister	1	6	7	6	20
other	11	20	21	20	72
Total	49	62	55	70	236

If the presence of one brother can screen the existence of many others with ties that are not quite as close or as compelling, then conversely we must accept the cruel realities of family survival. When we are given such an heir as a first cousin twice-removed, or a second cousin, as the nearest (if not the dearest), we are seeing the darker side of fertility and survival. The law's search for a (next or closest) heir, for purposes of inheritance, might not tell us about the existence of other relations beyond that heir, or about the contrast between the relatives of the genealogical table and those of cooperation or affection, but it is a source of information well worth some examination. In the absence of sons and their sons, the law proceeded to work its way through a fairly strict hierarchy of relationships. The next heirs would be daughters (and then those daughters' children), then brothers, then sisters. After that it became a little vaguer, and more distant and fairly exiguous kin sometimes come forward. The demands of the law, perhaps compounded by the curiosity of the jurors, usually meant that some answer had to be forthcoming. However, an Inquisition Post Mortem rarely conveys any impression of the competition between equal, or equally distant, heirs to an inheritance. When a first cousin-once removed is named, we are left with the impression that, in his absence, we would be resorting to other claimants, even further out, rather than to would-be rivals of an equal or similar status. When there was more than one woman in a critical category, they (and their direct heirs, if some of the women were already dead) would be named as co-heirs, and when descent was through sisters or daughters, subsequent children of either sex might put in a claim. The distinction between primogeniture and impartible inheritance for a male heir of real property (unless his claim were transmitted through a woman) and egalitarian, partible inheritance for heiresses was presumably not meant as a distinction designed to dignify and elevate heiresses. It was sufficient, in the eyes of the common law, to accept girl-children as better than no children at all.

The gradations of "next-best," as well as the incidence of the resort to such alternatives, along with their ages upon inheritance, are set out in Table II-1. When a man had no sons or no son's sons, he was more likely to be succeeded by a daughter (or a group of daughters) than by a (male) relative linked to him along the horizontal or collateral plane. Siblings were not very likely or common substitutes, and the men and women bracketed together in the medley of "other" relatives in the table were resorted to about as frequently as were brothers or sisters. Given that the deceased property-holder was usually the eldest male child of his own generation, the limited need to resort to brothers is a little surprising. Logically, there might well have been many more of them (and their sons), still around and waiting hopefully, though they fail to make much impact upon our records.

Table II-1 also indicates that the universe of other heirs (that is, heirs other than sons) was likely to be called upon at any point in life. Though the Inquisition Post Mortem does not guide us to the age of the deceased, except by inference, we are obviously looking at the deaths of a group of propertied men who had been anywhere from their mid-teens into their 70s or 80s. Of the daughter-heiresses, approximately two-thirds (49 of 71: 69 percent) inherited before they reached (the male legal age of) 21. Of the daughter-heiresses, 29 were aged 10 or less: clearly a group whose fathers had died young. Had some of the deceased fathers lived longer they might well have been able to do their proper patrilineal duty and produce sons. Accordingly, these particular daughter-heiresses were now profiting from the untimeliness of death. But no stigma should accompany the fortune of being in the right place at the right time, and quite possibly a longer-lived father would simply have meant an older daughter at the moment of her inheritance or perhaps the existence of still more sisters with whom she would share the patrimony. When our attention is focused in this way on girls and women, we might get a rare domestic touch, as when the jury identified the heiress as a 24-year-old daughter, and then added that her husband was also 24, and that they had a 2-year-old son.[6]

Because heiresses divided and shared the patrimony, and because an Inquisition Post Mortem gives all their ages,[7] the instances of daughter succession offer an occasional glimpse into the chronology and demography of families who were without surviving sons. In Table II-1, for simplicity or clarity, we only give the age of the eldest daughter, whereas the Inquisitions often provide the age of a whole string of girls. In some cases the heiresses are very close together—the children of a pre-contraceptive world, the fortunate survivors of safe and proximate births. But in other cases the spacing between the living daughters suggests gaps in the birth order, probably indicating intervening brothers and sisters who had died before the moment of record-creation, and sometimes also at the likelihood of a second marriage on their father's part. Some men must have died young, leaving behind a group of closely spaced daughters of little age: girls of 10, 8, and 6, or of 4, 3, and one-half years.[8] Other men left heiresses of more years but of similar ages in relation to each other: three daughters, one aged 35 and more, one 34 and more, and one 30 and more; or girls named as being aged 19 and more, and 18 and more; or of 18 and more and 17 and more.[9]

The laconic records give little hint of the sorrow that must have been occasioned when a man died and left as his heirs daughters aged two and one[10] or—as we are told regarding the two daughters of Philip Darcy of Nottinghamshire—aged two-and-one-half and fifty months, and of one year and one month.[11] Such examples are obviously unusual ones, and even among the 29 cases shown in Table II-1 where young girls inherited, they were rarely that young. The deceased fathers whose girls were eight, six, and five, or seven and one, or six and three, are a bit more common.[12] The church allowed woman to marry younger than men, without need for a dispensation, and these heiresses often were able to take control of their property while in their mid-teens. The sexist logic behind this differential treatment was that heiresses would come under the control of their husbands (who but took over from their guardians), and therefore could be safely transferred from one blanket of dependence to the next. In conformity with this reasoning, we learn that when Thomas Rollaston of Yorkshire died in 1415 both his daughter heiresses were already married: Margaret, now aged 16, and Ellen, now aged 15. Furthermore, lest we think there had been a sudden rush for their hands (and lands) in the interval between their father's death and the time of the inquisition, we are told that they had both been married before his demise. Since their deceased mother Beatrice had been an heiress of the Mauleys, and since Beatrice's brother Robert had pre-deceased her, it would not have taken any exceptional acumen to associate, some years before, what delightful wives and partners the young girls would eventually prove to be. In another case, with less at stake, there was less need for precision and the jurors might simply return that a man's heirs were his two daughters, both aged 16 and more.[13]

The spacing of children, as well as the question of their survival, was not an easy matter to decipher within the medieval family. When an Inquisition tells us that four daughters were 17, 13, 5, and 3, we surmise either an instance of remarriage and a "second family," or else the death of a number of intervening children between the second and the third daughters.[14] The impression of the father's remarriage is even stronger when the four daughter-heiresses are listed as being 32 and 31, and then 12 and 8.[15] But when the girls are listed as being 14, 8, 5, and 4 we are less inclined to speculate about the family's untold or hidden story, and it is hard to speak with any great confidence about parental survival and the frequency of pregnancies when the five daughters are listed as being 32, 30, 22, 17, and 14.[16] There might be two sisters, one married and 30 and more, the other but 8 years old, or perhaps one of 40 and more, her sister but 17.[17] Sometimes the jurors were thoughtful enough to provide the kind of information we long for. Lord Furnival's daughters were indeed by two wives. The elder girl, Maud, now 15 and more, was the daughter of Joan (the Furnival heiress) and the younger, Joan, just some 3 years and more, was the daughter of Ankarette, who now survived her presumably older husband.[18]

The resort to daughters could open the door for odd and intriguing combinations of heirs and heiresses. From time to time we encounter a string of sisters, some alive and some already dead but with direct heirs (of their own bodies), living and ready to inherit in their stead. In such cases the living sisters came in for equal shares, and then the heirs or heiresses of the deceased further divided their portion. The Yorkshire Inquisitions give us a good example of how this pattern was implemented. When Edmund Holand, earl of Kent, died without children in 1401, his sisters were named as his nearest kin and heirs.[19] The eldest, Eleanor, was dead, and her son (Edmund Mortimer, earl of March) received her share, that is, one-fifth of the inheritance. The four younger sisters were still alive, and each inherited in her own right: Joan, duchess of York, aged 24; Margaret, countess of Somerset, aged 22; Eleanor, countess of Salisbury, aged 21; and Elizabeth Neville, aged 20. This was an important political inheritance, but not a particularly exotic case of division in such circumstances. In a less exalted case the three claimants proved to be daughters of 50 and of 22, plus the son of a deceased daughter, now aged 25.[20]

Daughters, whatever their problems and burdens as females, were accepted as their fathers' children and were apt to be tied to him by a whole complex of links, comparable to if perhaps generally weaker than those between the father and his sons. Though it is a large topic, and beyond our immediate interests here, families of substance were expected to recognize their obligation to provide their daughters with suitable marriage portions (and partners), and *inter vivos* settlements, beyond the ken of a study relying so heavily on wills, probably assured that in many (if not most) cases the fathers would "do the right thing." Whether such settlements, and any affection they created or preserved, served as a bridge to a new network or were simply seen as an inescapable and dubious obligation, they had to be accepted as one of the consequences of the ill-fortune of having had daughters instead of just sons. Though we cannot say or even try to speculate regarding the proportion of all living daughters who were mentioned in their fathers' wills—an insoluble puzzle for a medieval social historian—we can say what proportion of wills did mention daughters. The level, in the extant collections, is reasonably high, and later we will enlarge a bit on this particular relationship. So in brief, the ties between fathers and their girls were preserved at both the legal and the personal level. When needed, daughters were frequently available to fill the breach left by the absence, or the prior decease, of their brothers. The law's own logic held that if a man were so bereft as to have no sons, he was probably better off with a daughter than with the nearest male relative picked from some more distant circle of kinship. Blood was, sometimes, thicker than gender.

But there could also come a time when the move sideways, along the horizontal plane, was necessary. Then the brother (and then his sons) was the next alternative. However, Table II-1 shows us that this resort to a male sibling only had to be taken in about 4 percent of the cases we have tallied. While this alone tells little about the ties between brothers, it does indicate that they were rarely linked, in life and death, in pursuit of the common patrilineal enterprise and its attendant ideology that we looked at in the preceding chapter. When they did work closely, it was apt to be on some new project, some bond or enterprise forged in their generation, rather than on an inherited one. In the customary realms of activity the accepted hierarchy of birth order usually governed personal relationships. We saw that fathers' wills usually posited a rank ordering of the brothers, and then acted so as to perpetuate such a rank order. If we should not infer hostility, we should also be reluctant to make an *a priori* assumption about equality or cooperation. "Different roads" was probably the route most often chosen.

A man's own duty to his ancestors either was fulfilled by the production of his own children *or* it was not fulfilled. If he died without a son and if his father had produced another son who was now awaiting his death, that might be to the older father's credit, but only his; the successful grandfather was entitled to his kudos. Most of the brothers who were named as heirs in the inquisitions were already of legal age: 32 of 38, or 84 percent of the small total. And of this group of 32, 25 (or 78 percent of the subtotal, 66 percent of all the brothers) were named as being age 30 or more. This means that they were usually needed because their brothers had had no success in fathering children (or surviving children), rather than because the older brother had died while still too young to have had his own proper opportunity. Sisters were but rarely identified as the heir, and they too were apt to be older women.

We find a fair sized group of the deceased whose specified heirs were farther out in the kinship circles. Sometimes the heir was just one further step, as when it was a brother's son or a sister's son. At other times it really could be a more distant relative, named at the end of an investigation that supports what we have said about the widespread concern for uncovering one's roots. Of these "other" relatives shown in Table II-1, about one-half were still below legal age, an indication that many were probably in a generation at least one down from that of their deceased (and unwitting) benefactor. Juries could usually confine themselves to a range of common alternatives, but when there were no suitable claimants in the more familiar and closer circles, they seem to have had little trouble extending their gaze. In extreme instances it might never fall upon a proper subject—as in the bleak and lonely instances we quoted, the men who died with no known heirs. But usually the search reached a definite if distant goal: Among the church's interest in marriage and genealogy and the documents that accompanied the possession and transmission of property and the ingenuity of folk memory (which alone might have sufficed at village level in innumerable instances), many a tangled thicket was eventually cleared to show a public right of way, even if it proved a tortuous one.

Sometimes the "other" category could contain a fairly straightforward candidate, as when the Nottingham jurors identified 7-year-old Henry, son of Elizabeth, daughter of William Phelip: a grandson through a daughter.[21] In some instances we have classified heirs as belonging to this category of "other heirs" because they were a mixed group, and various claimants, in different circles, were coupled together. One odd combination was that of two first cousins: One was the daughter of the deceased man's father's sister, aged 34 and more and married, and the other was a son of another sister, aged 24.[22] Hugh Cressey was succeeded by a 30-year-old sister *and* by a 9-year-old nephew, son of another (and now deceased) sister.[23] When a nephew was a brother's son, the tie seems obvious and fairly close, at least in the absence of better alternatives, and there are several dozen instances in the inquisitions of succession by either a nephew or a great-nephew. Though few of the boys (that is, the nephews) seem to have been very young, at least seven were between ages 11 and 20, six were in their 20s, and another ten or so were over 30. There were also some nephews who were identified as sisters' sons, as well as those who were brothers' sons,[24] and great nephews, identified in the genealogical detail as a brother's grandson.[25] Obviously, the John Bowghton who died and was succeeded by a nephew or a great-nephew, now aged 40, had been an elderly man,[26] but the number of such cases are too few and the ages of the deceased too uncertain for more than rough generalizations.

Even more exotic relationships turn up with some regularity. Sometimes they can only be deciphered if the compressed statement of the jurors is expanded into a genealogical table, a procedure made all the more necessary by the repetitious use of a limited number of Christian names within a family. One poor soul seems to have had no one closer than a third cousin, which is a pretty good stretch for any society's powers of record-recovery, if not for his family's pattern of fecundity.[27] This makes Hugh Cressy's heir—his first cousin once removed, the 28-year-old Alice—almost seem like an old intimate.[28] Second cousins once removed, or second cousins twice removed, surface from time to time, as do less complicated links between collateral kin.[29] In one instance the next-of-kin was just a first cousin, but what catches our eye is that he was aged 60 and more. Clearly, this family tree was singularly devoid of leafy branches.[30]

Combinations of relatives as co-heirs certainly give variety to the reports of the jurors, as when they reported that there was to be a divison between two aunts (aged 62 and 60) and a third aunt's child, a cousin, aged 26.[31] If such mixtures did not turn up very frequently, they were a puzzle that any given group of jurors might have to unravel every now and then. One man's two grandsons were by different daughters, and in another case the two granddaughters, by a deceased son, were 17 and more and 15 and more, and both married.[32] Links through (deceased) sisters might lead to various complications or permutations: a sister's granddaughter or a half-sister's 11-year-old daughter.[33] The latter case was made even more complicated because the young girl's father was still alive. Some combinations yoked three sisters' daughters or perhaps a sister, three nephews, and two nieces.[34] Groups of cousins could become very tangled. A man might be succeeded by a group of relatives consisting of a first cousin, a first cousin once removed, and a first cousin twice removed,[35] or by two third cousins once removed and a third cousin thrice removed![36] After this a mix of three sisters (aged 42, 40, and 30, and all married) and two half-sisters (aged 12 and 11, and both married) hardly sounds very exotic, though the younger set of siblings had certainly been eased into early domesticity.[37] There clearly was a great deal of ground that could be covered. Jurors were perhaps reluctant to admit that "who his next heir may be, the jurors are fully ignorant."[38] Nor were the king's agents particularly inclined to accept such a return, even if escheat might be the lands' ultimate destiny.

The prosaic conclusion to all this genealogical variation seems to be that most men of property could be fitted into a vertical, patrilineal axis, when it came to establishing their next-of-kin, and most others had, as their closest heir, a daughter, a daughter's child, a brother or sister, or a brother or sister's child. As such we probably have a universe, revealed by the four sets of Inquisitions, wherein the nearest legal descendent or heir was not apt to be so distinct or so distant from those with whom one was likely to have some regular personal relationship or interaction, apart from the ultimate question of inheritance. Of course, sisters (and female relations in general) represent one possible qualification: they might effectively leave the family of paternal origin and of elder brothers, upon marriage, regardless of the strength of former ties. But they did not necessarily or regularly break their bonds with their own paternal kin, and marriages were often contracted for the sake of looping old ties to new ties. A sister's value might be enhanced if she continued to function as a bridge, though the likelihood that she moved to a new household put some qualifications upon future contacts. In a world in which women were about even money to marry more than once, the paternal family of origin might be one of the few fixed stars, as we will see when we look at some widows. It was only when the jurors named such heirs and heiresses as great nieces or second or third cousins once-removed that we encounter horizontal links and webs of inheritance that stretch well beyond what we think of as the customary circles of proximity, affinity, and cooperation. But even here we cannot be certain, and nominally distant relatives may have had some regular interaction, especially when closer kin were not available to fill in the picture. Village life and close-knit urban life, even more than aristocratic life, could maintain a dynamic of interrelationship at a diverging but ascertainable level.

Before we end this discussion of legal heirs we will make one last assault upon the citadel. In our discussion of patrilineal continuity and violent death we noted that many of the peers who were killed or executed were also men who left no sons. Their rate of patrilineal failure was above the average rate of failure encountered in the total male universe of the inquisitions, as it obviously was above the average for the peerage as a whole. In fact, it was high enough to suggest that maybe the Wars of the Roses really did help kill off the English nobility. We will now look at those peers who fell to violent death *and* who died without male heirs of the body to determine who was the next heir, and how the distribution of these "other" heirs in Table II-2 compares with that of the larger group reflected in the data of Table II-1.

TABLE II-2   PEERS DYING BY VIOLENCE, NOT LEAVING A SON AS THE HEIR

Peer	Year of death	Age at death	Heir
Period I: violence stemming from Henry IV's accession			
William Scrope	1399	49	father & brother
Thomas Percy	1404	61	died unmarried
Thomas Mowbray	1405	20	brother, 13
Thomas Holand	1400	29	brother, 17
Thomas Bardolf	1408	39	daughters, 19 and 17
Henry Scrope	1415	42	brother, 17
Period II: the French wars			
Duke of Kent	1408	25	only sisters
Earl of Suffolk	1415	22	3 daughters; brother, 19
Duke of York	1415	42	nephew, 5
Duke of Clarence	1421	32	no direct heirs; 2 brothers
VII lord Roos	1421	24	brother, 15
II lord Abergavenny	1422	25c.	daughter, 7
Earl of Salisbury	1428	40	daughter, 22
IV lord Bourgchier	1431	41	no direct heirs
Period III: the civil wars of the 1450s			
No peers who died in this decade were without direct male heirs			
Period IV: the 1460s and 1470s			
Lord Bonville	1461	68	great granddaughter
Humphrey Bourgchier	1471	33	niece
Randolf Dacre	1461	30–35	brother, 25
XIV earl of Devon	1461	29	brother, 27
XV earl of Devon	1469	30	no surviving children
XVI earl of Devon	1471	39	2nd or 3rd cousin
lord Ormond	1461	39	brother, 34
lord Rougemont Grey	1461	40	no close heirs
VII lord Scales	1460	62	daughter, 24
Duke of Somerset	1464	32	unmarried
Earl of Warwick	1471	43	daughters, 20 and 16
Period V: after 1480			
Duke of Buckingham	1521	43	no male heirs
Duke of Gloucester	1485	33	no legitimate heirs
Earl of Lincoln	1487	25	father alive
Lord Lovel	1487	41	2 sisters
Earl of Rivers	1483	43	brother
III duke of Suffolk	1513	41	daughter, a nun
Earl of Warwick	1499	24	unmarried

We have divided the peers' violent deaths into five (chronological) groups: those killed in the violence and rebellions centering around Richard II's deposition and Henry IV's accession; those killed in the French Wars; and then the three chronological sub-groups of those who died in internal English strife—in the 1450s, in the 1460s and 1470s, and then in the 1480s and afterward. In each group—except for that of the six men who died in the 1450s—the proportion of those dying without a son (or a son's son) was very high. In the respective chronological brackets it was 6 of 14, 8 of 12, 0 of six, 12 of 32, and 7 of 13, or 43 percent of the entire universe (and in respective terms for each group, 42 percent, 67 percent, 0 percent, 38 percent, and 54 percent). In aggregate we see that 33 men, of the 76 who died by violence, did not leave direct male heirs of their body. Perhaps there is a positive correlation between the absence of an heir of the body and a propensity for the kind of behavior that often led to violent death. As John S. Roskell has speculated, regarding the political vagaries of the elderly and childless lord Wenlock: "He was without close kinsmen to advise him. The possession of direct heirs might have steadied him. The present and future interests of children . . . might have made him give pause before he committed himself. It is perhaps a disadvantage that he had nothing to lose but his own [life]."[39]

In looking at these 33 aristocrats who left no sons, what can we say about their "other" heirs? In some cases the identity itself is hard to establish, for the death in question marked the end of the peerage title, often soiled by a sentence of attainder, and less effort was made to determine the next of socio-biological kin when there was neither a title nor wealth to be transmitted. When Thomas Courtenay, XIV earl of Devon, was beheaded 1461, after the battle of Towton, still unmarried at age 29, his younger brother John was readily identified as his heir, and he was restored in 1470 to the family honors. But when the brother was likewise executed, at Tewkesbury in 1471, likewise unmarried and now in his late 30s, the heir and next earl proved to be his second cousin once removed. However, had there been no title, or no political *volte face* that caused Henry VII to elevate the second cousin to the earldom in 1485, we might be hard pressed to trace the heir. When Francis, lord Lovel, disappeared and presumably died in 1487, his two sisters were never serious claimants for the title or property, though we can identify them as his heirs and closest relatives.[40]

For men of property in medieval society marriage was almost universal. Therefore it is worth noting that 5 of the 33 peers who died by violence (or 15 percent) were unmarried, and in these cases no one closer than brothers or nephews or cousins could have claimed their worldly honors. Brothers were the most common "other" alternative, though sometimes they too had to bear some burden of misfortune on their journey. The earl of Ormond was killed in 1461, his brother (five years his junior at his death) inherited, only to die unmarried 16 years later, when the patrimony went to a third brother who did survive and continue the line.[41] Sisters could be the next of kin, but neither they nor their husbands and sons might receive much tangible benefit from such an inheritance. There was an occasional exception to this, as when lord Lisle's sister's daughter Elizabeth brought the Lisle title to her husband, Edward Grey. Daughters were a safer conduit for an inheritance, as the earl of Warwick's two dutiful sons-in-law (George, duke of Clarence, and Richard, Duke of Gloucester) knew full well when they fought over their claims to shares of the Montagu, Beauchamp, and Neville inheritance after the Kingmaker's death in 1471.

The examination of these aristocratic next-of-kin gives us a distribution not so different from that revealed by the larger tallies of the Inquisitions Post Mortem, though the resort to the odd sorts of heirs is proportionately greater. Daughters and brothers were the most common alternative, even if peerage law and political necessity tended to push the former aside at times in favor of the latter. Otherwise, sisters, a few nephews, an occasional cousin, and in one instance a great-granddaughter were named, along with some cases where attainder or an impoverished lineage produced no name for inheritance and succession. All 33 of the violent deaths without sons mark the end of a patrilineage in the strict sense in which we have been discussing this peculiar institution. In some instances the male line, as traced from a more distant common progenitor (as a grandfather, when brother succeeded brother, or a great-grandfather, when first cousin succeeded first cousin) stumbled but resumed its forward progress: The next male stepped in and put things right. We see this happen when Thomas Mowbray died in 1405, executed without trial after archbishop Scrope's rebellion. His younger brother was named as his heir, and the line of the dukes of Norfolk resumed its forward course for three more generations, until John Mowbray—grandson of the useful brother of 1405—died in 1476 and John Howard succeeded (as a grandson of the I duke, Thomas's father). Howard was the nearest collateral heir, and his claim to the dukedom was not seriously disputed, though partisan considerations may have weighed as heavily as genealogical ones. The de la Poles enjoyed a similar recovery, for the earl of Suffolk who died at Agincourt was followed by a brother, the I duke, who began another three-generation patrilineal chain (which ended when the III duke was executed in 1513, leaving only a daughter, a nun, and perhaps a younger brother who was a cleric).⁴² But some families never recovered stride at all, and the resort to an "other" heir often signals the real end of continuity and power, almost as surely as it does of the patrilineage. Daughters or other female heirs could convey a title and transmit estates, but there is little doubt that they were very inferior alternatives.

This review of "next-of-kin" leads us into a fairly mechanistic view of family links. Horizontal and collateral relationships, singled out by the law as critical ones, were not necessarily the stuff of which warm family life was built. Sometimes, no doubt, the absence of closer heirs helped forge positive bonds between these more distant kinsfolk. But in other instances, we suspect, resentment, frustration, and a hostility born of contemplating the inevitable serve to push people even further apart. Marriage, obviously, was a Janus-faced affair in terms of the push and pull between husbands and wives and the husband's family and the wife's family. Why should other links have been any different? And yet, in balance, there is no reason to conclude on a negative tone. We saw above that people were concerned to know who their relatives were, distinct though the pursuit of such knowledge might be from a feeling of affection towards those it uncovered. An awareness of bonds could lead to companionship and cooperation, and shared enterprise and outlook might result. In addition, the relationship between a landholder and a distant kinsman who was the potential heir might be different from the relationship between the would-be heir and other, even more remote kinsmen, pushing behind him in the same queue. How we behave is determined, to no small extent, by where we stand: who is in front, who is behind, the length of the line, and the probable duration of the wait.

Volition and Some Qualitative Decisions

The identity of the legal heir was not something over which one normally had control, especially after death. As such, an examination of horizontal family links based on the resort to the alternate and collateral heirs, in the absence of direct heirs of the body, only gives us a certain kind of information. It supplies what we might call structural or definitional data about different categories of kin beyond or other than direct descendents, as tested against factors found in some specific circumstances. It tells little about the strategies of affection and identification that existed and that could be cultivated and utilized for a wide variety of purposes. If the latter are not necessarily more important than structure, they at least offer an alternative approach for an investigation of the horizontal family and an assessment of its strength, appeal, and utility. To expand upon their possibilities we will now examine some wills for information about the ties between ego (that is, the testator) and the circles and aggregations of kinsmen and women who stood outside or beyond the vertical axis that tied him to his father and progenitors and to his sons and their sons.

The heir at law, for purposes of inheritance, was usually named on a fairly mechanical basis: *if* he (or she) existed it was an eldest brother, or sisters, or a brother's eldest son, and so forth. This was mostly beyond much individualized control. A will, on the other hand, can offer some combination of what was possible and what one chose. One could not name beneficiaries who did not exist: a testator with an only child was not going to leave bequests to a brood of five sons and four daughters. But on the other hand, in that great and open-ended world of kin where one was free to pick and choose, not everyone with five brothers and four sisters (and some appreciable number of brothers-in-law and sisters-in-law and the consequent collection of nieces and nephews) *had* to name any of them. They were likely but not compulsory candidates for bequests and for the set of burdens and reciprocities that went with such inclusive memory. Therefore as we look at wills, we are moving towards an assessment of the degree of overlap between the possible and the preferred, the chosen.

The networks of relatives actually named in wills range enormously in size and scope, as did the pool from which they were being chosen. The network covers all manner and all sort of kin, including kin by marriage, the spiritual kin created through the church's definitions and legislation, god-children (who might also be blood relations) and the step- and half-relatives in a bewildering assortment.[43] The inclusion of a group of beneficiaries within a will, all of whom are related to ego, turns that collection of individuals into a social group or unit, at least in the eyes of the testator (and the modern student). This unity was perhaps one that had only a formal or nominal existence, created merely by the act of being (passively) named and aggregated in the document of record, and existing in no other shape or form. At the extreme, the men and women mentioned as ego's kin in a given will need never have actually met, let alone had any direct form of interaction. But the names in the will are not a random shopping list, and to be mentioned in a kinsman's will was not just to be singled out as a recipient of a gift or bequest. Rather, it was to be recruited—perhaps unknowingly and perhaps even unwillingly—into a world of people who now could be called upon to accept reciprocal obligations and responsibilities, usually for prayer, but maybe for the care of younger children or of the widow or of the real and personal property and debts with which the testator now charged them. In return for the receipt of some tangible benefit or bequest there was the obligation to return prayers, personally or vicariously through the use of a subsidized alternative, either a clerical professional or such of Christ's flock as those deserving poor who would come to the funeral and collect some combination of alms, food, or clothing. Furthermore, by being included among the beneficiaries, one might become subjected to all sorts of conditions and contingent obligations. The kinsfolk named as beneficiaries might be brought, even without their prior consent and against their wishes, very close to that ridge that divides the valley of affection from that of authority, the benevolent pastures of harmonious reciprocity from the harsher slopes of social control. Fathers could impose conditions of varying degrees of severity upon others than just the son-and-heir, and supervisory duties, usually by the old over the young, were not uncommon.

Other considerations served to make the kinsfolk named within a single will into a kind of social group. They were related to ego, if not necessarily to each other, and ego was the point of convergence for the lines radiating to and from all the marriages, including those of children and collateral kin, as well as from the ties of the spiritual relationships with whom one shared baptismal sponsorships. Though most of the beneficiaries identified in a will as relatives of the testator probably knew each other, their views regarding their ties and their rights could vary considerably. Tangible benefactions differed in quality and quantity, as did the strong if silken threads of reciprocal obligation. As in most social groups and networks, some of the named beneficiaries occupied central positions in the testator's firmament, some stood out towards the periphery. In addition, this kin-group so named and so constituted was also a peculiar social unit because some of its members might well be dead. Nor, given its spiritual and religious as well as its secular purposes, was such a distinction necessarily that important. We may think of services rendered to the dead as being more one-sided than the links forged with those now about to outlive ego, but it was at best a matter of degree, not of absolute priorities. The dead (and the soon-to-be dead) included not just the testator, but perhaps some from among the ranks of parents and ancestors, as well as some from the ranks of his own generation (such as wives and siblings) and even children. A typical, if expansive, provision could ran thusly: "An honest prest for to syng yerly . . . for to praye for me and Anne my wyff, Waltier Tyrell my fadur and Alianore hys wyff my modur, Sir John Tyrell and Sir William Lysle knyhgtes, Richard, Tomas and Wylliam my brethern and John Basyngeborne and for all tho that I am bownden to praye for and for alle crysten sowles etc."[44] Or the same impulses might be expressed a bit more tersely: "ad celebrandum pro animabus parentum meorum, anima mea et animabus filiorum meorum et anima Willelmi fratris mei."[45] The reciprocities between the testator and his beneficiaries were not limited to an exchange of temporal enrichment in return for prayers and the acceptance of worldly responsibilities. They could include obligations that tied the obligations and duties of collateral kin onto those that had been imposed, in an even stronger fashion, upon the members of the nuclear family. We can almost say that *he* sought to catch *them* in the skeins of *his* network, vertical and horizontal, living and dead. Put this way, the hard bones of coercion and manipulation show beneath the comely flesh of common spiritual endeavors.

The complex of kin named in a will can be seen, therefore, as an idiosnycratic social group, created and shaped by the testator at or near the moment of death. No two testators, not even spouses or siblings, were likely to name the identical list, certainly not if the will were at all lengthy or expansive and written to reflect commitments contracted over any appreciable stretch of time. The family network chosen for this final occasion, this last "event," illustates the concept of the family as a multi-generational entity, stretching vertically through time and horizontally across several generations and embracing a miscellaneous set of *chosen* kin from various circles of intimacy. Each will coupled a unique blend of the dead and the living and fastened its own mix of obligation and of egocentric ideology and identification upon the entire group. Seen in this way, the will, a document of impressive empowerment, assumes an emotive force far transcending its obvious use as an instrument for the (re)distribution and transmission of property. Insofar as each beneficiary received his or her stipulated share and simply had to fulfill the reciprocal obligation of prayer, the acts of benefaction constituted a series of individual contracts between giver and receiver, supervised and administered under the eyes of canon and civil law. But insofar as the bequests carried conditions of social control or clauses covering the future disposition of property, they brought the beneficiary into a series of circles wherein he or she was caught up with others in the group and thrust ahead towards some prescribed course of voluntary or involuntary action. Contingent bequests could make economic prospects and future behavior depend upon the wishes, the longevity, and the fertility of others.

Who was actually included in the wills, and how were the members of the networks of blood and of marriage referred to and treated? Though a man's last will was, to a considerable extent, an exercise in free will, there were usually perimeters within which even the richest or the most eccentric were likely to operate. Three such restraints come to mind. The first was the almost universal propensity to give more—of both affection and of worldly goods—to nearer relatives than to distant ones. Such a flow coincided with the probable incidence of interaction and of personal as well as of structural intimacy. The spouse and the children were usually bound more closely—for better or for worse—than were the horizontal and collateral kin. Though we argue against the idea of rigid boundaries between categories of kin (except perhaps between the son-and-heir and all others), there is no disputing their value as a general guide to behavior. It is simply that we should follow statistical data rather than or in addition to prescriptive definitions of behavior. Any given testator could, at least in theory, ignore children for nephews and cousins, though in truth it was most unusual to do so. More often one distributed bequests (with their attendant obligations) within an inner concentric circle and only then moving outwards to the next and the next. A smaller and smaller proportion of testators reached each successive circle as we leave the center. But custom and conventional choices, not rules, governed the disposition of these matters. We should not view groups or categories of relatives mentioned in a will as if they stood in formalized rivalry to each other. The family was not meant to be a battleground, with a team of younger sons arranged for a formal joust against the team of nephews and/or first cousins. Furthermore, once one tapped a particular circle of kinship, one was still free to choose only some within that circle from among all the candidates who might be waiting there. Not even Dante tried to speak to all the residents of each level of Hell before moving on to those who would catch his interest in the next.

But we should not overemphasize volition and voluntary activity. The realities of birth and of survival imposed a considerable degree of restraint upon a testator's putative freedom to pick and choose. Such truisms carry a more powerful emotional burden than their simple logic necessarily admits. One could not leave bequests for and establish reciprocities with relatives who did not exist, though it is hard to say if the more poignant losses were for kin who had never been born or who had been born but who had not survived. Bequests for sons were only meaningful if one had sons (or at least a pregnant wife), and so with other, slightly more distant categories. Though the wills rarely leave traces of an explicit lamentation, had we the table talk of such men we would no doubt hear much on such themes. The conditional clauses were designed in part to temper the once-and-forever aspects of a last will and testament: "to the child in my wife's belly." For the most part, however, one had to operate with the universe of kin actually in existence at the given moment. *If* a pregnant wife produced a child who survived, or *if* a child married and had children, or *if* a son died and left the testator's brother as his heir, and so forth—these are the kinds of contingencies that occupied the thoughts of dying men. One's death-bed ability to alter these undetermined demographic and marital vectors was limited, to say the least. Testators had mostly to devise last wills that dealt—both by inclusion and exclusion—with the universe of reality as it was likely to be on the day they were both alive and dead.

A last and by no means least restraint upon a testator's freedom was that imposed by the competition for finite resources, both material and of affection. Few were so wealthy that they could stretch to cover "everyone," whether the qualification arose more from the limits of their worldly endowment or from the excess of kin. The competition among ego's relatives—who might not all be related to each other—could extend to emotional links as well as to those of tangible enrichment and exchange. The most expansive wills, coming mainly from the most affluent members of society, are intensely partiarchal documents. They were written (or dictated) for this very purpose by the testator, and they were presumably received and interpreted in this context by his beneficiaries. The father-figure distributed his great largesse to a huge brood, bound to him in obligations, in dynastic loyalty, and in shared worldly ambition, if not always in strong blood ties or with much personal warmth.

John of Gaunt's will, written in February, 1397, offers an excellent illustration of these points. Duke John scattered his worldly goods, his patriarchal blessings, and his clutch of future obligations across a wide expanse of kin: his third wife, Catherine; his royal nephew Richard II; his brother the duke of York; his son Henry Bolingbroke; his daughter Philippa, queen of Portugal; his daughter Catherine, queen of Castile; his daughter Elizabeth, duchess of Exeter; his son John Beaufort, marquis of Dorset; his son Henry Beaufort, bishop of Winchester; his son Thomas

Beaufort; his daughter Joan Beaufort, countess of Westmorland; Boling-broke's sons Henry (the future Henry V) and John (future duke of Bed-ford); a son-in-law; and his step-son, Thomas Swynford. The children of two (of his three) marriages, plus some of their partners and children, plus a brother and a dead brother's son: a wide cast indeed. In addition, many of the personal goods carry the same bond of patriarchal labeling that we saw among the lords Scrope. Such provisions were of the sort that gave a cup to his wife Catherine Swynford, which the earl of Wiltshire had given the king, "and which he gave me upon going into Guienne . . . and the robes I bought from my dear cousin the Duchess of Norfolk [Edward I's granddaughter]."[46]

Lesser men, lesser exchequers, and lesser families rarely reach the level of this vast aristocratic model. The more prosaic status of most exchanges was accepted by all parties. But even lesser versions of family largesse could still be widely distributed among a variety of recipients representing a va-riety of kinship bonds, despite a limited gross value; a huge net of kin could still be hauled in by a man of more limited worldly means. John Coventry, mercer and once sheriff of London, was affluent if hardly in the duke of Lancaster's league. However, his goods and his sentiments did stretch to cover a stepmother, two sons, a daughter, three brothers, a sister, a wife, and an unspecified "consanguine mee."[47]

The great gulf in this patrilineal world was that between those bonds made with a surviving son-and-heir and those made with all others. Some wills show this bifurcation very clearly, while in others it remains a gray area. Extensive real property was often conveyed in advance, or else through the semi-automatic channels of common law and primogeniture, and the son-and-heir might only be singled out here for some smallish share of the personal possessions. Personal property and cash could be re-distributed very widely and expansively, whether or not a single individual stood to receive the bulk of a landed patrimony. The strength of the father-son chain did not invariably depend upon the provisions of the last will, and that document was often oriented towards the other children and out-wards into the horizontal testamentary network. As a last judgement, ren-dered upon the trials and errors of a lifetime of kinship interaction, the will might reflect a final and uncharacteristic wave of generosity and of recip-rocal bridge-building. But in either case, its magnanimity did not depend, in more than some limited degree, upon the existence and strength of the father-son link.

Men with a son-and-heir, or a group of sons, were not especially prone to lavish personal property upon them, as a category, to the systematic exclusion of other relatives. The "conditonal clauses" regarding patrilineal contingencies show that testators thought about and tried to arrange for a future that could accommodate the uncertainties of life and death. Since the law would identify the next of kin, irrespective of personal wishes, so the testator could specify a "natural" but stipulated pecking order for the transmission of property among those now gathered, figuratively or literally, about the death bed. One man left bequests to two sons and a nephew, but if the sons pre-deceased the nephew the latter lost as well: the residue went to pious uses.[48] The frequent resort to daughters, siblings, and nephews—if all the sons should die without heirs of their body—is an indication of how people were conditioned by demographic realities to switch their hopes for the lineage from horse to horse. We have seen that horizontal and collateral relatives had to be countenanced, as the direct or immediate heir, in about 20 percent of the cases, and they appeared much more often than that in a supporting testamentary role of some sort. It were best if they were not held at too great remove from the father's first option, the vertical transmission to and the bond with the son. Whatever despair was in the father's heart over those whom he was about to leave, he usually made a brave face towards the future. Edward Tyrell had but one minor son between himself and the end of the patrilineage. His worry, "yff the sayd Edward my sone dye without yssue of hys body" was a legitimate one, for the boy had not yet "come to pleyn age of xxj wynter." But there were two daughters and then a nephew. He ranked them in this order of contingent inheritance, and there is every reason to read this as a likely guide to the rank order of his affection.[49]

As Edward Tyrell's will demonstrates, a man's immediate kin and his "natural" heirs, after his son(s), were his daughters. The relationships between fifteenth-century fathers and their daughters constitute a whole chapter in the story of family life, and we hardly plan to tell it here. While we know that the manipulative and instrumental aspects were often those uppermost in the father's plans, the discrepancy or gulf between his schemes and his daughter's level of compliance speaks well for the independence and spirit of the perpetually underprivileged. But while sparks of anger and of autonomy were not uncommon on her part, we should also note that they were not the model (nor the modal) behavior. It is likely that fathers and daughters tended to share a similar if not an identical world view, and that arranged marriages were an institution whose virtues were usually apparent to, or at least accepted by the younger as well as the older generation. Family records and correspondence indicate that a father often took his daughter's wishes into some account, as she in turn often displayed a willingness to accept what was proffered. The intricacies of marriage *per se*, with the complications that today attend the diplomacy between nations and the financial arrangements of multi-national corporations, are not particularly relevant here. Instead, we will glance at the links between the father and his daughters as illuminated by such behavior as testamentary benefaction. As the wills guide us, father-daughter links were common, and the existence of the preferred brothers did not serve to dissolve or even to weaken them, though they may have severely limited the worldly value of the tangible items that marked the reciprocity. It was expected that marital or claustral futures for young daughters would be taken care of, in the wills if not before, while for their older and now married sisters there were personal bequests, admittedly often of a symbolic or merely sentimental sort.[50] Such were the common currencies of this exchange. The Inquisitions Post Mortem showed that daughters as heiresses did make a regular appearance, and wills reflect the same richness, as well as the possibilities of competition between children of equal stature. Roger Flore had four sons to provide for, and such obligations confined his remembrance of his daughters to family heirlooms: "Also I wull that Anneys my doughter haue the standing pece that was my faders, keuered, and my gilt pece that Steneby gaf me . . . and my doughter Iohanes a keuered pece of siluer, the which the provest of Coderstoke gaf me, and six siluer spones."[51] Most of the will covered the problems raised by the uncertainties of the sons' survival and the possible affront of the widow's remarriage.

Perhaps the limited volumes of personal goods transmitted from fathers to daughters meant that much that changed hands was apt to carry a strong personal meaning, as with Roger Flore's trinkets to his girls. John Wodehous offered a similar solution, giving goods and money to each of five sons, and to his five daughters, personal items: "cuilibet quinque filiarum mearum . . . unum par de pater noster de corall' de illis corrall' quas Katerina regina Anglie michi dedit."[52] Lord Burgh had two sons, plus his heir's sons to worry about, and his two daughters again received the customary if lesser items, for example, a book of gold and enamel that had been his mother's, the three great rubies that had come from his wife, and a variety of chapel ornaments.[53] There are many instances of transmission between these particular parties that are low in quantity but high in quality, with a genuine personal value attached to the items by way of compensation: "Lego Beatrici, Margerie et Margarete filiabus meis scilicet cuilibet ipsarum unum anulum aureum valoris centum solidorum."[54] Younger daughters, as yet unmarried and unsettled in the world, often came in for more lavish treatment. Thomas Hoo wanted his executors to put up land in Hastings Rape for sale, to subsidize their future marriages. But to emphasize that permanent family interests were not to be sacrificed to meet immediate needs, he asked that "my brother to by it afore ony other man, yf he lyst."[55]

We saw that fathers put the obstacles of conditional behavior between their estates (or themselves) and their sons. Daughters too could be subjected to the dance of social control, and parental whims—rather than the question of whether the girls were the principal heirs—seem to have been the controlling factor. Again, the conditions might hinge on factors of survival and/or of her life choice. Was Richard Graveley of London being a realist: "To my doughtour Kateryn xx li to hir maryage yf she leve so longe, & yf she passe to god or she be maryed, y woll that my wyf haue that money."[56] If she were to choose the cloister, one young girl could lose her share to her brother.[57] This in turn raises the question of how genuinely free she was to decide in favor of, or to reject, the religious life. But presumably even daughters had some freedom to be willful and wayward. If so, curb them: "In caas . . . they bothe disagre to be governed by the saide Sir Tomas, my wief and the feffees, that thenne the said lxxx li. be receyved to the use and profitz of my sone Jone and my chylder that I have by my wief that now is."[58] A bequest left to a prospective son-in-law, *if* the man's daughter married him, raises more speculation about manipulation and coercion.[59] And here, as in all of the other contingent cases cited above, we have some idea of what the father had hoped for, little idea of what "really happened" after his death.

The existence of male heirs and the father's need to provide for them did not work to exclude other relatives, though such standing commitments obviously restricted what was available for outward distribution. The goodly combination of relatives we have seen above consisted mostly of those called forth from the younger ranks of kin, that is, those of the next generation after the testator. But brothers and sisters might also be included, along with their children and even their grandchildren. John Daubriggecourt was a pious and important old man when he wrote his will in 1415.[60] He left bequests to three nephews and a great-nephew, to step- or god-children and their spouses. This was in addition to bequests to three daughters and to his sons. And in this case many of the bequests were more than nominal. There was £10 to nephew Nicholas, and £10 and

then £20 per annum to Nicholas's brother Eustace, a 4 mark *ciphum* to a
stepson, 20 marks to great-niece Joan for her marriage, a 5 mark *ciphum* for
a stepdaughter's husband, and so forth. Robert James left a will that emphasized the strength of female connections within his family. There were
bequests for no male relatives, while his wife, a daughter, a sister, and an
aunt all received bequests. His wife was also his executrix and was entrusted with the disposal of the residue of the estate, to be used for his
soul.[61]

Nor is this sort of thing unusual. Richard Bankes remembered his
daughters and his brother's children, of either sex, plus his brother,
brother-in-law, and wife.[62] John Lumley provided rather handsomely for
three daughters and two sisters and a brother: money for the women's
marriages alone was supposed to amount to 1,100 marks. Of course, they
all had to be dutiful: "if she wille bee mariet bee ye avice of my brothre
marmaduke," as a typical provision ran.[63] The earl of Warwick presumably
had no trouble stretching his resources to cover bequests to a daughter, a
brother, two sisters, and a niece beyond and apart from what he left his
son and heir.[64] Other choices within the many circles of kinship emphasized the testator's degrees of freedom. He could take advantage of his last
opportunity to shape some aspect of that world of which he was still the
center, perhaps for but a few fleeting and final moments. Under these circumstances odd and idiosyncratic examples of this volition and manipulation are not surprising. The earl of Arundel singled out an otherwise
obscure relative, in return for her special labors at his time of need: "Lego
Elizabet Arundell' consanguinee mee pro bono et diligenti labore et servi-
cio que fecit michi tempore infirmitatis mee."[65] The earl of Devon's
younger son William was to receive the handsome settlement of 1,000
marks from family lands, *if* he were loyal to the king.[66]

Several recent studies have analyzed the identities of relatives named
in wills, regarding both prayers and the transmission of tangible items.[67]
They have reported a strong tendency to prefer members of the vertical
and the nuclear family over those of the horizontal. This is much as we
would expect. Though we generally hold against an inclination to put different categories of kin into mutually exclusive compartments, we certainly
assume a positive correlation between the legal and economic gradations
of kinship and the personal and affective ones. In a society where sons were
almost always of preeminent importance and great-nephews but rarely so,
it would be perverse to look for the latter as frequently as it would be to
expect the former to appear but rarely.

This analysis is not to assert that people invariably confined themselves to the straight and narrow paths of kinship. It is rather a reminder of our ignorance regarding their range of options, as well as the consequences that followed from their choice from among the options. When John Bount asked for burial with his brother and sister, at St. Mary Redclyf, Bristol, in 1404, we infer that he was childless. And when he leaves land to enfeoff "Thomas Bokeland my brother on my mother's side," we become more confident. Finally, when Bount finally says that in the event of Thomas Bokeland's death the land is to be sold to the next of kin on his mother's side, and "at a better price than to any stranger," we can begin to speak with some certainty.[68] Others controlled the flow of goods so as to emphasize their roles in the family. William Nobles, a man who died with at least one son and one daughter, still was concerned with his place in a chain that stretched from the previous generation. His brother and his sister were to share "all those goods which my mother bequeathed to us."[69]

In general, these distribution patterns, and the underlying ideologies they make manifest, do not come as a surprise, not unless we are trying to argue for a nuclear family that was exclusive in its embrace and that acted in direct competition with an extended group network of kinsmen and kinswomen. There is little evidence in these data for such a competitive and jealous creature. The metaphor of the concentric circles, or of the family as a series of prioritized choices with the incidence of preference usually going first to inner circles over outer ones, seems sufficient. The family of affection and of authority, or of voluntary bonding and of functional networks, was comprised of some mix of those whom blood, marriage, proximity, and personal ties had shaped (and continued to reshape). For virtually any purpose—though usually short of the transmission of real property held in chief—one was at liberty to cross kinship boundaries and to bind and unbind the disparate groups with whom ego had kinship links.

Men who were without sons, of course, faced a death-bed prospect that was doubly unwelcome. But here the need for alternatives was even greater. It is unlikely that all relatives within the larger, outlying categories were ever apt to be remembered, at least not when they existed in any appreciable number. But those who were named as beneficiaries were sometimes but not invariably profiting from the peculiar chance of the absence of a son as heir. This missing son may have opened up possibilities that approximated a free scramble for favor (and inheritance). Whether there would be a partition of the patrimony among daughters or significant transmission to a brother or nephew or cousin, the rivalry within this universe of second-best choices may have been keen. On the other hand, from a monetary perspective, testamentary bequests might be intended by the testator to redress the inequities inherent to the distribution of property in a world that placed so much emphasis upon sex and birth order. The bequests afforded an ultimate opportunity to help those whom the law did little to aid, those innocent victims of primogeniture, of impartible inheritance, and of sexism. Sometimes the testators chose to use the opportunity, sometimes the vote was negative.

Seen in this way, the mix of relatives brought together in the will of a man now facing death without direct male issue can be seen as a group of rivals. But in the testamentary rhetoric of the fading patriarch little of the competitive side of family life appears. The inclusion of a medley of relatives conveys the impression of the harmony and unity of the lineage, rather than of despair of the testator and of the competition among his beneficiaries. The Inquisitions carried no hint of disputes over next-of-kin status or of the concomitant controversies about inheritance that could be lurking just around the corner. Similarly, the wills disguise much legacy hunting and a fierce jockeying for the inside rail. Edmund Thorpe, after a public career of four decades and more, left a will in 1418 that reveals an old man, still intent upon imposing law and order upon his heirs and descendents. If the first daughter died without heirs of her body, then to the second daughter, and then to each of two nephews, and then to the nephew's sister, and then to the outer reaches of kinship where relationships are not precisely identified.[70] If the odd members of this small universe were not already rivals, they were certainly being arranged in Edmund's will so that each had a strong interest in the mortality and (in)fertility of those ranked before him. There was nothing like a string of clauses talking about "pur defaute d'issue de son corps engendre . . ." to concentrate ones attention while waiting in the queue. John Rokewode set up a strategy of inheritance and transmission that opened with his brother, then moved on to his brother's sons, and then concluded with his brother's daughter. But if any of them crossed Rokewode's executors, they were to lose out: "Perturbaverint, impedierint, impedire perturbareve procuraverunt tunc nichil haberant de predictis lectis, calicibus et aliis necessariis supra specificatis."[71]

Men who faced death without sons, we have been arguing, faced death with an awareness of failure. To what extent is this reflected in their wills: an expression of bleakness or bitterness, as they took final stock? We saw how embittered lord Berkeley was by his final plight, or so his chron-

icler chose to interpret the tale. We can look at the wills of other peers who
were similarly bereft and see if the family situation is reflected in the emotional timbre of the will, as well as note which kin were included. After all,
when there was a son, bequests to other relatives talk to such issues as
patriarchy and sentiment, not to the basic transmission of the patrimony.
When there was no son, it was very different.

When Ralph, III lord Cromwell, died in 1455, his heirs were two
nieces, Maud, wife of Robert, lord Willoughby, and Joan, wife of Sir
Humphrey Bourgchier. Cromwell had outlived their mother, his sister
Maud Stanhope, as well as his own wife, Margaret Deincourt. His will
leaves no family bequests of any sort, and though his list of executors and
supervisors included such eminent figures as the bishop of Winchester, the
archbishop of York, and Sir John Fortescue, no links of blood or marriage
were to be seen.[72] A lonely ending, in his case, produced a bleak will. But
few men, even at the end, appeared so disinterested. Some of the testamentary clauses that we have talked about in the context of social control and
as reflections of an incurable desire to worry about the family's future can
also be read as signs of a determination to fight the anomie of approaching
death. To keep interested was to keep up ones spirits. When John de Vere,
XIII earl of Oxford, faced death in 1513, there were no children, and the
next earl would be his younger brother's son. The old earl was about 67
when he wrote his will, 71 at his death. Nevertheless he refused to admit
defeat: "I woll that if I haue yssue male of my body laufully begoten that
than my same yssue male shalhaue the goods and Juells feraftir ensuyng viz
First myn Image of the Trinitie."[73] There were some more realistic clauses
in which the earl simply left goods to his heir (whom he would not name,
in a fashion foreshadowing Elizabeth I and James I), to be transmitted
when the latter came of age: "to be deliuered by myn Executors vnto myn
heire at his full age."

The language used to address and refer to relatives is too flexible and
imprecise to be more than suggestive. The way in which kinsfolk spoke of
each other, or to each other, offers no sure guide to the quality of the sentiments involved; conventional modes of address, reticence, and a desire to
cover the shifting currents of personal relations must all be taken into account. When we looked at the huge net of benefaction that John of Gaunt
spread over many of his kinsfolk, we also were looking at a will with numerous interesting touches of expression. His son in the church, Henry
Beaufort, was referred to as "the most reverent father in God and my dear
son [reverent pier en Dieu et mon tresame fitz l'evesq]," while Henry's

secular brother John Beaufort was simply "mon trescher filz." Gaunt's brother, Edmund of York was "mon trescher et tresreverent bienaimee frere," and York's son, Gaunt's nephew, was "mon trescher et tresentiere-ment bien ame nevue Edward." His wife—once his mistress and the mother of many children—was "ma treschere compaigne Katerine," while her son, Gaunt's stepson Thomas Swynford, was "mon tres cher bachelier." Gaunt's grandson, the future duke of Bedford, was "mon tresame filtz John . . . filtz de mon filtz." Nor was this usage exceptional in tone. A few years later the earl of Westmorland's brother, lord Furnivalle, referred to the earl as "venerabili et magnifico domino meo," which is probably accurate but surely a bit fulsome.[74] But we have so little of such usage, and most of it contained within such narrow conventions, that neither its presence—as in the Paston Letters—nor its frequent omission or loss can be read as signal-ing a consistent message about either affection or estrangement.

*   *   *

We can explore a different stretch of the boundaries between the world outside and the family within by looking at some clerical wills. As the clergy could not have (legitimate) heirs of the body, such wills only admit to material affecting horizontal and collateral kin, though there could also be a strong vertical axis linking the testator upward to his pro-genitors. Successful and lengthy clerical careers were often more peripa-tetic than secular ones, and some of the bonds we might expect to find with siblings and collateral kin may have been frayed by years of physical and geographical mobility. Likewise, family bonds may have weakened because useful links in the church forged during the years of clerical careerism were ultimately adjudged to be the ones most worth honoring. But on the other hand, the family of origin might remain a fixed point in a world of shifting orientations, and clerics had fewer relatives and fewer categories of rela-tives than did the typical worldly veteran of several marriages and of a gen-eration of procreation and patriarchy.

We can readily analyze the 76 clerical wills found in *The Register of Archbishop Chichele*. This good sized selection is biased towards the great men of the English (and Welsh) church, men who mostly died with full years, full coffers, and much vocational peregrination behind them. In giv-ing us many eminent older men, *Chichele's Register* also offers us a universe wherein the interval between the nurturing years, in the putative family bosom, and the moment of testamentary decision-making is probably far

greater than the average. Major figures in the church had both the economic resources and perhaps the spiritual equivalent of a patriarchal definition of self to impel them to include kin, of both sexes and of varying
degrees of relationship, within their testamentary network. Though lesser
clerics might not be so moved, their world was likely to have remained
more provincial, closer to that of their relatives and their families of origin
in both geographical terms and in its definition of self.

Of the 76 clerical wills in *Chichele's Register*, 52 call for at least some
token bequest to a beneficiary who is explicitly identified as a kinsfolk. Because there seem to be no comparable studies of such behavior, it is hard
to say whether this 68 percent response rate is high or low. Of the 24 bishops included among the 76 clerics, 17 (or 71 percent) were so minded. Episcopal behavior in this regard ran pretty much across the spectrum. Some
major fifteenth century bishops did not choose to remember family at all,
and some did so only in the most meager way, mere asides in wills replete
with bequests to ecclesiastical institutions and to ecclesiastical personnel
encountered in a lifetime of service; others were generous, thoughtful, and
expansive. John Mascall only bothered to reach out once to William Gase,
"consanguineo meo," with a bequest of £30.[75] Edmund Stafford, bishop of
Exeter, left a long will that included bequests to several peers of the realm,
but only one kinsman: "nepos et meus heres."[76] Richard Clifford was a
bishop of aristocratic family, but he was hardly expansive: only his brother
Robert, his executor, was mentioned or identified as a kinsman.[77]

Other bishops were more generous and their princely stores of personal or private wealth were expended to cover bequests to numerous relatives. Robert Hallum, bishop of Salisbury, wanted to ensure prayers for
the souls of his parents, and he left items to two brothers as well as to a
niece and her husband.[78] But this reasonable level of family remembrance
and generosity was nothing besides that of John Clyderowe, bishop of
Bangor. He mentioned a brother ("Ricardo fratri meo") and three sisters
("Alicie sorori mei," "Elianore alias Alyn sorori mei," and "Iohanne sorori
mee"). Then Richard's children were to share £40 for their marriages,
while Richard's wife Alianore was to receive cash and personal items. Alice's children also received gifts for their marriages, as did Eleanor's two
nephews, boys named Nicholas Stodert and William Clyderowe, along
with money and goods. And in a final burst of affection, Richard Clyderowe, William's father, was referred to as a brother.[79]

Men such as Clyderowe were unusual, even for bishops and even for
patriarchal figures who came from large families. Though most bishops did

remember a relative or two, such benefactions have to be assessed against a much larger group of *other* recipients. Roger Whelpdale, bishop of Carlisle, left his sister and niece a tenement in Beverley, in order to subsidize prayers for himself and for one Thomas Povys.[80] John Wakeryng, bishop of Norwich, left £5 for his sister-in-law, Matilda: "nuper uxori fratris mei."[81] But if these men represent a considerable descent from the plateau on which we found Clyderowe, they regain a respectable status when we consider how many bishops left no family bequests. Some of these men were the most insignificant of ecclesiastical princes, and Robert Rede of Chichester and Richard Young of Rochester are hardly names with which to conjure. But Philip Repingdon was bishop of the great see of Lincoln for 15 years (1405–20), and we may well wonder at both his family situation and his personal outlook. The fact that he was elderly and an Augustinian canon may help explain his withdrawn behavior.[82]

Of the clerics below the level of bishops whose wills appear in *Chichele's Register*, 35 of 52 (70 percent) named relatives who were linked in some fashion or other. The variation in identifying the beneficiaries ran from a most perfunctory bequest to a recipient identified simply as "consanguinee mee" to the wide net cast by a number of men with avuncular or patriarchal views of their lineage. Thomas Felde covered a network that would have graced the last wishes of an affectionate bishop. He talked of a mother, two brothers, a sister and her husband, a nephew, and a second brother-in-law.[83] Walter Medford was a man who might well have gone even higher in the church, and his will bespeaks the princely style in which he, as dean of Wells, had lived. He offers us the clerical version of a patriarch's role: The prayer network alone is that of a man with many ties and a rather grand view of self. Nor was he less expansive with his goods. Elizabeth Talbot, "consanguinee mee," received a whole treasure chest: £20 in cash, plus books, household items, and chapel ornaments and furnishings. Walter's sister, Alice Hunt, was to receive £10, "sub ista condicione quod nichil petat de legatis sibi relictis in testamento Ricardi Medford." Alice's son, Walter's god-son, was remembered, as were a sister Eleanore; her husband John; nieces Alice Shotelsbroke, Eleanore Fithnycoll, Margaret Holeot; each of sister Eleanor's children; each child of sister Agnes Daundesey; and various other nieces, nephews, and people simply identified as "consanguinee mee." This will is the winner in our competition, and no other clergyman in *Chichele's Register*, regardless of ecclesiastical level, matched its comprehensive generosity.[84]

Of those clerics who remembered a few relatives, most singled out between one and four recipients, and the bequests took a variety of forms and values. They could be purely secular, usually in cash, as to Alan Frere, "filiolo meo, xx s.," or to Robert Robertson of Stykeswold, "cognatur meus habeat iijs. iiijd."[85] Others received small personal items of interest or sentimental value, though bishop Chaundeler's bequest to his brothers was of a distinctly practical nature: "octo boves cum quadam biga vocata wayn' et toto apparatu."[86] Some bequests bespoke the testator's own calling and choice of life path, as when clerics left books or other such items for young relatives, no doubt with an eye on their future career choices. A northern bishop, Walter Skirlaw, left 10 marks to his brother's widow and 1,000 marks to the poor.[87]

*   *   *

Variety, as we said at the start, is the essence of the presentation, and the data we have offered in this chapter have been chosen to support our argument. Each person had a specific and unique set of defined kin, and of cooperating kin. Even what would seem as an externally controlled social phenomenon—the extended or horizontal family—was a malleable one, once it was translated from the purely formal to the functional. In some of the contexts we have considered, one did not choose one's kin. In others, one did. And very often social interaction and the kinds of behavior for which we are searching took place at the meeting point of these two lines, the intersection of the world one shaped and of the world by which one was shaped. Much of family history consisted of those instances of cooperation, of transmission and inheritance, and of testamentary disposition and obligation that we have been considering. They were its historical events, its tides of daily intercourse writ large. Few men of substance were so bereft as to have no one to whom they were related and with whom they would choose to be linked and identified; even most clerics—after a life of separation and celibacy—harked back to that aspect of their original, pre-clerical identity. There is no way of knowing whether people thought of themselves as being constricted or supported by the many circles of kin within which they so often moved. Or rather, there is no single answer to this question. The wills seem to indicate that they often looked expansively upon their beneficiaries among their kin. After all, such a universe gave them all that many more people—besides their sons and their widow—

over whom they could exercise a posthumous control, towards whom they could display the better side of patriarchal pride and possession.[88]

Some Case Studies

The importance of the family network in pre-industrial or late medieval society is virtually axiomatic. No one would deny that ties between members of the horizontal family, the collateral kin, were among the more important ligatures binding individuals. Such bonds often linked family members of two or even three generations, and they could persist—with appropriate changes among the *dramatis personae*—for as long as we care to plot their course. The spokes that radiated out from siblings, from parents' siblings, and from siblings' children lead us to multitudinous ties and alliances among individuals, and they provide the underlying strata for many structures of common action and types of choice and response.

However, our interest here lies neither in genealogy nor in demography. How many such collateral kin any given person "had" is not a question for which we can often provide a meaningful answer. We are interested rather in the intersection of or the dialectical relationship among the relatives one had and the relatives with whom one chose to interact. There are innumerable ways in which such interactions can be examined. When we looked at the kinship network as revealed by wills, we saw a wide spread inclination to include some—but rarely all and probably not even a very high proportion of the potential beneficiaries—in the network being shaped by volition, gift giving, and reciprocity. One was tolerably free to do as one chose. There were some strong expectations and conventions covering the structures of the testamentary network: bequests for the church and funds for burial and prayers, money and personal goods for the family, remembrances for friends, servants, creditors, executors, and so forth. But how any individual recipient within a particular category or circle of kinship came to be singled out, let alone which sub-categories of potential recipients were chosen, was an idiosyncratic matter. Though sons were obviously (and almost invariably) remembered more than nephews, no specific rules existed to cover their proportional shares or the incidence of inclusion and exclusion.

Wills have offered us an entree to the complicated channels and shifting sands of the family networks. As a source they probably overemphasize the formalistic aspect of human relationships. In addition, because they are death-bed or near death-bed documents, they contain an element of retrospection that can differ markedly in tone from the sustained one of worldly give-and-take. They focus the universe of benefaction and reciprocity upon the testator, and he usually stands at the centerpoint of all the concentric circles and their occupants. In life there was rarely such an uncontested focus: not even all of John of Gaunt's beneficiaries always looked just to him as the center of their world. Competing loyalties and distractions took their toll. And despite the many instances of posthumous social control that have emerged, the general tenor of a will is usually one of generosity and benevolence. Consequently, though the will is a source of great value, we must not overlook or make light of its inherent limitations.

To illuminate some of these limitations, and to offer a slightly different perspective, we will look at some case studies of family networks in operation. There are an almost unlimited number of such networks, had we data and time to pick and choose, and there are a fair number of perspectives.[89] The mere existence of the network is rarely in much dispute, and when we look at people about whom any reasonable amount of precise data is available, we readily identify groups of men, related by blood or marriage and seen to be working in some degree of concert. Of course, that many colleagues within almost any social and political circle were also likely to be related through some sort of kinship tie is neither startling nor, by itself, particularly helpful. If all (or many) were apt to be so linked, then obviously the mere existence of such links becomes of limited value in explaining behavior. Rather, how men, linked through such definitional ties, also chose to work together and to exhibit a common identification is our tale. That they were part of some kind of extended family *and* that they interacted in some positive or dialectical fashion is what makes their activity of interest. A common course of action or policy, a high degree of interaction (perhaps sustained for decades or generations), and some sense of common identification are perhaps the three criteria that help define a fully developed family network in a functional as well as a definitional sense. But if we are flexible in our definitions, we can identify lesser or ephemeral family networks that appear, make their presence felt, and then perhaps become diluted or completely disappear from sight. Men moved in many circles, and we must be careful not to confuse the inevitable coincidences of a heavily intermarried and interrelated world with those of concerted action and common identification.

A specific example of what *may* be seen as coincidence is provided by looking at the leaders of the Southampton plot of 1415, that peculiar conspiracy against Henry V that was uncovered just before he embarked on his French campaign. The actors in this sordid drama were linked in a would-be coup, supposedly designed to put Edmund Mortimer, earl of March, on the throne of England. But they were also linked to each other through the byways of marriage and relationship. One of the major conspirators, the earl of Cambridge, had been married to Anne Mortimer (d. 1414 or a bit earlier), the earl of March's sister, so Cambridge was presumably scheming on behalf of his quondam brother-in-law. In addition, there were links with the Percies, progenitors of early rebellions against the house of Lancaster. Anne Mortimer's aunt, Elizabeth, had been married to Hotspur, heir of the earl of Northumberland, while Cambridge's second wife, Maud Clifford, was the sister of the man who married Hotspur's daughter Elizabeth. Henry, lord Scrope of Masham, another noble conspirator who now paid with his life, had married Joan Holand, Cambridge's stepmother (and widow of Edmund Langley, duke of York) and Edmund Mortimer's aunt. And to finish off the tangle, we take note of Sir Thomas Grey of Heton, one of the lesser figures in the plot. Grey's sister-in-law had married Hotspur's son-and-heir, while Grey's son Thomas had married Cambridge's daughter Elizabeth.[90]

Though it is unclear to what extent this clumsy plot was genuine, let alone a genuine threat to the king and his dynasty, it is not difficult to imagine that the links between the men are part of the explanation for their original involvement. The earl of Cambridge might not have been as sympathetic to this fatuous affair had a Mortimer not been its intended beneficiary, and we can extend such speculations to the other conspirators. Eccentric and even irrational behavior does not necessarily preclude a rational social bond. If the plotters in this instance hoped for a political effect that neither proves nor depends on their peculiar webs of marriage and blood, we can easily continue in this direction and offer other instances of such linkage without evidence, pro or con, of a great deal of concerted action. Students of the peerage and of political history are fond of noting that four brothers of the Bourgchier family sat, simultaneously, in the House of Lords: Thomas, archbishop of Canterbury, Henry, earl of Essex, John, lord Berners, and William, lord Fitzwarin. Though they may generally have leaned in the same direction in political matters, mere propinquity and kinship never served to make them a major force in the great division that split the upper class between the 1450s and the ascendancy of Henry VII. There may have been a Bourgchier interest, but it never took such root that it grew to become a Bourgchier party.[91]

A propitious marriage could give a would-be patriarch the raw material from which he might mold a large network of marriages, of sons- and
daughters-in-law, and then of collateral and affinal kinsmen and kinswomen who resulted from such unions. A prominent local figure could
hope to emerge as the center point of a whole set or series of circles, even
though there is little indication beyond the genealogical table to indicate
that he was the real center point, the prime mover of political and social
organization. Sir Thomas Parr of Kendal provides us with such an example, and depending upon how we choose to view the material, he was either the focus or a neutral conduit through which ran other men's
schemes.[92] The question we should ask is whether he was actually able to
use the marriages of his children, plus their ties with their new families, to
elevate himself, along with his eldest son-and-heir, to a new plateau of local
prominence. By such lights he seems to have had fair success, though like
most medieval climbers whose ascent we can follow, he had actually begun
fairly well up from the bottom when he enters the records that enable us
to tell the story. Sir Thomas was sheriff of Westmorland from 1461 to 1475,
and his wife was the daughter of Sir Thomas Tunstall of Thurland, Lancashire. Sir Thomas had three sons, and the two who survived to full age
certainly fulfilled the old man's ambitions. Sir William, the son-and-heir,
became a Knight of the Garter, sat in the House of Commons for Westmorland, and married (as his second wife) the daughter of lord Fitzhugh.
His brother John was sheriff of Westmorland, though he strayed a bit
afield—geographically if not socially—in his choice of a bride: she was the
daughter of the lord mayor of London. A third son, Thomas, was killed at
the battle of Barnet.[93] But the real test came with the fortunes of the bevy
of daughters, and here in at least five of the six cases we have all the visible
signs of success and advancement. The girls married (or were married to:
where do we place the active predicate?) Sir Thomas Radclyffe of
Derwentwater, William Harrington of Cartmel, Sir Christopher Moresby
of Moresby, Sir Thomas Strickland of Sizergh, and Humphrey, lord Dacre
of Gilsland. Apart from the obvious fact that these men represented
extremely good matches, they were all the raw material or the potential
personnel for the formation of a powerful local network, with the father-
in-law, old Parr, as the unifying link. Where we run short, in this case, is
when we have to judge the strength of the entire edifice. There is little
indication that Parr or his son became the recognized nucleus of a powerful
local network because of the girls' marriages. On the other hand, Parr was
able to use his status to contract marriages and alliances that at the very

least helped to preserve status with which he had begun and probably helped to enhance it by some appreciable degree. The Radclyffe were feoffees of the earl of Northumberland, and as such they moved with the Scropes of Masham. These were at least useful connections.[94]

We can go beyond these purely structural ties and look at some case studies that may take us closer to the questions of "team spirit" and group interaction. Since we are analyzing a society that assumed such links between countless individuals, we must go farther than the mere identification of genealogical bonds to build a case for some shared and common identity as the real sign of a collective, dynamic kingroup network. Can we find people who acted in concert with kinsmen and who—by word as well as by deed—reveal the central nature of such principles of organization? We will examine two case studies that involve families that are clustered around powerful clerics, *inter alia*. These offer a special element of interest because a major cleric, once safely moving up the ladder of careerism, was perhaps less tied to his family of origin than were ambitious laymen. Thus a family network in which he was critical was a work more of art than of mere biological or political necessity. Or so—in the absence of more detailed prosopographical studies—it seems possible to argue.[95]

The Chichele family, primarily of importance in the first half of the fifteenth century, offers a good case study of the creation and preservation of a family network. Since the bedrock of methodology is always near the surface of our investigations, and we will use the case studies to pose more questions than we are likely to "prove." How can the levels and values of interaction between members of a collateral kin network be determined? Can we measure and assess their mutuality in comparison with other forms of social interaction? The case studies have to be recreated from such recorded phenomena as common public and private service, mutual involvement in a range of joint activities, and common patterns in biography, benefaction, and testamentary bequests. There might well have been many other forms of interaction, perhaps on an almost daily basis. Such collections of family letters as have been preserved indicate how often brothers and nephews could concern themselves with the larger family enterprise and, in felicitous circumstances, express themselves in the idiom of common identification. And though such rich epistolary veins are rare, even the laconic and formulaic records of the fifteenth century tell us something about the degree to which the members of the group bonded together, though usually they only betray a minimum of explicit discussion regarding the personal motives behind the cooperation and common endeavor.

The three main members of the Chichele network were Henry (1364–1443), bishop of St David's (1408–14) and archbishop of Canterbury (1414–43), and his two brothers, William (d. 1425) and Robert (d. 1438 or 1439). The three brothers were the sons of Thomas Chichele of Higham Ferrers, Northamptonshire, and through the course of their three successful careers—one in the church and two among the *haute* bourgeoisie of London—the brothers remained in close contact with each other and seemed to share a view of mutual aid and interaction that drew in and embraced other members of the family, plus some of the in-laws acquired along the way, and some measure of their posthumous benefactions.[96]

William Chichele, the oldest of Thomas's sons, was long prominent among the burghers of London: a member of the mystery of grocers in 1373, thrice master of the company (1385, 1396, and 1406), and one of its first companions (1386). He served as an alderman of the City (1407–20), a member of parliament for the City (January, 1398), a warden of the bridge (1401–04), and sheriff (1409) and auditor (1411–13) of London. Though he was buried at the family's old point of origin, Higham Ferrers, he was a generous benefactor of London institutions, and two of his children married into his familiar world of the bourgeois aristocracy of the City. One son, William, entered the church and rose to the position of archdeacon of Canterbury.

The second of the brothers, Robert, makes his appearance in the records of the London Grocer's Company in 1397. He was sheriff of the city in 1402, and an aldermen from the ward of Aldgate from 1402–07 (as was his elder brother William immediately afterwards). Then he moved on to become alderman from the Vintry ward, 1407–26, and he was twice Lord Mayor (1411 and 1421), master of the Grocer's Company (1413), and a member of parliament in 1414 and 1415. He was buried in the parish church of St. Stephen, Walbrook, London. The number of career rungs common to the two secular brothers is striking, even in a public world familiar with family networks, patronage, and nepotism, and even within the large but confined world of the city of London.

The career of the third brother, Henry, is well known and need not be covered in much detail here. He blazed a wide trail through the forests of ecclesiastical preferment, and his example, along with his direct or indirect support, helped open the way for nephews and cousins who followed. Henry began with an education at New College, Oxford and eventually earned a doctorate in civil law. He held his first rectory, Whitechurch in Denbighshire, in 1391, and he accumulated such ecclesiastical plums as post of advocate in the Court of Arches and the chancellorship of Sarum before he was nominated to the Welsh episcopate in 1408. He was translated from St. David's to Canterbury, after six years of Welsh service, and in his long rule as primate of the church in England he also filled such positions as royal councillor, legal advisor, and diplomat.

Separately, each of these three tales provides a reasonable vignette of upward mobility and careerism, combining well-rewarded service in "the public sector" with profitable enterprises in "the private sector." But it is when we look at the three careers in tandem that we see how intertwined the brothers' lives were. In addition, we should recall that, as archbishop of Canterbury for almost a generation, Henry spent more time through the course of the year at Lambeth and Westminster than he did in the unexplored depths of Kent: physical proximity to the world of his brothers, as well as understanding and personal affection, enters the tale. Given these general observations it is no surprise to discover such instances of fraternal involvement as when William and Robert sat together on such proceedings as that of 13 October, 1408, when Drew Barrington was elected Lord Mayor of London, before "an immense commonalty assembled."[97] But the network is more tightly woven than just the high coincidence of common actions, and it touched the next generation, and eventually the next plus one, in addition to the obvious bonds between the three brothers.

William had a son, another William, who entered the church.[98] Young William's road, needless to say, was hardly made more difficult by his uncle's position and his willingness to offer visible support. Nor, as we shall see even more strongly below when we consider the Booth family, was there any feeling for a decent reticence on the part of senior and influential relatives when it came to helping younger ones to move ahead. Henry Chichele had been bishop of St. David's, 1408–14; Nephew William became a canon of that cathedral in 1412 and he held the sinecure until his death in 1424. Henry had been a canon of Abergwili from 1400 until 1404; William became chancellor there in 1417. Henry had been archdeacon of Sarum from 1402–04; young William was likewise the archdeacon from 1410–20. William eventually rose to be his uncle's right hand man, as archdeacon of Canterbury, and he was installed into this high position, personally, by the archbishop and the king in the royal tent during the siege of Melun in 1420.

Nor was this case of uncle and nephew, patron and protege, the only example in the family's annals. There was a great nephew, Thomas, who was also coming along the road.[99] He concentrated more on northern and midland benefices than had William, but again there was some overlap or

near-overlap with Henry and with what had proved to be the stepping
stones of a great career. Henry had been rector of Sherston Magna, Wiltshire, 1400–03; Thomas was rector of Sherston Pinkney free chapel from
1426–44 (which was during about two-thirds of Henry's archepiscopal
reign). While Henry was archbishop of Canterbury, Thomas was master
of East Bridge hospital in Canterbury, and then he too became archdeacon
of Canterbury from 1433 until his death in 1467. Henry had once been a
canon of Lincoln; Thomas eventually held the Lincoln canonry of Bedford
Major. And at the end, Thomas was one of his great-uncle's feoffees for
the building of All Souls College at Oxford and he served as a general
executor of the archbishop's last will.

As a founder and benefactor of the church and of education, Henry
had two great (realized) ambitions. One of his creations, All Souls College,
belongs more to the realm of his public life.[100] But the other was the college
he founded and built at Higham Ferrers, and Henry spoke with pride of
being in a position to so glorify the place of his birth. He planned a college
of eight secular canons or chaplains, along with a goodly complement of
clerks, choristers, a grammar master, and some other specialized staff.
Henry and his brother William were allowed to acquire the suppressed
alien priory of West Mersea in Essex, for the college, and they were further
licensed to alienate land worth up to 40 marks in annual value towards its
endowment. At the dissolution in the 1530s, it was stated that the College
had a clear annual value of £93 1s. 9½d.[101] What is of special interest to us,
however, is the appeal of the home town project for the archbishop's
brothers. William died before the new instición was fully built, and
though a Londoner of many years standing, he requested burial "in oure
lady chapel at Hiegham like as it is ordeined bisyde my fader."[102] But some
years later Robert bequeathed a whole packet of London tenements and
properties to the master and college of Blessed Mary and St. Thomas Mar-
tyr and Edward the Confessor, as founded by "Henry, most revered in
Christ, lord of lords," and his brother.[103] Robert's specifications for the
prayers he was buying, in return for his endowments, included the mention of his parents' souls, plus those of Thomas and Agnes Chichele, of his
three wives, of his late brother William and of William's widow Beatrice,
among other and more generalized parties. He also remembered the fabric
of the parish church at Higham Ferrers (where his father and brother William lay) with a gift of £20, and the town bridge there was to receive £10
for repairs and upkeep.

Nor were the testamentary entanglements and coincidences of the brothers confined to their old home ground in the midlands. The London careers of William and Robert had often run together, as we have seen, and the overlapping and intertwining of their benefaction and beneficiaries add yet another dimension to the tale. William's bequests within London touched the gildhall, the Grocer's Company (for the construction of their hall), London bridge, and the parish churches of St. Stephen Walbrook and "Seint Benettes Shorhogge." In life Robert had helped raise money to build the parish church of St. Stephen, and his laying of the first stone there, in May, 1429, is an indication of how seriously his acquired London commitments were grafted atop those of an older and provincial or natal loyalty. Robert also followed his brother William's testamentary lead, and he left money for work on London bridge and on the gildhall of the City.

Both lay brothers remembered their kin networks when they listed their own beneficiaries. William left books to his sons, John and Thomas, and to his daughter, Florence (and then to her son, Thomas, and then on to Florence's cousins, John's daughter, Anneys). The archbishop was empowered to dispose of his brother's lands, for the sake of the dead man's soul, after the death of William's widow Beatrice (who was to hold them for life). Beatrice and her son John were to be the executors, brother Henry the supervisor of the will. Robert's will contained bequests for brother Henry, for nephew John, and for William's daughter Florence, by now (1439) the widow of John Daryll. Robert left a bequest to St. Antholin's parish church, London, where Thomas Knollys, father in law of his nephew John, had recently been buried.[104] William's daughter Florence received many of her husband's goods and lands, to hold for life. But her husband, John Daryll, had been steward to the archbishop, his uncle by marriage, and Daryll was not likely to jeopardize further good relations with the Chichele connection that might be so helpful for the young children he was leaving behind.[105] Nor was this all. Robert Chichele and John Daryll were both benefactors of the bridge at Rochester, and John's executors received land in the parish of St. Stephen, Walbrook, where the older Chichele brother had been an active figure and donor.

So the whole picture is one of a family whose ties—to each other and to each other's special projects—were strong and continuous. The senior or founding members provided leadership and blazed the trail; the junior ones followed with the proper degree of obedience and dedication. Whatever the archbishop's other (and fancier) connections in this world, he always was able to find time, money, and interest for his birthplace, for his secular brothers and their children, and for the ecclesiastical and administrative careers of his younger relatives and their spouses. And despite their strong London ties and their success in the metropolis and the southeast, William and Robert seem to have looked upon family prosperity and family roots and ties as a common obligation. Their benefactions overlapped, they followed their ecclesiastical brother's impressive lead as well as striking off on their own, and they worked to include their in-laws and their children's in-laws within the family orbit. By the end they were erecting a Kentish connection to match the London one and the old Northamptonshire one. But, as a testament to the strength of their common bonds, they do not seem to have abandoned older obligations and commitments as they cultivated new ones.

＊   ＊   ＊

The Chicheles present a case study of a horizontal network that centered mainly around three brothers, though we tend to view the archbishop as the *de facto* head of the family, if hardly as its only bright light. If we move onwards for a generation and cast our gaze northwards, we can look at an even larger and more cohesive network, again one in which the ecclesiastical lead was obvious and this time honed to an even finer edge. The network of the Booth family is larger and more complex than that of the Chicheles, and a recent study of William Booth, its eldest member, aptly introduces him as being but "the first of what became a virtual episcopal dynasty."[106] This well-placed north midland and northern family produced four bishops between the mid-fifteenth-century and the early years of Henry VIII: William Booth, bishop of Coventry and Lichfield (1447–52) and archbishop of York (1452–64); Laurence, bishop of Durham (1457–76) and archbishop of York (1476–80); John, bishop of Exeter (1465–76); and Charles, bishop of Hereford (1516–35). William and Laurence were half-brothers, John their nephew (as the son of a third brother), and Charles a great-nephew. The mere accumulation of so many high ecclesiastical offices within a single family is noteworthy. But the Booths are not just collectors. They formed a real network, with a concomitant realization of a common or collective purpose. The network, which we can almost call a family enterprise, embraced three generations of collateral kinsmen within the church, as well as a broad span of secular relatives, linked both by blood and by marriage. Again, common enterprises and mutual aid indicate a well understood if implicit policy regarding careerism and family traditions of mutual aid. Nepotism and favoritism were part of their standing order; almost, we might say, of their hereditary make-up. It has been suggested that "mentoring" is perhaps the way to interpret this tradition of aggressive support, and such a view indeed moves the matter from one of clandestine or shame-faced partisanship to that of an overt tradition, a predictable behavioral pattern.

William Booth was the only fifteenth-century bishop whose formal, higher education had been at the inns of court, rather that at the university or in the cloister. He was in orders by 1420, and he quickly began the customary climb through the *cursus honorum* of service and advancement without which one rarely reached the episcopacy: a canon of Southwell, prebendary of Oxton and Cropwell, archdeacon of Middlesex, and much more of the same. He attracted the support of the duke of Suffolk, then became Queen Margaret of Anjou's chancellor, and eventually a bishop and then an archbishop—at the same time proving adept at serving both the Lancastrian and the Yorkist kings in a variety of offices and functions.

William's half-brother, Laurence, was illegitimate. Despite this token obstacle he began with a distinguished career at Cambridge, and he too was soon climbing in the church.[107] The signs of an older brother's hand are not hard to find. While William was an influential cleric in the chapter of St. Paul's, Laurence received the rectory of St. Mary Magdelan, Milk Street, London, which he soon resigned in favor of the living of St. Botolph's, Bishopsgate. He followed William as the queen's chancellor, was keeper of the privy seal from 1456 to 1460, served as an ambassador for Edward IV, and was the king's chancellor from July, 1473, until May, 1474. Though the family had originally been strongly identified with the Lancastrian cause and had risen in some part because of intimate service within the royal household, their value and their versatility kept them in favor even after the coup of 1461. Laurence, like William, had no trouble learning the family game, and a modern observor has paid him an appropriate, if back handed compliment: "Though a bastard, a true Bothe in his appreciation of the merits of his relations."[108]

Next came the brothers' nephew, John, son of their brother Roger. Like Laurence, he had studied law at Cambridge.[109] He began his ecclesiastical climb as the warden of Denwell hospital, in Cheshire, in 1452, and as rector of Thornton-in-the-Moore, Cheshire, of which church his father conveniently was the patron. In 1457 he became treasurer of York, where—wonder of wonders—uncle William had been presiding as archbishop for some five years. Then he became archdeacon of Richmond in 1459 (as uncle Laurence had been a few years before). He was king's secretary from 1462 to 1465, when he was consecrated as bishop of Exeter. Charles Booth, the last of the great success stories, took law degrees at both Cambridge and Bologna, and was holding his first benefice by 1493.[110] He collected such positions as the treasurership of Lichfield (where William had once been bishop), the archdeaconry of Buckingham, and a canonry at St. Paul's, among others, before he (too) became bishop, of Hereford, in 1516. Though he is mainly beyond the chronological boundaries of our tale, his career reminds us that our self-imposed boundaries do not always fully cover the logical extensions of the story.

The Booths, especially the three older ones, offer us an exceptionally clear picture of the intertwining of lives and career paths. The senior men worked with each other, along with various younger members of the family (who will soon make their appearance), and their separate "projects" are easily seen as being but the separate segments of a larger exercise in collective action. We can look at some examples of one aspect of family interconnection, drawing from the sphere of private rather than governmental or episcopal activity. In 1450 William was moved to found and build a large and imposing chantry chapel, within the parish church of St. Mary Virgin, at Eccles in Lancashire. This was a new venture, a manifestation of the family's burgeoning desire for self-glorification, and over the years many Booths dipped a rich finger into this spiritual pie.[111] In the royal license that enabled William to launch the project, the founders were nominally listed as William, Sir John Byron—his brother-in-law—and Richard and Laurence Booth, and subsequent grants and licenses were issued to William and Robert Booth, plus Seth Worsley, treasurer of Lichfield and a member of a family that intermarried with the Booths for some decades.[112] When a second chantry was founded in Eccles church, William acted in concert with Nicholas Byron, Sir John's son, Robert Clyfton, his brother-in-law, Richard Booth, esquire, and Seth Worsley.[113] And in addition, further chantry chapels in St. Mary Southwark and in York cathedral were being founded, around this time, by the smooth-working team of Richard Booth and Nicholas Byron.[114]

Nor was cooperation confined to private and family projects. The records of chancery indicate how closely the various public careers intersected, how members of the "clan" were apt to be collectively involved in public business of both a secular and an ecclesiastical nature. When William Booth was still a canon of St. Paul's, he and Robert Booth, esquire, were among the five men involved in a quitclaim over land at Clapton, Hackney.[115] Some years later land in Surrey was at issue, and again we find lord

Stanley negotiating with a coterie that included Laurence Booth, now bishop of Durham, John Booth, clerk, and Richard Booth.[116] Other relatives appear at other times as members or partners in these amalgams: Robert Booth of Stratton, George Booth, and William Booth of Erleston, Derbyshire along with his son Henry, all figured in a quitclaim in 1465.[117] One Alice Booth, a widow of Ypeswich (Ipswich), made a gift in widowhood of all her lands and goods, "within the realm and overseas, and of all debits to her due":[118] The gift was made to Laurence Booth, bishop of Durham, and to the dean of St. Paul's. Laurence, as bishop of Durham, and John Booth, now bishop of Exeter, stood together as witnesses of a similar transaction in 1474.[119] When William was bishop of Durham and Laurence archbishop of York, the latter received a bond of 800 marks from the former as a pledge regarding the "repair and dilapidations" of the temporalities of the see of Durham.[120] When archbishop Laurence had to post bond, until he could realize the debts owed him from Durham, the bond was posted by dint of joint action on the part of Laurence, Ralph Booth, a clerk in the archdeaconery of Richmond, and of John Booth, esquire, son and heir of Robert Booth.[121]

Many men who led active lives in public service constantly moved in and out of networks of relatives and associates, and we must not make more of "the Booth connection" than it warrants. Though it was probably richer and more complex than many others we could find, this network was unusual more by matter of degree than by the mere fact of its existence; quantity, perhaps, rather than quality. Nevertheless, family shoulders and elbows often rubbed together. William, an archbishop, and his half-brother Laurence, as keeper of the privy seal, were natural associates on commissions, such as the important one appointed for "the counsel and care of Edward, prince of Wales."[122] But it is when we look at the latter (and lesser) ecclesiastical careers, those of the second and third generations of Booths, that we begin to appreciate fully how much God was inclined to help those whose relatives also lent a hand, as the Booths themselves might have expressed the matter.

With the Booths we not only find the links of cooperation and association, but we find, to an unusual extent, explicit tags and labels by which men of the subsequent generations proclaimed their membership on the team. When John, future bishop of Exeter, was appointed treasurer of Lichfield, he was identified in the documents as the son of Roger Booth, esquire: a lineage already considered well worth stating.[123] One Peter Booth, a rising young scholar of Lichfield diocese, "whose father and uncle are knights," was moving along the well-blazed path that marked the early stages of a successful career.[124] More often than with most other fifteenth-century families of climbers and petitioners, the links and ties between the various Booths and between their different generations were clearly—if not always accurately—given. Laurence was the "carnal brother of William":[125] John Booth, clerk, was "son of Roger Booth, esquire;" and then there was a further reference to William, "whose nephew he is."[126] Such a link could be variously expressed, as in "a nephew of the archbishop of York by his brother."[127] Henry Jule, now about to receive Yoxhale parish church (which he would hold for the rest of his life), was another "kinsman of William, archbishop of York," as though in this case the different surname were an obstacle that could be leveled through the use of such a clause of identification.[128] Then there was Edmund Booth, "a nephew of the archbishop and the son of a knight," now rising in the church as rector of the valuable living of St. Mary le Bow, London.[129] Thomas Booth, clerk, received permission to study and simultaneously to hold a benefice while but in his fifteenth year: very much what we might expect when examining the early days of "a nephew of William, archbishop of York."[130]

The extant family wills contribute still another set of variations on this theme of close interweaving. Laurence and William were both buried in Southwell Minster. Links with that church were neither new nor confined to the two senior members of the partnership. Laurence had been in the process of endowing a two-chaplain chantry there, at the end of his life, while William left £40 for the vicars choral and was such a local cult figure that miracles supposedly took place at his tomb. In addition, the parish church of Kneesal, Nottinghamshire, was appropriated to Southwell, in 1459, and the advowson was bestowed by none other than our old friends, Nicholas Byron, Robert Clyfton, Richard Booth, and Seth Worsley.[131] Laurence's executors included Thomas Byron, Robert Booth, and Gervase Clyfton.[132] William had been even more expansive. He left 250 marks to each of the four daughters of the late Nicholas Byron, knight, to be used for their marriages.[133] There were further gifts designated for the large family chantry within the parish church at Eccles, cash bequests for Richard Booth, money for the marriage of John Byron, and money for the marriage of Sir William Booth's daughter. William's executors included Robert Clyfton, Richard Booth, esquire, and Seth Worsley, and all of them received handsome cash bequests in return for their duties. One Robert Booth, who died as dean of York in 1488, endowed prayers for the souls of Laurence, as well as for himself and his parents, to be said for "as many years as my estate can cover." His nephew Philip was to work, with Gervase Clyfton, to distribute money for additional services, and one Richard Booth was to serve as an executor of this will.[134] Agnes Clyfton, Gervase's widow, chose in her turn, in 1503, to leave £17 to Laurence Booth's chantry in Southwell Minster.[135]

Nor are we necessarily at the end of this. We have not tried to elaborate every possible link in the long chain, and quite possibly not all the Booths found in the records of the northern church were related within meaningful circles of acquaintance or cooperation. But neither should we rush to jettison possible kinsmen. The Thomas Booth who was advanced to a benefice at age 15 was later collated to Wolstanton parish church by Laurence Booth.[136] Edmund Booth succeeded his uncle Laurence in the lucrative deanery of Stow, in 1452, before he moved to exchange it for the church of St. Mary le Bow, another family favorite.[137] Hamo or Hammond Booth was perhaps a brother of the bishop of Exeter, and he held the rectory of St. Clement Danes.[138] The nephew John eventually reached the treasurership of Lichfield, another valuable office that almost seemed a family holding.[139] A Ralph Booth was canon and prebend of Norton, still another living within Laurence's web of patronage.[140] And what do we make of Robert Booth? At first he received a dispensation to enter orders because it was held that he was the illegitimate son of a married nobleman and an unmarried woman. Now, it seems, his father was an unmarried nobleman.[141] Perhaps not even the Booths understood all the familial and genealogical ramifications of their coming and going.

By now sufficient examples have been adduced to support the larger point. When we look at the more prominent men in each of these two family groups—the Chicheles and the Booths—we might be inclined to expand upon the theme of upward mobility. But actually they all started at the level of healthy gentry or burgher origins: If they indeed go forward (or upward), we should at least be clear that there are no rags-to-riches stories here. The original Thomas Chichele had been a prosperous midland burgess, while the Booths were of good north midland and northern landed stock.[142] Moreover, neither family represents a dynasty: They were networks. Neither family—in their secular or collateral branches—lasted with any prominence much beyond the three generations that completed the proverbial cycle of rise and decline.[143] The family webs we have illuminated are the kind of ports in a storm that men (and women, of whom we sadly hear so little) always seek. Such ports were not antidotes to or safe havens from political danger and civil disruption, nor were they alterna-

tives to political partisanship, loyalty, and service. But they were an extremely powerful and attractive form of social organization, of social
bonding. That we have little trouble finding them and tracing their many
byways indicates that they, like the proverbial justice, were to be seen to
be done.

*   *   *

Of all the great and complicated family networks of fifteenth-century
England, that of the Nevilles, in and after the lifetime of Ralph, I earl of
Westmorland (1364–1425), is perhaps the most intriguing and the most
complicated. Biographical information on many of the individuals and an
analysis of the earl's marital strategies for his many children is available and
familiar.[144] What we hope to do here is to extend these useful expositions
beyond the obvious realms of political and economic history, and to look
at the earl's activities in terms of family network building, with a regard for
both its positive and negative aspects. Like the networks of the Chicheles
and the Booths, the earl's strategies, though complex, were hardly devious
or foreign to the customary run of family strategies pursued by his contemporaries. In tracing some of the ramifications of his activities, we are just
offering a more detailed analysis of a form of social action that combined
obvious public policy with equally evident but more private schemes.

In demographic terms alone the Neville network was vast. Where we
concentrated only upon three senior Chichele men, and upon a slightly
larger number of Booths, this was a different world. The earl had eight or
nine children by his first marriage, to Margaret, daughter of Hugh, II earl
of Stafford, and 14 by his second, to Joan Beaufort, daughter of Catherine
Swynford and John of Gaunt and half-sister to Henry IV.[145] And of the
earl's many children, seven and nine from the respective marriages lived to
marry. Nor was the network of Neville children and their own families
merely a large one. It attained a level of social and political eminence fully
on a par with its magnitude.

The earl himself had sat in the House of Lords, along with two brothers, Thomas, lord Furnival, and John, lord Latimer. Five of the earl's sons
(the earl of Salisbury, the bishop of Durham, and lords Fauconberg, Latimer, and Abergavenny), plus six of his sons-in-law (the dukes of York,
Buckingham, and Norfolk, the earl of Northumberland, viscount Beaumont, and lord Dacre), sat at various times in the House of Lords. But
above all else, from our viewpoint, the Neville network was a construct, an

elaborate mechanism or enterprise whereby a mighty horizontal and collateral web of kin was put together so that in almost every matter of public life, as in the private lives of many northern families and their enterprises, a Neville or a close Neville link was involved. For this kind of clan-building, the risks might be as great as the rewards, and not all of the earl's sons, grandsons, and sons-in-law were inclined to lie down together, though it is often unclear as to who was the lion, who the lamb.

We have mentioned that close kinship and personal affinity did not always march hand in hand. The earl himself contributed no small part to a family division when he in effect disinherited the sons of his first marriage in favor of those of his second. Partially as a consequence of this unpaternal behavior, the network of which he was the center quickly proved to be so complicated that, even before the death of its founder, a single melody and a common rhythm were proving almost impossible to achieve. Another consideration is that much of the bridge-building only took place in the last 10 or 15 years of the earl's life. The fruits of earlier efforts had been so successful that, we might argue, he eventually turned his sustained and increasingly ambitious efforts in this same direction when he was well into his autumn and still with the large brood of young children produced by his second marriage on his hands. Also, the political opportunities of the day, combined with the slow-healing wounds of the Percies, may have drawn him toward more ambitious schemes than in his earlier days.

Earl Ralph was of an ancient and distinguished family. From his youth he had been surrounded by close kin of importance. Figure II-1 shows how his own life span fit, chronologically, between those of his influential kin of his father's generation and those of his own. Of the earlier generation, he was virtually the last survivor (except for his second wife), though he died at 61, a respectable but hardly an awesome quantitative feat. But survival and inheritance, plus political service and lucrative office holding, plus the decline of the rival Percies in the early years of Henry IV, contributed to his growing eminence. The earl's opportunities, as created by his own diligence and good luck, were greatly reinforced and enlarged by the good fortune of his two well-placed and fertile marriages. He was married to Margaret Holland by about 1380, and by her he had two sons and seven daughters. Margaret died in June, 1399, and a second marriage to Joan Beaufort—Henry IV's half-sister—meant even brighter political light as well as an additional nine sons and five or six daughters.

Figures II-2a and 2b show how Westmorland stood, chronologically, in relation to his many children. Their age spread meant that the eldest

FIGURE II-1 COHORT OF RALPH, EARL OF WESTMORLAND[a]

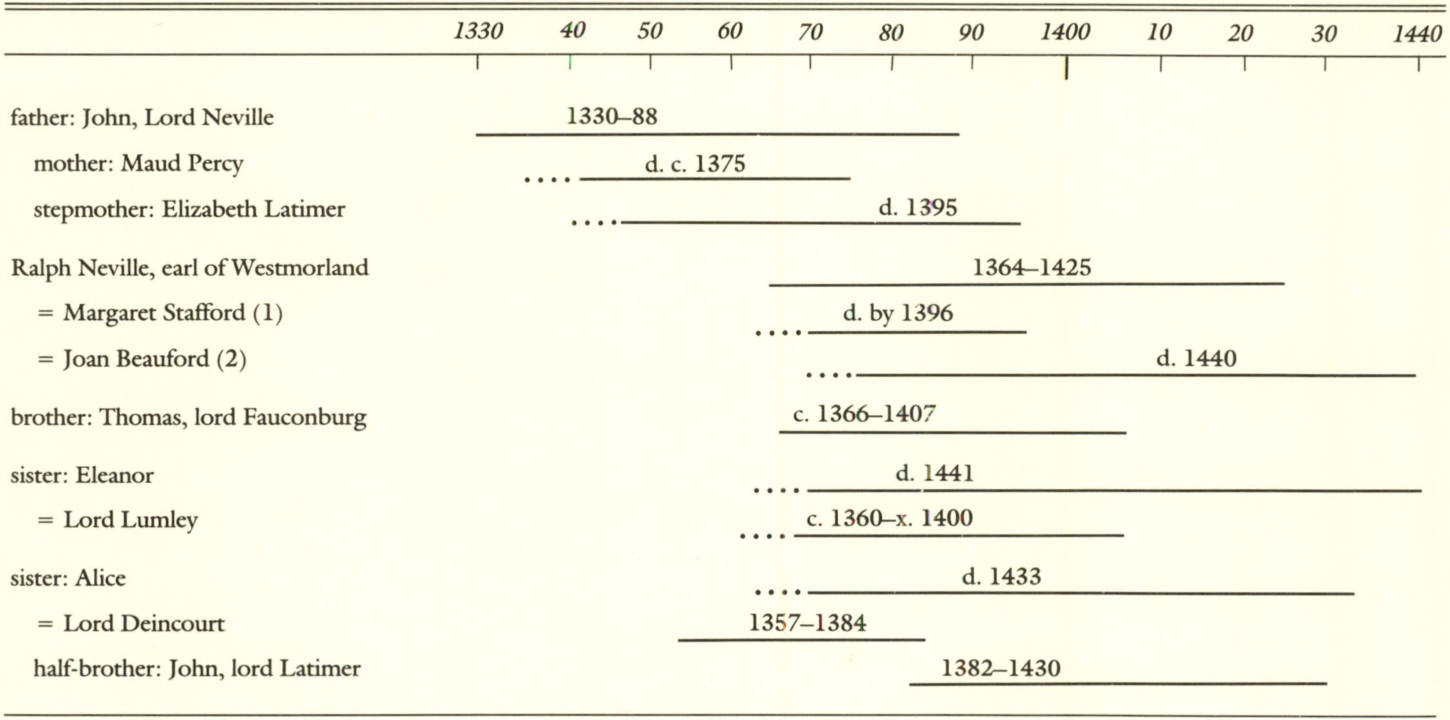

	1330	40	50	60	70	80	90	1400	10	20	30	1440

father: John, Lord Neville — 1330–88

mother: Maud Percy — d. c. 1375

stepmother: Elizabeth Latimer — d. 1395

Ralph Neville, earl of Westmorland — 1364–1425

= Margaret Stafford (1) — d. by 1396

= Joan Beauford (2) — d. 1440

brother: Thomas, lord Fauconburg — c. 1366–1407

sister: Eleanor — d. 1441

= Lord Lumley — c. 1360–x. 1400

sister: Alice — d. 1433

= Lord Deincourt — 1357–1384

half-brother: John, lord Latimer — 1382–1430

[a] Here and below, x. = died by violence

FIGURE II-2A SURVIVAL OF EARL RALPH'S CHILDREN FROM HIS FIRST MARRIAGE

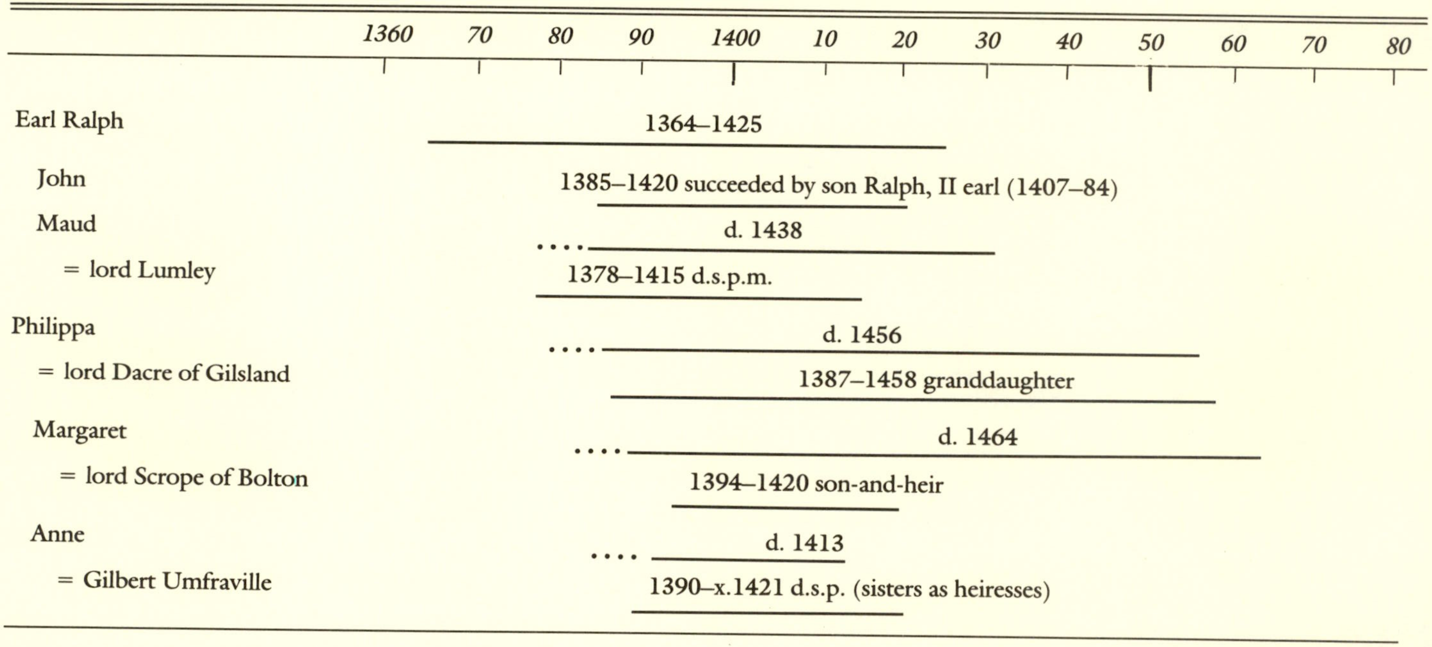

	1360	70	80	90	1400	10	20	30	40	50	60	70	80

Earl Ralph
1364–1425

John
1385–1420 succeeded by son Ralph, II earl (1407–84)

Maud
d. 1438
= lord Lumley
1378–1415 d.s.p.m.

Philippa
d. 1456
= lord Dacre of Gilsland
1387–1458 granddaughter

Margaret
d. 1464
= lord Scrope of Bolton
1394–1420 son-and-heir

Anne
d. 1413
= Gilbert Umfraville
1390–x.1421 d.s.p. (sisters as heiresses)

FIGURE II-2B   SURVIVAL OF EARL RALPH'S CHILDREN FROM HIS SECOND MARRIAGE

	1390	1400	10	20	30	40	50	60	70	80	90	1500

Earl Ralph — 1364–1425

Richard, earl of Salisbury — 1400–1460

William, lord Fauconburg — 1403–1463 d.s.p.m.

George, lord Latimer — 1409–1469

Edward, lord Abergavenny — c. 1419–1476

Robert, bishop of Durham — d. 1457

Catherine — d. 1485

= John, duke of Norfolk — 1392–1432

Eleanor

= Richrd Despenser (1) — d. 1414

= earl of Northumberland (2) — 1393–x. 1455

Anne — d. 1480

= Duke of Buckingham — 1402–1460

Cecilly — 1415–1495

= Duke of York — 1411– x. 1460

children of the first marriage were more than ready for marriage and parenthood by the time the very youngest were moving into the nursery. Much of the childrens' lives were lived after the earl's death. He himself had been of reasonable age when his parents died. His own first son, John (who predeceased his father and whose son Ralph became the II earl), was only born in 1385, too late to have any independent link with an older cohort that harked back to the mid-fourteenth century, to the world of a vigorous Edward III and the Black Prince. In all the obvious considerations Westmorland stands as a great patriarchal figure. But in this case the status of the patriarch and the transmission of the patrimony proved a stumbling block, and to some extent the earl's ambition, plus the exceptional fecundity of both wives, ultimately served to hamper some aspects of the larger plans that he may have harbored regarding family unity and cohesion.

As a patriarch Westmorland had obvious limitations, for the move to support and endow Richard, the first son of the second marriage and eventually the earl of Salisbury, carried many seeds of self-defeat. This eccentric move can be explained in part by reference to the strong character and ambitions of Joan Beaufort, the earl's second wife. Regardless of the origin or the wisdom of the scheme, it does show that the earl's flair was perhaps for matrimonial alliance rather than for the real consolidation of power. He was an important figure in government and politics, but never really a "kingmaker" or a major domo. He was only an earl in a game that was coming to feature more and more dukes. He was best at finding and arranging a bevy of matches for his children, ranging from the merely useful to the politically dazzling. But beyond that uxorious vision, the limits of his own horizons seem to have posed some self-generating or self-perpetuating problems that he should have been able to anticipate and perhaps, with good fortune, to remedy. Did he expect the older children to acquiesce and be pleased? Had he ever heard the story of Jacob's older sons and their relations with Joseph and Benjamin?

As far as marriage went, he certainly tried to do his duty. For the sons of his first marriage he was able to arrange for such brides as Elizabeth, daughter of Edmund Holland, duke of Kent, and his wife Alice, daughter of the earl of Arundel. His daughters also did fairly well: their husbands were lord Mauley, Sir Thomas Grey, lord Scrope of Bolton, Thomas lord Dacre of Gilsland,[146] and Sir Gilbert Umfraville. These men were mostly northerners, of some considerable wealth and prominence, and surely the sort of collection of sons-in-law that could, with a bit of leadership, be turned into a useful network. They were not so different from the sons-in-law of Sir Thomas Parr, except that they were mostly about two rungs farther up the socio-economic ladder and that the father-in-law was at least *primes inter pares*.

For the children of the second marriage the earl (and his countess) did even better. Many of these marriages were arranged in the last years of Ralph's life, when his ambitions were presumably soaring and his family was able to radiate the appearance of success that made others eager to join. His second batch of sons married the heiresses of three peerages: she of the Montague earls of Salisbury, she of the lords Fauconberg, and she of the Beauchamp lords of Abergavenny. His daughters married such men as the duke of Norfolk, the earl of Northumberland (after she had already been left a young widow by the death of Richard Despenser, son and heir apparent of Thomas Despenser, Richard II's earl of Gloucester), the duke of Buckingham, and the duke of York. If the children of each of the marriages can be seen as a wave of advancing infantry, the first battalion had already carried the hill by the earl's death, and the second was beginning the charge that would pretty much take them, with their spouses, to the very crest.

Figure II-2 presents a chronological scheme for the lives and marriages of the children, and for the lives of their spouses. Figure II-2a covers the children of the first marriage, II-2b those of the second. By their father's death in 1425 almost all of the children were married, which was hardly surprising given his moderate longevity and the aristocratic proclivity for early marriage. The creation of the network of useful sons-in-law and daughters-in-law, accordingly, is clearly a feat for which the earl should receive full credit. In fact, for some of the youngest children there may have been a concerted push towards settled and concluded marriages while the old man was still on the scene. The arrangements for some of the youngest were quite recent: Richard Neville married Alice Montague in 1421; William Neville married Joan Fauconberge in 1422; Edward Neville married Elizabeth Beauchamp in 1424; for the daughters, Anne married the Stafford heir around 1424, and Cecilly married Richard, duke of York, before October, 1424. By the earl's death in 1425 the only child yet to marry—of those who ever did—was George Neville, who became his uncle's heir and was eventually summoned to the House of Lords as Lord Latimer. He married Elizabeth Beauchamp before 1437 (and was declared a lunatic in 1451). Three or four of the earl's daughters spent their lives as nuns, and

Robert, the fifth son of the first marriage, entered the church and rose to become bishop of Durham.[147]

It is easy to look at this great network—with its full generation span between the eldest children of the first marriage and the youngest ones of the second—and simply to say that it was too big, subject to too many internal and external strains, to hold together. Unlike those relatively small and closely connected systems of the Chichele brothers and of the Booths, the Nevilles and their affines were *too* numerous. They represented too many competing interests to display the sort of sustained unity of their lesser counterparts. After the split between the children of the earl's two marriages, there would have had to be some sagacious *modus vivendi* between at least two would-be patriarchs. There was the elder line, headed by the II earl of Westmorland (the son of the eldest son of all), and then the younger, the Beaufort-Neville faction, under the lead of the earl of Salisbury (and, to some extent, his brother-in-law, the duke of York, as political factionalism became more important). But we must not allow hindsight to color our picture. The old earl did take the one critical and divisive step that pretty much guaranteed a disunited network, and his second wife and her children never worked to heal the rift. But in other respects he was the master family craftsman of the age. Some of his ventures were gambles, and some of them paid off handsomely. One such success was the emergence of Elizabeth Beauchamp—Edward Neville's wife since 1422 or earlier—as her grandmother's heiress in 1435. She eventually proved to be the conduit through which the old Abergavenny peerage (and patrimony) would be transmitted to the Nevilles, though Edward was not summoned to Lords for that peerage until 1450, two years after Elizabeth's death. Another lucky effort, ultimately of much greater value, was the inheritance acquired by Alice Montague in 1428, when her father, the earl of Salisbury, died of wounds in France with only a daughter-heiress. Her husband, Richard Neville, was summoned almost at once as the earl of Salisbury, some seven years after their marriage and three years after Westmorland's death.

We have to set these successes against some of the obvious difficulties the earl also helped to create. In addition, much of the subsequent factionalism was caused by extra-familial problems. Who had any reason to foresee, as Westmorland lay on his death bed in 1425, that the three-year-old Henry VI would never be able to assert himself over his baronage or that the wars in France would deteriorate so badly within the next three decades? The Wars of the Roses were neither inevitable nor predictable.

With these caveats in mind, our awareness of the bloody divisions imposed by events and personalities upon English politics, some 25 or 30 years after Westmorland's death, should not color our view against the way in which an old schemer tried to read the future in the early and mid-1420s. He had indeed been on guard to arrange marriages that generally avoided the most obvious divisions that were opening before his feet in the early years of Henry VI's long minority. If Westmorland's marriage alliances were not especially likely to bring opposing factions together, neither were they particularly incendiary. The children of his first marriage mostly married in the north, while those of the second were well spread across the landscape. This change in policy—if it were perceived and articulated—regarding the marriages of the two sets of children probably reflects the wider opportunities that came his way after his second marriage. But as well as mirroring the grander aspirations of the later years, the new policy may indicate a sensible desire to separate, at least in geographical terms, the vital interests of the two competing groups, the two sub-dynasties he had fathered. Furthermore, the earl did pull off one great stroke of irenic statesmanship when he wedded his daughter Eleanor to Hotspur's son, the Percy heir, in 1414 or thereabouts. This was just when young Henry Percy was coming of age and beginning his long quest for the recovery of the family's land and status. If the Percies were ever to approach their position, the presence (and identity) of the new countess—who bore the earl some 10 or 12 children in her long marriage—might blunt the edge of future rivalry between the two greatest northern families.

We have referred to such actions as the writing of a will as an *event* in the social history of the family. The paths of testamentary distribution the will creates, through and among the network of potential recipients, reflect the world view of the testator and create, in a limited sense, a specific, limited social group (of beneficiaries). He or she who writes such a will and who remembers and distributes, as some spirit of kinship and affection dictates, is turning a select number of kin and potential beneficaries into a precise complex of recipients. When we looked at the Scropes of Bolton, we were especially interested in the use of the wills as the tools of patriarchal and patrilineal craftsmanship. For the Nevilles the interest is in comparing the strength of the vertical links with those of the horizontal. How much attention was focused upon the patrilineal axis, how much upon those of the collateral kin, the network so carefully created by means of those marriages, and by the children who were their result?

The family of the earl of Westmorland has been quite cooperative in the matter of leaving extant wills. Were they as helpful regarding their willing involvement in the family network? The earl's father, though hardly the matchmaker his son was to be, had pursued a similar course with his own testamentary bequests, nor had he been a slouch at family brokerage in his day. While the earl himself was his father's principal heir of both personal and real property, the will of John, III lord Neville (d. 1388), had also singled out younger children, a brother-in-law, a son-in-law, and grandchildren.[148] Lord Neville's son Thomas (later lord Furnival) and three of his daughters were among his beneficiaries. Of these daughters, one was already well married in 1386: Eleanor, wife of Ralph, I lord Lumley (beheaded, 1400). A third daughter, Alice, was named in the will: she was already the widow of William, lord Deincourt.[149] A younger daughter, Elizabeth, was provided for, whether she entered religion or stayed in the world. This was clearly network building, though a will alone does not indicate whether such behavior was a continuation of older policies or rather a final stab in a new direction. We suspect the former, but it is best to avoid the appearance of certainty when the sources are so remote.

It is when we come to earl Ralph himself that we find the happy conjunction between family policy-making and the web of testamentary benefaction. He was expansive in death, as he had been in life, to at least a fair number of his vast band of children. We might well expect favoritism towards the children of the second marriage, and we find some indications of such an inclination. Earl Ralph's will, written in October 1424, leaves bequests to his second wife, six sons, and eight daughters.[150] The grand scale was the only appropriate stage for Neville family affairs, and this is what we discover in a will that leaves goods to sons who were (or who would become) the earl of Salisbury, lord Fauconberg, lord Latimer, and lord Abergavenny, among others. Because some of the sons were still young, their marriages might be arranged but their futures not yet fully assured: It might be years before the contingences of a marriage with an heiress or a presumptive heiress were worked out in detail. If young William Neville's wife, Alice Fauconberg, were to die without children of their marriage and her surviving spouse did not gain her inheritance, then William's father said that his son was to receive family land worth £100 per annum. There proved to be three daughters of this Neville-Fauconberg marriage, though their mother (d. 1490) outlived all her progeny. Young Edward Neville, who married the Abergavenny heiress, was authorized to sell the London property he was about to inherit, if he needed the money to complete his marriage arrangements. Such clauses show that matchmaking, until the couple were safely in bed, could never be taken for granted. Experience gave the earl skill, along with an understanding of the need for caution and a healthy respect for unforseen difficulties.

The earl's daughters came in for the fairly standard, smallish bequests of personal items, mostly the jewelry and valuable household possessions that often characterized amicable or unexceptionable father-daughter relationships. The girls of the second marriage would probably receive more of the same when their mother died (in 1440), but her will has not been preserved. Westmorland's bequests to his daughters were more by way of tokens of affection and of affiliation than transfers of significant wealth. There were married daughters: had they needed economic support for their marriages, it presumably had been provided, separately and previously, as part of the arrangements that prefigured and accompanied such important mergers. But also of significance regarding identities and affiliations, each daughter is explicitly referred to by her married name, that is, by her husband's name (and in several instances by his title). The girls were enumerated as Katherine, countess Marshall my daughter, Countess Stafford my daughter, Cecilly of York, and so forth. Since some of them were still minors when their father drew up his will in 1424, as were some of their husbands, this was one of the earl's last opportunities to tug at the strings. Though many of his sons-in-law were of greater stature, as long as he lived he was determined to assert that he was the center of the circles: the ties between members of the network were to go through him as the central exchange. The daughters mentioned in the will were children of both the earl's marriages, and there is less difference between the way the two groups of girls were treated than was the case for their brothers and half-brothers.

The rift between the sons of the two marriages eventually snapped any bonds of affiliation their father might have hoped to fasten. The rift killed much of the family spirit, on the part of some members of the older faction, towards the younger. They had already tasted ashes, and in a very public fashion, and never again would some of them be wholly trusting after their father had distanced himself from their interests. Westmorland's first son pre-deceased him, dying by the spring of 1420 (and his wife, a Holland heiress, was dead by 1429), so the old earl's heir to his title was his grandson, Ralph, II earl Westmorland (1407–84). But a lesser personality, a lesser political prominence, and a lesser fecundity marked the II earl's life and career, as it did those of most of the other men of this line, through the remainder of the century. None of them ever came near their founding father's record, either for political activity or for procreation. The II earl outlived all his children, and subsequent family wills of this branch are mostly jejune and unrevealing. The I earl's daughter Matilda married and long outlived Piers, V lord Mauley. The marriage produced a daughter heiress, and when Matilda died (1438), her bequests were for her husband's heirs (through his sisters), rather than back towards the Nevilles.[151] Philippa, the earl's daughter who married lord Dacre of Gilsland, died shortly before her husband (in the late 1450s), and their heiress was their grand-daughter Joan, the child of their deceased son Thomas. Neither Philippa nor anyone else of this group gives testamentary evidence of any sustained Neville ties.[152] Mary, the earl's daughter who married Richard Scrope of Bolton, preserved some family ties because she was left a widow with young children in 1420, and her own family helped protect her interests during the difficult years of minority that followed. However, she made a *déclassé* second marriage with William Cressoner, lived until 1464, and eventually moved away from the world of aristocratic magnificence into that of the comfortable gentry. She was buried in the house of the Austin Friars at Clare, Suffolk, far from the old Neville headquarters and areas of great influence.

Do the children of earl Ralph's second marriage display a greater de-gree of bonding than do their half-siblings? In purely political terms they did, as we know: The earl of Salisbury and his brother-in-law of York were the main strands from which the Yorkist cause was woven. However, we should keep in mind that this more-or-less unified faction was really born and nourished by the circumstances of Henry VI's incapacity, circum-stances that took shape two or three decades after Westmorland's death. In the Wars of the Roses the elder line of the Nevilles, that is, the earl's chil-dren by his first marriage, tended to stay with the House of Lancaster, and surely family hostility as well as larger political allegiances helped deter-mine this choice. Nor were they men of any prominence, either in counsel or on the battlefield. In terms of political choices, the Beaufort-Neville fac-tion did display considerable bonding. But in terms of testamentary be-quests, most of these younger children died so long after their father that intervening conflicts and intervening loyalties more than covered over the arrangements of the 1420s. Figure II-2 shows that the earl's five sons who lived full lives survived him by an average of 41 years, and their three sisters for whom we have data outlived him by an immense average duration of 62 years. Clever schemer and builder though he was, we can hardly hold the earl at fault for the fact that his younger children chose biographical paths and public roles that diverged over the course of the next two generations.

We do not mean that the wills of Westmorland's children contained no bequests to other members of the Neville network. It is rather that we cannot assume the original motivation and the same bonding impulses, in a will of the 1460s (let alone in one of the 1470s, the 1480s, or even the 1490s), that we identified in one of the 1420s. Thus when we look at the will of Elizabeth, widow of George Neville, lord Latimer, the earl's third son by Joan Beaufort, we are seeing intermarriage and intertwining, but also the intervention of many years. Elizabeth died, around age 63, in the 1480s, by which time her husband had been dead for 11 years. She was a younger daughter and co-heiress of Richard Beauchamp, XIII earl of Warwick (d. 1439), and as such was related on her own to her husband's nephew Richard, now earl of Warwick (who had married Anne Beauchamp, the XIII earl's daughter and the co-heiress of Henry, XIV earl), as well as to his brother Edward, lord Abergavenny (d. 1476, husband of Elizabeth Beauchamp, daughter of heiress of Richard, II lord Abergavenny). But in her will she requested burial with her own father and her paternal kin. This was a bit unusual and perhaps it was a kind of final assertion that the earls of Warwick were even more impressive than those newcomers, the earls of Westmorland. Her burial was also to be alongside her son "Harrie" and her son-in-law, Oliver Dudley.[153] Family bequests were to daughter Katherine and to Henry's son, Thomas. Elizabeth's daughter-in-law, Joan Bourgchier, had died in 1470, and Joan remembered such Nevilles as Lord Latimer, in addition to many of her patrilineal kin: her father, lord Berners, her mother Margery Berners, her brothers Thomas and Humphrey, and her sister Elizabeth (who had married lord Welles).[154] So the network opened and closed, as we look at it over time and as we compare the founding father's early successes against the effects of the centrifugal forces that were an inherent part of family dynamics. How do early successes compete against and soften the appeal of the competing networks to which everyone, except perhaps the patriarch himself, also belonged. He had built a great network, though he sacrificed some individuals and some sentiment towards his larger ends. Some of his plans bore rich fruit before his own death, some ripened later, and some turned sour on the tree.

The answer to the entire question about the strength of these constructs is that no one could build *and* hold a sprawling network for very long. The Booths and the Chicheles enjoyed their appreciable measure of success in no small part because the leaders were princes of the church, not

of the secular realm. They were men who had no sons with whom to identify, upon whose survival and procreative success lay the more distant future of the line. Bishops and archbishops could display a degree of relative
disinterest and of avuncular patronage, to nephews, great nephews, and
cousins, that few worldly fathers could affect. Even men and women who
rose to power and wealth because of the Neville connection were not likely
to remain bound within. Its opportunities and affinities helped launch
them to new, higher plateaus, and the last will was always more likely to
gaze back with affection upon the last landscape that upon its prior variations.

   Moreover, life's experience argues that the gaps between individuals
were likely to widen with the passing of time. The I earl of Westmorland's
brother Thomas married Joan, the Furnival heiress, and the bequests of his
will fall within the Neville network to a striking degree. Though Thomas
was buried with Joan and her father, William, IV lord Furnival, at Worksop priory, in obeisance to his Furnival title, he did leave an appreciable
bequest to his sister Alice (d. 1433), now widow of William, III lord Deincourt (1357–81). There were also bequests to his daughter Joan, to the earl
of Westmorland (now his great-nephew), to his nephew Robert Lumley,
and to a William Neville.[155] Thomas's elder daughter, his heiress, married
John Talbot. Talbot became the earl of Shrewsbury, but Maud Neville-
Furnivalle was eventually buried at Worksop priory—proclaiming a paternal lineage that then hearkened back to a maternal one. Thomas's sister,
Alice Deincourt, left gifts in her will to numerous children, but only to her
sister, lady Lumley, among the many potential Neville beneficiaries. Alice
had also become identified with the midlands: her husband had been buried in Kirkby Bellars, Leicestershire, and she at Thurgarton.[156]

   If we look some years ahead we see fewer crossings of the old paths.
The I earl's most important son was Richard Neville (1401–60), earl of
Salisbury from 1429. He was married to Alice Montagu by 1421. In Salisbury's will—written in 1458—he asked for burial at Bisham priory, the traditional burial ground of his in-laws.[157] Alice was interred there in 1461, as
was their son Thomas, also killed at Wakefield with his father, his uncle,
Richard of York, and his first cousin, the earl of Rutland. The Montague
magnetism was clearly greater than the Neville, and Nevilles who married
heiresses regularly seem to have identified with their in-laws, with older
lines whose lands and titles they inherited through their marriages. The
earl's son-in-law, Richard, III duke of York, was buried with his progenitors of the house of York, at Fotheringay College in Northamptonshire,

though little of Richard's wealth came from this line. With him, eventually, went his wife, Cecilly, the earl's youngest daughter. The scattering of bequests and the dispersal of the burials is only natural, and we would hardly expect to find anything else. In the preceding chapter we saw how unusual it was to build a chain of direct father-son links that ran much beyond the traditional three generations. Here, in looking at the complexes of "other" kinsfolk, we are presented with two doors, and each leads to a truth about how families functioned. Through one we proceed to a field of folk, related in various and sundry ways, and we marvel at how many casually come and go. Through the other we go to an ordered assembly, and we marvel at how long some semblance of order and common purpose can hold them together. People, then as now, lived with both truths, though sometimes one chose one door over the other, and sometimes the "choice" was more in response to being pushed than to being freely wooed and freely won.

Notes

1. Linda Clarke and Carole Rawcliffe, "The History of Parliament, 1386–1422: A Progress Report," *Medieval Prosopography* 4, 2 (1983), 9–41. See also Josiah C. Wedgewood, *History of Parliament, 1439–1509: Biographies of Members* (London, 1936), passim.

2. On the Cannings-Young network, see James Sherborne, *William Cannynges, 1402–74*, Bristol Branch of the Historical Associations, Pamphlet 59 (Bristol, 1984); Wedgewood, *History of Parliament*, under the entries for Thomas and William Cannyngs and Thomas and Sir John Young. J. S. Roskell, *Parliament and Politics in Late Medieval England* (London, 1981–83), vols. II, III, for reprints of his biographical studies of the speakers of the House of Commons. Information about their networks—of birth, marriage, and collegial activity—is a standard part of each biography.

3. For crimes among and between relatives, see Introduction, note 17 (James Given, *Crime and Homicide*, and Barbara Hanawalt, *Crime and Conflict in English Communities*, 151–83. For a social or family strategy apt to cause hostility, see Alain Collomp, "Tensions, Dissension, and Ruptures inside the Family in Seventeenth and Eighteenth Century Haute Provence," in *Interest and Emotion* ed. Hans Medick and David Sabean (Cambridge, 1984), pp. 145–70.

4. A good bibliography covering much recent work on medieval marriage is in Michael Sheehan, "Theory and Practice: Marriage of the Unfree and the Poor in Medieval Society," *Mediaeval Studies* 59 (1988), 457–87.

5. For peers, the next heir to the peerage might differ from the next heir of the blood, because of political considerations. For examples, see the earl of Kent (*CP*, VII, 159–62) and Thomas Fitzalan, earl of Arundel (1381–1415). Arundel left three sisters as heirs for the Arundel inheritance: his male heir, and the next earl, was his

second cousin, John d'Arundel (1385–1421). For the peers (and peeresses), where no specific source is given, the biographical and demographic material is taken from *CP*.

6. *Chancery*, number 943.

7. Unfortunately, we have no details in a case where a man's heirs were ten daughters, all aged 18 and more: *Chancery*, number 1178.

8. *Chancery*, numbers 6 and 886.

9. For a daughter aged 26 and more, see *Chancery*, numbers 175, 148, and 174.

10. *Nottinghamshire*, I, 143.

11. *Nottinghamshire*, I, 168; see also *Yorkshire*, 142: Philip, VI lord Darcy, died 2 August 1418 (aged 20–22), and his barony fell into abeyance. By his wife Alianore Fitzhugh he left two daughters, Elizabeth, aged two-and-a-half, and Margery, aged 1. His brother John (aged 15 and more) was his male heir. John married Joan, daughter of lord Grey and lived until 1454; he was never summoned as a peer. This seems to be a case where the coincidence of a young and unimpressive male heir, plus just daughters, combined to cause social demotion.

12. *Chancery*, numbers 621, 1134, 1169.

13. *Yorkshire*, 97: Thomas Rollaston had held the land, of his late wife, for life; when she had predeceased him, she had already outlived her brother, whose heiress she had been. Thus upon Thomas's death the Mauley estates, which he held by courtesy of marriage, went to his two daughters. See also, *Chancery*, number 1195.

14. *Chancery*, number 457.

15. *Chancery*, number 530.

16. *Chancery*, numbers 707, 821.

17. *Chancery*, number 117: also, number 252: a case of two daughters, one aged 40 and more, one but 17.

18. *Yorkshire*, 59: Thomas Neville married Joan Fauconberg, c. 1379. She was daughter and sole heiress of William, IV lord Fauconberg (d.s.p.m. 1383), and Thomas was summoned as lord Fauconberg, 1383–1406. After Joan's death in 1401 Thomas married Ankarette, daughter and heiress of John, lord LeStraunge, and widow of Richard, lord Talbot. Thomas d.s.p.m. 14 March 1407 (and Ankarette died, June 1413). Thomas's eldest daughter, Maud, married John, second son of Richard, lord Talbot and of Ankarette—her stepmother.

19. Earl of Kent's heirs are not particularly difficult to unravel, but they show how high aristocratic families were able to perpetuate their status. The son and heir of Thomas Holland was Edmund Holland, earl of Kent, d.s.p.m. in September 1408 (killed in Brittany). Edmund's heirs were his four sisters and/or their heirs. His earldom became extinct and no earl of Kent was summoned until a new creation in 1465.

20. *Chancery*, number 801.

21. *Nottinghamshire*, II, 14. For William Phelip, *CP*, I, 420–21. He married the Bardolf heiress and was styled as lord Bardolf, but it is not clear that he was ever summoned to Lords or that he carried the title in a formal sense.

22. *Chancery*, number 71.

23. *Nottinghamshire*, II, 14.

24. *Chancery*, numbers 532 (aged 11), 607 (aged 40), and 946 (aged 17).

25. *Chancery*, numbers 619 (aged 19), 997 (aged 24).

26. *Nottinghamshire*, I, 148.

27. *Nottinghamshire*, I, 170.

28. *Nottinghamshire*, II, 37.

29. *Chancery*, numbers 688, 742.

30. *Chancery*, number 166.

31. *Chancery*, number 21. The landholder died a minor, and his heirs were his two aunts, each aged 62, and the 26-year-old child of a deceased third aunt.

32. *Chancery*, number 611, *Chancery*, number 235, where the heir is a grandson of seven and more, the son of a daughter; *Chancery*, number 248, where there are two married granddaughters. One was a son's daughter, now aged 17 and more, the other a daughter's daughter, aged 15 and more.

33. *Chancery*, numbers 816, 1049.

34. *Chancery*, number 1086: also, 681, where the heirs are a sister, three nephews (sons of three different sisters, all deceased), and two nieces (daughters of two different sisters); 278, for three married nieces, of 40, 35, and 30. In this instance the propensity for round numbers—sufficient for heiresses so clearly above legal age—seems to have triumphed.

35. *Chancery*, number 205.

36. *Chancery*, number 974.

37. *Chancery*, number 820.

38. *Nottinghamshire*, II, 8. The inquisitions contain other combinations of heirs that are of interest. *Chancery*, 181, for a man who had left a week-old son, who subsequently died. The inheritance then reverted to an aunt of the dead man, his father's sister. She was now 40 and more, and married. In addition, the dead man's mother was alive, holding one-third of the property as her dower share. Also, *Chancery*, number 1059, two daughters, aged 22 and 21, plus a grandson; *Chancery*, number 999, for a 60-year-old uncle; *Chancery*, number 1083, for three daughters, aged 19, 18, and 14, and all now married; *Nottinghamshire*, I, 195, where a son's daughters were 25, 24, 22, and 17; *Chancery*, number 130, where the heirs were two married sisters and two sons of two other sisters, now dead. No ages are given, though the jurors did return that only one of the nephews, of the entire crowd, was not yet of age. *Chancery*, number 294, three cousins, once-removed from the deceased, shared the estate.

39. John S. Roskell, *Parliament and Politics*, II, 231.

40. *CP*, VIII, 223, for the sisters and heirs of Francis, lord Lovel: they both made good gentry marriages, but there was no question of a revival of the peerage.

41. On the end of the de la Pole dukes of Suffolk, *CP*, XII, 1, 451, and *CP*, XII, 1, appendix, 20–25: John, duke of Suffolk (d. 1492) had seven sons. Two predeceased him (including the earl of Lincoln, killed at Stoke, 1487), one was executed in 1513, one died in the siege of Pavia in 1524. None left legitimate male heirs. Edmund (x. 1513), left a daughter who was a nun at the London house of Minoresses, and there may have been a son who had entered orders.

42. For a family that flirted with disaster through most of their days in the sun, the de la Poles lasted a goodly time. For some early troubles, John S. Roskell, *The Impeachment of Michael de la Pole, Earl of Suffolk in 1386* (Manchester, 1984). But

when their luck ran out, it is interesting to observe that none of the early sixteenth-century Poles who attended Oxford were eager to proclaim any putative affiliation (though Reginald Poles's pedigree was too well known for his own explanations to have made any difference), A. B. Emden, *A Biographical Register of the University of Oxford, A.D. 1501 to 1540* (Oxford, 1974), pp. 452–55.

43. Alan Macfarlane, *The Family Life of Ralph Josselin*, 156–57, for the diagrams of his "intimate, effective, and peripheral kin" refered to above.

44. *Chichele*, 631: the path of transmission of the land was from wife to son, then to two daughters, for life, and then "to Thomas Tyrell my nefew and to hys eyres male . . ." This sounds like a case of his own children all appearing likely to end up childless.

45. *Chichele*, 369; for more examples, the wills on pages 23, 34, 116, 135, and 276.

46. *TE*, I, 223–39. A typical example: "grant hanap d'or lequelle le counte de Wyles donna a Roy mon seignour, et il donna a moy a mon alee en Guyen."

47. See *Chichele*, 404; also 34. See p. 171, for an instance of three nephews and a brother; p. 452, where the wife, a sister, a daughter, and an aunt are mentioned. This latter is another example of the strong female connection we sometimes find.

48. *Sharpe*, I, 376.

49. *Chichele*, 628; also 35, 547.

50. *TE*, IV, 260, for a will indicating unusual sensitivity regarding a daughter's freedom to choose between the cloister and the world.

51. *Fifty*, 57.

52. *Chichele*, 438.

53. PCC, 30 Vox.

54. *Chichele*, 519; 90, for two daughters, three sons, and the residue to the wife. John, IV lord Darcy was very generous when his thoughts turned, at age 34, to his three unmarried daughters: *TE*, I, 356–57.

55. British Library, Add. Ms. 27,402, ff. 21–22.

56. *Fifty*, 87.

57. *Chichele*, 185.

58. *Chichele*, 547.

59. *Chichele*, 171.

60. *Chichele*, 53.

61. *Chichele*, 451–53.

62. *Chichele*, 66.

63. Robin L. Storey, ed. *The Register of Thomas Langley, Bishop of Durham, 1407–37*, Surtees Society (1956–71), II, 191–94.

64. Lambeth Palace, Archepiscopal Registers, Arendel, I, 179b.

65. *Chichele*, 75.

66. PCC, 15 Bennett.

67. J. T. Rosenthal, *The Purchase of Paradise* (London, 1972), pp. 12–28; Peter W. Fleming, "Charity, Faith, and the Gentry of Kent, 1422–1529," in *Property and Politics: Essays in Later Medieval English History*, ed. Anthony J. Pollard (Gloucester, 1984), pp. 36–58, with 50–51 for a discussion of "where testators asked to be buried . . . a predominantly patrilineal family feeling"; R. G. K. A. Mertes, "The Household as a Religious Community," in *People, Politics, and Community in the Later*

Middle Ages, ed. Joel T. Rosenthal and Colin F. Richmond (Gloucester, 1987), pp. 123–39.

68. *SMW*, I. 11–14.

69. *SMW*, I, 63–64.

70. *Chichele*, 143.

71. *Chichele*, 273.

72. PCC, 5 Stokton.

73. PCC, 11 Fettiplace, and printed *in extenso*, with discussion by William H. St. John Hope, "The Last Testament of John de Veer," *Archaeologia* 66 (1914–15); for the gloss see pp. 275–309, and pp. 310–48 for the text.

74. *TE*, III, 40.

75. *Chichele*, 106.

76. *Chichele*, 153–58. He was extremely generous to his cathedral at Exeter and to other institutions of the town and the region.

77. *Chichele*, 224–26.

78. *Chichele*, 126–30.

79. See *Chichele*, 532–34, and Langdon's will, *Chichele*, 556–58: bequests to a brother, to an unspecified female relative, and to his brother's children (and if they died, the money was for prayers for the bishop's parents); *Chichele*, 133–35, for Stephen Patrington's bequest to "Iohanni Jolym cognato meo" and his wife and children; *Chichele*, 178–86, John Catterick's bequests to two sisters, £20 for the marriage of a sister's two daughters, and, to a nephew, "omnes libros meos in utroque iure et eciam de capella"; *Chichele*, 540–41 for Robert Fitzhugh's bequests to two brothers, a sister-in-law, and two sisters.

80. *Chichele*, 237–40.

81. *Chichele*, 311–14.

82. *Chichele*, 285, 36, 165, 298, 347, 415, and 482.

83. *Chichele*, 163–64: to his nephew, "omnes libros et quaternos meos de facultatibus . . . iuris canonici et civilis."

84. *Chichele*, 250–56: the various nieces and nephews mostly received cash, in the neighborhood of L5 or 10 marks.

85. *Chichele*, 420, 284.

86. *Chichele*, 450–51.

87. *TE*, I, 308, for Skirlaw's will; also, *Chichele*, 131, 133, 232, 477, and 561.

88. If a man did not have a son to push around, he might turn to a nephew, as when John Stourton stipulated that a bequest was to go to a younger relative, *but* "if . . . [he] shall make complaint . . . for any things which belonged to William his father, and if he be not content with what I have bequeathed him . . ." *SMW*, I, 146.

89. We referred above to such forms of bonding as brotherhoods in arms and the fraternities of the municipal guilds. There were also criminal gangs linked in dastardy; Ralph A. Griffiths, "William Wawe and His Gang, 1427," *Hampshire Field Club and Archaeological Society* 33 (1977), 89–93; for an earlier period, see Edward L. G. Stone, "The Folvilles of Ashby-Folville, Leicestershire, and Their Associates in Crime, 1326–47," *TRHS* 5th series, 7 (1957), 117–36; and for a general treatment,

see John Bellamy, *Crime and Public Order in England in the Later Middle Ages* (London, 1973), pp. 69–88 ("Criminal Bands"), with bibliography, 208–09.

90. See Frank Taylor and John S Roskell, eds. and trans, *Gesta Henrici Quinti: The Deeds of Henry the Fifth* (Oxford, 1975), pp. 188–89, for these entanglements. Anyone with any experience in a family business could have warned the earl of Cambridge that the plot was too inbred to be kept secret. Thomas B. Pugh, "The Southampton Plot of 1415," in *Kings and Nobles in the Later Middle Ages*, ed. Ralph A. Griffiths and James Sherborne (Gloucester, 1986), pp. 62–89, and *Henry V and the Southampton Plot of 1415*, Southampton Record Series 30 (1988), xi–xiv, 64–121, 187–88, on the conspirators and their ties to each other: xii, "there was no plot in 1415 to assassinate Henry V . . ."

91. For the Bourgchier family, John Enoch Powell and Keith Wallis, *The House of Lords in the Middle Ages* (London, 1968), pp. 467–68, 486; *CP*, V, 137–39 (for Essex).

92. John W. Clay, *Extinct and Dormant Peerages in the Northern Counties of England* (London, 1913), pp. 157–59.

93. Cora Schofield, *The Life and Reign of Edward the Fourth* (London, 1923), I, 121–22, says he was killed at Wakefield. J. W. Clay says he died at Barnet, which gives him another decade of life.

94. *TE*, III, 309. Parr's daughter Mabel, who married lord Dacre, had an adventurous middle age. Before she died in 1508 and left money for a "Mabelles Chaunterie," for her parents and in-laws at Lanercroft, she had been in trouble, "accused of having ravished one Richard Huddlestone, a ward of the late king": *Letters and Papers of the Reign of Henry VIII*, ed. John S. Brewer, James Gairdner, and R. H. Brodie (London, 1862), I, letter 380. She spent nine months in prison, and the mother's suffering had killed her daughter Elizabeth, who suffered from such "heaviness and sorrow" when her mother was "so unrighteously daungiered and troubled." It sounds like a good example of Tudor despotism and the "over mighty subject." For other Parr connections, see *TE*, III, 280–81.

95. Kenneth B. McFarlane, *The Nobility of Later Medieval England* (Oxford. 1973), p. 12: "It is not surprising therefore that most bishops' families ran to priests and that archdeacons were often bound by ties of blood as well as gratitude to their diocesans."

96. For biographical information on William and Robert Chichele, see *Chichele*, 646. For the archbishop, see Emden, *OU*, I, 410–12; Ernest F. Jacob, ed., *The Register of Henry Chichele, Archbishop of Canterbury, 1414–43* (Oxford, 1938), I, xvi–xl, and Ernest F. Jacob, *Archbishop Henry Chichele* (London, 1967).

97. Reginald R. Sharpe, ed., *Calendar of the Letter Books of the City of London: Letter Book I* (London, 1899–1912), p. 69: also pp. 222, 226, on the common involvement in the election of sheriffs in the City.

98. Emden, *OU*, I, 413. For his collation to livings directly in the archbishops control, see Jacob, *The Register*, I, 138, 164, 247, 196; this last citation pertains to his institution as archdeacon, "master William Chichele, the archbishop's kinsman (consanguineo suo)."

99. Emden, *OU*, I, 412–13. Jacob, *The Register*, I, 115, 298,236, 261 (instituted to the mastership of the hospital in Canterbury); 281 (to the archdeaconry of Can-

terbury); also, IV, 294–95, where a John Chichele is referred to as "dilecti consanguinei nostri."

100. For the endowment and construction of All Souls, see Ernest F. Jacob, "The building of All Souls College, 1438–43," in *Essays in Honour of James Tait*, ed. J. G. Edwards, V. H. Galbraith, and Ernest F. Jacob (Manchester, 1933), 121–33; see also Jacob, "The Warden's Text of the Foundation Statutes of All Souls College, Oxford," *Antiquaries Journal* 15 (1935), 420–31; Jacob, "Two Lives of Archbishop Chichele," *Bulletin of the John Rylands Library* 16 (1932), 428–68, and Jacob, "An early booklist of All Souls College," *Bulletin of the John Rylands Library* 16 (1932), 469–81.

101. *VCH Northamptonshire*, II, 177–78. By 1425 Henry was quite explicit about the pleasures of founding such an institution in the town of his birth.

102. *Chichele*, 339–41.

103. *Chichele*, 564–69.

104. *Chichele*, 519–26.

105. *Chichele*, 568–71. John Daryll was buried in the London Charterhouse, with bequests of land to wife Florence to hold for life along with half his goods. There were also bequests to the archbishop (if he prays for Daryll's transgressions). Land in the parish of St. Stephen Walbrook would go to the executors (Florence and brother William Daryll).

106. See Albert Compton Reeves, *Lancastrian Englishmen* (Washington, 1981), p. 265, for the quotation; 265–390, for a full biographical treatment. For the family, Ernest Axon, "The Family of Bothe (Booth) and the Church in the 15th and 16th centuries," *Transactions of the Lancashire and Cheshire Antiquarian Society* 53 (1938), 32–82. A. Compton Reeves and Michael Bennett are contemplating an exhaustive study of this fascinating family. The comment on "mentoring" was from Compton Reeves, while discussing the Booths, at the XXV Congress of Medieval Studies (Western Michigan University, May 1990).

107. Emden, *CU*, 78–79.

108. Axon, "Family of Bothe," 56; and on William, 49, "He showed with his brother Laurence a family affection so strong that it might be thought to be nepotism. This was not confined to those nephews of the Bothe family . . . besides them there were very many men bearing Lancashire names, probably all relatives, who became dignitaries and incumbents in the church of his successive dioceses in his time. Also, *TE*, III, 250 n., and 282 n., "Like other members of his family, [Laurence] brought whole troops of his Lancashire friends and kinsmen to batten off his offices and preferments."

109. Emden, *CU*, 77–78.

110. See, Emden, *CU*, 77; see also, Arthur T. Bannister, ed., *Registrum Caroli Bothe, Episcopi Herefordensis, a.d. MDXVI–MDXXXV*, Canterbury and York Society, 1921. For Charles's will, see his register, pp. ix–xiv, and PCC, 25 Hogen. He too had a foot in London, with such livings as St. James Garlickhithe and a canonry in St. Pauls. In the north midlands, he fastened onto the treasurership of Lichfield.

111. *CPR 1446–52*, 322.

112. See *CPR 1452–61*, 375; 526, for joint endowment by William and Robert

Booth. Reeves, *Lancastrian Englishmen*, p. 276, for involvement by Seth Worsley, treasurer of Lichfield. See also, *CPR 1461–67*, 86.

113. James Raine and James Raine, jr., eds. *A History of the Chantries Within the County Palatine of Lancashire*, Chetham Society, 59–60 (1862), I, 134–36. *CPpL 1458–71*, 258–67, 369–71; *CPR 1452–61*, 526; see Reeves, *Lancastrian Englishmen*, p. 303, regarding the souls to be mentioned in the prayers said at the chantries. For further family interest and support, see *CPR 1452–61*, 275, 512; *CPR 1461–67*, 86.

114. *CPR 1452–61*, 512; *CCR 1441–47*, 483; *CCR 1454–61*, 360, 479; *CCR 1461–67*, 307. For cooperation regarding efforts to bestow the advowson of Netherwollop, *CCR 1454–61*, 360, 373, 442. Among those involved were John Booth, Robert Clifton, Richard Booth, and Seth Worsley.

115. *CCR 1441–47*, 483; *CCR 1454–61*, 360.

116. *CCR 1454–61*, 479.

117. *CCR 1464–67*, 307. Five different Booths were involved in this one quit-claim transaction.

118. *CCR 1468–76*, 783.

119. *CCR 1468–76*, 1359; also, 1154.

120. *CCR 1476–85*, 371, 395. These agreements covered damages caused by "guile, negligence, or failure."

121. *CCR 1476–85*, 396. For another, and earlier, example of many Booths in action, see *CCR 1447–54*, 335.

122. *CPR 1452–61*, 359.

123. *CPR 1452–61*, 505.

124. *CPpL 1447–54*, 26.

125. *CPpL 1447–54*, 125–26.

126. *CPpL 1447–54*, 128–29.

127. *CPpL 1455–64*, 630.

128. *CPpL 1455–64*, 543.

129. *CPpL 1455–64*, 87.

130. *CPpL 1455–64*, 434–35.

131. *CPR 1452–61*, 512.

132. For Laurence's will, see *TE*, III, 248–50.

133. *TE*, III, 331–33, for a will of 26 August, 1464. For problems encountered in the execution of William's will, *CPR 1467–77*, 577; and for Laurence's will, *CPR 1476–85*, 283.

134. *TE*, IV, 30–32, for Robert Booth's will.

135. For the will of Agnes Clifton, Gervase Clifton's widow, *TE*, IV, 242–44; and *TE*, IV, 64–71, for Gervase Clifton's will (of April, 1491): he left bequests for the chantry in Southwell Minster (including money he had received from Laurence's will; land at Woodhouse; a debt of £17 owed him by Trinity priory, York; the altar goods he had received from Laurence), £10 to Thomas Bryan, and bequests to William Booth's chantry at Eccles. Also from this Booth circle, *TE*, III, 155–57, for the will of William Worsley, dean of St. Paul's.

136. For Thomas Booth and various other Booths—perhaps related but perhaps not—see Emden, *CU*, 73, 77–80: *TE*, III, 250n; Axon, "The Family of Bothe (Booth)," 57–58.

137. Axon, 66 ff., and Emden, *CU*.

138. Axon, 68–69.

139. Axon, 59–61; Emden, *CU*, 80.

140. Axon, 72–73; Emden, *CU* 79–80.

141. Axon, 569; Emden, *CU*, 73, 77–80: there are 16 Booths given by Emden and none are positively eliminated from kinship; *CPpL*, 1471–84, 6.

142. For a discussion of how such a world was closely interconnected, Michael J. Bennett, *Community, Class, and Careerism* (Cambridge, 1983), pp. 21–40: p. 26, ". . . ties of kinship and marriage. Even with the limited genealogical data available, the degree of interrelatedness is remarkable"; Nigel Saul, *Scenes from Provincial Life*, 28–72; A. J. Pollard, "The Richmondshire Community of Gentry During the Wars of the Roses," in *Patronage, Pedigree, and Power in Later Medieval England*, ed. Charles Ross (Gloucester, 1979), pp. 37–59, and 47–49 with details of intermarriage within the gentry; R. G. K. A. Mertes, *The English Noble Household, 1250–1600* (Oxford, 1988), pp. 161–69 (though she is too prone to accept Stone on the lesser emotional investment in children who would perhaps soon leave the scene); and Cicely Howell, "Peasant Inheritance Custom in the Midlands, 1280–1700," in *Family and Inheritance*, ed. Jack Goody, Joan Thirsk, and Edward P. Thompson (Cambridge, 1976), pp. 112–55, with a discussion of the spread of relatives named in wills, pp. 140–42.

143. Ralph V. Turner, *The English Judiciary in the Age of Glanvill and Bracton c. 1176–1239* (Cambridge, 1985), p. 186: "Despite efforts . . . to build up great blocks of lands, their ambition of founding dynasties to stand alongside the old baronial houses was unfulfilled. The chances of birth—too many daughters and not enough surviving sons—thwarted their ambitions."

144. For an extensive and perceptive analysis of the marriages of the earl's children, with particular interest in their political and economic aspects, Ernest F. Jacob, *The Fifteenth Century* (Oxford, 1961), pp. 319–26: p. 323, "The Neville family well illustrate a tendency to be remarked in the fifteenth-centry baronage: the absorption of the smaller units by the larger, corresponding perhaps with the economic tendency of the rich to get richer but fewer." Also on the family, see Jack R. Lander, "Marriage and Politics in the Fifteenth Century: The Nevilles and The Wydevilles," in *Crown and Nobility, 1450–1509* (London, 1976), pp. 94–126, and Lander, "Family, Friends, and Politics in Fifteenth-Century England," in *Kings and Nobles in the Later Middle Ages*, ed. Ralph A. Griffiths and James Sherborne (Gloucester, 1986), pp. 22–40.

145. *CP*, XII, 2, 544–48, for earl Ralph.

146. *RP*, VI, 44, for the gift that his father settled on the young couple.

147. For Robert Neville, see Emden, *OU*, II, 1350, and *DNB*, XIV, 300–302. He was bishop of Salisbury, 1427–38, and then bishop of Durham until his death in 1457. The records covering unmarried daughters are always sketchy, there seem to have been two daughters of the first marriage and one of the second who entered the church: Margaret became abbess of Barking, Elizabeth a nun at London Minories, and Jane a nun at some unspecified house.

148. PRO, E 327/774.

149. William, III lord Deincourt, died in 1381, Alice not until 1431, which makes her a near recordholder for survival as a relict of a peer.

150. PRO, E 327/776.

151. *TE*, II, 66.

152. Nicholas H. Nicolas, ed. *Testamenta Vetusta* (London, 1830), p. 390.

153. Nicholas, *Testamenta Vetusta*, 357–62.

154. PCC, 31 Godyn.

155. Lambeth Palace, Arundel's Register, I, 235b–236a.

156. Alfred Gibbons, *Early Lincoln Wills* (Lincoln, 1888), pp. 159–60.

157. PCC, 22 Stokton.

III Widows

Widows and Widowhood

The Wife of Bath is the most familiar woman of late medieval England, though Margery Kempe may be closing the gap. Chaucer's famous figure arrests our attention because of her flamboyant sexuality; any odd moments of grief at burying one husband or another along the way are submerged by her sense of excitement at the next marital and domestic adventure. Her cheerful and frank appraisal of her life makes her a creature of immediate sympathy. Also in her favor is the harsh fact that she has been winning at longer and longer odds and that the avalanche of patriarchy and of male domination is perhaps about to catch up with and quench her blithe spirit. Her romantic proportions as wife, widow, and frequent participant in the games of the marriage market seem to be much larger than life. But in a sober perspective we can see her in a much less jaunty setting: a much-widowed figure whose life has been a long series of new identities and new roles thrust upon her by the death of successive husbands. In many ways her experience and personality have been formed by the fact that she really is the *widow*, not the *wife*, of Bath. In this grayer guise, not in her louder and gayer robes, she would have been more at home with, if less exciting to, Chaucer's contemporary audience. We can even argue that she goes onto the offensive so quickly because she sees this as her best defense against the closing walls of patriarchy; she has been lucky but her time in the sun is perhaps about to end.

Family dynamics, as we have had occasion to state, were mostly about men: fathers, sons, brothers, and, when better alternatives failed, nephews and cousins. The social role of women was almost never as important as their biological role, and even when an individual woman became the key in the transmission of a patrimony or the preservation of a lineage her individuality was soon subsumed by the males whom she bore to the new patrilineage. Her temporary import was a fluke or, at best, a convenience, a peculiar social institution called into operation at a crucial moment for (temporary) want of men who could provide the needed link. She was never seen as much more than a bridge, a second-best alternative to father-son succession.

But if patriarchy was the prime model that largely defined interpersonal and family relations and that guided the enduring realities of interaction and inheritance, it did not mean that the secondary position of women was translated into an iron law of inferiority and subordination. There were institutional as well as personal lines of defense: allies could be found in all sorts of strange places. The ecclesiastical support of marriage as the free exercise of personal volition, plus the ecclesiastical emphasis upon the mutual obligations of partners, were great helps in the struggle.[1] The spiritual grace that accompanied and grew with the proper fulfillment of marital goals was a sexually balanced and symmetrical blessing within the confines of Christ's church. As real people, rather than as legal entities, daughters and sisters and wives and other female relatives were provided for, respected and trusted, and obviously loved and valued above and beyond their instrumental value or their legally defined sphere. Within the sober boundaries of family and social history such literary and theological tropes as women as the vessel of sin, women as seducers of a more perfect *mankind*, and women as the sirens of betrayal and lechery make but little appearance.[2] Within the circles of their lesser roles and lives, women presumably worked to carve what individual niches they could, and the overpowering realities of class and wealth often may have meant as much in countless specific and practical situations as did those of gender. Women of substance, at least, often had useful weapons at hand.

Beyond the many particular instances of push and pull, and related to but separate from the question of equality or inferiority, lies the fact that women were very different from men. Their life experiences and life lines could diverge considerably from those of their husbands, fathers, brothers, and male social equals. They truly were the second sex, the *other*, and their lives were often a series of roles differing from those of men in both biological and social categories, comprising some distinct admixture of the passive—the object role—and the active. As unmarried daughters, their identity or role as object was heavily underscored. As wives they were usually meant to be seen mainly as a complementary projection of their husbands' role, their identities at least in part derivative from their sexual and social union with a man (or a series of men). We may know that a particular strong minded woman could well be setting the family policy, but in the eyes of the law and the political-economic framework within which families existed, it was *his* doing, she but a loyal lieutenant or counselor. And husbands versus wives, both as a (comic) literary convention and as a too-frequent theme of "real" family life, was generally a battle fought on a field that had been measured by male-oriented and male-defined laws of war. We tend to side with her, in so many instances, in large part because she was the irreversible underdog.[3]

But to see the woman in her role of maximum isolation, in the role most emphatic of her otherness and her loneliness, her vulnerability and her alienation, we can best turn to the widow. In this role or status much of the essence of female existence surfaces, both in its most meager and dependent, and also in its freest and most opportune. In its very definition and its wide boundaries, widowhood leads us to women at a point in time and circumstances when they come closest to an identity determined and shaped by *their* view of identity. It also takes us to women when they have entered a wholly new status, but through an entrance or by means of a *rite de passage* over which they have no control. Widowhood is the screen on which we can get our clearest images of the multiple identities of the woman and of the complexities of her life line. The best and the worst of her life come into focus when we explore some of the varieties of widowhood.

Life is a series of stages or roles, as Shakespeare reminds us in *As You Like It*. There is an inevitable progression as we climb the hill upwards to the crest of maturity and independence, an equally inevitable retrogression as we come down the other side. A man moved across this terrain as a youth, then as a mature man—a would-be patriarch—and, if he survived, as an old man. Somewhere along the line, if he did not enter the church, he was apt to marry (though there are probably some qualifications for younger sons in large and/or poor families), probably for the first time about when he was crossing the broad chronological boundary between youth and early maturity. Along the course of this linear progression he might lose a wife or two, and he was statistically more likely to remarry than to remain a widower. But along the entire course of the line he was and would always remain the same person, carrying the same surname and belonging to the same patrilineage. The children of *his* marriages—no matter how many marriages and how many children—were *his* children. Eventually, as an old man he would be identifiable as the logical end product of the mature man, as the mature man had been of the youth. His life course was some combination of social roles and age roles: personal, familial, and marital history were woven into one fabric, and it was pretty much the same fabric that encompassed or embraced his public roles.

A woman's life, if she married and was widowed, did not necessarily have this neat linear progression. When she married, she began a series of basic changes. She took a new surname. She left her patrilineage, or her father's family, and she became part of a different family. The children of her marriage(s) were, in most vital matters before the law and in the eyes of her peers, his children. If he died and she remarried, she underwent still another mutation of identity, and now the possibility of stepchildren and of more children from her next marriage—half siblings to those of her first marriage—only compounded the pattern of her life. For the man, the domestic life was not at odds with the public life. His status in the world was obviously affected by family considerations, and these would enhance or diminish his prospects, fame, and fortune. But for the wife the public life was largely an expression of her status and role within the domestic life, and this status was altered much more fundamentally by such factors as marriage or widowhood than any comparable set of factors that existed in the world of men. In the eyes of the law she was not the same person through the course of her life.

Both demographic and social factors conspired to make the widow—and not necessarily the first-time widow—an extremely common figure in late medieval society. In this introductory portion of this essay we have two purposes. One is simply to indicate what a common phenomenon widowhood was and to show how the widow stood apart and, whatever her individual freedom, how recognizable she was as the occupant of a special if not a desirable role. The other is to argue that she is too easily made the subject of romanticized or wish-fulfillment treatment. She rarely had a life of great joy or ease, and if widowhood "really" was preferable to marriage in terms of wealth and independence, such a judgment must be seen as an attack upon marriage more than a positive statement about or a vindication of widowhood. Chaucer has led us astray. His own granddaughter made some exalted marriages and buried two or three husbands as she moved up the ladder. Which was her favorite among the Tales?[4]

A brief look at some exalted case studies quickly takes a bit of the polish off widowhood. The dowager queens, at the highest level of all, exemplify many of the common and lugubrious themes of their lesser sisters. The English kings of the fifteenth century were not a long-lived group, and they left a group of royal widows whose subsequent lives were often unhappy and who, even in their more fortunate moments, offer some bleak testimonials to the fraility of women's fortunes. And though queens are hardly typical of their sex or of women of widowed status, their life in a glass house was difficult enough to allow us to look for a balance between their privileges and pleasures and the unsympathetic standards by which they were judged. At his deposition and death Richard II left behind the young wife of a political, unconsummated marriage; Henry IV a second wife who was already the widow of the count of Brittany; Henry V a young wife and an infant son; Henry VI a tough young wife and mother; Edward IV another royal woman who was now widowed for the second time. In the lives of these five royal widows are found many of the characteristics we have referred to in general terms, and their lives emphasize the picture of women enmeshed in passive and derived roles, forced so often to live a vicarious and once-removed existence.⁵ The varying biographical and post-marital tales of the five dowager queens also offer, in essence, some idea of the diversity of existence that widowhood could embrace. The five women were, respectively, Isabel of France (1389–1409), Joan of Navarre (c. 1370–1437), Katherine of Valois (1401–37), Margaret of Anjou (1430–82), and Elizabeth Wydeville (c. 1437–92). That four were French and only one English further indicates the instrumental nature of high marriage, and brings home the way in which even the most exalted women's lives were ornate chessboards on which other people moved the pieces for the sake of international diplomacy. Joan of Brittany had come to her marriage with Henry IV having already borne eight children, and Elizabeth Wydeville had had two sons by her first union. In each case these prior life entanglements complicated their loyalties and obligations in the operative marriage and made the wives suspect to some of their husbands' partisans.

A queen's life, after the death of the king, was neither an easy nor a happy one. All of these women knew personal tragedies in addition to the royal death that marked the onset of their widowhood, and they all suffered varying degrees of public obloquy for the way they played their undefined but demanding royal role. Isabella of France was but 9 when she was contracted to Richard II, 14 when she left the land of her first marriage and returned to France, 19 when she married the duke of Orleans, and 23 when she died in childbirth. After Richard II had been deposed, the several years she spent in England were an unhappy and unedifying tale of house arrest, of nominal involvements in Richardian plots and rebellions, and of enforced idleness while Henry IV balked at returning her dowery and talked of marrying her to the future Henry V. No wonder she rejoiced to set foot once again on the continent in 1401. She was the child bride, the child widow, and the child pawn of medieval statecraft, *par excellence*.

The queens who followed young Isabella onto the English throne and then into royal widowhood lived longer and perhaps had more measures of joy to mix into their cup of sorrow. Joan of Navarre married Henry IV in 1402, when she had been a widow for three years, he for eight. She had borne eight children by her first husband, John IV, count of Brittany, of whom seven were still alive, while Henry of England had had three sons and three daughters by his marriage with Mary Bohun. Joan received a splendid dower settlement upon her remarriage, and life in England went smoothly, not only during Henry IV's lifetime, but under her stepson Henry V, until 1419. Then she was accused of witchcraft, placed under nominal restraint, and only restored to good grace in 1422. She then lived quietly, if rather grandly, until her death, around age 70, in 1437. But during her life in England she had to smile through years of such additional burdens as her son Arthur's captivity after Agincourt, and the diplomatic hostility to her new kingdom sustained by her son, the Count of Brittany.[6]

Katherine of Valois, daughter of Charles VI of France, married Henry V in 1420. She bore him a son who was nine months old when the king died on 31 August, 1422. By 1425 it was becoming known in court circles that her relations with Owen Tudor were not of a platonic nature. The queen's private life, of course, was public business, and the scandal of Katherine's behavior was all the greater in that Owen Tudor was but a minor courtier, *and* a Welsh one at that. Parliament passed a statute in 1428 making it illegal for the royal dowager to remarry without the consent of the king and council. The statute is another classic instance of bad timing about when to close the barn door, as Katherine had borne or was about to bear a daughter, Tacino (who married Reginald, lord Grey of Wilton), plus three sons, Edmund, Jasper, and Owen.[7] The political and parliamentary harassment, largely fostered by the duke of Gloucester, was intended to shame the queen mother and to emphasize that she was to have little role in the realm, now that royal widowhood should have spelled the end of her sexual and breeding functions. She too was subjected to the polite house arrest deemed appropriate for an errant queen: in this case it was at Bermondsey Abbey, where she died in January, 1437.

Henry VI was in his mid-20s, Margaret of Anjou but in her mid-teens, when they were married in 1444 (and 1445). The signs were hardly auspicious; the court party had agreed, as the price for Margaret's hand, to surrender various English strongholds in Maine that the hawks considered invaluable to their continued presence in France. When she arrived and took stock of her husband's weakness, and then produced the obligatory heir in 1453, she thought a new role as a power behind the Lancastrian throne to be an obvious one for her to assume. Though we tend to blame her personality and her lack of understanding of English institutions, along with her unrealistic expectations of wealth and court ceremonial, for her heavy hand in the political quarrels of the 1450s and 1460s, she was a victim at least as much as a malevolent and partisan force. Her effective widowhood began in the mid-1460s, and after the death of her son and of her husband in 1471 she really was as pathetic as Shakespeare depicts her in *Henry VI* and *Richard III*. She died in 1482, after six pitiful and impoverished years back in France, a paltry object of royal and aristocratic charity.

Elizabeth Wydeville, like Joan of Navarre and Brittany, was twice wed, twice widowed. Her first husband was a Lancastrian, Sir John Grey, son of Edward, lord Ferrers of Groby. He had been a casualty of the second battle of St. Albans (1461). He left her with two youngish sons, and her pursuit of her dower claims brought her into close contact with Edward IV. Her marriage to the king produced two more sons (who survived infancy) and four daughters who lived to marry, one who became a nun.[8] After Edward died in 1483 and her son was deposed by her husband's brother, she was in a dreadful position. Richard III's accession meant not only the disappearance and probable death of the princes, but the execution of her brother, Anthony, earl of Rivers. When Henry VII married her daughter Elizabeth, five months after Bosworth, Elizabeth's position became relatively safe if not wholly regularized. Her son-in-law gave her reasonable dower rights in 1486. However, he distrusted her behavior at the time of Lambert Simnel's uprising, and she too was forced into Bermondsey Abbey, with a pension of 400 marks (raised to £400 in February, 1490). In the Abbey the poor dowager queen led "a wretched and miserable life," and in her will of 1492 she talks of her inability to leave bequests because she was bereft of worldly goods.[9]

Taken together these are melancholy tales, the feminine analogues of Richard II's desire to sit and tell sad tales of kings. Many of the woes suffered by and inflicted upon these women stemmed from the anomalous political and constitutional role of the queen. To be a queen was to receive a hand with many losing cards, and only by great luck and skill could one hope to avoid a heavy share of misery. But the worst problems came with the king's death, for nothing and no one was as redundant as a foreign dowager. Of these women only Katherine of Valois was a queen mother after her husband's death—if we except the short interval between Edward IV's death and Richard III's coup—and to be a useless and unwanted foreigner, stripped of husband and without a normalizing and accepted role, was clearly an awful fate. Affluence may have dulled the sharp edges of personal privation, but even there much of the economic support depended on the good will and whims of others. What was given was frequently taken away. If women in general were expendable commodities, royal widows were but left-overs, relicts whose potential for embarrassment and trouble was infinitely greater than any positive wisdom or contribution they might be allowed to offer.

So many royal widows, all without role or purpose, may be a little unusual for the royal houses within less than a century. But that such women were so generally prevalent in society was obvious to any observer. In the secular male wills published in *Chichele's Register*, 116 men were about to die and leave wives behind, while only 52 men seem to have been the final survivor of the (final) marriage. The percentage of last marriages that ended with his death (69 percent) may not tell us anything about the incidence, length, or success of the marriage, but it speaks clearly to the question of longevity and ultimate survival. The data for the fifteenth-century peerage tell a similar story. There were approximately 262 peers, summoned between Henry IV's accession and 1500. Of these men, 189 (or 68 percent) left living wives at their death. Insofar as these two statistical samples are reliable and typical, they reveal a world where about two of every three men left a widow, only one man in three was a widower.[10]

Women as widows means, once again, women as defined by some activity of their husbands, though here it was one in which he was usually an involuntary and unenthusiastic participant. But society, and the essential life experience itself, requires some frame of reference, and for the *other*, it was appropriate that it be a passive one, one in which she was—at least at the point of entry—the object rather than the active mover. By starting with a group of women defined in terms of their husbands (that is, after their husbands' deaths), we make their marriages into their normative life experience, and to speak of the woman as a widow is to begin counting her as a separate entity only from the moment at which she survived the marriage. This *modus operandi* pays little regard, at first glance, to where and how that particular marriage fitted into *her* life pattern. Some examples from the pool of aristocratic widows illuminate this point, though we shall spend more time on such material later on. When we see her primarily as a widow, we play havoc with her own biographical trail; later we will work to disentangle the knots created by a life with a dual identity, her double "contextualization."

There is some statistical material on the length of the different segments that comprise her life line. Between the husband's death and her own, how long an interval elapsed: for how long was she a widow (if she never remarried)? The queens survived the kings for an average of 14 years, though widowhood was shorter because Isabella married Charles of Orleans, six years after Richard II's deposition, and Katherine of Valois married Owen Tudor about nine or ten years (or possibly sooner) after Henry V's death. We have comparable data on survival for 168 of the 189 aristocratic widows. The data strongly confirm that what we assume to be the common life experience for these widows, that is, that their marriages with peers were really but one personal and chronological segment along the entire course of their lives. Thirty seven of the widows outlived their aristocratic partners by five years or less, 48 by some 6–15 years, 37 by 16–25 years, and 46 by 26 years or more. This means that 49 percent of the women lived at least 16 years longer than the partner we have been watching (and using as the biographical bedrock on which to ground our definition and our statistics). And of the widows, 52 (27 percent of the 189) were already widows when they contracted the marriage that brings them to our attention. When a woman became a member of such a universe (that is, that of aristocratic widows) would seem to be a simple, factual matter, based on her husband's aristocratic status, the fact of their marriage, and that of his subsequent death. Of the peers' widows, 77 (41 percent) remarried, as did two of the five royal widows. So for some of the women the aristocratic marriage was undoubtedly the principal or modal life experience: they had entered it as maidens and they never remarried, no matter how long it lasted and how long they survived their husbands. But for other women such a marriage was but one section of a more complex pattern, representing one of a number of marriages, perhaps the first, perhaps the fourth. In span it may have represented a goodly portion of their alloted years, or it may have been a temporary episode, perhaps sandwiched between more prosaic marriages and/or a try at the single life.

These considerations are presented to suggest some of the differences between the female life line or pattern and the male. The amount of distinction varied, of course, not just between the sexes but between almost every set of individual cases. For some men and women there was but one marital partner, an extensive sharing of common life experiences and of a common network of relatives, with the same children and collateral kin as participants in the mutual enterprise. Such partnerships are not hard to find. John Beauchamp (lord Beauchamp of Powicke from 1447) was born c. 1417. In or before 1434, he married Margaret Ferrers. He died in 1475—having been exempted from attendance in Lords because of age and debility—and she followed him in 1487. They were buried together in the Dominican friary at Worcester. They had produced a son who followed his father in the peerage, and presumably they shared a long and at least a tolerable life venture.

But there are also women whose lives were exotic in that they married and remarried a number of times, changing names, families, and perhaps even identities to some extent, and later we shall look at a few of these women, and their marital careers, in more detail. Such women, doubtless to be found at all social levels, went from marriage to marriage, from family to family, until he or she proved to be an ultimate survivor as the game came to its end. For many, one particular marriage may strike us as the central one, as defined either in length, fertility, or social standing. For others, life was clearly a series of ventures where each new partner was perhaps roughly indistinguishable from the previous one, and it is hard to know which experience served to shape a woman's identity as against those that were but ephemeral events. Elizabeth Dinham, sister of a minor peer, married Fulk Bourgchier, IV lord Fitzwarin, some years before his death in 1479. Then, before December 1480, she married Sir John Sapcote, a second marriage of some 20 years duration. Sapcote died in 1500, and by 1507 she had moved on to a third marriage, though of but a few years, with Sir Thomas Brandon. Brandon died in January, 1510. Lord Fitzwarin had been buried at Brampton parish church, the third husband at Black Friars, Ludgate, and the widow (who died 19 October 1510) at the Grey Friars in London. Her first marriage had produced three children whom we know of, and had served to create or at least to consolidate her social status: her eldest son was summoned to Lords as his father's heir in 1492, and his own marriage in 1499 was to a peer's daughter (Cicely, daughter of lord Daubeney and sister of the earl of Bridgewater). Her second marriage was the longest in duration, while her third must have brought a few years of comfort and companionship as she aged, with her children grown, established in their worldly places and well settled.

There is no simple way of determining whether the first, or the second, or even the third marriage was *the* critical experience or the main element in defining her ego and identity. Furthermore, such a woman was involved in a large number of the kinds of networks we looked at in the previous chapter. To the members and kin of each family that she passed through—a member, for a while at least, because of marriage—her identity as one of them might have seemed the operative identity. But from our perspective we can say that the view of each set of beholders was but a segment of the total reality of her life; her life was both a subject and an object, an internal reality to her and an external or objective fact to a great many others. If such complexities bedevil our efforts to untie the knot, they must have been that much greater for the widow whose life was composed of so many tangled skeins as she moved along, living and experiencing the ups and downs of her fortune.

Dying Husbands and Surviving Wives

It was the husband's death that turned the wife into the widow. Therefore, except for those infrequent instances when she actively encompassed his death, she was just a passive participant in the transition.[11] And since her new role and her new identity were defined by the act or event of his demise, we begin this treatment of widows and widowhood by looking at *her* new status in terms of *his* final view of and final attempt to control their relationship. It was customary for him to make an effort to set the conditions and terms of her status, and he wanted her to enter widowhood through a corridor built to his design. The dying husband was apt to fix a firm eye upon his surviving partner, and the imminence of his departure generally concentrated his attention towards her. The wills of few husbands fail to make some provision or to say something about her, and more often than not it was complimentary. What we can label as *their* last relationship can be divided into a number of sub-categories, though in any given partnership there was probably an emotional climate that subsumed the sub-segments of the relationship; his testamentary terminology, the proportion of bequests that went to her, the degree of final and posthumous responsibility with which she was being invested, and his interest in her future. On the other hand, varying degrees of wealth, the prior dispositions of real and personal property and of children, and of individual reticence and a degree of haste all entered in. Our generalizations about dying husbands and surviving wives embrace a range of behavior, in virtually every relevant set of particulars, that pretty much covers the entire market place.

The common law had an interest in the widow's right to a share of her husband's estate, and by the fifteenth century his responsibility for her support seems to have been generally accepted.[12] The dower share of real property was meant to ensure her against the worst bite of the winter wind. This share was not ordinarily at the mercy of the husband's volition, and her success in securing it and in living upon its proceeds will be considered later. Here we look, instead, at the testamentary bequests that he chose to steer to her, covering the transmission of personal (and some real) property and the sets and circles of bilateral obligations he erected to surround such transfers. The husband, to some extent, saw her as his partner in their collective enterprise, and how she was about to perform her future duties towards their children, the estate, and his posthumous projects could be fairly critical in terms of the success and stability of the next generation, as it was to his final peace of mind. The preservation of patriarchy and its accompanying patrimony would depend to no small degree upon the mother, the surviving partner. But between the partners there must also have been an element of ambivalence and of jealousy. There was competition as well as cooperation in their relationship. She had beaten him, and she now was about to score still more runs in the game of survival. How did husbands actually refer to their soon-to-be widows in their last wills?

As far as the husband-wife dialogue goes, the most striking answer is that few men added any personal touches to the wills, beyond the mention of their names' and identity. Even in wills that in other ways bespeak great loops of cooperation and trust, terms of affection or phrases that reveal his view of their private or intimate life are rare. Neither does her prior identity—either as daughter or as wife and mother from some earlier marriage—often enter in, and only a rare will goes so far as to drop its guard and even to say "my enterly belovid wife."[13] We know from other studies that wives were named as executrixes and supervisors in at least half the wills of any group of dying husbands, a clear mark of affection and confidence.[14] But perhaps bound by the same conventions of discourse that made family and private letters so tight-lipped, we rarely find much explicit discussion of the cooperative side of spousal relations in the wills.

Of course, there were variations and considerable room for individuality, if and when one wished to be assertive. John of Gaunt used tender words towards his survivor, as he did for her two predecessors, as we saw above. Sometimes a husband might pay tribute to his wife's impressive family credentials, and might be very decorous about identifying his relict. Lord Mountjoy, a minor peer, married Anne Neville, daughter of the earl of Westmorland and widow of Humphrey Stafford, duke of Buckingham, a direct descendent (through female lines) of Edward I and Edward III. Mountjoy began his will by asserting that he was "husband unto the right high and mighty princess Anne, duchess of Buk'."[15]

Fortunately for the widows, bequests of tangible goods were much more common, as well as of better value, than were terms of endearment. Such transfers of personal property are mostly above and beyond the widow's dower share of real or burgage property. In almost every will of a married man, there is some mention of and some provision for the widow, and if any relative at all was mentioned, it was almost sure to be the late partner. But given that variation is the theme of our tale, we can fully anticipate the transmission of the immense range of bequests we actually encounter. The extremes of personal wealth were one factor in the spectrum of behavior, but so was the prior disposition of property, the warmth of feeling, the presence or absence of children, the existence of competing claims upon personal items, and other ephemeral conditions. Had we enough controlled cases, we could attempt to plot a behavioral graph for such variables as the age of the couple, the years of marriage, the existence of prior marriages (on his and/or her part) and the presence of children of such marriages, the number of children by each marriage, their age, sex, and marital status, and so forth. The chances are that we might identify certain propensities and patterns, but that we would still have to fall back, time and again, upon the assertion that idiosyncracy was perhaps the strongest determinant of all. These caveats about social control and ambivalence are not designed to lead us, inescapably, into a world of relentless competition and manipulation. There are almost as many versions of the husband-wife relationship as there are partnerships, and we can find examples to illustrate virtually any current or theme we choose. For an example of what we can define as generous treatment, combined with genuine if contained enthusiasm toward the wife, we can look at the will of Seman de Tonge.[16] He was about 80 years old when he drew up his will on 14 November, 1414; the wife he was about to leave was his third marital partner. As such, she presumably had had but limited involvement in some of his life-long enterprises, and both her age and her own prior life experiences suggest that she may have had her own material resources to fall back upon, beyond the provisions of de Tonge's will. He left her 100 marks, plus 100 marks' value in cattle, "iuxta disposicionem executorum meorum." This was hardly niggardly treatment, by any standards of the gentry or the bourgeoisie. It is, instead, a good example of extremely decent treatment being accorded a late partner, one who had to match her own interests in the estate against those older claims of other relatives and of the children of his earlier marriages: a daughter, a son-in-law, various god children, a brother, and a sister all figure, along with the widow, among the old man's beneficiaries. Then there was competition against those resources he choose to devote to the dead; the souls of Seman's parents and of his previous wives drew money away from survivors and towards his new ecclesiastical project, the chapel of Holy Trinity, to be built in Faversham parish church. Nor was the widow named as an executrix or supervisor. So we see, in this relationship of companionship rather than of youthful passion and long-lasting partnership, a very reasonable financial settlement, probably made upon a woman of fewer than his 80 years but still of some fair age. The testamentary settlement hardly tries to link her or her future life and responsibilities to the commitments that mark his prior or entire life span or to his other kin and his older enterprises. Very proper and decent, and with circumscribed warmth and controlled generosity, is perhaps the best assessment of the husband's regard for his wife. It is certainly more companionable than when she could only collect her share if she "content herself with the portion of goods" that he specified for her, or if she maintained a chantry for his soul as a condition for the receipt of the bequests.[17]

Urban wills talk of property and of estates resting upon a different economic basis, and a fair share, in the literal sense, may have represented what society dictates as constituting a decent regard for her interests. In addition, burgage tenure and local customs often cut her in for more than the common law gave those whose wealth rested on land, whether held in chief or by lesser tenure. In a society where London women were profiting from a "golden age," we can assume that they often did better, in practice, than in the strict wording of their husbands' memorial bequests.[18] Robert Schapman of Haringay left her "alle the goodis that be moeuablis," and since there are other indications of esteem between them we should accept this as positive treatment.[19] Henry Ranfield, who died in 1418 at the siege of Rouen, seems generous enough, but leaves—for us if not for his widow—only a series of unanswerable questions.[20] Joan was to receive one-quarter of his goods, up to the value of 80 marks: But were they really worth that much, and how well informed were people about their estate's true evaluation? In addition, she was to receive the £40 her husband was owed by one Richard Aunger of Hampton. But did Aunger ever pay the debt? She was a war widow, and the customary uncertainties of widowhood were surely not diminished by the circumstances of his death, across the sea. Nor was she the only widow whose prospects hung on variables beyond her control, or beyond our ability to determine. The earl of Westmorland's son John made his wife Anne his executrix, and commissioned her to collect the "c. marc due to me by my lord her fadir of hir mariage, if she can secure yt."[21] Could she secure "yt," indeed?

Usually the widow of an affluent man drew her income primarily from her dower share of his property (plus what she might have held as an heiress in her own right, and perhaps from *inter vivos* agreements with her husband or with his male heir), rather than from the personal bequests of the will. Nevertheless, we can look to some of the most handsome testamentary treatments as evidence of his concern for her welfare, his pride in the fact that even after death he could afford to keep her in the style to which they had both aspired. Great nobles had no trouble reaching this standard, or so it would seem. We have already looked at John of Gaunt's testamentary network. His long inventory of items to Katherine Swyneford is what we would expect: chapel utensils and furnishings, jewels, household and domestic furnishings, presents he had received from such luminaries as Edward III and the duchess of Norfolk, presents Catherine had given him (including some from before their marriage), and all the goods and jewels he had given her.[22] But men well below Gaunt's level of splendor could also fill pages with their careful listings of goods for the widow. Lord Hungerford left household and personal goods,[23] but John Stourton, of an aristocratic but rural turn of mind, left his wife the paraphernalia and property of rural life: ". . . 14 oxen being at Preston, with the waggon, ploughs, yokes, iron chains, 'dragges,' harrows with all the apparatus to the same, and which belongs to husbandry there." She had to take care of the estate: we are not completely removed from the world of Charlemagne's capitulary *De Villis*.[24]

Not that one had to be of high born and affluent family to revel in such detail. Richard Brigge, perhaps about to die without surviving children, found time for such elaborate if unnecessary details as: "integra pro sacerdote, exceptis dalmatica et capa, cum libro missali et uno calice, una paxbrede deaurato, una compana argentea cum duabus fiallis argenteis."[25] Sometimes the mere tone of the description conveys a sense of warmth, as when John Dalton simply left his wife the house, "to have and hold and to rejoise durynge hir life."[26]

The transmission of items of sentimental value often struck the testator, if not the beneficiary, as being of great moment. We saw this when we looked at fathers and sons and at patriarchs and their collateral and extended networks. Similar ties between dying husbands and surviving wives are only to be expected. Edward Cheyne was a man of some importance and wealth, and he had an interest in rolling the details of his household and personal possessions across his tongue, as though he were dividing the realms of christendom among his issue.[27] On the two full pages needed to list the items he was giving his wife, we find such choice bits as a "halle and docer and ij costours steyned with the sege of Troye," and again, "the bed of red worstede with the hole sile of the largest assise embrouded with the hole armes of Edmund Cheyne on that parte and the armes of Sr John Cheyne [his father] on that other partie." He could hardly have been more circumstantial if he were dividing the armor of Achilles.

The provenance of personal items was often considered worth mentioning, and the nobility were inclined to trumpet individual status and a sense of collective and genealogical bonds by such statements. The earl of Suffolk left his countess a book, "qui nuper fuit comitis Stafford patris sui."[28] He also threw in some items of greater tangible value, such as life control of the de la Pole manor at Courthall by Kingston on Hull, with all the lands and tenements and their returns. Nor were the remembered items necessarily of exotic or lofty origin. John Stourton's chalice, intended for his widow Katherine, had simply "belonged to mag. Richard my brother."[29] Among the many and valuable bequests between Richard and Katherine Brigge was the "ciphum deauratum quem magister Sancti Iohannis dedit michi."[30]

But dying husbands were not simply (or invariably) cheerful and willing conduits through whom flowed household and personal goods. They too wanted their pound of flesh, in the form of our old companion, social control. We saw such forces in operation when we looked at fathers and sons, and we can see them even more openly when we look at husbands and wives. After all, in some ultimate sense, the father's goods also were (or eventually would be) the sons'; while for the widow, dower was but a form of usufruct, a use-repayment for the services of body and soul she had rendered during, and now, after the marriage.

The main avenue of social control that husbands sought to utilize concerned the remarriage of the widow. This was an even stronger theme, in articulation, than material support and future comfort. The specter of her remarriage seems to have haunted a sizeable number of men as they gazed into the future. By her remarriage their property would be diminished or used to enrich and comfort another in their stead. This bothered them. Their children might be neglected if she were young enough to bear more or if the new husband came with his own. This also bothered them. But more importantly, if we correctly catch a tone that they were reluctant to speak too loudly, their exclusive control of her sexuality was now being placed in jeopardy by the mere prospect of her remarriage, let alone by its consummation, as we see in the oft-expressed wish that she "remain a chaste widow." This last consideration, though never clarified beyond its general allusions to chastity and the narrow boundaries of public morality, seems to have bedeviled dying men. They held out to their wives the promise of bequests, of favors, and of public signs of trust that might all be withdrawn if the widows failed to remain chaste, bereft, and single. The collective testimony of so many clauses of this sort is a striking indication of jealousy, worry, and a frustration over the inability to control the future with any confidence. It is hard to read all of these worries as tokens of unselfish love: The concern with her remarriage seems to transcend the legitimate concern that she be distracted from the care of the estate and the raising of the children. From a purely practical view, executors and feoffees could assume responsibility for such obligations. But in fairness, there was no reason why a purely practical view had to be uppermost in the mind of the dying husband. Though we have little information on how many widows were actually denied a share of the estate because of their subsequent behavior, whether within the bounds of the normally permissible or not, the tone was often a hectoring one, even if the motivation could pass as unexceptionable.

Roger Flore was about to take his last leave of four sons and two daughters, and it may have seemed appropriate for him to worry about how his wife's future life would affect the children and the estate.[31] He certainly tried to cover as many alternatives as possible. He left various conditional tiers of bequests to cover all sorts of possibilities and contingencies: *if* she took a vow of chastity, *if* she remarried, *if* she remarried after more than a year of widowhood, and *if* she simply remained a widow without benefit of formal ecclesiastical vows. Needless to say, the sliding scale of benefaction worked against her if she remarried, and the more she wanted to be free to follow her own inclinations, the more she had to pay for her freedom. She had to balance "if she take the mantel and the rynge and avowe chastite . . ." against "if my said wif take hir an husbond, thanne wul I that my said ioint feffes make astate to Robert, my son." In Flore's case, the aggregate value of the estate and the need to provide for the children may honestly figure strongly among his motives for trying to control her, though we may also suspect the power of the unspoken personal

considerations. The value of the estate may also have affected her inclination regarding her wifely obedience.

The line between a concern that she have undivided future loyalties
and a desire simply to dictate her future may have been a fine one in most
instances, especially when there were (young) children to be cared for.
Richard Welby left five children, and some at least were minors.[32] His
widow's remarriage would have diverted her from what he saw as her
proper future role, and he, like Roger Flore, left the inducements of behavior modification: "if my wyff can fynde sufficiat suerty to myn executours that she shall nevir have housbond after my decesse, that thanne she
be my chief executrix."[33] And were the clauses and conditions that followed
elaborated simply for economic reasons, or was he trying to preserve the
"old fashioned" household and family values as a bond for the future: "if
my wyff wol not dwelle in my place and kepe householde, that than Richard, my sone, imediatly after my decesse, have the said place and all the
landis of tenementes"?

Sometimes the widow was presented a simple choice: *if* she remarried,
then the property would go to "my son and to the eyres of his body com-
myng."[34] John Whyte's widow received all his utensils if she did not remarry, and if she did she was to get £20 while the two sons would divide
all the goods.[35] Such a provision might imply that the value of the household possessions was greater by some considerable fraction, or maybe she
would have to make a choice at some future time. Perhaps the Goodman
of Paris had been more realistic regarding the future, when he said that his
training would help her in another marriage or show her off to advantage
among her friends.[36] So, we may suspect, was the Oxfordshire man who
simply said, "And whenne it happenith Agnes, my wife, to marye ageyn."[37]

Not all the posthumous concern was oppressive. In this discussion we
are deliberately mixing the positive and negative currents of the husbands'
wills, looking at the complexities of personal and institutional bonds that
depended on some blend of collaboration and of separateness. Dying husbands, more often than not, named the surviving partner as either an executor or a supervisor of the will. In addition to this formal responsibility,
she was often named to receive and then to disburse the residue of the
estate, perhaps for the sake of his soul. We see, even then, the reluctance to
let go: "to Johanne, my wif, she to do and dispose thereof at hire own fre
wyll, trusting that she will remembre and the good guyding of my said
childre and hers lyke as she wold that I should do in cas lyke."[38] After Robert Schapman bequeathed his moveable goods to his wife (whose Christian

name never appears in the will), he proclaimed that, "sche to be my prinsepall secutur . . . to dispose the goodis for me like as they wole anscwere to-fore gode atte the day of jogement."[39]

The former partner was one of the favorite executors, since as a party with an abiding interest in the property her diligence could be assumed, and her sex was evidently not a serious obstacle in the performance of the attendant duties. A common package for the wife was receipt of the residue of the estate along with the task of executor or co-executor.[40] John Walden cast the net a bit more widely, and his wife Idonea shared these responsibilities for the estate with two clerics, a Londoner, and a man from Tottenham.[41] In this will there had been no personal bequests and the main task was to oversee the distribution of a goodly batch of ecclesiastical endowments, including money, for the souls of Richard II and the testator's brother, Roger Walden, bishop of London.[42] Sir Thomas Brooke seems exceptionally solicitous for his widow, and his will conveys a tone that is almost apologetic. After all, if she was about to outlast him in one competitive arena, he at least had the solace of having no further responsibilities. If any of Brooke's children tried to prevent his old servants from realizing their bequests, "my wyff, with alle the lordeshipe and frendshipe that she may gete, socour hem, helpe hem, and defende hem, from the malice of myne oune children."[43] Concerns could be expressed in peculiar way, as the husband's fancy and the situation demanded. Philip Love ordered that "my executours take none of my wife's dettes whiche is dew unto her by the resone of her 3 furste husbondes."[44]

A further sign of trust between husband and wife was the oft-found clause that left the future of young children in her hands. Such a clause is to be expected: to whom else was he apt to entrust them?[45] But even so, the deliberate phrases sometimes reveal his need to choose between the alternate routes of coercion and cooperation. The desire to exercise control over the wife was tempered by the desire to exercise—often with her help—control over the children. Since the latter impulses often proved stronger than the former, she might emerge as his accomplice and partner. Her help might become the vital bridge between the enterprise of his generation and his hopes for the next, and his instructions could be fairly harsh. Richard Chamberlayne was clearly in no mellow mood on his deathbed when he gave his draconic instructions: "Sonne William . . . be reuled by his moder tylle he come to the saide age of twenty six yeres."[46] In a society and a situation where trust was perhaps difficult to establish, one was inclined to invest in already-proven partners, and the wife was entrusted with an emotional (as well as a legal) power of attorney. The cooperative side of the marital partnership might put a distinct edge to a husband's last wishes.[47]

Widows, as we have said, had little to do with the creation of their status. The husband died, and the wife immediately and automatically took on a new persona. It is easy to project a view of widowhood that carries a false luster of affluence and independence. But there were, at best, compensations and consolations for the burdens now imposed upon the survivors. For many women, widowhood doubtlessly offered such an escape, and the data on remarriage show that many widows of substance—whatever fate befell their poorer sisters—were presumably free to avoid a remarriage and that they did exercise this negative freedom. But for some women the abrupt and short step from marriage into widowhood had awkward and even dangerous aspects. Their husbands not only left them alone to face an uncertain future, but his identity, and sometimes the occasion and manner of his death, carried peculiar problems and risks. We see this with particular clarity when we look at some aristocratic widows, but again it seems possible that analogous dilemmas confronted women at other social levels. Later we will look at some of the problems related to the recovery of property and dower shares. But there might be even more basic difficulties, and they could befall her while her grief was freshest, her life most disorganized.

Thomas, lord Bardolf, died of wounds after the battle of Bramham Moor in February, 1408. Because he had been a rebel against Henry IV, he suffered the posthumous fate of being quartered and of having the sections of his body displayed in various parts of the realm, *pour encourager les autres*. In April, 1408 his wife petitioned to recover the grisly segments and to give them decent burial. On 13 April, 1408 the king ordered the sheriffs of London, Lincoln (where the head was on display), Lynn, and Shrewsbury to take the relics down from the city gates and to permit burial.[48] Hardly a cheerful beginning to a widowhood that poor Amice Bardolf— who began life quite comfortably as lord Cromwell's daughter—was to preserve until her own death in 1421.

Bardolf's fate was unpleasant but not especially hazardous for his widow, though it may be easier to assert this from a safe distance than it was in 1408. But sometimes the risks were patently closer. After Richard Neville, earl of Warwick, was killed at Barnet in 1471 his widow, Anne, "appears to have expected no justice at the hands of King Edward, and to have seen little safety even for her person."[49] Her own vast inheritance, as the Beauchamp heiress, was gobbled up by her undutiful sons-in-law, the royal dukes of Clarence and of Gloucester, "as if the said countess were not naturally dead."[50] In the mid-1470s she may well have suffered some form of house arrest, at the hands of Richard of Gloucester. Not until 1487, 14 years after she had left her original sanctuary at Beaulieu for what turned out to be genteel captivity (reminiscent of that in which several of the dowager queens had been held), did an act of parliament reunite the dowager countess and her rightful lands. But even now all was less than milk and honey, and Dugdale says that "it appears that the same year by a special feoffment . . . she conveyed it wholly unto the King, entailing it upon the issue male of his body, with remainder to herself and her heirs."[51] Granted, these tribulations were most unusual, and they are better seen as part of the special risks of those of exceptionally high rank rather than of widows *per se*. But they likewise indicate that neither sex nor status was an absolute protection, and that of all society's vulnerable groups, widows could be among those with the fewest safe resources and the fewest reliable friends.[52]

These political problems, and all others to a lesser extent, were not ones that husbands deliberately imposed, but rather ones that happened to befall the woman, as her husband's *other*, as the silent partner in whatever had been his business, his partisanship. This whole discussion of her new status emphasizes how directly it sprang from his last views of her future. Eventually, of course, the dower share would (usually) be turned over, and she could slowly begin to assert herself, to build whatever sort of new life she could have. But at first it was very much a case of his control, his plans, his conditions. Her first transitional steps from marriage into widowhood usually were negotiated with his voice still ringing in her ears, his conditions weighing upon her shoulders. Insofar as the jaunty and free wheeling widow of literary depiction was a reality, the chances are that it was a persona she only came to develop and enjoy with the passage of time. The date on the remarriages of the aristocratic widows show that most who did remarry did so fairly soon, within five years or less. Those who did not remarry had anywhere from one or two to forty or fifty years of survival, and their styles as single figures no doubt grew and matured over the years. Some women perhaps were turned away from subsequent marriages by their husbands' wishes and the burden of their husbands' conditions, and others might already have had their fill of the married state regardless of their husbands' testamentary sentiments and directions. But a husband's frequent injunctions against his wife's remarriage were hardly likely to help expand her choices or her freedom to pick among them. Late medieval society's repressive views of sex, of female chastity and celibacy, and of sexual subordination under a double standard could only have been amplified by such frequent words from the home front. Trust was frequently there, but hardly much encouragement for what we see as liberation and an expansion of life's possibilities. Few wives received the personal reinforcement that lady Daubeney got from her late husband, of whom it was reported, "forthwithe the said knyghte wt oute ony tarrying saide my wyf shal haue hit. This was his last wille."[53]

Dower Shares and Survival

In theory, society wanted its widows to be well provided for. It spoke, through the voice of the common law and in the diversity of local custom, of a generous dower share, a widow's portion that was to represent one-third of the late husband's real property or a larger proportion if he had held in burgage tenure. Though young widows with children to raise might not find this overly generous, the same share befell those without such responsibilities. And, of course, the real question went beyond the counsel of law: What was the size of the pie from which one-third was about to be sliced, how accessible were the dower holdings, and could she realize the resources without falling back upon intermediaries who would profit at her expense from their labors? Even at the top, the dower share of an aristocratic or landed estate was not only a large block of land(s), but carried with it dominion over that servile infrastructure that worked the land and over that bureaucratic one that served to funnel those profits upwards. In contrast, the widow's share of a struggling artisanal enterprise, let alone of a cottar or villein's marginal holdings, was hardly the magic carpet leading to the new life of independence, affluence, and seasonal pilgrimages with the rich and famous of the fifteenth century. Many a bourgeois widow survived and even prospered, but only by dint of hard work and through the realization of organizational skills the possession of which may have been a surprise even to her, let alone to those around her. The range of possible futures across the topography of the realm was immense, and in perhaps no other aspect of widowhood was the locality and sociolegal setting as important as it was in setting the economic table for her opportunities and her problems.[54]

As the widow was a virtually ubiquitous figure in society, so presumably were dower divisions and shares among the landholding classes.

When the peers conducted a self-assessment of their landed incomes in 1436 they provided a list of the men and women who were holding the baronial estates of the realm.[55] The list contains the names of 68 parties—47 men, one set of feoffees, and 20 women, in control of the 51 baronies. Some of the 20 women held land by virtue of their status as independent heiresses, and a few were direct recipients of special royal grants, made in deference to their high status. But most of them figured on the list because, as peers' widows, they held dower shares of their late husbands' patrimonial estates. Their incomes varied considerably, as did those of the peers themselves, and there were financial and social light years between the £1,958 that Anne, dowager countess of Stafford, was to receive annually, or the £1,333 of Margaret, dowager duchess of Clarence, and Elizabeth Audley's dower holding worth but £100 *per annum*, or that of Margaret Clinton, evaluated at £52 *per annum*. Nevertheless, at a time when the peerage was pretty much in command of English government and society, almost 25 percent of the ranks of the high and mighty consisted of wealthy widows.

If widows were such a strong and common thread at the very top of the pyramid, then surely their presence and their role in towns, villages, and through the countryside could likewise be tracked were the data available. For any given family—at any level of affluence—there was a reasonable correlation between a series of short-lived men and long-lived widows, on the one hand, and the weakening of that family's grip upon its always precarious social and political perch, on the other. In looking at patriarchs we had occasion to discourse on the dangers, to the family as an entity, of early death and too many minors. Early death and too many long-lived widows posed a comparable set of hurdles. We can see this for some aristocratic families. Thomas Fitzalan, Earl of Arundel, died at Harfleur in 1415, aged 36. His widow, Beatrice of Portugal, lived until 1439. Thomas' heir, his second cousin John, died in 1421 (also aged 36), again leaving a widow who long outlived him (Eleanor Berkeley, d. 1455). John's heir was his son John, who died in 1435, and whose widow died in 1436. This means that for a short period immediately after June, 1435, when the younger John had died, three dowager countesses were on the scene, each holding a share of a share of the Fitzalan estates. Young John's heir, Humphrey, died when aged nine, in 1439, and his heir was his uncle, William, who lived from 1417 until 1487. By the time William was summoned to Lords in 1441 the widows' knots were beginning to come unraveled, the dowagers were finally passing away. But we can readily see how, for some years, the family had been forced, by the diverging fortunes of male and

female demography and longevity, to acquiesce in a protracted partition-
ing of its extensive but finite landed resources. The Mowbray dukes of
Norfolk and the lords Roos offer similar stories of young men, old women,
and dower holdings that just went on and on, invariably to the detriment
of the family's overall position.[56]

The dower pendulum could also swing the other way, and a man
awaiting a landed inheritance might have good luck when it came to the
deaths of the dowager ladies. Richard, duke of York, moved to recover his
vast complex of estates, in 1432, when he was a few months short of his
legal majority.[57] While a year or two earlier he might have feared a future
very like that which faced the three consecutive earls of Arundel, the situation changed rapidly, and steadily in his favor. On 19 July, 1432 he confirmed the dower share of the huge block of Mortimer estates held by his
uncle's widow. But she was dead before 26 September, and by 20 November, 1432, he was incorporating her lands, "notwithstanding that no inquisition of the premises after the death of the said Anne has been returned
into chancery, and that the said Duke has not proved his age."[58] So exited
a dowager countess on his mother's side. His father's side of the family
proved just as obliging regarding two dowager duchesses. York's grandfather, Edmund Langley (d. 1402), had been twice married, and his second
wife, Joan Holland, was now considerate enough to die in April, 1434. This
freed lands that she had been holding for a generation. Richard's uncle,
Edward (d. 1415), had also left a widow, Philippa Mohun, who had also
just recently departed from the scene, in July, 1431. So in this case a great
inheritance was quickly consolidated, its lord now able to finance his serious role in the adult (and male) world that stretched before.[59]

The perspective of this discussion of widows and their stubborn reten-
tion of their dower holdings is very much the perspective of the men, waiting to recover and to reunite their full patrimony. It defines widows as
obstacles and impediments, their long lives as but trials to be borne or
outlasted, often with little sympathy or patience. But from the widow's
point of view the matter of acquiring and keeping the dower share was
neither inequitable nor particularly easy. It was very well for the law to say
that she was entitled to her full share, for life, of the late husband's estates.
Even when there were no legal, political, or genealogical obstacles to
tangle the process, full recovery relied upon the smooth mesh of many
gears of government—at central and at local levels—and some time was
sure to pass before all could be accomplished. John, IV lord Darcy, died
on 2 December, 1411, and his will was probated on 18 February, 1412. On 14

June, 1412 Margaret, his widow, petitioned for £40 per annum from his estate, "in consideration of her poor estate and because she has the charge of maintenance of one son and four daughters who are not yet married or otherwise promoted." But there were other commitments, and Henry IV had promised his friend, Henry, lord Fitzhugh, £100 per annum from these lands, as Fitzhugh "has laboured so much for the king." By late October 1412 young Philip Darcy, John's son and heir, was being allowed to receive some revenues from his lands, filtered through the hands of their new warden, Thomas Darcy. Finally, on 11 November, 1412—almost a full year after her husband's death—Margaret was assigned her dower share. She had a full taste of the life of the aristocratic widow, and before July, 1421 she had remarried, to Sir Thomas Swyneford of Kettlethorpe, Lincolnshire (perhaps John of Gaunt's step-son or the step-son's son). Swyneford died in 1432, and Margaret survived, now a widow throughout, until 1454.[60]

The bigger the matter at stake, the more complicated the process. A great dowager like Katherine Neville, widow of John Mowbray, II duke of Norfolk, had a dower partition that included lands scattered through Norfolk, Suffolk, Surrey, Sussex, Essex, Hertforshire, Salop and the Welsh marches, Warwickshire, Leicestershire, Middlesex, Nottinghamshire, Derbyshire, and Bedfordshire and Buckinghamshire. Her recovery of her share proceeded with proper dispatch: the duke had died on 19 October, 1432, and by 18 Feburary, 1433, the various escheators were being ordered to give the duchess her livery.[61] Nor was her firm hold loosened, nor her charms diminished, by her subsequent marriages to Sir Thomas Strangeways, to John, viscount Beaumont (killed at Northampton in 1460), and ultimately to the young John Wydeville.

Eventually the dower share fell to the widow, the "system" worked, and if the share were sizeable she was henceforth economically free to pick up whatever life awaited her as an affluent widow. But the tale of women's lives, like that of true love, runs smoothly only in the infrequent instance. The records—admittedly more attuned to reflecting the problems of life than its many instances of easy passage—offer frequent glimpses into the woes of widows regarding dower: it was too small, they could not recover and take control of it, they were already deeply in debt, they were being overborne by rapacious guardians, and similar difficulties, all too familiar to the woman who was without power and without a male partner. We saw how long it took lady Darcy to recover her lands. Given that the Darcy estate was only valued at £121 in 1436, it is not surprising that the widow had to petition for immediate help, nor that the king was willing to allow, "in consideration of her poor estate and because she has the charge of maintenance of two sons and four daughters who are not yet married or otherwise promoted, of £40 yearly from the issues . . . late of her said husband."[62]

Nor was poverty (or alleged poverty) the only source of an embarrassing public scrutiny of a widow's life. Before they received their dower, widows could be ordered to take an oath that they would not remarry without the king's permission,[63] and at least one poor woman was set a task more typical of modern bureaucracy, that is, the need to demonstrate in 1400 that a marriage consummated back in 1392 and now ended by death had been a legal one.[64] But as with lady Darcy, poverty and the obligations of life without a partner, burdens that were both financial and psychological, were sharp spurs. Lady Neville put the matter with no little poignancy, as she made the familiar plea: "To the grete hurte and hevynesse and uttermost undoing of your Suppliaunte, considering that she hath not whereof to finde hir her children and servauntes."[65]

The quest for the rightful share of the real property was a critical one for women at all social levels. The varying levels of success and the varying degrees of ease with which success was realized are just further testimonials to the series of dependencies and dependent conditions that formed such a large part of a woman's life experience. Not infrequently the obstacles were indeed overcome, and sometimes women found chivalrous (or interested) friends and relations who would put in a crucial word when it was needed. We have looked at the dangers some widows incurred because of their husbands' political stance. Needless to say, such women could run into further problems regarding their cut of the property. But sometimes—as when the widow of the traitor happened to be the king's sister—such haste and consideration could be shown so that her standard of living barely dipped. The duke of Exeter was attainted on 14 January, 1400. His widow, Elizabeth, was granted 1,000 marks, for maintenance, almost immediately, out of cash and goods available in the exchequer. By the summer of 1400 she was receiving some of her late husband's lands. By the end of 1400 (before 12 December), she had married Sir John Cornwaille, and they were soon petitioning, together, for 200 marks' worth of land, of which Elizabeth was "dowable," notwithstanding Exeter's sentence of forfeiture or for any other impediment.[66] She lived, no doubt in considerable style, until 1425. Some widows had an easier time getting over their tragedy with its accompanying practical problems than others.

High born ladies could enlist this kind of support, and dower might be readily realized, thanks in part to "the advice and assent of the lords spiritual and temporal, and at the special request of the commons in Parliament."[67] And when the mills of government ground too slowly, a powerful woman might get interim support, as with "the arrears of the annual grant of 20 marks a day to sustain her dignity."[68] We suspect that such boons were reserved, if not exclusively for the highest and mightiest, at least for those with influential friends and relatives. Many more women may have been driven to litigate, through years of poverty, and success might never have been forthcoming; borrowing and cadging from relatives was also a universal tactic in times of need.

The records of the king's chancery and of the City of London reveal a further side to the complicated quest for the recovery of the dower share. When a widow sued for and was allowed to receive her proper portion, she might have to produce sureties before the escheator, parties who would stand as guarantors of her honesty and as assentors to the transaction. There were the parties with an interest in the full estate, perhaps represented by their attorneys or other relatives. Sometimes they might be the widow's own children, for example, a son or a married daughter and the son-in-law. The law made such parties potential rivals, if not adversaries to their mother, and sometimes family feeling was stretched by necessity or ambition. For her to acquire what the law accorded only by means of a proceeding where she obtained the assent of such parties as her own children certainly argues strongly for her lesser and dependent status. Typifying such a transaction is the entry contained in the *Calendar of the Close Rolls* for 1405, when the escheator of Gloucester was instructed, "In presence of Lewis Grevylle, son and heir of William Grevylle of Campeden and of full age, to assign to Edward Benstede and Joan, his wife, who was wife of the said William, dower of her husband's lands."[69] In this case the operative words concerning the son's role are "in presence of." Sometimes the widow's diminished or controlled individuality is brought home to us by the telling phrase, "as with the assent of" her son.[70] Nor does the presence of two sons-in-law and a daughter exactly enhance her dignity and independence. She was to give her oath, "in the presence of John More, who has taken to wife Alice, one of the daughters of her late husband, and of John Harecourt, who has married Anne, a second daughter, and of Margaret Deschalers, the third daughter."[71]

Nor were close relatives the only ones who might be involved in the supervisory procedure. Margaret Holland, sister and heir of the earl of

Kent, was the widow of John Beaufort, earl of Somerset (d. March, 1410). In October of that year the wheels of government had finally turned so that she was about to come into her own. The extensive dower lands involved in this proceeding, lying in Leicester, Cambridge, Northampton, Middlesex, Lincoln, Somerset, Dorset, and London, were to be assigned to her "in the presence of the next friends of Henry, son and heir of John, earl of Somerset, or of their attorneys."[72] The widow's oath might be rendered "in the presence of the next friends of Simon Blunt, son and heir of her husband, a minor in ward of the king, or of *their* attorneys."[73] Other combinations and other parties also had their day: "the next friends of Joan and Elizabeth, infant daughters . . ." or "in the presence of brother and heir of the said William . . ." or "in the presence of Robert Sterne, son of Joan, sister of the said John, being his cousin and next heir, or of his attorneys."[74]

All, however, was not impoverishment and degradation. Widows of men who had held offices of the crown, or who had been in business, could even receive dower shares and income that were drawn from resources other than his real property. Agnes Whetyden's husband had received revenues from the farm of Canterbury, and she was to be allowed 44s. 8d. per annum from this source, 14s. 10d. at Easter, 29s. 10d. at Michaelmas.[75] Small stuff, on the national scale, but presumably important in its lesser context. Robert Savage had been keeper of the wardrobe in the city of London, and the widow was told that the office could now be "occupied by herself or by deputy," with issues and profits coming from the duchy of Cornwall.[76] At his death Thomas Ratforde had been owed £1,082 17s. 2d. by the king's government, and to help her realize this sum, the widow was given a French prisoner of war, being held in the tower, as one of her dower resources.[77] John Walden's widow had to surrender his share of a tenement lease in London, but she immediately received it back, "for a term of 4 years at the same rent as formerly."[78] One London fishmonger's widow argued successfully that she, as well as her late husband, had been "a merchant sole," and she was therefore allowed to "enjoy the benefits of the custom relating to the same."[79]

Dying husbands often became pious and sentimental as they entrusted their young children to their widows. How a widow actually managed these responsibilities is harder to judge. As part of her financial responsibilities, the children sometimes appear in the guise of further causes of her distress, as lady Darcy had claimed in her tearful (and successful) petition. Children also enter the records when their custody, and its accompanying share of the patrimony, were officially placed in the hands of their mother, often acting now in concert with her *new* husband. Seen in this fashion, the children and the duties they entailed were not necessarily a further burden of widowhood, and their new fostering arrangement reminds us of how much happier society was when she reassumed her dependent and vicarious role, that is, when she remarried (with an appropriate partner). Dying husbands might not want wives to recommit themselves, but most others probably did. Though the *Letter Books of the City of London* record innumerable instances of the mother (as a widow) being formally granted the guardianship over and the patrimony of her own children,[80] it was no doubt preferable when the awarding of the youngsters could be made to such a couple as "John Adenard, mercer, who had married Johanna, widow of the said Simon," along with his wife.[81] But it was a tough world, and the corporation of London was not inclined to give anything away. When the guardianship of three children was granted to their mother and stepfather, it might only be for five years, "if the said orphans so long live and are not married."[82] When the patrimony was supposedly worth £1,000, the mother could not only choose to be the guardian, but might be happy to exercise control, "until the said orphan reached the age of twenty-four years."[83] The son's assumption of full majority, delayed though it might be, would probably put a wrinkle in her own financial position.[84] Among the aristocracy the widow would often have at least a share in the guardianship, whereas at the bottom of the ladder the trick was rather to find anyone willing to assume responsibility.

Later we shall look at the widows' movement toward remarriage. They remarried for any number of reasons, we may imagine, but one was simply that a single woman's life was not an easy one. The private life of a widow might be all too public. Sexual activity between widows and clergymen seemed a likely possibility, in a society of many single women and many unmarried (if not celibate) clerics. Some reported incidences of misconduct suggest an interest by others that seems more prurient than disinterested or public spirited. The beadle of Lymstreet ward in London told of a chaplain, celebrating in St. Botolph's church, who was taken in adultery with a widow, as it was so quaintly put.[85] A chaplain of St. George's, Puddinglane was caught with a widow at about 11 at night, while another was found with Margaret Ryver, "other called 'Shepster' " at 3 o'clock in the morning.[86] Were the neighbors more concerned about widows' behavior, or clerical morality, or trysts held after curfew?

Presumably upon remarriage the new couple followed the economic fortunes of the more prosperous and settled partner, which was not invariably the new husband. This means that in some instances they resided in *her* house, and that he labored to keep up *her* business or to till *her* fields. But the new marriage might also mean a change in her role and position, moving her away from a former residence and from her accustomed level of dignity and solidity. A peculiar problem encountered by some urban widows arose when their late husband's apprentices sued for their freedom, because "she had not provided him or instructed him in the trade of her late husband."[87] Another apprentice won his freedom, since she "kept no shop" and so had failed to keep her side of the original bargain.[88] A chandler's widow "did not carry on the trade and could not instruct him or present him for the freedom when his term was completed."[89] These laconic entries give the impression that sometimes a widow had to close down the old concern and perhaps suffer a corresponding loss of income and status. At least in the last quoted case the complaint was against the widow and the new husband, a man "who had no shop within the franchise," but who perhaps could provide for her from other forms of endeavor.[90]

This glimpse at the fortunes and fates of some widows is not meant to depict a scene of unremitting gloom or of unceasing struggle. Rather, it seeks to show that many women had very attractive possibilities, as widows, but that the realization of the possibilities was hardly automatic. The law's delay and the insolence of office compounded the personal and familial burdens of widowhood that the average married woman was likely to be called upon to assume at least once in her lifetime. If she were in financial trouble, or if his business were one that she could not readily step into on her own, or if resources were tied to place or specific skills or offices, the woes were apt to be that much greater. Many widows made a smooth and profitable transition, and so enjoyed their new status that they remained permanent residents of the far-flung kingdom of widowhood. Others visibly suffered at each step along the road of pain. Long before the period we have been discussing, St. Hugh of Lincoln had returned a widow's ox, to which he was entitled as bishop of Lincoln, after the death of her husband. His steward took him to task, as the foil to the saint is expected to do in hagiographic literature. But St. Hugh responded: "This woman has but two workfellows; death has robbed her of the better and shall we rob her of the other? God forbid that we should be so covetous; for she doth more deserve our consolation in this moment of supreme affliction, than that we should vex her further."[91] When we reflect upon the frequency with which a Hugh of Lincoln surfaced in a position of administrative responsibility, we have an index of the likelihood of such charitable treatment being meted out on a regular basis.

Family Situations and Patterns of Life

We have been talking of widowhood as though it were a very simple matter: they married, he died, she was left behind, a widow. In addition, the data and the situations we have been dealing with mostly focus upon the incidence of widowhood. Life was more complicated, and in many instances women married over and over, so even the incidence of widowhood was not always a unique life experience. The life patterns of some women could become very complex, and mountains of strategy, advice, and decision making must be veiled by the clouds of time. The problems that arose with each instance of widowhood were solved or dealt with, by some women, by withdrawal from further domestic entanglements, and by others through remarriage, a remarriage that in turn could open the door to further widowhood.

To a considerable extent, women's lives must be seen as dependent variables, caught between the stronger legal and social forces personified by fathers, husbands, brothers, and guardians. Some women struggled—and with a marked and commendable degree of success—to swim against the traditional currents of patriarchal domination, and battles for some reasonable measure of equality and of independent dignity were no doubt fought and won at all levels of society. Some women waged their struggle before marriage, some while in wedlock, and many after their partner's demise. Some women emerged from a terminated marriage with a reasonable share of worldly goods, with some mark of their late partner's trust, and with some form of family estate or business to which they could now turn a guiding hand. Many of these women never remarried: We can only hope that their status was respected, their rewards commensurate with their efforts.

But to judge from the aristocracy about half of a group of widows would remarry.[92] Whatever the supposed freedom and opportunity of the widow's independent status, about as many abandoned it as chose to remain within its embrace. Widowhood, after all, was an involuntary state into which one had fallen. Some women chose to remain there, some perhaps either had no choice or died before they could alter the situation. Others moved with reasonable dispatch to leave it and to reenter the most paradigmatic form of adult male-female relationships, marriage. We have a reasonable amount of data concerning the widows of the 262 peers summoned to the House of Lords, through the course of the fifteenth century, and we can analyze their patterns of remarriage. But even the formulation of this question is not as clear-cut as it might seem. Of the 160 women who emerge as the widows of these peers, there are still problems of classification. How do our tallies take into account the life patterns of the 29 women who had had prior marriages with commoners? or the 45 women who went from the critical aristocratic marriage to a subsequent marriage with a commoner? or the 28 widows whose remarriage was with another peer of the realm?[93]

Can a comparable spread of behavior be projected for other groups of women, at other levels of society? No clear line of argument is all-convincing. On the one hand, rich women had the substance to maintain and support an independent status, if they so chose. But at the same time, they were also extremely attractive, in a financial if not in a personal sense, with dower shares, their own wealth as heiresses (as were 36 percent of the peers' widows, in their own right), and the extensive personal property we have seen being transmitted and directed through many a husband's will. We have encountered landed widows, with dower shares from one or two marriages, and we have looked at urban widows, with a going business and perhaps some years of guardianship over well-heeled and very young children. The new husband could expect to share her portion of the old husband's patrimony. Women at other social levels did not need the duchess of Norfolk's great estates to be considered comely, and a widow's inheritances from a London shoemaker or brewer could be more than ample. As we move downwards in socio-economic terms, the plight of the unattached woman no doubt becomes bleaker, her potential for a material contribution to another marriage steadily diminishes. But it was a relative matter, and a garden plot, help for a village widower with child-care obligations, and companionship in bed and at the table may have been enough for young or even middle aged widows, if luck ran with them and they sought remarriage.

Because of the relative abundance of material about the top rungs of society, the ranks of the peeresses are the ones that provide us with our best glimpses into the tangled and complicated lives that many women wound up leading (or following). To go with some of them through their marital careers is to get a good view of the distinctions between the male life pattern and the female. The man's course was usually a fairly straightforward affair. Assuming he married and had children, he went through life with a clear direction or model, and he followed the patriarchal path from childhood onwards until he reached the moment when he had to dictate his testamentary instructions. His identity remained the same, the children of his marriage(s) were his children. He followed his father, and he in turn set the course for his son-and-heir. But not so for the woman. When she married she usually left her original home and family. She changed her surname, and to a considerable extent this connotes a change of ego-identity as well as of social role. This was true when she married for the first time, and again if she remarried in her widowhood—a process that might occur two or three times in the course of her life. Who, indeed, was she? Which name was her *real* name, which self her *real* self? Furthermore, the lives of her mother and of older sisters were not apt to be models she could follow, as they too had scattered, and now belonged, to some extent, to other families with other webs of kinship and reciprocity. Thus, when we talk of the widows of the peers, we seem to be making a simple reference to a fair sized universe of women who just married and subsequently outlived a peer. But beyond the mere incidence of widowhood stands a vast arsenal of social history, stocked with a great variety of complex life patterns that are hidden by our resort to generic terminology.

There were some fairly exotic life patterns among the aristocratic widows, particularly those woven by women with three or four marriages. A little unraveling shows this to some advantage. John Fitzalan or John d'Arundel was a cadet of an old aristocratic family, and he was summoned to Lords in 1416 as the earl of Arundel. Upon his death in 1421 (at age 36), he left a youngish widow, Eleanor Berkeley, daughter of Sir John Berkeley of Beverstone and of Elizabeth, daughter and heir of Sir John Betteshorne of Sopley, Hampshire. At his death John Arundel and Eleanor had been married for some 14 or 15 years, and their marriage had produced at least two sons. With her husband's death Eleanor enters our universe of aristocratic widows: She has already made one successful social jump as an heiress from the wealthy gentry into a cadet but rising branch of an old noble house, and she will figure in the family genealogies as the mother and grandmother of future earls of Arundel.[94] However, there was to be no withdrawn and quiet widowhood for her. She was still a young woman, with most of the race yet to run. Within two years of Arundel's death she married Sir Richard Poynings, son and heir of lord Poynings. However, Sir Richard died in 1430, still in his father's lifetime, so Eleanor accumulated little by way of new titles or dower holdings from her second marriage.

Before the end of the decade, however, she has married again, this time to Walter, lord Hungerford. She was his second wife, and now the step-mother to the four sons and one daughter he had had by his marriage to Katherine Peverall, an heiress from Cornwall. Hungerford died in 1449, aged 71, while Eleanor lived until 1455. Later we will look at her again and try to assess how she handled her many identities and roles as a transient member of three important families (plus her family of origin). It suffices here to note how she entered and left a string of different and fairly important families throughout the course of her life.

Obviously, such a pattern of life experience was more complex than the average one. But at least 29 of the aristocratic widows married three or more times, and Eleanor Berkeley's career has several dozen analogues. Such lives almost always had to be long ones, and not infrequently the oft-married peeress still wound up a widow at the end, as did Eleanor. Joan Cobham was the granddaughter (through her mother) and heiress of John, lord Cobham of Kent, who died a very old man in 1408. Joan had married Sir Robert Hemenhale of Norfolk before 1380, and he was dead by 1391. She then married Reynold Braybroke, who died in 1405. Next came Sir Nicholas Hauberk, wed in 1406, buried in 1407. John Oldcastle—summoned to Lords as lord Cobham and executed as a Lollard in 1417—was her husband from 1408 until his death, and his heterodox behavior landed her in some serious trouble for a while.[95] Finally, she married Sir John Harpenden, still alive and her spouse at the time of her death in 1434. She was buried at Cobham, with Braybroke, the father of most of her children, along with her own paternal ancestors. She outlived all of her sons; eventually her daughter Joan Braybroke, who married Sir Thomas Brooke, was her heiress. What a confusing identity. The Wife of Bath made light of a comparable career, but dead sons by two husbands, plus her imprisonment while her fourth husband was an outlawed and hunted heretic, rather spoiled some of the fun. Katherine, duchess of Norfolk, likewise may have had moments of less than hilarity, and we have briefly looked at her storm-tossed marital career. She began life as one of Ralph Neville's daughters, and she had 20 years of marriage to John Mowbray, II duke of Norfolk, before his death in 1432. Then she married Sir Thomas Strangeways, though they had to seek a royal pardon for marriage without a license. Then, after Strangeway's death, she married John, viscount Beaumont, as his second wife. He fell, one of the Lancastrian casualties at Northampton, in July, 1460. In 1463 Edward IV forced Katherine to marry the young John Wydeville, one of his queen's brothers. But this last move was part of the king's counterproductive efforts to elevate his in-laws, rather than a normal marriage negotiation. Contemporaries had no hesitation in labeling the union a "maritagium diabolicum."[96]

A number of these aristocratic widows with complex life patterns have left wills. How did such women identify themselves? And how can we sort them out regarding their views towards family involvement, loyalty, and identification? Eleanor Arundel-Poynings-Hungerford, née Berkeley, has left us her will.[97] She begins by identifying herself as lady Mautravers and Hungerford, a style that commemorates or denotes her rank from her first and her third marriages. She asked for burial with John Arundel, her first husband, at Arundel College, one of his family's pet foundations. She left bequests to her son William Arundel and his wife, Joan Neville, daughter of the earl of Salisbury. In addition, her daughter, Eleanor Poynings, now married to Henry Percy—soon to become VIII earl of Northumberland—received £100 and such personal items as a silver basin with the Poynings family arms gilded thereon. Then there were bequests to her step-son, Robert Hungerford, now lord Hungerford and Moleyns, and to Robert's wife, Margaret. Since Hungerford had been forced to pay a bankrupting ransom for his release from French captivity, Eleanor's bequest of 100 marks and the wool of her Heytesbury manors was welcomed as more than a token bequest.[98] Finally, in a slightly unusual touch, she remembered her family of origin: her brother, Sir Maurice Berkeley, his wife Laura, their son Maurice, plus two other nephews. These recipients were to receive the usual mixture of cash, personal items, and household furnishings. Her brother was also given some silver work on which were the Hungerford arms, plus some jewelery that Eleanor had received from their parents. Nephew Edward Berkeley would get 100 marks if he married with the consent of Eleanor's son William, now earl of Arundel. So in this case the will can be interpreted as a document of integration: in it Eleanor not only thought of all four of her families, but worked with her bequests and reciprocities to bring them together. If her most basic identity was ultimately as a Fitzalan, made by her first marriage the mother of subsequent earls of Arundel—as witness her burial site and the roles given to those children—there was no rejection of any of her other roles or identities. In fact, by putting a Fitzalan son in charge of a Berkeley nephew, she was making a bold attempt at knotting together some of the separate strands. But she was opting for the most important family of the four, and she may also have been signaling that her first marriage was her major life transition or experience.

Most women, however, were a bit less inclusive. Some made choices for rather obvious reasons, such as of status and prestige or in keeping with the chronological order of marriage, and some followed personal motives that can be guessed at but are not made explicit. George Neville, IV lord Abergavenny, married, as his second wife, a woman who was already thrice a widow. Elizabeth Neville had been married to a Lord Mayor of London, who died around 1480, then to Richard Naylor of London, whose will was probated in 1483, then to John Stoker of St. George's, Eastcheap, whose will was probated in 1485, and only then to Neville. He died in September, 1492; she, in 1500. Her will, with only a few personal and family bequests, asks for burial with Naylor, in St. Martin's, Outwich, London. Thus her last marriage—and the one that puts her among our ranks of aristocratic widows—was clearly a fairly short one (lasting but some five to seven years), as it was childless (though Neville had had six sons and two daughters by his first marriage, to Margaret Fense, d. 1485), and could hardly have been a union of fireworks and rockets. On the other hand, Neville treated her decently enough, and in his own will he left her personal items and 40 marks, "so that she be comformeable and aggreable to the execucion and performans of this my last will."[99] But she was not among his six executors, and presumably she fell back in her remaining years upon the social circles of an earlier life.

The wills of these two aristocratic women offer some contrasts in the way widows might look upon themselves and upon the various families to which they had belonged. Usually the choices were less clear-cut, though they are almost always relatively easy to follow. The duke of Exeter's third wife took him as her third husband. But he made her an executor of his will,[100] and when her turn came she asked to be buried, by him, in St. Katherine's by the Tower, London, where he was already lying beside his first wife.[101] When the earl of Salisbury was lynched by a mob at Cirencester, in January 1400, he left a widow who had already buried two husbands of much lower rank. But she had also borne Salisbury at least five children, and she was content, now, to remain a rich dowager countess until her death in 1424. In this instance it comes as no surprise that she saw herself as a member of his family: burial at Bisham, prayers in that Montagu family house, bequests to her daughter Anne ("carissime filie mee"), and Anne named as an executor. But there were bequests for Alan Buxhill, her son by her first marriage and her legal heir.[102] John, lord Wenlock, died childless, killed at Tewkesbury in 1471. His widow, Agnes Danvers, had had two previous husbands, and she remarried yet again, to Sir John Say, speaker of the House of Commons in the parliaments of 1449, 1463–65, and 1467–68.[103] She asked for burial with her second husband, Sir John Fray, chief baron of the exchequer, at St. Bartholomew the Less, London. Children, grandchildren, and stepchildren all join the list of her beneficiaries, while her executors included a Henry Danvers, either a brother or a nephew. Since Wenlock had been a newly created peer, and was without children, his own cadet or collateral heirs were of little social importance.[104] Agnes would have had but limited reason, from a practical or material standpoint, to stick with off-shoots of her in-laws and her choice with her family of origin and with that of an earlier marriage is an understandable one. Philippa Mohun married Walter, IV lord FitzWalter (d. 1386), then Sir John Golafre (d. 1396), and then Edward, II duke of York (d. 1415). After that she rested, and was finally buried in Westminster Abbey, in 1431. She bore no children in any of her marriages, but her will remembers FitzWalter's stepchildren, and Thomas Chaucer and Sir John Cornwaille are among the executors. The duke of York had been brought home from Agincourt and buried at Fortheringay College in Northamptonshire. She solved the problem by presenting herself as a member of several families. Young Lord Fitzwalter, her stepson, was referred to as her son, while she emphasized her royal links by her choice of burial site.[105]

These wills all contain statements about self-identity, some expressed in words, some in strategies of testamentary disposition. The widows could be quite explicit when the matter interested them. Elizabeth, a daughter and co-heiress of the earl of Warwick, married a son of the earl of Westmorland. When she died, after outliving both the Neville spouse and a second husband, she asked for burial with her father and her son Harrie, "natural born" and killed at Edgecot, and her son-in-law, Oliver Dudley, in the traditional Beauchamp burial site of Our Lady, Warwick. George Neville's identity had been impressive, but her own was as good or even better.[106] Though many instances of multiple identity and even of competing identities can be found and deciphered, they may not be typical of the masses of poorer widows with less complicated lives. Many a woman of decent but modest substance was satisfied, or even proud, to be identified as her former husband's one-time partner. If one woman was content to begin her will as "ego Agnes Vaunce, vidua,"[107] another, with similar credentials, was a bit more elaborate: "Ego Johanna Est nuper uxor Willelmi Est de Radenache."[108] Former status was worth asserting: "I Agnes ye whilke was wyfe of Richard of Shirburn squier."[109] Widowhood, like matrimony, was an honorable estate.

For widows of property, remarriage involved more than self interest and a personal decision. Children, her dower share, and even the future of his patrimony were to be affected. And for women of political import, the king was among those with a concern in their future choice. Accordingly, we find that a number of well placed widows were obliged to buy licenses to remarry as they chose, and a number of others—along with their new husbands—paid fines (and even went to prison) for having remarried without the king's prior permission. This was a fairly common business, and one wonders why so many seemed to have had trouble complying with the standards of control that they should have known were apt to be imposed. Perhaps many other widows escaped surveillance, or took their chances against a system wherein fines and even the threat of severer penalties were always negotiable.

After Ralph, V lord Greystoke, died in 1487, his widow, Beatrice Hawcliff, obtained a royal license (in July 1490) to marry whomsoever she wished. She exercised her privilege with Robert Constable of York. And in her will, of 1505, after four years of a second widowhood, she too was prepared to make her testamentary bequests; to her own children and their spouses, to Constable's brother, and to a fair number of Hawcliff relatives. At least her efforts to obtain the license for remarriage had led to what appears to be a successful marriage and an integrated family life.[110] Sometimes widows remarried in haste and then, at a leisurely pace, sought pardons for their transgressions: Edward Brooke, lord Cobham, died in the autumn, 1464, and by 8 November, 1464, his widow, Elizabeth Tuchet, was pardoned for remarriage with Christopher Worsley, a servant of Edward IV's household.[111] Joan Fauconberg, whose idiocy or feeble mindedness was more than balanced by her status as the heiress of her father, remarried within two months of William Neville's death in 1463, and had to be pardoned for her rash act. Politics and economics, as we know, ran together and when Margery and John Cobeldyke were pardoned for marriage without a license, she was also given her dower share of her first husband's property.[112]

Permission to remarry was a form of social control, of power exercised over widows. It was a natural extension of old feudal controls that regulated the lives of those who held land and sizeable amounts of wealth. When such women and their new husbands chose to ignore the stick, it could land heavily upon them. At the top, the fine for remarriage without a license might reach the 2,000 marks the dowager duchess of Norfolk had had to pay after she took Sir Robert Goushill as her third husband.[113] Nor was this the full extent of royal anger. When the dowager countess of Oxford married Sir Nicholas Thorley, again as her third husband, the bridegroom spent time in prison before all was forgiven. What we cannot recover is any impression of how many marriages were never contracted, or just became casual liaisons, because of the heavy concern with activity that only gradually completed their odysseys from the public to the private realm.

One way of forestalling the problems posed by the wayard widow was to extract a promise, in advance, that she would not remarry without royal permission. Obviously, one could not put too much trust in any future course of action, even if she had "taken of her an oath that she will not remarry without the king's consent," but it was at least worth a try.[114] Of course, her feelings about taking the oath were not unrelated to her concern with the recovery of the dower share.[115] Such high and mighty ladies as the duchess of Buckingham had to take such oaths, along with others holding but modest worldly goods and aspirations.[116]

There is little impression that fifteenth century- widows were systematically coerced into remarriage, though such pressure certainly existed and occasionally did shape a woman's future.[117] More pressure existed to check than to foster remarriage, and if we had to decide, the chances are that the widow was much freer to choose (or to reject) a partner than the maiden had been some years before, just as she was much abler to back up her personal inclination with cash to cover a license or a fine. Unlike their predecessors of the high middle ages, widows rarely seemed to have been forced to dig deeply just to stay unmarried. That a number of aristocratic widows made subsequent remarriages with men of lower social rank or origin does not by itself argue for love matches, but it does turn our thoughts in that direction. It likewise indicates that a woman of good background and with a reasonable dower had some freedom to move around, socially as well as geographically, and that her freedom could stretch a fair distance. Sometimes her family or her in-laws might view her next union as declasse, but in many instances she seems to have been free to follow her fancy with only limited regard for social categories.

Though many women did move down the social scale upon remarriage, we have seen enough instances of mobility in the opposite direction to check any idea that a widow was less attractive *per se*. Margaret Bromfleet was both an heiress (and a *de jure* claimant to the Vescy barony) and lord Clifford's widow when she married a mere county knight, Sir Thomas Threlkeld of Cumberland. Even very great ladies might be content to take a social plunge, and we have seen that when Henry IV's sister Elizabeth recovered her dower share of the duke of Exeter's estates she married Sir John Cornwaille. This marriage lasted from 1400 until her death in 1425 and it never carried much social cachet: Though he is referred to as lord Fanhope, he was not summoned to Lords until 1432. Among the aristocratic peeresses who married three or four times, some mix of titled and common husbands (usually of the rural gentry) was most often found. Neither was there any particular order in which the women moved from one social camp to the other as such ranks were represented by successive partners. But snobbery and social barriers were of concern, even in a world of reasonable mobility. When lord Roos's widow (Margery, the Despenser heiress in her own right) followed her inclination, a year or two after Roos had been killed at Beaugé in France in 1421, the allegations were that she had "married herself dishonorably without a license from the king."[118] She outlived, or lived with the stigma, for over half a century, and in her will of 1477 she left bequests to various children and grandchildren, plus a bequest of books and silver to Queen's College, Cambridge.[119]

Freedom of choice should not be overemphasized. Few people dance just to their own music, regardless of sex or social status. We can find occasions when widows complained about undue pressure: the vulnerability of the woman's social position always lies near the surface. A London woman complained of a bond that had been constructed in order to frighten her into marriage with one Robert Snell, "who thought her to be a widow."[120] If a widow claimed in the ecclesiastical courts that she had been coerced into remarriage and that she acquiesced through fear, she at least received a hearing.[121] However, we do not know whether she received her freedom. The complications of successive promises and of marriage and of remarriage could baffle the wise men at Lambeth (or of the Court of Arches), Westminster, and Rome. What can we say about her freedom in a case where originally she contracted a straightforward marriage. Then, in her husband's lifetime, she contracted a second and *de facto* marriage, *per verba similia*, and cohabited with the second man. Then the first husband died and she sued the second for divorce or nullification. The local authorities were not inclined to be helpful in her quest for freedom (to remarry again?), and the record only picks up her story when she was appealing to her bishop and to Rome.[122]

In theory, remarriage for the widow always remained an option she could pursue. Consequently, we can never say that she would never remarry, but rather that death sometimes just came before she managed to do so. However, we can look at those aristocratic widows who only married once (that is, who never remarried after the aristocratic husband died), and we can calculate the interval between the husband's death and their own. For some 91 aristocratic women, the duration of widowhood, or of ultimate widowhood, was as follows. Twenty-nine women outlasted the marriage for something between one and five years after their (last) husbands' deaths and their own, 17 survived by 6–10 years, 20 by 11–20 years, and 25 by 21 years or more. Since remarriage for women of the aristocracy (and probably for those of other social groups or categories, had we the data) usually took place within five years of their husbands' deaths, we have here a group of widows who mostly would never have remarried: 50 percent remained widows for over a decade, and some for an impressive duration. Clearly, for all our scepticism about the advantages of freedom a woman earned in this fashion, prolonged widowhood was often her preferred alternative.

Did the widows in the course of these tangled and dependent lives get lost? We can look at their Inquistions Post Mortem and at their wills in order to get some idea of their family situations, and to gauge whether the currents pushing them towards alienation, loneliness, and anomie were met and matched by benign countercurrents carrying them towards family and support networks. By definition widows had lived longer than their husbands. This means, at their deaths, that their mutual heirs were older than such folk had been at the moment of the husband's death. Accordingly, such heirs were more likely to be of legal age, more likely sometimes even to be dead. Did this now give us a universe of an old (or older) woman, cut off by time and mortality, from close kin and old friends? Or was it rather one of easy companionship, in contrast to the toils and burdens she perhaps had been forced to assume at that bleak earlier moment when he had died?

Table III-1 shows the heirs of the widows as reported by the juries in the Inquisitions for Yorkshire and Nottinghamshire, and for the chancery of Henry VII, 1485–1500. We see here a heavy proportion of widows' heirs who were already of legal age at the moment of inheritance, that is, at the moment of her death. We expect the drift in this direction. The Table also reveals a heavy proportion of her children among the categories of heirs. In two-thirds of the cases, the heirs were children of her body (82 sons, 23 daughters, for 67 percent of the 156 widows), and in another 21 percent of the cases grandchildren were named as the next-of-kin. For children of the women's bodies, there were 15 sons and daughters aged 10 or below, 19

TABLE III-1   WIDOWS' HEIRS, FROM THE IPMs[a]

Heir	Age as given in IPM			Total	
	0–10	11–21	21+		
Son	12	17	59	88	55%
Grandchild	7	15	15	37	23%
Brother or sister	0	1	9	10	6%
Daughter	4	5	16	25	16%
Total	23	38	99	160	100%
	14%	24%	62%		

[a] The findings of the four sets of IPMs have been aggregated.

between 10 and full legal age (of 21), and 71 beyond their majority (68 percent of the 105). For the men reported in these Inquisitions, the proportion of direct heirs who were under age was considerably higher.[123]

Though the widows' own ages are not given in their Inquisitions, those of their heirs appear as a regular feature, and aged heirs mean a high incidence of aged widows. In the Chancery Inquisitions for the first 15 years of Henry VII, we find instances of daughter-heiresses aged 60, of two sisters of 60 and 45, of three sisters of 48, 44, and 23, of two married sisters of 50 and 48; and of three married sisters of 50, 40, and 35. These figures clearly argue for mothers of 60 and 70 and 80, at least on occasion. They provide some statistical basis for the familiar vignette of the long-lived aristocratic widow and dowager, and they also extend this picture a bit farther down the social ladder. When Henry IV's dowager queen Joanna died in 1437, her heir was her son, the count of Brittany, listed in the English Inquisitions as being 50 and more.

In about half the cases where a daughter was named as heiress, she was the sole (or sole surviving) child, and in about half the cases, there were two or more girls to divide the property. To balance the picture of elderly widows succeeded by daughters in their 30s or 40s, there are other instances of women being succeeded by groups of younger daughters: girls of 17, 15, and 13; of 9, 7, and 4; of 9, 6, and 3.[124] Some left daughters of middling age, of 30 and 26 or thereabouts. The age of the grandchildren is a further argument for the relatively advanced age of many of the widows. Few of the grandchildren were really young, and 12 of the 33 were of legal age upon succession, with the oldest being identified as 30 and more. Of course, individual cases offer the usual range and variety. We find grandchildren of 31, or of 25, or the two married granddaughters of a widow, one now 36 and more, her sister 32 and more.[125]

There are a fair number of cases of "mixed heirs," where some combination of daughters and grandchildren—usually the sons or daughters of other daughters, now dead—were present for their joint claim upon the patrimony. The odd and mixed groups of heirs we saw for men also come forward, with outstretched hands, when widows were about to pass on their property. There are mixes of children and grandchildren, the sons and daughters of other children who had pre-deceased. A widow's heirs might be identified as a daughter and a daughter's son or a daughter of 30 and another's son, now 18. One woman left four granddaughters by one daughter, a great-grandson by another. Another left married daughters of 24 and more and 23 and more, plus two grandsons of 17 and 10, children of a third daughter, now dead. Younger women, clearly, left younger children. Katherine de la Pole left daughters: one had been nine on the previous 6 May, one seven on 22 July, and the youngest had turned four on 4 June last. This was peculiar as well as precise information, and its appearance is almost unique among the Inquisitions. A son's young daughters could also come in handy, and sisters of 13 and ¾ and of 11 might turn out to be first in line.[126]

The overall picture is that in about eight or nine cases of each 10 there would be a child or a grandchild as the widow's heir or closest kin. Thus we seem to have a universe of widows who give an indication of being integrated into some sort of multi-generational or lifelong family network, at least insofar as the existence of close relatives is a sign of good relations. Since the "other" categories of heirs were only mentioned in the Inquisitions when there were no children or grandchildren, their relative absence is no reliable guide as to the probable plenitude of siblings, nephews and nieces, cousins, and so forth. Their identity was simply screened from sight by the existence of the legally preferred heir or heiress. In those cases in which the jurors did name a sibling as the next heir, such a person was almost always of legal age. Given the necessary life pattern or biographical trail of the widow, this is to be expected. In addition, the sibling-heir need not have been younger than the sister who is at issue, unlike the sibling-heir of a man.

We saw that only a few men were so bereft of children and siblings that the search for the closest kin and heir had to reach far out into the circles of cousins, nephews, or nieces. But sometimes it was necessary, and so on occasion it was necessary with the widows. A great nephew or a resort to a first cousin was hardly a great stretch as families were counted. And to fall back upon a nephew of 50 or an aunt was even less so. But there were times when the quest reached more exiguous folk: a third cousin once-removed, or second cousins, or the division by three nieces (aged 30, 28, and 26). At the far end, we discover that women also ran the occasional risk of ultimate isolation. The jurors might return that "they do not know who is her next heir," or that "she died without an heir of her body," or—more tersely—that the next of kin is simply "unknown."[127]

Such statistical information about widows' heirs, for all their methodological and emotional shortcomings, helps fill in some background. Some widowhoods were short: the women whose heirs were their own minor children had obviously not survived their husbands by many years. Those men who died while expressing worries about children conceived but still in the womb obviously were reflecting on the not unlikely contingencies of an uncertain world. The lives of the surviving mothers, as well as those of the young or the unborn children, were clearly at high risk, and probably would be so for many years.

The Inquisitions Post Mortem looks for the single heir, the best next-of-kin, at the moment of her death. As with the husbands, the search in the legal process is only for the single successor or for a group of heirs, if they are sisters or daughters. But widows' wills speak of and to the wider network of family. The family and kinship web of their wills can run both to the three-generational horizontal family of the widow—her children, and her grandchildren—and outwards to that familiar horizontal network of siblings, nieces and nephews, and cousins. Like the wills of the men, widows' wills are both passive and active statements about kinship, in that they had to accept the relationships that were in existence, but wherein they also could exercise volition concerning beneficiaries, conditions of inheritance and transmission, and power to impose posthumous responsibilities and social control.

The widows' Inquisitions indicated that 67 percent of a group of such women of property had either a son or one or more daughters alive at the time of death. How do widows' wills complement such information? The questions for the wills are more complex and more interesting, for while the law only cared for the eldest son the woman herself was more likely to worry about all her sons and all her daughters. What can we learn from the wills about her links with her children, both regarding their numbers and their relationships and ties? By the time of her death her children were not the same as they had been at the time of her husband's death. They were older, of course, and by now they were apt to be the recipients of whatever settlement their father had made, whatever largesse he had ordered distributed amongst them. In addition the widow was more likely to be surveying a family of grown and married children who were by now trailing their own children along, and her testamentary dispositions were more concerned with personal goods and relationships than with the future of the patrimony.

The Inquisitions gave us a picture of widows that featured the customary presence of children, grandchildren, and siblings. As we read these sources, we posit a universe of women who were not, for the most part, condemned to live out their last years in isolation, bereft of relatives and family networks. Rather, we generally have widows who are surrounded by at least a modicum of close kin. It is possible that the class bias of the source makes us see an atypically high and helpful level of such support, mostly enjoyed by those of property, just as the Inquisitions may hide appalling tales of poverty and isolation for those beyond the pale of possession and material comfort. But whatever our suspicions, the data we do have are an historical artifact of some value, for at least some of the women, some of the time.

The wills of fifteenth-century widows are not so different from those of their husbands. We find the same worries over the inability to control the future and the same endeavors towards posthumous social control. We find testamentary conditions that reflect a concern over the uncertainties of demography and of survival and the imposition of conditions that reflect a desire to run children's lives. Some widows either had few relatives or chose to ignore them, and they left their money and goods instead to the church, friends, servants, and pious causes. Others had—and named in considerable detail—huge spreads of kinsfolk. There could be relations from a variety of marriages, from the family of her origin, from such groups as her children's in-laws, plus all the stepchildren and god-children she might have accumulated during a life of marriage and remarriage. The widows transmitted the same kinds of items as their husbands: personal goods, household and chapel furnishings, cash, jewelery, books, and all manner of items with a provenance or origin considered worthy of specific mention.

Men, with or without sons as their heirs, often distributed personal goods to a wide network of relations. They also constructed descending hierarchies of transmission; so land and goods would move on from son to son, to daughters, and then perhaps to nephews, and so forth, if and when each heir in turn died without children of his or her body. Widows, less encumbered by the need to build a base for the prosperity of the next generation, had or chose to exercise even more discretion and fewer constraints when they turned to distribute their goods to a wide network of kin. Elizabeth Gray, lady Fitzhugh, survived her husband by a couple of years and was buried beside him in Jervaulx Abbey. They had had a large family with at least four sons and five daughters who survived childhood. In her will, Lady Fitzhugh was appropriately expansive.[128] There were bequests for four sons and five daughters and two god-daughters (who may well have been granddaughters). Cash and personal goods were freely distributed, and the unmarried children were to divide the residue of the estate.[129] This all seems very natural. But it is matched by the comprehensive generosity of Elizabeth Scrope, who ended her life (in 1537) as the widow of both William, II viscount Beaumont, and of John de Vere, earl of Oxford. She had no children by either marriage, and therefore her will is as close as we can come to an exercise in volition rather than in prescribed or "natural" expectations. There were bequests to the present earl of Oxford, to three or four god-children (including lord Bulbeck and his wife, Lady Vere, and Elizabeth Darcy), a sister-in-law and her daughter, to "my brother" Sir William Kingston, to the siblings of some of the god-children, to four other women identified as "my sisters," to a nephew, and to a cousin. This was all what we might call a surrogate or constructed family, though they were her relatives by the definition of consanguinity, affinity, and spiritual bonds, of a world that was about to change rapidly at the time of her death.[130]

Such vast networks of beneficiaries are hardly the norm. Fewer resources, fewer relations, and less inclination to give served to cut many wills down in size and scope. Alice Stury was twice a widow, the second time of the notorious Lollard, Sir Richard Stury.[131] She was not noticeably without resources, but her only mention of family is a mention of prayers for her mother, and a pair of basins, covered with silver, to go to "mon cosyn Sr Hugh Loterell." Nor was the countess of Salisbury herself much more expansive. She and her son were to be buried beside her husband, at Bisham, and there were some prayers at Twynham for "malme mez progeniteurs."[132] Her sister and brother-in-law, the duke and duchess of York, received a few personal and household items, and an unspecified "monsier Richard Mountagu" was to come in for "une hanape dargent covere." From a woman who was a Mohun heiress and then either countess or dowager countess of Salisbury for about 50 years or more, this was certainly restrained. It was also rather bleak: her only son, William, had been killed in a tilting match with his father in 1382, and he had left no children by his marriage to Elizabeth Fitzalan.

We should not end on a note of sentimentality. Widows of property were often quite as willing as their late husbands had been to assert their wishes from beyond the grave. They too now had the carrot of bequests to dangle before their heirs and beneficiaries. A Buckinghamshire widow left her tenements in town to her daughter, but the revenues had to be used to support a chantry in Huddersfield for at least one year for the mother's soul.[133] Mothers may traditionally have more sanguine views of their sons' behavior than fathers do, but Alice Neville was not taking any chances that her wishes would go unheeded. Son John was to get the house and land, *if* he would give other properties in Holbeck to two poor women who would pray for his mother's soul. If one of the women died, John was to replace her, "but put in no man." At the annual rate of 13s. 4d., paid in six installments, the poor women were pretty sure to remain poor, though they might be a bit holier and a little better fed. But Alice talked as though she were distributing the loot of monastic dissolution, and John had to agree to honor her wishes: "on this condicion, that as he will answere to God at the daye of dome, and by the othe that he hath moade to me uppon a boke."[134] Property and the privileged status that came with the death bed were powerful forces. Sometimes they worked to soften stony hearts and to loosen rusty purse hinges. Sometimes they worked to focus dying thoughts upon children, just waiting to cut loose. Such natural inclinations could not be denied, but they could certainly be hamstrung. Last wills were wonderful tools for such purposes, and widows were as canny as the deceased husbands had been.

The Church and the Pious Life

The pious widow is as much a commonplace as the emancipated and bawdy widow. Both are probably exaggerated figures. We have encountered relatively little evidence of the carefree widow, and we will see that the sort of documentation that might support the picture of a world heavily populated by elderly ladies, living like lay nuns, is a bit thin as well. There were certainly a fair number of widows who found comfort and security by wrapping themselves in the blankets of religious routine. However, despite accepted opinion, their number was probably quite limited.

Most widows seem to have had a view of personal religiosity, of their debts to and links with mother church, and of their own testamentary identification as sinful creatures that was, once again, much on a par with that displayed by their late husbands. It was part of their make up, but hardly a predominant strain their self-identification.[135]

Men and women of property, when dictating wills, invariably directed some share of their worldly goods towards the church. This was an accepted spiritual and social convention, and neither diversity in religous expression nor personal idiosyncrasy served to diminish its appeal. For convenience we see such bequests as falling into three categories: the money and goods that accompanied burial and that were given to the burial church and its personnel, those designated for other ecclesiastical institutions and clerics, and those dedicated to what we might call social welfare and "do good" purposes. The three species of benefaction fall within the same larger genus of social and spiritual activity, since the purchase of prayers was the reciprocal service called for, explicitly or implicitly, in the transmission of material goods.

Any survey of how men handled these social expectations and obligations is primarily a tale of variety, and the normal distribution pattern—with very few (if any) either giving nothing or almost everything, with most giving something—certainly prevails within any imaginable group or universe of any significant size that we can isolate. The tale for the widows seems to be very similar. Widows' wills, of course, centered less on the transmission of the patrimony and more on the personal goods of domestic life. But within these slightly different parameters the same themes of individual variation and of a collective normal curve or distribution of behavior seem the prevailing pattern. Some widows gave great bounties to the church. Others, even when we combine our three categories of benefaction, offered no more than a respectable or perhaps a passable or token minimum. Nor does overall wealth seem to have been a governing factor, in a proportionate sense, for a small estate can be cut into fractions as easily as a large one. Neither does age of the testatrix offer much guidance. It is the personal equation that usually prevails as an explanatory device, with adjustments for family traditions and individual circumstances. We emerge with a picture of piety and ecclesiastical endowment, based on widows' wills, that argues against a view of them as being exceptionally devoted to the church as an institution or to testamentary and posthumous philanthropy as a form of voluntary activity.

Men often left money for elaborate funerals and funeral processions,

and they not infrequently specified that interment was to be beside deceased relatives in a specified church or churchyard. Widows, as we know
from our previous discussion of their multiple identities, might have to
pick and choose from among various husbands and families for identity,
for benefaction, and for burial. But for most women, as far as the wording
of the will runs, the final choice was set forth in fairly straightforward
terms. A powerful noblewoman could cover the canvas with bold strokes.
As a granddaughter of Edward III, countess Anne was likely to have been
neither in the midst of an "identity crisis" nor in the rapids of economic
disaster: "I Anne countesse of Stafford, Bokingh'[Buckingham], Hereford,
and Northampton and lady of Breknoc," as she summed herself up.[136]
Burial was to be at Lanthony by Gloucester, "in the place wher I have
beforn ordeyned and do mad my tombe." But as with other issues we have
looked at, the bourgeoisie were not necessarily less assertive, as we see from
the way an urban widow of the day identified herself, "Alicia Galiot relicta
Thome Galiot civis dum vixit et waxchaundeler civitatis London'," with
burial in St. Michael le Quern, "in tumulo in quo corpus mariti sui mortui
iacet humatum."[137]

   The women also were free to wander around in most of the other
discretionary areas in which their husbands had once roamed. They too
constructed elaborate routines for prayers for those odd medleys of souls,
living and dead, male and female, related and unrelated. Masses were the
coin of this realm, and lady Alice West used £1,700 to purchase 4,400 of
them, "for my lord sir Thomas West-is soule, and for myn, and for alle
cristene soules, in the most hast that it may be do withynne xiiij nyght after
by deces."[138] The prayers might be bought for mother ("malme de ma
mere"),[139] or for a brace of father, mother, husband, children, and sister,[140]
or for the near and dear plus "alle my good doers and alle cristen soules."[141]
Women, like men, were given to the conventional but oddly moving comments about their worthless selves and the uncertainty of the day of
death.[142] To speak of the mercy of Christ the creator, his mother, and a
familiar range of saints was always a good idea, and wise women followed
the convention.[143] In a brief will, God, the Blessed Virgin, and all saints
was at least an all-inclusive category,[144] and for those with more time there
was no harm in naming as many as possible.

   Choices regarding expenditures on pomp and splendor were also to
be made. Few people, regardless of sex or wealth or marital status, were
likely to try to match the countess of Warwick's style. She only survived
her husband by a matter of months, and she asked for burial at Tewkesbury

Abbey, a traditional resting place for her natal family, the Despensers. She requested a tomb with "my Image to be made all naked, and no thyng on my hede but myn here cast bakwardys, and of the gretnes and of the fascyon lyke the mesure that Thomas Porchyln hath yn a lyst, and at my hede Mary Mawdelen leyng my handes a crosse, And seynt Iohn the Evangelyst on the ryght syde of my hede, and on the left syde Saynt Anton, and at my fete a Skochen of myn Armes departyd with my lordys, and ij Greffons to bere hit vppe."¹⁴⁵ Others cared more about the procession than about what happened when it reached its final destination. The aged countess of Suffolk was concerned with determining the number of torches that would accompany her body, while Elizabeth Byconyll of Glastonbury wanted 30 masses and 30 diriges, for 30 days, from each of "iiij discrete preestes," with more details regarding the service books and the rotation of the men.¹⁴⁶

Our image of the funeral procession as public theater is reinforced by a consideration of the care with which people could describe their own procession. The liveried servants we associate with sworn retainers and the reciprocities of bastard feudalism were replicated, on a higher spiritual but a lower social plane, by such as the 12 "pore men . . . al clothed in blak at my cost," which lady Clinton called for as part of her funeral march.¹⁴⁷ The unceasing pleas for spiritual intercession could be subsidized, as when lady Bergavenny asked for special mention of her welfare in "the first mass in the mornyng" and "the last masse thay ys doon in the day."¹⁴⁸

Generosity to a circle of ecclesiastical institutions, especially to those within a given geographical radius, was one of the customary forms of patriarchal largesse. Widows could follow suit. Insofar as they took their husband's lead, and that of his family, they were showing an identification with his patriarchal traditions, as well as with the sort of socio-economic leadership that he had cultivated in a region or a particular branch of the church through the concerted exercise of pious bequests. Rich ladies, especially when they belonged to families with traditions of generosity, could bestow their benefactions with weight and self-confidence. When the countess of Salisbury was buried at Bisham in 1414, where her husband's family had gone for about three quarters of a century, she directed her wishes towards both intensive and extensive benefaction. At Bisham, as part of the funeral ceremonies, 24 poor men were to participate, in return for 20d. apiece, and 4000 masses were to be said "en tout la haste."¹⁴⁹ The prior of Bisham was to receive 13s. 4d., each priest-canon 6s. 8d., others 3s. 4d. A new two-priest chantry (founded with a bequest of £12) was to function at Bisham. Nor did this family foundation monopolize her attention. Money was left for prayers to be said at Bruton priory, Christchurch, Christchurch Twynham, and Montacute priory, and in parish churches at Donyatt, Curry Rivel, Chedesey, Marstock, Yarlington, Charlton, Henstridge, Goathill, Wichenford, by friars at Ilchester and at Bridgewater, by the Austins and Carmelites of Bristol, by the Franciscans of Bristol, by those in the leper houses at Taunton and Langport, and in the abbeys of Torre, Newenham, and Cleve. Nor were these merely token bequests. Apart from the substantial sums that Bisham would realize (coming in all to several hundred pounds) the countess was distributing such sums as 10 marks, £20, 1 mark per priest, and one-half mark to those without ordination, £5, 5 marks, and enough vestments to clothe her private army of spiritual retainers.

Such commanding instructions could also be cut on a much smaller scale. Some widows of modest means still managed to distribute their largesse to a wide circle of ecclesiastical recipients. While barely giving, *in toto*, as much as the countess left just to the friars of Ilchester ("pour prier pour malme x marcs"), Matilda Raget, with very limited resources at her disposal, spread such gifts as 6*d*., 4*d*., 2*s*. 6*d*., and six sheep to six institutional beneficiaries as well as to four rectors or parish priests.[150] Another widow stretched out the distribution of £3 13*s*. 4*d*., plus vestments, books, chapels ornaments, and a harness to enrich four churches and three priests or chaplains.[151] From the institutional perspective, we have to assume that even Salisbury cathedral was quite willing to be the recipient of a bequest of 2*s*., the churches of Hernam and Layngford of a mere 1*s*. apiece.[152] One wealthy widow, lady West, reserved part of her estate for what we might today label a feminist ecclesiastical network. As well as the customary recipients we find in most of the expansive wills, she clustered bequests to "the Religiouse wommen, the menchouns," of Shaftesbury, Romsey, and Wilton, and to "the Religiouse Wommen the Menoursesse" without Aldgate, London.[153]

Chantries were relatively inexpensive and easy to create, and widows certainly number among their founders. The souls of the widow and her late husband were to receive the daily attention of one chaplain, "ydoneum et honestum," for two years, for an endowment of 18 marks. Joan Beauchamp had extensive resources, and she felt free to draw upon them to support "v prestes to synge for me xx wynter," along with a good collection of other souls.[154] Two of the men were to sing at Rocheford, three in Kirkby Bellars, Leicestershire. Sometimes widows were more circumspect, and they concluded the will—as did many a husband—by simply asking that their executors devote any residue, after debts and bequests, for the good of their souls.

Were widows any more charitable or compassionate than their husbands had been? Within the world of spiritual reciprocities, did they bend any more of their bequests towards the unfortunates of their world than had their fathers, husbands, and brothers? Many were generous, in this direction, but again it is hard to identify trends or behavioral patterns as being characteristic of, let alone peculiar to, widows. Their benefactions, like most of their other forms of pious and spiritual activity, were so routinized that gender hardly emerges as an independent variable or a reliable guide to action, though if we had to choose we might say they were a shade more sympathetic or thoughtful. But it is only a matter of degree, not a significant quantum leap.

As with most other impulses and forms of voluntary behavior, bequests for the amelioration of social ills and the human condition followed fairly standardized channels. Roads, bridges, and thoroughfares—the bailiwick of our departments of public works—were traditional recipients. The matter could be extremely prosaic, as one did what one was supposed to do but with limited enthusiasm: "Item to Twykenham brygge iiij d."[155] Or it might be spelled out with a bit more concern: "I be whethe to the amendyng of evel waies and febull brigges there as my executours seen moste nede is xx markes."[156] Other causes were a little less uniform. The poor were apt to be mentioned. The two most popular sub-groups of this ubiquitous and eternal universe were the poor of her own estates and those poor who attended her funeral. A generous if fairly standard bequest of this sort ran thus: "I wol that euery teneaunt in Ochecote haue dim. quarter of wete and dim. quarter of malt . . . All the remenaunts of whete and malt . . . (to) other poer townes that be here abowte."[157]

Sometimes general categories of unfortunates might be mentioned, and presumably it fell to her executors to decide on the method and scope of charitable distribution. A bequest could be exceptionally vivid: land was to be sold and the revenues to go "to pore husbandes plough men in the contrey suche as have wyf and childres and pore wydowes and other suche pore diligent laborers in pore village."[158] The imagery here is closer to the great body of late medieval poetry of social commentary and protest than to the laconic wording we have come to expect in this context. Some wills covered all of these categories, plus such others as the relief of prisoners and the marriage of poor (but virtuous) maidens. Money was certainly appreciated when it was "yeven and dalt among bedred men and other poer peple dwellyng in the lordschippe that I have."[159]

These categories of benefaction and of *noblesse oblige* were, in aggregate, catch-alls for almost everyone with sufficient material worth to merit a will. If only a few wills touched all of our bases, very few missed out completely. But heading the church's honor roll of patrons and benefactors were those who moved to create, *de novo*, an ecclesiastical institution of some sort. However, by the fifteenth-century such munificent ranks are rather thin. That the century was a period in which lay interest in monasticism and in either new regular or mendicant houses flickered low is a generalization standing in little need of qualification or revision. Most of what large and ambitious lay support the church was able to attract—beyond that devoted to the foundation or enlargement or re-subsidization of chantry chapels—went towards hospitals, almshouses, and perhaps smallish educational enterprises. Were wealthy widows especially disposed to give money for such purposes? To build such an institution was the late medieval equivalent of putting ones name in lights.

Benefaction to create or to enlarge on a grand scale required both moderate wealth (or something beyond that) and some strong personal motivation. In a world where even most of the most generous tended to be laconic about the reasons for their gift-giving beyond the standard formulae, it seems likely that membership in and identification with a family that had an older tradition of generosity usually provided the special motivation. Of course, every such family had need of a member who had once begun the tradition. But beyond such a family tradition—as the Scropes of Bolton had toward St. Agatha at Richmond, or the Chicheles toward Higham Ferrers, or the Nevilles toward Staindrop College—the smallish fruits of fifteenth-century endowment were largely the result of a series of individualized if linked inspirations. However, the flash of piety and self-centered generosity that led Henry VI to found Eton and King's College, Cambridge came but infrequently, and not often even to the wealthiest widows (any more than it had to their husbands). They played their role and contributed their share of gifts, but there is little evidence for a picture that highlights them, in any consistant or regular fashion, as the group towards whom enterprising ecclesiastics were apt to turn when they tried to spin their dreams into gold. And sometimes, when gifts came from the widow, they were rather the culmination of plans once made by the married couple, with her now acting as the agent to further the traditional patronage of his (or their) house.

An old scholarly survey of the hospitals of medieval England gives fifteenth-century activity less credit for foundation and elaborate support than it would probably receive were the study to be redone.[160] Nor do widows, in any medieval century, come in for many kudos. Rotha Clay's tabular presentation of foundations, arranged by counties, shows one woman as a founder in Cambridgeshire, one in Devon, one in Essex, one in Gloucestershire, three in London and Middlesex, two in Suffolk, one in Sussex, and three in Wiltshire. A small catch, and of these 13 hospitals, only one foundation (and one foundress) fits into our chronological universe of our ladies. The one relevant case was the almshouse at Westminster, founded by Henry VII's mother, lady Margaret Beaufort, around the turn of the sixteenth century. Lady Margaret's general role in educational bene-faction and "social welfare" projects was more that of a king's mother, which makes her the exception that proves a custom, if not a rule.[161] So whatever mark widows made as patrons and benefactresses of the casual sort, they left little mark as founders.

Did they lean more toward educational endowment? A recent and thorough examination of the schools of York diocese hardly gives more credit to our group. Jo Ann H. Moran's list includes "every notice of a school within York diocese that has come to my attention,"[162] so not every single testamentary bequest made, if to an already known institution, nec-essarily figures in her tally. On the other hand, any activity that even ap-proaches or approximates an instance of foundation or of extensive endowment has been treated with care. The results are what we can antic-ipate by now: disappointing. For 221 schools that can be identified with some degree of certainty, no widows are cited as founders. Widows' wills are only listed as a source of benefaction and endowment (and serve as data to help establish the fact of the institution's existence) for 13 schools. In addition, the bequests are not only small, but usually in the form of charity connected with her funeral and the attendant obsequies, now distributed to scholars of the house on an individualized basis: a penny to each scholar of Richmond, "yt hayff a surples for their dewty doyn at messe and dirige," or a penny to "every scholar belongyng to the quere" of Wakefield gram-mar school.[163] None of the bequests went to the schools themselves, and so none did much to further learning as a social, intellectual, or economically useful activity.

These approaches to the philanthropic inclination of the late medieval widows are perhaps formulated as rather harsh questions. In fairness, no particular social group, singled out for some secular aspect of its identity, is likely to be outstanding for its philanthropic support of any particular set of recipients. Several recent studies of the fifteenth-century episcopate show that even the bishops were something less that outstanding when put to this test.[164] But, as has been argued in their defense, bishops were not chosen for their philanthropic proclivities or their death bed inclinations,[165] and widows even less so. We are hardly surprised that the latter groups are not prominent among the limited ranks of those who founded regular or mendicant houses, colleges at Oxford or Cambridge, hospitals, alms-houses, or grammar schools. But any study of those who did so build and so create forces us to cover a good deal of uneven ground, and all sorts of people, for all sorts of reasons, have to be sought and found. That widows were no less pious and no less generous than their men, regarding testamentary benefaction and the institutions of the church, seems about as far as we can go. Nor is this meant as a mean spirited assessment. As the women of their families, both great and small, they had hardly been schooled towards the assertion of an identity stressing a sense of independence, individuality, or innovation. Many widows, after a husband's death, simply remarried and rejoined the protected legions of women with men. Those who did not remarry were either busy coping with the problems and burdens they had been forced to acquire, or—if they were older and/or women of substance—they became quiet caretakers of family wealth and family cohesion. They were mostly content to run along familiar, well traveled rails.

The piety and personal religious life of widows could veer towards one particular end followed by neither their menfolk nor their married sisters. Numerous widows took formal vows of chastity. They thereby made a commitment to henceforth live a single, celibate life, and their bond was duly recognized and watched over by the church. A few widows actually entered the cloister, though popular imagination probably exaggerates their confines as a recruiting ground of and final resting place for elderly women in the orders. Some entered regular houses as lay sisters and residents, as did the widow in the diocese of Lincoln who received permission to try the life of an enclosed anchoress, in the chapel of St. Edmund by the Bridge at Doncaster, for one year.[166] Some widows received papal indults to enter and stay within monastic precincts for a set duration on some annual or regular basis, as when the duchess of York was allowed to enter "as often as she pleases" with five or six honest matrons or virgins, and to stay for three days and three nights, but no more at any single time.[167] But this was exceptional latitude, as was the right to visit up to six or seven times a year, though it was to be exercised "without eating or passing the night there."[168] Some widows set up and governed households that achieved a level of piety, without benefit of explicit vows, that would have graced many an old and honorable Benedictine foundation, and later we shall look at one such private, if rather grand, establishment.

But a simple vow of chastity was a fairly common course. Furthermore, it was taken, with appropriate ceremonial, by young as well as by elderly widows, and its weight was enhanced by the majesty that ritualized behavior and public ceremonial helped inspire. Some of the women moved in this direction while their grief and bewilderment were still green. Others followed later, either when alternatives had proved disillusioning or when the early responsibilities had diminished and when old age and the grave began to claim a larger share of their attention. The vows were fairly simple and, once again, standardized. A Lincolnshire widow, "not wedded," committed herself before the bishop of Lincoln for "the purpose of chastite aftir the rewle of Saint Paule."[169] Such touches as a declaration that she was "wydow, and not wedded, nor vnto no man ensured," were to guarantee that she was indeed free and able to make a proper commitment.[170] But there was also a recognition that such a promise might not be easy to keep, and Agnes Baldwin vowed to "our lady and to all the companye of hevyn . . . to be chaste of my body and treuly shal kepe me chaste from this tyme forward as longe as my liff lastyth."[171]

We saw that dying husbands often became obsessed with the possibility (or probability) of their wives' remarriage. The male view of female sexuality, from this perspective, was not a flattering one. Both lust and irresponsibility resided within the female form. Consequently, in the sources that speak with the male voice, unflattering statements about a widow's occasional slip, or of her desire to change her mind, creep in; the tone of condescencion often vies with that of Christian concern. One young widow had been so "pierced with grief" that, by age 27, she had taken the vow of continence. But then she worried lest she not be able to resist efforts to ravish her: the solution in this case was permission to contract marriage.[172] So too, a Yorkshire widow's vows had been hastily made. Because she feared that she would slip, due to the frailty of human flesh, she received permission to contract marriage, for which she now had to repay the church (that is, commute her vow into other works of piety).[173] Churchmen seem to have had some sympathy, but they could not always resist the temptation to smirk when they granted the petition.

They should not have been so patronizing. If the widows of fifteenth-century England were not the canon fodder from which a new army of regular religious was to be recruited, they seem to have been dutiful sisters of the church, as they were dutiful subjects of their many kings. If they set no new standards, they hardly let down their families, their dependents, or their sisters.

Some Case Studies of Widows' Lives

The rich widow who presided over the great household is not hard to find. Data exist to support this conventional picture, and many a dowager lady seems to have been quite willing to lead her life so as to conform to our model or stereotype. When such a widow really was the long-lived dowager of a house with a patrimony of considerable substance, her own household and domestic complex served a number of roles. It could be the haven and vocational training school of the young and unmarried children of the family, especially of the girls, and it might serve a similar role for the children and grandchildren of friends, political and economic allies, and the socially subservient families of the region. In the wills of the widows, there is a markedly greater incidence of bequests to grandchildren and to godchildren than in those of their husbands. To a considerable extent this simply bespeaks the widow's greater age at the end. But it also suggests that the dowager household served as a headquarters for socialization and acculturation for the third generation and for offspring and cadets of the horizontal family to a degree that had been less common in the patriarchal household, that is, while the old man had still been alive.[174]

The wealthy widow, the dowager mother-figure, also functioned as a link between the generations. Her household could preserve some of the grandeur of a former day, and her level of entertainment and her display of piety would redound to the credit of the line. Inventories of widows' households and estates, usually made shortly after their deaths, illustrate the level of affluence and comfort that was an accepted and regular part of such establishments. An inventory of the estate of Elizabeth, lady Clifford (wife of Thomas, lord Clifford), shows gross assets of almost £700, a sum that includes £138 18s. 6d. owed to her from the marriage portion of Elizabeth, daughter of the earl of Northumberland. From these gross receipts £223 6s. 8d. went for the funeral and clerical expenses, and after all the other debts and obligations were deducted there was a clear (that is, a net) value of £106 19s. 6d. This was life in the fifteenth-century jet set. A lesser

Yorkshire widow of the day, Elizabeth Sywardby, left an estate with a gross value of £110 2s. 10d., and debts, legacies, and funeral expenses left her (or her heirs) with a net gain of £29, most of which was to go for a monument, three years' of masses for her soul, and for the expenses (£10 7s. 11d.) of a niece who was entering a nunnery. So at the different levels, we see relative affluence and the allocation of resources. Some of the resources were clearly free for discretionary purposes; conspicuous expenditure for spiritual ends was always an accepted form of medieval behavior.[175]

An inventory is a static presentation, an account of possessions (and their whereabouts), with little hint of their frequent or infrequent use or of their intrinsic or sentimental value. For a more dynamic view of the life of a great dowager, and of the stewardship that the maintenence of her household entailed, we can turn to the household book of lady Alice de Bryene. There are numerous accounts of the household of important widows from the thirteenth century onwards, and by comparison nothing in Lady Alice's lifestyle is out of the ordinary, given the social and economic plateau on which she lived. Life in the castle, or even in the imposing manor house, was usually life in the fast lane of contemporary society. We know something about how matrons and dowagers organized these large administrative-domestic complexes, and women of the day give every indication of being as capable as earlier medieval women or as their contemporary male counterparts at assuming supervision of imposing establishments.[176]

Alice de Bryene was the daughter-in-law of Guy, I lord Bryene (Brien), and the widow of his son and heir, Guy, who died in 1386, four years before his father. There were two daughters of Alice's marriage, still minors at the time of their father's death (aged nine and more, and five and more, in the Inquisitions Post Mortem of 10 Richard II), and Alice held her dower share and perhaps her daughters' portions, as well, until they came of age in the 1390s.[177] Alice lived a long time and presided over a substantial if not quite a magnificent establishment. Her household book for the year that ran from September 1412 to September 1413 takes us into the detailed accounts of an elaborate domestic institution, controlled and supported by a woman who now had been a widow for over a quarter of a century. Dame Alice must have been both hospitable by nature and/or training and clearly concerned to remain a figure in county society. In the month of May, 1413, to take a typical one-month span, she entertained visitors, friends, and hungry neighbors about as regularly as she herself sat down to eat. At breakfast, in that month, she had between 3 and 12 people each day, with a total for the 31 days of the month amounting to 219 mouths (for a daily average of about seven per day): the dinner groups ranged between 18 and 30, and they totaled 625 (for an average of almost 20); the supper groups were 6–24, with a total of 387 (average, 12). While it is impossible to know how well so many mouths actually fared, in that month their needs called for the purchase of stores that included six quarters of wheat, barley, and drage, eight of malt for brewing, two beef carcasses, four pigs, 20 chickens, 238 pigeons, 350 red herrings and 450 of the white variety, plus various amounts of mutton, capons, salt fish and stock fish, and other miscellaneous victuals and condiments. In the household book the total for the amount of wine bought is left blank, so the collective thirst—no doubt compounded by the consumption of some 800 herrings—can only be guessed at. Such tallies conjure up a picture not only of squirearchy at its hungriest but also of the not inconsiderable legion of domestic servants and administrators needed to buy, cook, serve, and clean up. We see her as a major employer as well as a well-born hostess.

This indeed was the widow's version of life at the top. Usually, as we have argued, she experienced some mixture of ups and downs. We have tried to avoid an overemphasis upon her freedom, affluence, and independence. This is not to denigrate the valor and the resilience of so many brave and capable women, but rather to stress how irremediably patriarchal and oppressive society was. This is true, with adjustments for the appropriate socio-economic context, for queens and dowager duchesses as it is for yeomen and burgher widows, let alone for single mothers among the peasantry and the permanently oppressed and depressed. One way in which we have tried to shed light upon the feminine chapters of the human condition is by keeping in mind the dependent nature of a woman's life: from father or brother to husband, and then—for many of our women—into widowhood and then perhaps into remarriage and then, often enough, into a second widowhood. Her identity shifted; her loyalties became spread out or even stretched thin. She entered and sometimes left a whole series of families. Some widows, we saw, asserted themselves in a very positive fashion, and they not only proclaimed their membership in a number of families but they worked, in their wills, to yoke them together.

The widow who had been the mother, who had borne the children who would carry the patriarchal family forward in time, was always a member of that family, or so the logic of medieval patriarchy and of our behavioral analysis would seem to argue. This was the case, even if she subsequently moved on, perhaps to bear more children—even more heirs—in a new marriage. But if she had not borne children at all, or if they were not the heirs, her role was clearly more peripheral or transient, even regarding her first acquired family. Her identification with this family might well survive her husband's death, and the dowager step-mother or dowager sister-in-law could continue to be counted as among the near and dear. But conversely she might pass well beyond their affective pale, and either disengage herself or be disengaged. When that happened she could fall back on earlier family links, or forge new ones, or just become another unwilling recruit in the vast army of the alienated and the isolated.

The Scropes of Bolton provided us with some good material for our reconstruction of the patriarchal family and male bonding. Their father-son chain ran through the course of the century, and the separate men worked serially with sufficient sense of continuity to cultivate such useful family traditions as Richmondshire benefaction and Yorkshire philanthropy. They learned how the profits of political investment could bring home handsome dividends. They also learned how to sail near the political wind without capsizing. For men of moderate wealth (by aristocratic standards) and—after Richard, I lord Scrope (1327–1403)—of only moderate ability and modest national prominence, they held their own for a long time in a competitive and often dangerous game.

The Scrope lords also are of interest because they left behind a series of widows; the importance of the men turns us toward "their" women. When we look at these women we see our views of gender-determined life patterns once again reflected in a family case study. And in consonance with earlier impressions, common themes and ties between the various Scrope widows are more noteworthy for their absence than for their presence. The Scrope men were linked to each other by both biology and socio-political teamwork, moving successively along a narrow path and passing much the same baggage on from man to man. The women, by way of contrast, were all outsiders, taken aboard for a limited stretch but bound much less securely for the long passage. They might be wives and then mothers of the lords and patriarchs to come, but they were, at best, mothers-in-law of the next lady, the next potential family widow and dowager. A look at the widows, in aggregate, leaves us with little impression of common bonds and themes comparable to what we observed for their husbands and sons.

Richard Scrope, I lord, left no traceable widow: we are not certain whether he remarried after the death of Blanche de la Pole around 1380. Richard's second son, Roger, succeeded his father but died almost immediately. Roger had married a daughter of Robert, III lord Tibetot (d. 1372), as had his younger brother Stephen: the girls had been wards of I lord Richard. Roger's widow, Margaret (b. 1366, married around 1385), survived him by many years (d. 1431). After Roger's death she made a déclassé remarriage in 1405 or 1406 with one John Niander, and she eventually asked for burial in Holy Trinity, Christ Church, London, a church without any other Scrope family connections.[178] The son and heir of Roger and Margaret was Richard, III lord Scrope, who died (at age 26) in 1420. He had married Margaret Neville, the Earl of Westmorland's sixth daughter by his first wife. When Richard died, his widow, who had very young children to raise, naturally fell back upon the protection of the Nevilles, as we saw above. In 1427, after seven years of widowhood and presumably of concern for her maternal responsibilities, Margaret Scrope, née Neville, married William Cressoner.[179] In this instance there must have been some harmony between her two families, for years later her son, Richard Scrope, bishop of Carlisle (1464–68) left goods in his will to his stepbrother, Ralph Cressoner.[180] The next Scrope peer was Henry (1418–59), who married Elizabeth Scrope of Masham, a distant cousin, around 1435. She outlived him by almost 40 years, dying in October, 1498. Their son, John (1438–98), married thrice, being the first of our patriarchs since I lord Richard to bury a wife. In 1447 he received a dispensation allowing him to wed Joan, daughter of William, IV lord Fitzhugh, and Margery Willoughby. Joan was dead by 1470. John then married Elizabeth St. John, the widow of William, lord Zouche (d. 1468). Elizabeth died around 1490, after having lasted to serve as a godmother to poor young Edward V. Then, by the end of 1491, Scrope married for a third time, this time to Anne Harling. She was already the widow of Sir William Chamberlain, K.G. (d. 1462), and of Sir Robert Wingfield, sometime member of parliament (dead by November 1481). Anne died in October 1498, just two months after her last husband. John's son and heir Henry (by Joan Fitzhugh) had a short life (1468–1506). He married Elizabeth Percy, and we know that she survived him by at least six years.

Some of the patterns that emerge from this brief chronicle of the marital history of one family are probably relevant for many families and their women. If we exclude I lord Richard, of the six men under consideration only John, V lord, married more than once. And in every case except that of I lord Richard, the woman outlived the husband: six men were outlasted and buried by their five widows. For each marriage, in respective order beyond that of I Richard, the wife's life span after the Scrope marriage compared pretty favorably with the duration of the marriage; II lord Roger and his wife were married for 18 years, she lived another 28; III lord Richard was married for seven, she lived for another 44; IV lord Henry for 24, she perhaps for as long as 60 more; V lord John was married (for the third time) for about nine years, she survived for two months; VI lord Henry's marriage is hard to plot, but his youngish widow survived him by at least six years. So the Scrope marriages were an important part of each of the women's lives, no doubt. However, in mere numerical terms these unions hardly occupied the major segment of their life spans. What can we offer concerning what we have referred to as her identity; did the women, in their own eyes, become Scropes for life? Two of the wives re-married, and in each case the subsequent marriage lasted as long as or longer than the first. Neither remarriage was with a peer, which may argue that Scrope widowhood—falling on women already of aristocratic birth—had little effect in either direction on their social status. Or, conversely, it may argue that social demotion was the price they might have to pay in return for the right to exercise a choice for remarriage. V lord John had a checkered marital career, as did his third wife, and we have to assume that she was a middle-aged or elderly woman who came to him with her own complement of material and emotional fixtures and furnishings. So in many ways the Scrope wives-cum-widows hardly constitute a social group. What they had in common is apparent: their Scrope marriages made them peeresses, and they bore a series of sons who would be summoned to par-liament as lords of the realm. But the Scrope marriages were only one part of each separate life. Had this particular set of husbands been men of less import, we might well have missed that particular segment of each woman's biography that might generally be seen by the historian—in po-litical if not necessarily in arithmetic or even in personal terms—as their major life experience.

The arithmetic of the matter indicates that the Scrope widows were not strung as uniform beads on a common necklace. What other forms of family experiences might they have had? Is there any reason to think they had been integrated into the family of their in-laws by the peers and peer-esses of an older generation? Roger's wife had been a Scrope bride for 15 years before her father-in-law died, and as a young orphan she had been his ward. So she, at least, was as much an insider in the family as one could hope to find, just as was her younger sister who had married Roger's younger brother Stephen. But III lord Richard's wife had married him some eight or ten years after her father-in-law had died, and by the time of her own wedding her mother-in-law had already remarried and was gone from the Scrope fold. She presided as the only woman of the family and the household, child-bride though she might appear to us. IV lord Henry's wife came into a similar situation: a dead father-in-law, a remarried (and departed) mother-in-law. V lord John's first wife did have some years of marriage while his father was still alive, while his own mother may have outlived all three of his wives. VI lord Henry's wife is hard to pin down, but she did have a few years as the family dowager and as the sole survivor of an earlier generation. Thus, when we put father, mother-in-law, husband, and wife together as a series of consecutive family units, the generational overlap is usually pretty thin. The wives may have preferred entering families where they could take over the great household at the time of marriage, that is, without mother-in-law or father-in-law to compete with their growing self-assertion. However, in terms of family continuity and the preservation of tradition, the Scropes' high level of success may have been due more to their sons than to their wives and mothers. Whatever else the Scrope ladies were, they were not the dedicated matriarchal keepers of the patriarchal arcana.

The wills of the Scrope men gave us material for the construction of an impressive edifice of patriarchy. But none of these wills are particularly helpful regarding marital bonds between husbands and wives, or the widows' family ties and identities. I lord Richard left bequests to his two Tibetot daughters-in-law (and his younger son Stephen's wife was referred to as "carissime filie mee"), but he made no reference to his long-departed and very well born wife. II lord Roger made his wife ("praecarrissimam") one of his exectutors, but her own will of 1431 makes little reference to the Scropes: she refers to herself as the daughter of Robert Tibetot, now dead some half century.[181] III lord Richard made no reference in his will to his wife, and when she died, some 44 years later, she asked for burial in the Austin Friars house at Clare, perhaps to lie beside her second husband or his family.[182] John, V lord, was more intertwined with his third wife, to whom he had been married for less than a decade, than any of his predecessors had been to their partners. He left his "lovyng wife" his possessions south of the Trent, the £100 due him from outstanding debts (and in return for money he had borrowed from her before their marriage), and some manorial revenues. She was asked to serve as an executor but was given the option of refusing, without any of the penalties sometimes attached to this bogus exercise in free choice. When Anne died, a scant two months later, she left behind a family network of few or no children but of many collateral, fictive, and spiritual kin. Her Scrope stepchildren and their spouses and children were among her beneficiaries, as were various Wingfields and Chamberlains, relatives and probably descendents of her previous two husbands. It was a generous will, gracing the final days of an old woman who was now looking back upon many worldly possessions, a long and full life in which three prosperous marriages must have figured prominently, and no direct heirs of her body.

Once again, of course, we have been looking at the women from the male or patriarchal perspective. What kind of group did the widows of the lords Scrope of Bolton constitute, and how do they stand in terms of membership on the Scrope team? For the men, there was only one life pattern, that of being *the* Scrope of Bolton. But for their wives (and widows), in aggregate, it is clear that their Scrope marital experience was, at least for some, only *one* of the major life experiences. Their separate trails all converged and ran with the highway of Scrope patriarchy, at least for a while, but mostly they branched off, sooner or later, on their own. Demography and mortality (among the men) may have caused the diversion, but the women give little indication that they cared overly much about turning back and sticking to the main course. At the end, they could look back upon lives in which the Scrope chapter had been of importance, but the chapter had hardly comprised the longest or the most critical part of the entire narrative. That two potential dowagers remarried out of five, puts this issue of identity into sharp focus; another died young, before she had the opportunity to chart the longer voyage.

We pick up a different perspective by looking at the long widowed life of Cecilly, dowager duchess of York. She was the youngest of the earl of Westmorland's 23 children. She had married Richard, III duke of York, by October, 1424 (when she was about nine), and they eventually had eight children (who survived infancy), between the births of their eldest, Anne, in 1439, and their youngest, Ursula (c. 1455). Duke Richard of York was killed at Wakefield on December 30, 1460, along with their second son Edmund, earl of Rutland, as was Cecilly's eldest brother by their father's marriage to Joan Beaufort, Richard, earl of Salisbury.

The widowhood into which Cecilly was suddenly plunged was to last until her death, almost 35 years later (on 31 May, 1495). Those 35 years comprised a life of extremes. She lived, at one level, in great affluence and comfort, as the mother of Edward IV and of Richard III and then as the grandmother of Elizabeth of York, Henry VII's queen. Simultaneously, she lived amidst so much personal tragedy that it is hard to relate it without a touch of bathos: The deposition and death of Edward IV's two sons; the death (and probable murder) of her son George, duke of Clarence; the death in battle of Richard III (shortly after his only legitimate son had died); and lesser if far from pedestrian family woes. Cecilly had an imperious and stately side, as we shall see. Her pious side was probably noteworthy even among her aged and wealthy contemporaries. Which of the many Cecillys was the true one? All of them, no doubt, and taken together they highlight the peaks and the depths of widowhood: wealth, dependence, vulnerability, piety, an extensive family circle, and assertive matriarchy amidst the monuments of the fecundity and the mortality of two or three generations of descendents and kinsfolk.

Figure III-1 shows how her long life was set into the context of an ongoing series of family lives and deaths, some coming from human causes, some from natural reasons. She began by losing a husband, a son, and a brother on the same day. She saw two of her sons die by violence (three, if we include the executed Clarence), and there may have been an element of fratricide in the death of Clarence in 1478. Even Edward IV, who died safely in his bed, was only 43 at his end. And there was ridicule and shame, as well as tragedy. When Richard III was in the process of claiming the throne he did not scruple to question his mother's marital fidelity, along with his late brother's legitimacy.[183] Nor were Cecilly's daughters a secure source of comfort, and as survivors they were hardly ahead of their brothers. Only Ursula, of the girls, survived her mother. Neither were the fates of some of her grandchildren, through her sons, much cheerier. Other than the princes in the Tower, Edward had at least one son (George) who died young, as well as a daughter (Margaret) who was to marry the king of Denmark but who died in 1482, before the arrangements had been set. Richard's son, Edward, Prince of Wales, predeceased him, and after Richard's death at Bosworth there was only an illegitimate child from that ill-fated branch of the tree. Clarence had two children die by execution, but at least they were considerate enough to postpone their fate until after their grandmother was dead. Cecilly's daughter Elizabeth married John de la Pole, duke of Suffolk, and their son, the earl of Lincoln, was killed at Stoke in 1487.

However, the personal and family situation of a veritable queen mother cum dowager duchess might be relatively free from some of the worries attending physical and economic well-being. At the time of his death the duke of York had had an annual landed income in the neighborhood of £5,000–7,000. Though Cecilly suffered some uncertain days, and

FIGURE III-1 FAMILY OF CECILLY, DUCHESS OF YORK[a]

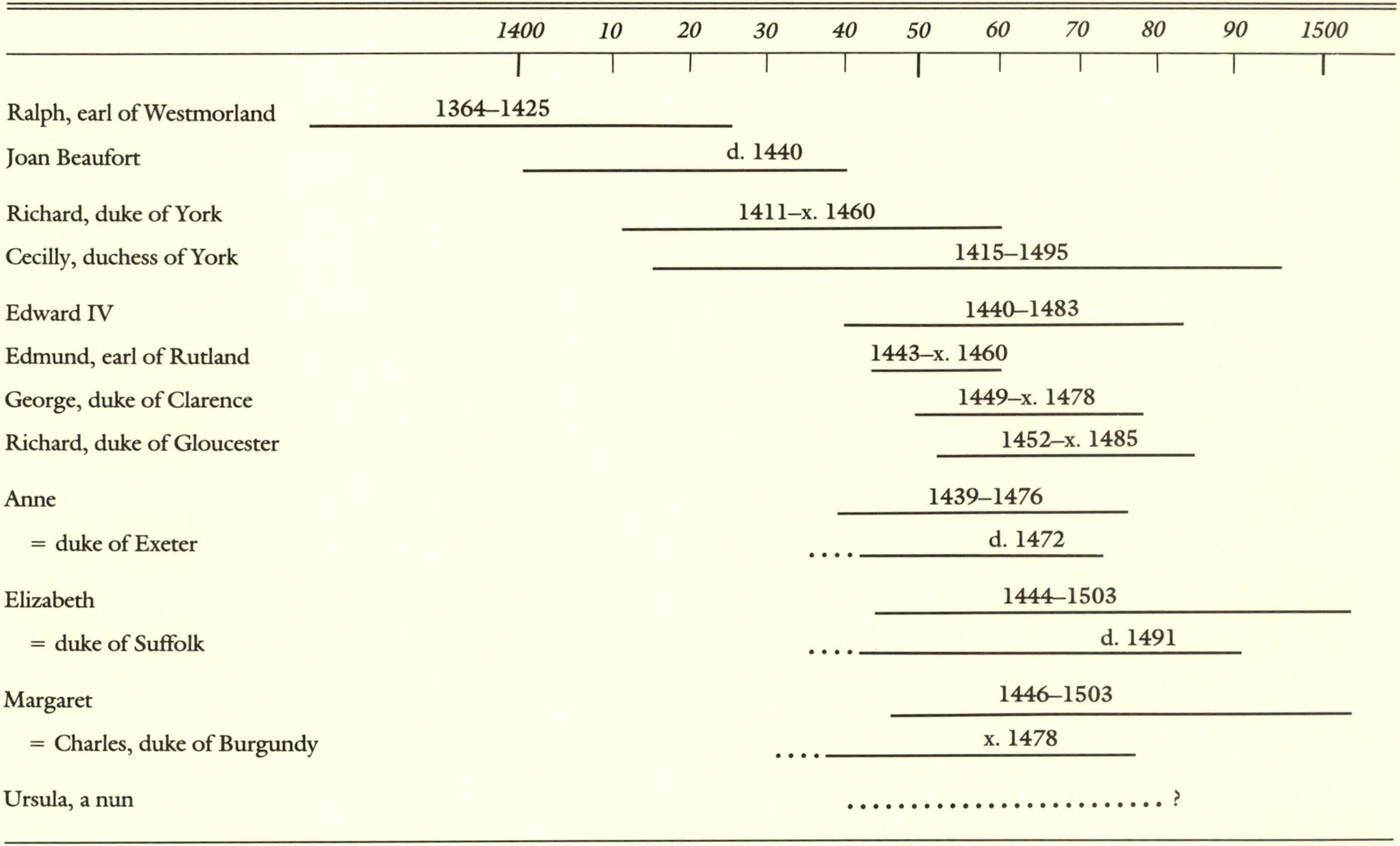

	1400	10	20	30	40	50	60	70	80	90	1500
Ralph, earl of Westmorland	1364–1425										
Joan Beaufort				d. 1440							
Richard, duke of York			1411–x. 1460								
Cecilly, duchess of York			1415–1495								
Edward IV					1440–1483						
Edmund, earl of Rutland						1443–x. 1460					
George, duke of Clarence						1449–x. 1478					
Richard, duke of Gloucester						1452–x. 1485					
Anne						1439–1476					
= duke of Exeter						d. 1472					
Elizabeth						1444–1503					
= duke of Suffolk						d. 1491					
Margaret						1446–1503					
= Charles, duke of Burgundy					x. 1478						
Ursula, a nun					?						

[a] x. = died by violence

even some danger, along with other women of the York-Neville connection in the interval between the Coventry parliament of the autumn, 1459, and Edward IV's accession in the spring, 1461, she was quickly reestablished at her rightful level of affluence and respect once the house of York was on the throne.

Though she was well supported during the generation of her widowhood, there were regular fluctuations in the allocation of revenues, and over the years she regularly relinquished old grants and gained new ones. In addition, as the children grew up and the stately household became more a dowager's retreat, her financial need probably declined a bit. But the duchess, through most of her long life, held a special position in the realm, and her economic and social status was usually subsidized at the appropriate level. Royal grants took the form of land, mainly bits of the duke of York's estate holdings, along with grants of cash and the control of offices which returned a profit, plus all sorts of odd franchises and perquisites. Shortly after his accession Edward IV took steps to establish his mother in the courtly style to which she would become accustomed. By 1 June, 1461 he was moving to bestow upon her, for life, land with a yearly value of 6,000 marks.[184] Along with large bits of her late husband's estate, she was to receive such oddments as £400 per annum from the customs revenues of Hull, £289 6s. 8d. from those of London, and £100 from those of York. Many years later we find that she, like the rest of humanity, was having trouble collecting what was owed her, and she, or her attorneys, were allowed to dip directly into the revenues that came from the export of wool and woolen cloth until she realized the £689 6s. 8d. due her from the customs.[185] When the Tudor dynasty replaced the Yorkist, she continued to sail on the high tides of subsidization: Henry VII renewed the older grants, and if the monies due her from the customs were not forthcoming, she could collect her allocation from other sources by way of compensation.[186]

Even as a queen mother, Cecilly's exalted status is a reminder of a woman's vicarious identity: she was a great lady because of her father in the first instance, then because of her husband, and lastly because of her sons and her grandson-in-law. Nevertheless, she seems to have had little trouble coming to grips with these identities, and any misgivings she may have felt are well covered over by layers of imperious behavior and the subservience of the lesser creatures who surrounded her. One measure of her status is the diameter of the circle of patronage of which she was the center. By virtue of the lands she held and the various offices she controlled, she could dispense some fair measure of what we might term "good ladyship." The patent letters of chancery indicate that the king's government regularly endorsed her appointment of old family and partisan servants, part-time retainers, and household officials to numerous profitable positions and sinecures. Often the post was a reward for "good service to the king and the king's father,"[187] and the appointment might embrace such a position as that of the porter of Fotheringhay Castle, or that of parker of Brimmesfield, or of Marshwood (to Ralph Kyrisshawe, esquire, one of the sewers of her chamber), or of Bardefield, Essex, or of Southfrith (to her "sergeant at arms" and to a "yeoman of her chamber"), and so forth.[188] That the royal chancery mostly recorded these transactions in the form of confirmations of Cecilly's own letters patent is but a further sign of the dignity and scope of her own secretariat and of the elaborate nature of a great dowager's household.

We would hardly expect, in the courtly world of Edward IV, any fall in the level of decorum. A letter of chancery could assert both dignity and genealogy: "The king's mother Cecill, duchess of York, late wife unto Richard, rightful king of England."[189] When young Elizabeth Stonor wrote from London, where she was sight-seeing in the company of the duchess of Suffolk, she recounted, in tones that still convey her sense of awe, how they "wayted uppon hyr to my lady the kynges modyr," and then saw "the metyng betwyne the kynge and my ladye his modyr." To her eyes, it was "trewly . . . a very good syght."[190] But shrewd Londoners also knew that Cecilly's favor was worth cultivating, and they were quite happy to seek a word on their behalf from such an exalted and possibly influential widow.[191]

Cecilly's household was noteworthy for its piety. The same domestic ordinances that contain the regulations for her world of feminine religiosity also regulated the great dowager's secular ceremonial routines through the course of the days, weeks, and months.[192] She ran a large establishment, usually residing at Berkhamstead Castle, Hertfordshire, and the regulations that have been preserved refer to the huge hierarchy and variety of regular servants and officials: carvers, cupbearers, sewers, "offycers" and "heade offycers," waiters, gentlemen ushers, cofferers, "clerke of the kytchen," marshalls, cooks, "the scullery," the "sawcerye," porters, bakers, purveyors, "cators," "ladyes and gentlewomen," yeomen, and others. Meals were served at set times, and while lesser attendants were fed at four o'clock, it was not until "five of the clocke" that "my lady and the household" came to supper. The menu, probably spare by aristocratic standards of the day, featured boiled beef and mutton plus a limited number of roasts on Sunday, Tuesday, and Thursday, only the boiled meat on Monday and Wednesday. On fast days the assemblage was reduced to eating "salte fyshe and two dishes of fresh fishe." The ordinances also discuss the payment of the household accounts (on a weekly basis), plus those bills that were settled monthly and the quarterly payment of wages. In addition, there was to be a settlement in the Berkhamstead market, on a quarterly basis, with any vendors and purveyors who disputed the honesty of the household accounts. The administrative arrangements that were generally hidden in the earlier household records of Dame Alice Bryene emerge here, and there are provisions to cover the distribution of food and supplies ("lyvery of bread, ale, and fyre, and candle") and the care of the sick and the aged and feeble who had given good service in better times.

The impression is that while household pomp was *de rigeur* and hardly an oppressive burden upon the duchess, it was in her pious routines and ecclesiastical involvements that she found the most pleasure or the best source of personal consolation. There are all sorts of signs, beyond the household regulations, of half a life spent just this side of the church. Prayers were said for the high and mighty, as a matter of course, and in itself to be named as an object of such pieties by others says little. But Cecily's involvements exceed the usual formalities, and they argue for a regular policy of moral and financial support for matters spiritual. The monks of Syon Abbey, one of Henry V's royal foundations, put in a particular good word for the mother and the father of the Yorkist dynasty. "The vii obit is in Ester . . . for alle frendes and benefactours and specialli for the duke Richard and Cecillie his spouse parentes unto kynge Edward."[193] The London Charterhouse noted a gift of £13 6s. 8d. from "the most serene Lady Duchess of York," and she helped them procure a boon for men and women who made visits and gave alms.[194] Her position as a member of the confraternity of the Black Monks represents the recognition of her moral support, but in addition it probably indicates the receipt of various forms of tangible aid.[195]

The deep piety of the dowager duchess's household is reflected in its ordinances. But in addition there are numerous references to the staff of clerics who filled its rooms and clustered about its central figure. We have a record of dispensations granted to churchmen who went from service for Cecily to advance a claim to ecclesiastical advancement. A clerk "who alleges that he is a counsellor" of Cecily was given absolution and promotion to the priesthood.[196] Thomas Canderer, a bachelor of civil law and

Cecilly's chaplain, received a dispensation to hold, simultaneously, two benefices.[197] An indult to have and to use a portable altar went to Richard Tessy, identified in the records as one of her counsellors.[198] There was also the usual involvement in the proprietary church, little though that speaks to any peculiar level of personal devotion. Cecilly was one of a group of important people who had control of the advowson of the parish church at Lechlade, one of Richard of York's Gloucestershire manors.[199] She also had a share of the collation of the next prebenadry to fall vacant in St. Stephen's, Westminster, and at her instance a license was granted permitting the foundation of a fraternity at Thaxstead.[200]

Atop these many links with the church, her domestic ordinances indicate a level of lay piety that may well have been burdensome for the younger and lighter spirits of her large household. The ordinances were set down in writing so we may "understand the order of her owne person, concerninge god and the worlde," and they show her in the constant company of the household chaplains, both morning and evening. A routine of an afternoon audience, followed by a short nap, then prayer "unto the first peale of evensonge," then wine or ale, then evensong, then supper, and then a lecture (that is, a sermon) is hardly the gay life. The lectures were to be along such lines of "holy matter" as "either Hilton on contemplative and active life, Bonaventure de infancia, Salvatoris legenda aurea, St. Maude, St. Katherin of Sonys, or the Revelacions of St. Bridgett." This is certainly an upper class, insular version of the *devotio moderna* that marks so much continental piety among the laity in the fifteenth century.[201] If it sounds dreary, it also carries a note of sincerity and personal commitment notable for its absence in most contemporary records of more casual ecclesiastical observance.

Nor was such deep involvement without its humane side. We like to think we see the mother's conscientious hand behind several of her sons' grants. There was one, made for life to Katherine FitzWilliam, "for her good service to the king's mother, duchess of York." She was to receive a deer called "a stagge of an herte," yearly, along with "a tun of red wine," as a boon of the king.[202] Another such royal gift took the handsome shape of an annuity of 20 marks, made to Joan, "late the wife of John Malpas, esquire, and afterwards the wife of John Peysmerch, knight, deceased, for her good service to the king in his youth and to his mother."[203]

When Cecilly finally came to the end, she was about 80 years old. She could look back upon carnage and family slaughter of appalling proportions—a kind of single family version of the battle of the Somme. It is not hard to imagine that religion, coupled with a severely controlled domestic life style, were ways of maintaining a balance. But whatever her own outlook, in public eyes she was a great survivor, a woman who had married while Henry VI had been a mere toddler, and who had been a widow for a period of years roughly equal to the average life span of about one-quarter or one-third of the adults of the realm. Her death certainly merited some public notice, and one of the London chronicles duly notes it: "Also this yere, in the moneth of Jun, dyed the Duchesse of York, modir vnto the noble prynce Kyng Edward the iiijth, upon whos sowles Jhesu have mercy."[204]

Cecilly's last will, written between early April and late May of 1495, is pretty much a summary statement of the themes we have tried to develop.[205] It is full of both the conventions of piety and the good things of this world. But is is also a poignant if mute treatise upon some high matters that were best left unsaid. She identifies herself as the wife of duke Richard and the mother of Edward IV, and the will's terms and conditions are to be carried out "at the kinges pleasure." No mention here of how the king (Henry VII) came to hold his throne, or why his pleasure towards her might have been such a shaky reed. By the end Cecilly must have been fairly removed from Tudor court life, because of both her age and her potential for representing embarrassing issues. If so, the will is another example of such a document, or event, as a deliberate bridge-builder: bequests to the king and the queen, to Henry VII's mother, Margaret Tudor (née Beaufort), to the Prince of Wales (Prince Arthur, her great-grandson) and to the duke of York (Henry VIII to be). There were bequests to ecclesiastical foundations with old Yorkist ties, as Fotheringhay (founded by Richard's grandfather, and to hold the bodies of Richard and now Cecilly and of their son Edmund, killed at Wakefield), and the college at Clare (an old Clare-York favorite), along with some of marked Lancastrian ties, as Syon Abbey (founded by Henry V).

Almost all of Cecilly's own children were dead by 1495, and Edward IV's daughters and other survivors came in for the personal-cum-pious bequests that often link wealthy three-generation families. Favorite treasures were about to go to the nearest and dearest: Bridget was to get a Legenda Aurea, "in velem, a boke of the life of Saint Kateryn of Sene, a boke of Saint Matilde"; Bridget's sister Cecilly received service books, and their sisters Anne and Katherine household items and furnishings. Cecilly's daughter Elizabeth and her two sons were remembered. Elizabeth's daughter, now prioress of Syon, received more items of instruction and devotion:

"a boke of Benaventure and Hilton in the same in Englishe, and a boke of the Revelacions of Saint Burgitte." Many clerics are numbered among the beneficiaries, and they received the appropriate bequests: Chausibles, stoles, service books, a "gospell boke," and a "pistill covered with ledder," copes, altar clothes, vestments of white damask, and the like. The great household also contained many servants who were now to be remembered, and it is with some pleasure that we see many women, married couples, and widows singled out for specific mention. Gentlemen of the household and clerics and staff from a variety of parish churches were mentioned, as were the yeomen (at £2 apiece), the grooms (at 26s. 8d. each), and the pages (they, at the bottom, to receive 13s. 4d. apiece). Cecilly ended the business by affixing both "signet and signemanuell," on the last day of May, at Berkhamstead Castle. An aged, pious, rich, and tragic lady finally went to her last rest. We can see her as an archetypal widow in late medieval society.

Notes

1. Much of the obvious and accessible material has already been cited above: Michael M. Sheehan, "Marriage Theory and Practice in the Conciliar Legislation and Diocesan Statutes of Medieval England," *Mediaeval Studies* 40 (1978), 408–60, and "Choice of Partners in the Middle Ages: Development and Mode of Application of a Theory of Marriage," *Studies in Medieval and Renaissance History* n. s., 1 (1978), 1–34; Richard H. Helmholz, *Marriage Litigation in Medieval England* (Cambridge, 1974); Elizabeth M. Makowski, "The Conjugal Debt and Medieval Canon Law," *Journal of Medieval History* 3, 2 (1977), 99–114; Frederick Pollock and Frederic William Maitland, *The History of English Law* (Cambridge, 1895: repr. Cambridge, 1968), II, 364–447.

2. Frances Lee Utley, *The Crooked Rib* (Columbus, Oh., 1944); Ruth Kelso, *Doctrine for a Lady of the Renaissance* (Urbana, Ill., 1956); Georges Duby, *Medieval Marriage: Two Models from Twelfth-Century France*, trans. E. Forster (Baltimore, 1978); Henry A. Kelly, *Love and Marriage in the Age of Chaucer*, (Ithaca, N.Y., 1975).

3. Simone de Beauvoir, *The Second Sex*, trans. H. M. Parshleg (New York, 1952); Eileen Power, *Medieval Women*, ed. M. M. Postan (Cambridge, 1975); Frances Gies and Joseph Gies, *Women in the Middle Ages* (New York, 1978); Vern Bullough, *The Subordinate Sex* (New York, 1974); Margaret Wade Labarge, *A Small Sound of the Trumpet: Women in Medieval Life* (Boston, 1986); Judith M. Bennett, *Women in the Medieval English Countryside* (New York and Oxford, 1987), pp. 142–76. For some recent studies of the topic in a continental setting, see Heath Dillard, *Daughters of the Reconquest: Women in Castilian Town Society, 1100–1300* (Cambridge, 1984), pp. 96–126; for the presentation of demographic and quantitative data, David Her-

lihy and Christiane Klapisch-Zuber, *Tuscans and Their Families*, pp. 130–231, 257–79.

4. For Chaucer's granddaughter, dowager duchess of Suffolk, *CP*, XII, 1, 447.

5. Each queen is covered by an article in the *DNB*. In addition, see Agnes Strickland, *Lives of the Queens of England* (London, 1905), vol. III. A few separate biographies are listed, see DeLloyd J. Guth, *Late Medieval England, 1377–1485* (Cambridge, 1976), pp. 37–38. For a recent view of the issue, see Anne Crawford, "The King's Burden? The Consequences of Royal Marriage in Fifteenth-Century England," in *Patronage, the Crown and the Provinces*, ed. Ralph A. Griffiths (Gloucester, 1981), pp. 33–56: one of the few efforts to deal with late medieval women. Most of what is available looks at the women of the early and high middle ages: Marion F. Facinger, "A Study of Medieval Queenship: Capetian France, 987–1237," *Studies in Medieval and Renaissance History* 5 (1968), 1–48; Lois L. Huneycutt, "Images of Queenship in the High Middle Ages," *Haskins Society Journal* 1 (1989), 61–71, with a bibliography covering recent work on Anglo-Saxon and continental society.

6. Alec R. Myers, "The captivity of a royal witch: the household accounts of Queen Joan of Navarre, 1419–21," *Bulletin of the John Rylands Library* 24 (1940), 69–84, and 26 (1941), 82–100.

7. Ralph A. Griffiths and Roger S. Thomas, *The Making of the Tudor Dynasty* (Gloucester, 1985), pp. 25–32, and Griffiths, "Queen Katherine of Valois and a Missing Statute of the Realm," *Law Quarterly Review* 93 (1977), 248–58.

8. Michael A. Hicks, "The Changing Role of the Wydevilles in Yorkist Politics to 1483," in *Patronage, Pedigree, and Power in Later Medieval England*, ed. Charles Ross (Gloucester, 1979), pp. 60–86; Jack R. Lander, "Marriage and Politics in the Fifteenth Century: The Nevilles and the Wydevilles," in *Crown and Nobility, 1450–1509* (London, 1976), pp. 94–126.

9. John G. Nichols, *A Collection of the Wills . . . of the Kings and Queens* (London, 1780: repr., New York, 1969), pp. 350–51 for Elizabeth Wydeville's will: p. 350, "I have no wordely goodes to do the Quene's grace . . ."

10. For some discussions of widows and widowhood, Joel T. Rosenthal, "Aristocratic Widows in Fifteenth-Century England," in *Women and the Structure of Society*, ed. Barbara J. Harris and Jo Ann K. McNamara (Durham, N.C., 1984), pp. 36–47 and 259–60, and Rosenthal, "Other Victims: Peeresses as War Widows, 1450–1500," *History* 72 (1987), 212–30; Rowena A. Archer, "Rich old Ladies: The Problems of Late Medieval Dowagers," in *Property and Politics: Essays in Later Medieval English History*, ed. Anthony J. Pollard (Gloucester, 1984), pp. 15–35, with 22–26 on the protection (or lack thereof) of dowagers; Barbara J. Todd, "The Remarrying Widows: A Stereotype reconsidered," in *Women in English Society, 1500–1800*, ed. Mary Prior (London, 1985), pp. 54–92. Information on these problems—and almost all others pertaining to wives and widows—is to be found in the various papers brought together by Susan Mosher Stuard, ed., *Women in Medieval Society* (Philadelphia, 1976).

11. Waldo E. L. Smith, ed., *The Registers of Richard Clifford, Bishop of Worcester, 1401–1407: A Calendar* (Toronto, 1976): Joan Smyth complained that she had been "maliciously defamed by statements of people unknown to her by name, that when robbers broke into the house and killed her husband, she sided with them" (p. 119).

Defamers were to be excommunicated, and the local clergy were to make the sentence known for three Sundays in Preston-on-Stour parish church. On defamation or bad-mouthing in inter-personal relations, J. A. Sharpe, *Defamation and Sexual Slander in Early Modern England: The Church Courts at York*, Borthwick Papers, 58 (York, 1980).

12. Pollock and Maitland, *History of English Law*, II, 399–436, on "Husband and Wife," for a discussion of dower and widow's rights.

13. *TE*, IV, 234; for John of Gaunt, *TE*, I, 223–39.

14. Rowena Archer and B. E. Ferme, "Testamentary Procedure with Special Reference to the Executrix," *Reading Medieval Studies* 15 (1989), 3–34; on widows' control of their children, see Sue Sheridan Walker, "Widow and Ward: The Feudal Law of Child Custody in Medieval England," in *Women in Medieval Society*, 159–72; see also Eileen Power, *Medieval Women*, 42, "Or when the lord perchance got killed, who acted as executor of his will and brought up his children? The answer to these questions, in nine cases out of ten, is—his wife. She had to be prepared to take his place at any moment."

15. PCC, 18 Wattys. Henry, III lord Scrope of Masham, referred to his wife as Joan, duchess of York: Public Record Office (London), E 41/364.

16. *Chichele*, 11–14.

17. *Sharpe*, I, 532, 560–61.

18. Caroline M. Barron, "The 'Golden Age' of Women in Medieval London," *Reading Medieval Studies* 15 (1989), 35–58; the argument is that there would be a decline, in Tudor times, from which we have not yet recovered.

19. *Fifty*, p. 80.

20. *Chichele*, 170–71.

21. *TE*, II, 46. The widow was Anne Holand, daughter of John, duke of Exeter.

22. *TE*, I, 223–39.

23. *SMW*, I, 186–93, printed from PCC, 17 Stokton.

24. *SMW*, I, 143–46, from PCC, 25 Luffenam.

25. *Chichele*, 188.

26. *TE*, IV, 24. There were other instances of generosity; Thomas Leventhorp, who left his wife all that had been hers before marriage, see *Bedfordshire*, 50; also, *Bedfordshire*, 61, 63, 77; Augusta Hawkins was to receive £100, "in satisfaction of a certain loan, and L9 which I had of her on two occasions," see *Oxfordshire*, 18.

27. *Chichele*, 46–47.

28. *Chichele*, 59.

29. *SMW*, I, 143–46.

30. *Chichele*, 188.

31. *Fifty*, 55.

32. *Lincoln*, 119; *Sharpe*, I, 355–56: she was to receive lands and tenements, "for life, or as long as she remain a widow," and only one third of this amount if and when she remarried; 379: only what common law allows, if she remarry; 435–36; land to the wife, "so long as she remain unmarried and well conducted to bring up his children becomingly." For an example that seems to show greater interest in

property than in sex, see *SMW*, II, 7: she to have the lands, for life, "if she live sole withoute empechement of waste."

33. *Chichele*, 122.

34. *TE*, II, 89.

35. *Bedfordshire*, 55.

36. Eileen Power, *The Goodman of Paris*, 42–43.

37. *Oxfordshire*, 74.

38. *Oxfordshire*, 47–48.

39. *Fifty*, 30.

40. *Chichele*, 97: *Chichele*, 90: a standard provision of this sort runs, "Item lego residuum omnium bonorum meorum Margerie uxori mee. Iten constituo et ordino executores meis Margeriam uxorem meam."

41. *Chichele*, 135–36.

42. *Chichele*, 135–36, "pro anima mea animabuseque regis Richardi secundi, Rogeri fratris mei, parentum et benefactorum meorum."

43. *Fifty*, 130.

44. *SMW*, I, 352–54.

45. *Sharpe*, I, 419–21, for an example of the wife holding authority over the children by his instructions. Also *Sharpe*, I, 439–40: She was to get his land, "so long as she remain unmarried and well conducted to bring up his children becomingly."

46. *Oxfordshire*, 55.

47. *Chichele*, 217; *Chichele*, 277: ". . . omnes pueri mei . . . cum omnibus bonis . . . in custodia et gubernacione predicte Margarete uxoris mea." *TE*, III, 203: She was to "reward theme [the children] aftir hir power for us bothe," in the manner "as natur and kynd requyres." But her power was to be used within the context of a "tendire and a faithfull luffe and favour."

48. For the problems of lord Bardolf, see *CCR*, 1405–09, 323: the quarters "of her husband's body" were to be collected from London, Lincoln, Lynn, and Shrewsbury. His head came from Lincoln, where it had been "set up over the gate." Also, regarding her dower, see *CCR*, 1409–13, 245–46, 262–63, 315–16, where her son-in-law gives surety, on 12 February, 1412, that she would be "harmless towards the king."

49. James Gairdner, *A History of the Life and Reign of Richard the Third* (Cambridge, 1898: repr., New York, 1969), p. 22; Lander, "Marriage and Politics," pp. where the topic is treated in a discussion of attainder; M. A. Hicks, "The Beauchamp Trust." Nor was this an isolated danger: Anne Crawford, "Victims of Attainder: The Howard and de Vere Women in the Late Fifteenth Century," *Reading Medieval Studies* 15 (1989), 59–74.

50. Crawford, "Victims of Attainder," 23: the quote is from the *RP*, VI, 100.

51. Crawford, "Victims of Attainder," 25.

52. *CPR, 1485–1500*, 304.

53. *CP*, IV, 101; also, *Oxfordshire*, 50: "She maie do therewith and dispose [of the residue] as she shall seime mooste to hir avauntage, pleasure, and profit."

54. For an appreciation of the range of possibilities that *might* be open, see the papers by Barbara A. Hanawalt, Judith M. Bennett, and Maryanne Kowaleski, in

Women and Work in Pre-Industrial Europe ed. Barbara A. Hanawalt (Bloomington, Ind., 1986); for data from the continent, and from cities, see Martha C. Howell, *Women, Production, and Patriarchy in Late Medieval Cities* (Chicago, 1986). This valuable study opens many windows into the dynamics of spousal relations. For a wealth of learning compressed in a few pages, see "Peasant Women," in Rodney Hilton, *The English Peasantry in the Later Middle Ages* (Oxford, 1975), pp. 95–110.

55. Howard L. Gray, "Incomes from Land in England in 1436," *English Historical Review* 49 (1934), 607–39.

56. For the Mowbray family tale, see Archer, "Rich Old Ladies." The lords Roos of Hamelake have a similar story. The men lived short lives: William, VI lord (1370–1414); John, VII lord (1385/90–1421: killed); Thomas, VIII lord (1406–30); Thomas, IX lord (1427–64: killed). Their widows lived long lives: William's widow survived until 1438, John's until 1478, VIII Thomas's until 1467, and IX Thomas's until at least 1487. Thus each outlived her eldest son, and the four women outlived their husbands by an average of 35 years. John's widow "remarried herself dishonourably without license from the king," and VIII Thomas's widow married Edmund Beaufort, duke of Somerset, killed at St. Albans in 1455. It is hardly surprising that Roos family fortunes were running down in these years. Edmund, X lord, was "declared of insufficient discretion to handle his own affairs" (*CP*, XI, 106) in 1492, and he d.s.p. in 1508, enfeebled son of an attainted father. Edmund's heir, his nephew George Manners, was never summoned as a peer.

57. *CPR, 1429–36*, 150, 207.

58. *CPR, 1429–36*, 242.

59. For Cambridge's widow, Maud Clifford, her will is printed, *TE*, II, 118–24, with other information, *CP*, II, 494–95. She left bequests to Clifford nieces and nephews, upon her childless death in 1446. Before she married Cambridge she had married and "divorced" John Neville, VI lord Latimer. On York's recovery of his inheritance, see P. A. Johnson, *Duke Richard of York, 1411–1460* (Oxford, 2988), pp. 1–27. Jack R. Lander, *Government and Community: England, 1450–1509* (Cambridge, Mass., 1980), 239, referring to the infamous Wydeville-Mowbray (Neville) marriage: "For thirty years the old woman had been a family nuisance, holding in jointure an unduly large proportion of the Mowbray family estates with which she had already enriched two successive husbands."

60. For lord John's will: *TE*, I, 356–57. On the dower, *CCR, 1409–13*, 403, 446.

61. *CCR, 1429–35*, 204–05, 208–14; *CPR, 1441–46*, 1441–46, 32, 50, 61 (for a £1,000 fine, for remarriage without a license); *CCR, 1461–68*, 225.

62. *CPR, 1408–13*, 402.

63. *CCR, 1454–61*, 11.

64. *Calendar of Inquisitions Miscellaneous, VII (1399–1422)*, number 9.

65. *CP*, IX, 504.

66. *CP*, V, 195–200; *CCR, 1399–1401*, 168; *CCR, 1402–05*, 424–25: in 1405 she was identified, in a writ *de inquirendo* sent to an escheator, as "Elizabetha uxor Johannis Cornewaill chivaler Comitissa Huntyngdon, nuper uxor Johannis de Holand nuper Comitis Huntyngdon."

67. *CCR, 1429–35*, 5–6.

68. *CCR, 1485–1500*, item 623; *CCR, 1461–68*, 24–25.

69. *CCR, 1405–09*, 19.

70. *CCR, 1405–09*, 197.

71. *CCR, 1468–76*, item 20.

72. *CCR, 1409–13*, 133.

73. *CCR, 1468–75*, item 26; Also, *CCR, 1485–1500*, item 12: friends of the three daughter-heiresses stood in for them when their mother claimed her dower share.

74. *CCR, 1468–75*, item 1223; *CCR, 1478–85*, item 1046; *CCR, 1429–35*, 276.

75. *CCR, 1461–68*, 27.

76. *CCR, 1461–68*, 172.

77. *CCR, 1429–35*, 79.

78. *Letter Book L*, 54.

79. Philip Jones, ed., *Calendar of the Plea and Memoranda Rolls of the City of London, 1437–57* (Cambridge, 1954), pp. 34–35.

80. *Letter Book K*, 41.

81. *Letter Book K*, 9.

82. *Letter Book K*, 42.

83. *Letter Book K*, 280.

84. *Letter Book I*, 242–43. *Calendar of Inquisitions Miscellaneous VII, 1399–1422*, item 543.

85. *Letter Book I*, 277.

86. *Letter Book I*, 282, 282–82.

87. Jones, *Calendar of the Plea and Memoranda Rolls, 1437–57* (Cambridge, 1954), p. 31. Martha Howell, *Women, Production, and Partiarchy*, and, for a case study of the enterprising widow, see Beatrice H. Beech, "Women Printers in Paris in the Sixteenth Century," *Medieval Prosopography* 10, 1 (spring, 1989), 75–93.

88. Jones, *Calendar of the Plea and Memoranda Rolls, 1437–57*, 46.

89. Jones, *Calendar*, 96.

90. Jones; also, *Calendar of the Plea and Memoranda Rolls, 1413–37* (Cambridge, 1949), pp. 230–31.

91. From Giraldus Cambrensis, as quoted in Rosamund J. Mitchell and M. P. R. Leys, *A History of the English People* (London, 1950), p. 87.

92. Rosenthal, "Aristocratic Widows," 37–41.

93. Rosenthal, "Aristocratic Widows," pp. 37–38. Todd, "The Remarrying Widow" for a discussion of the push and pull. Bennett, *Women in the Medieval English Countryside*, 146: ". . . few economic incentives for remarrying," because women had access to land and an independent economic life. Where land was scarce the remarriage rate was much higher.

94. *CP*, I, 247.

95. For Joan Cobham's troubles, as Oldcastle's wife, *CP*, III, 345, and *CP*, X, 47–48.

96. See Charles Ross, *Edward IV* (London, 1975), p. 93; Cora L. Schofield, *The Life and Reign of Edward the Fourth* (London, 1923), Vol. I, p. 376: "a woman whose years were almost four times as many as his own and who had been already thrice widowed!" But see Lander, chapter 3, note 59.

97. PCC, 3 Stockton.

98. Michael A. Hicks, "Piety and Lineage in the Wars of the Roses: The

Hungerford Experience," in *Kings and Nobles in the Later Middle Ages*, ed. Ralph A. Griffiths and James Sherborne (Gloucester, 1986), pp. 90–108.

99. PCC, 8 Horne.

100. Lambeth Palace, Archepiscopal Register, Stafford ff. 160a–161b.

101. PCC, 11 Stockton.

102. PCC, 2 Luffenam.

103. Roskell, *Parliament and Politics in Late Medieval England*, II, 153–74. For the marriage with Agnes, see discussion, pp. 168–69. A good marriage for him; her brothers were justice of common pleas (1450–67), justice of king's bench (1488–1504), and a retainer of bishop Waynflete. In addition the second and third, respectively, sat in the parliament of 1472–75.

104. Roskell, *Parliament and Politics*, II, 265, and *CP*, XII, 2, 479.

105. *Chichele*, 457: "jeo Phelippe duchesse de York et dame de lysle de Wyght . . ."

106. N. H. Nicolas, *Testamenta Vetusta* (London, 1830), p. 441.

107. *Buckinghamshire*, 69.

108. Buckinghamshire, 69, and 159: ". . . Ego domina Agnes Cheyne vidua et domina de Isenhamstede Cheyne . . ."

109. *TE*, II, 105.

110. *CP*, VI, 197: Lord Grey died in 1487. In 1490 his widow received a royal license to marry as she wished. She married Robert Constable, who died in 1501. Then she took the veil and lived until 1505.

111. *CP*, III, 346.

112. *CCR, 1399–1402*, 72.

113. *CCR, 1399–1402*, 381–82.

114. *CCR, 1468–76*, number 687.

115. *CCR, 1454–61*, 21.

116. *CP*, VIII, 450.

117. Sue Sheridan Walker, "Common Law Juries and Feudal Marriage Customs in Medieval England: The Pleas of Ravishment," *University of Illinois Law Review* (1984, #3), 705–18; see also Walker, "The Feudal Family and the Common Law Courts: The Pleas Protecting Rights of Wardship and Marriage, c. 1225–1375," *Journal of Medieval History* 14 (1988), 13–31.

118. *CP*, XI, 103.

119. PCC, 33 Wattys.

120. *Letter Book L*, 10.

121. *CPpL, 1458–71*, 435.

122. *CPpL, 1458–71*, 646.

123.   Ages of Children Named as Widows' Heirs

	21–30	31–40	41 +
Sons	33	15	7
Daughters	4	3	7
Total	37	18	14

124. *Nottinghamshire*, I, 165; II, 44; *Chancery*, p. 390. The daughters, respectively, were aged 17, 15, and 13; aged 9, 7, and 4; aged 9, 6, and 3; aged 30 and 26.

125. *Chancery*, 390, 522; *Nottinghamshire*, II, 41.

126. *Chancery*, 486, 1085, and 1165; *Yorkshire*, 139 (all three of the de la Pole daughters died unmarried); *Chancery*, 599; *Nottinghamshire*, II, 33, for a daughter's daughters of 19 and more and 17 and more, both married to men of same surname—presumably brothers.

127. *Nottinghamshire*, II, 38; *Chancery*, 189 (aged 14 years and more), 299 (aged 7 and more), 463 (aged 30 and more), 653, 309, 294, 1170, 418; *Nottinghamshire*, I, 173, II, 192; *Chancery*, 238.

128. R. L. Storey, ed., *Langley's Register*, number 691.

129. For the will of Robert Fitzhugh, bishop of London, *Chichele*, 540–41: There were bequests to his brother and sister-in-law, to each of his sisters, and perhaps to another brother as well, in addition to those to clerics, ecclesiastical institutions, and the books given to the Cambridge University library.

130. *TE*, II, 118–24.

131. *Chichele*, 7–10.

132. PCC, 2 Luffenham: she was buried beside her husband at Bisham. One of the Stonor ladies worried whether a grand daughter would be "lawfully begotten," *Oxfordshire*, 50; also, *Chichele*, 278.

133. *Buckinghamshire*, 195.

134. *TE*, III, 244–45.

135. Eileen Power, *Medieval English Nunneries, c. 1275 to 1535* (Cambridge, 1922), pp. 38–41, on the motives of widows and married women who sought to enter religion; see also Ann K. Warren, *Anchorites and Their Patrons in Medieval England* (Berkeley and Los Angeles, 1985), touching both widows' vows and widows' wills.

136. *Chichele*, 596.

137. *Chichele*, 553; *Chichele*, 15, for the countess of Salisbury's funeral.

138. *Fifty*, 6.

139. *Chichele*, 8.

140. *Chichele*, 267.

141. *Chichele*, 535.

142. *Chichele*, 535, for such commonly found references as those to "this wrecched and unstanble lyef . . . [and] my symple and wrecched body."

143. *Chichele*, 64.

144. *Chichele*, 78.

145. *Fifty*, 116.

146. *Chichele*, 95; SMW II, 72–73.

147. *Chichele*, 266–67; *Chichele*, 458, for the duchess of York's instructions for the 24 poor men who would greet her procession when it reached Westminster. They were to receive 20*d.* each, plus vestments.

148. *Chichele*, 535.

149. *Chichele*, 15.

150. *Chichele*, 263.

151. *Chichele*, 320.

152. *Chichele*, 471.

153. *Fifty*, 7.

154. *Chichele*, 536.

155. *Fifty*, 85.

156. *Chichele*, 267.

157. *Lincoln*, 42.

158. P. E. Jones, ed., *Calendar of the Plea and Memoranda Rolls of the City of London, 1458–82* (Cambridge, 1961), p. 104.

159. *Chichele*, 536.

160. For a list of the hospitals and their founders, see Rotha M. Clay, *The Mediaeval Hospitals of England* (Cambridge, 1909: repr., London, 1966), appendix II (pp. 277–337), for a list of all hospitals and their founders.

161. E. M. G. Routh, *Lady Margaret: A Memoir* (London, 1924), especially chapters 9, 11–13.

162. Jo Ann Hoeppner Moran, *The Growth of English Schooling, 1340–1548* (Princeton, N.J., 1985), appendix B, "Schools within the Diocese of York," pp. 237–79: the quote is on p. 237.

163. Moran, *English Schooling*, 267, 275.

164. Helen Jewell, "English Bishops as Educational Benefactors in the later Fifteenth Century," in *The Church, Politics, and Patronage in the Fifteenth Century*, ed. R. B. Dobson (Gloucester, 1984), pp. 146–67; Joel T. Rosenthal, "Lancastrian Bishops and Educational Benefaction," in *The Church in Pre-Reformation Society*, ed. Caroline M. Barron and Christopher Harper-Bill (Woodbridge, 1985), pp. 199–210.

165. Rosenthal, "Lancastrian Bishops," p. 207.

166. E. E. Barker, ed., *The Register of Thomas Rotherham, Archbishop of York, 1480–1500*, Canterbury & York Society, 69 (1976), p. 204.

167. *CPpL, 1404–15*, 132; 293: Lucy, countess of Kent, as allowed to stay for two nights only, and her sojourn was to be "at her own expense."

168. *CPpL, 1427–47*, 70.

169. *Lincoln*, 88. Sometimes the church thought it best to prepare its representatives against the moment when need arose, and the Abbot of Notley received a license to bestow veil, ring, and mantle of widowhood on various noblewomen within the archdeaconry of Oxford and Buckingham: Margaret Archer, ed., *The Register of Philip Repingdon, 1405–19*, Lincoln Record Society, 1963, III, #251.

170. *Lincoln*, 113.

171. *Lincoln*, 244–45; also, *SMW*, I, 294: "I . . . being in pure widiouhode professed and sacred to holy chastity, vexid with bodyly syknes nevertheles hole and perfite in mynde thanked by my Lord God."

172. *CPpL, 1447–55*, 55.

173. *CPpL, 1396–1404*, 536.

174. R. G. K. A. Mertes, *English Noble Households, 1250–1600* (Oxford, 1988), pp. 161–82; Nicholas Orme, *From Childhood to Chivalry: The Education of the English Kings and Aristocracy, 1066–1500* (London, 1984), pp. 5–65.

175. For Lady Clifford's household inventory, see *TE*, III, 85–87 (and II, 118–24 for her will): for Elizabeth Sywardby, *TE*, III, 161–64.

176. Margaret Wade Labarge, *A Baronial Household of the Thirteenth Century*

(London, 1965); Carole Rawcliffe, *The Staffords, Earls of Stafford and Dukes of Buckingham, 1394–1521* (Cambridge, 1978), passim, on the various countesses and duchesses who outlived their husbands and held and managed the family estates. For lady Alice, Vincent B. Redstone and Marian K. Dale, *The Household Book of Alice de Bryene*, Suffolk Institute of Archaeology and Natural History, 1931.

177. *Calendar of Inquisitions Post Mortem, 7–15 Richard II*, 352–55.

178. The marriage of Margaret (Tibetot) Scrope and John Niander was not a smooth affair. They married in 1405 or 1406: he had to flee the realm as a felon in 1414 for having killed the rector of Wensley "for opposing his matrimonial designs": *CP*, XI, 541–42. Margaret married John de Harwood, esquire, in 1421.

179. After Margaret (Neville) Scrope married William Cressoner, they had to pay £100 for a pardon for marriage without the king's license: *CPR, 1422–29*, 444. He was dead by May 1454, she by March 1464.

180. *TE*, III, 169.

181. PCC, 13 Luffenam.

182. *TE*, III, 297–99; Nicolas, *Testamenta Vetusta*, 470–71.

183. Charles D. Ross, *Richard III* (London, 1981), pp. 88–89: Ross sees this as part of the Tudor "smear" against Richard. Gairdner, *Richard the Third*, 80–81, is inclined to accept that Richard did indeed so "asperse" his mother. As things were put in more genteel days, "It was even, he hinted, doubtful if Edward himself and the Duke of Clarence were the children of the Duke of York, to whom they bore no resemblance. 'But,' cried the preacher, 'my lord the protector, that very noble prince, the pattern of all heroic deeds, is the perfect image of his father: his features are the same, and the very express likeness of that noble duke,' " as in Thomas Keightley, *The History of England* (New York, 1840), vol. 2, pp. 106–07.

184. *CPR, 1461–67*, 131–32: Cecilly was granted "the full recompense of her jointure, to the value of 5,000 marks yearly."

185. *CPR, 1477–85*, 441.

186. William Campbell, ed., *Materials for a History of the Reign of Henry VII*, Rolls Series 60 (London, 1873–77): I, 288, 460; II, 48, 62–63.

187. *CPR, 1467–77*, 184.

188. *CPR, 1467–77*, 439, 447, 538, 563; also 599, *CPR, 1477–85*, 218, 278, 283, 337; Campbell, *Materials for a History*, I, 204, 460, 468, 479, and II, 198.

189. *CPR, 1467–77*, 439.

190. Charles L. Kingsford, ed., *The Stonor Letters and Papers, 1290 to 1483*, Camden Society, 3rd series, 29 (1875–76), p. 14.

191. John H. Harvey, ed., *William of Worcester: Itineraries* (Oxford, 1969), p. 347.

192. *Society of Antiquaries: A Collection of Ordinances and Regulations for the Governing of the Royal Household* (London, 1790), pp. 37–39.

193. Charles A. J. Armstrong, "The Piety of Cicely, Duchess of York: A Study in Late Mediaeval Culture," in *For Hilaire Belloc: Essays in Honour of his 72nd Birthday*, ed. Douglass Woodruff (London, 1942), pp. 73–94; *CPR, 1461–67*, 145.

194. E. Margaret Thompson, *The Carthusian Order in England* (London, 1930), p. 196; for prayers in which Cecilly was mentioned, *CPR, 1461–67*, 161, 216.

195. William A. Pantin, ed., *Documents Illustrating the . . . General and*

Provincial Chapters of the English Black Monks, 1215–1540, Camden Society, third series, 54 (1937), III, p. 116.

196. *CPpL, 1471–84*, 106.

197. *CPpL, 1471–84*, 511.

198. *CPR, 1477–85*, 374.

199. *CPR, 1467–77*, 361.

200. *CPR, 1477–85*, 143, 227.

201. D. A. L. Morgan, "The King's Affinity in the Polity of Yorkist England," *TRHS* 5th series, 23 (1973), 21.

202. *CPR, 1461–67*, 335.

203. *CPR, 1477–85*, 374.

204. Charles L. Kingsford, ed., *Chronicles of London* (Oxford, 1905: repr., Trowbridge, 1977), p. 205. F. Sandford, *Genealogical History of the Kings and Queens of England* (London, 1707), p. 392: Cecilly's coffin was reopened, and "Dutchess Cecilie had about her neck, hanging on a Silk Riband, a Parden from Rome, which penn'd in a fine Roman hand, was as fair and as fresh to be read, as if it had been written but the day before."

205. J. G. Nicols and John Bruce, ed., *Wills from the Doctor's Commons* (Camden Society, 1863), pp. 1–8.

IV Family Lives: The Predictable and the Unpredictable

This collection of essays needs no formal conclusion: its themes have been covered, at least once, and apologies for topics that have not been treated are a little late. We have not set out to cover the family in a thorough or comprehensive sense, and wide tracts of life pertaining to childhood and nurture, to parent-daughter relations, and to ties between women of the family, whether of comparable marital and life status or not, have not received the attention they deserve. Instead, we will close with some reflections about aspects of family pathology, about ventures that went aground. The need to avoid sentimentality is a check upon the propensity to dwell too heavily upon examples of successful and harmonious family enterprises and adventures. In addition, patriarchy itself—oppressive as it could be, and supported by a vast complex of institutions and cultural constructs— was neither all-embracing nor invariably triumphant. We can offer instances of emancipation, as well as instances of anomaly. Between family members, affection vied with the desire for mastery and for the last word, and rivalry and hostility can be earmarks of the family along with the gentler emotions upon which the poets discourse.

As some generations have greatness thrust upon them, or so we are told, some men and women were fortunate enough to have complete and satisfactory family lives thrust upon them. The model was of a long and fruitful marriage, with a host of children perhaps further complemented by a legion of collateral kin. By now we have looked at enough statistical presentations and enough case studies to realize that this model was neither an impossible, utopian dream nor, in contrast, something that more than a major fraction of fifteenth-century folk would ever come to realize. Like other social models, it both described a desirable life pattern and enabled individuals to gauge whether their own course was placing them on, or near to, or perhaps diverging farther and farther from the main path.

The information about direct male replacement rates and the incidence of father-son succession showed that the patriarchal-patrilineal model was a useful guide to what would *probably* happen to most men. On the other hand, we saw enough men who had no son at the end, or only such a young son that there was a long and difficult path between succession and majority, to keep us very sober about what life might have in store. There were families where one or two sons per generation sufficed to preserve a successful diachronic chain. In others, the fecundity of the nursery proved illusory, and such a line as the de la Poles came to a bleak end (in the early sixteenth century) despite an apparent excess of male demographic riches. The same variations exist when we look outwards, at the horizontal family, or at the expectation of those girls or women who went as young brides from their father's to their husband's home. Some cases worked out quite nicely, from the standpoint of longevity and fertility, and we have seen aggregations of sons and daughters, grandchildren, in-laws, siblings, cousins, and nieces and nephews (still) held together by the network of benefaction in an old man's will or even in that of a powerful widow. Some efforts to stay on the path were challenged early and some met the test; others, as founders and progenitors of an ongoing family tradition and of lineal continuity, failed.

This view of individual and family survival places heavy emphasis on biological and demographic determinism. Obviously, as we have said above, nature always held the first card and might throw it on the table with a vengeance. But if nature were too slow, or apparently in need of counsel, society was usually ready to help out and to take a turn. Ideology, social institutions, and interpersonal relations—both positive and negative—could wreak a fair measure of havoc with the basic laws of the jungle and of survival. Society not only introduced complications and degrees into the bedrock verities of birth, copulation, and death, but it helped make some room for volition and strategy.[1] We have talked about ways in which individuals and even families could try to come to terms with the facts of demographic life: family traditions, fictive kin, the resort to cousins as heirs, the manufacture (and fabrication) of coats of arms, and the resort to and strategies of remarriage can all be seen as alternative lines of defense within the social fortress. If ultimately the fortress would always fall before the assaults of time and mortality, the fight could be both prolonged and extremely ingenious.

Social strategies and human emotion were two weapons in the struggle against the natural assailants of family happiness and survival. They operated, of course, within the boundaries mapped out by extra-social forces, but they could at times push pretty hard against these boundaries.

A life pattern that encompassed marriage, child bearing, collateral kin, and—for most women, perhaps—widowhood at the end was an easy one to grasp. From the beginning it illuminated a road that most perhaps recognized that they were likely to follow. For some people the early expectations proved to be realistic. For others the pattern proved harder to approximate. Sometimes serious obstacles appear at the very beginning: parental pressure towards a marriage that was just too odious, a marriage that soured very early, the failure to produce children, the ravages of infant mortality, or the early death of one of the partners. These were blows against which one could never be wholly prepared. When they fell, some people bravely coped with the immediate adversity but withdrew from further struggle, some fell prostrate, and some went on to fight some more and to try again.

Men and women who lost partners were both inclined to remarry at least as often as not. We have not looked at this form of the male experience, but our data about women indicate that half or slightly more, of any particular universe of widows, moved to a subsequent marriage, and remarriage was likely to take place within a few years of the husband's death. Some women not only put together a biographical necklace with two or more marriages, but they worked to integrate the separate and discontinuous pieces of their life experience. Case studies of successful integration are easier to investigate, since they help create and are reflected in the extant records of medieval society. Social disintegration and anomie leave fewer records, at least short of the law courts: The alienated and the isolated are less likely to reflect upon their sum of experience. As each individual and each family tale moved away from the high road we have referred to as the model or normative experience, so they were inclined to cover their tracks. Widows surrounded by children and grandchildren and great-nieces and great-nephews are more attractive, at the end, than lonely and neglected old women. Nor is it just a coincidence that the former often were of more concern to the king's officers and the ecclesiastical authorities than the latter. Which means, to turn the wheel, that our recreation of past life will focus more on mainstream lives than upon the marginal ones that we spot from time to time.

We do have a few windows into some of the broken life experiences of the day. When men and women married their expectations—whatever their feeling as we articulate the concepts of love and friendship—were that the union was at least for the life of one of the partners. At the same time we know that in practice no institution fully conforms to its definitional structure, and that (almost) every social byway is paved with the flagstones of exception and anomaly. The procedures and records of marital dissolution mainly lie within the domain of ecclesiastical legislation and litigation, and they have been well treated by modern scholars working in these realms.[2] Our interest here is not to cover all the well explored and charted ground, but rather to look at some of this marital data in the context of "broken" family lives: personal tales that not only leave the high road but actually pitch off into the areas of trespass and mire.

Margery Kempe offers a familiar example. She is now attracting a good deal of scholarly attention, and her story need not be repeated. However, she is usually presented as a rather eccentric woman, eventually liberated from the traditional course of life by her personal and extreme religious calling, which she expressed with what is to us an intriguing element of feminist self-consciousness.[3] Her difficult journey from conventional marriage to celibate marriage to separation to episcopal toleration is usually seen in terms of her spiritual quest. She offers us a rare case study of a difficult and highly personal effort to give fulfillment and meaning to her pilgrimage. Her despair in facing a life within the confines of the allotted and anticipated set of female roles certainly evokes our sympathy. But from a different perspective, she—like the fathers and mothers of the desert, and like St. Francis himself—put self above family (as Christ and Paul enjoined us). She broke up a traditional home and left a bewildered and angry husband. We have Margery Kempe's story, dictated when she was old and able to look retrospectively upon her travails. What would we learn if we had a series of memoirs from children, husband, and female friends of her early married days? Would they sympathize with a search for self-expression that led her to her final resting place? Or would they rather see her as a selfish and willful home-wrecker? Families and family-building were serious enterprises, fully on a par, in daily life, with personal quests and private roads to salvation. How tolerant were those still aboard ship of those who jumped off at some half-way port?

This alternate version of the familiar story, as it might have been told, obviously does not exist. No doubt, it never occurred to any of them to reflect, in writing, upon their common experience. Perhaps they would have been less laconic had they known how famous Margery would eventually become, how much support her version would eventually evoke. But this gap in the records is the usual situation, and the full story of the broken family almost never gets recorded. In other instances we have much less than we do here: occasional tantalizing views of rocks just below the water on which other marriages and other family ventures foundered. The sources that we have mainly speak through the procedures of appeals and petitions, and they express themselves in the aggrieved and partisan rhetoric of litigation. They may tell the truth, but they rarely tell the whole tale. Nor do we know, in most instances, how such briefs impressed contemporaries—whether lay peers and well-wishers, or the sterner judges of the ecclesiastical judicial structure.

Individual tales of woe about family units that became fractured or fragmented are easy enough to assemble. Each of them is some plea for help, uttered by an injured party, usually the woman. She now speaks from the disillusionment that has followed a fracture in one of the basic premises of social life, that is, that a marriage—once contracted and bound together—was for life. And now the voice of appeal dwells instead on the impermanence of the bond, or a union that turned out to be based on a foundation either in violation of canon law or that ran against the expected and tolerable course of behavior. Whereas the death of a partner or even of children was part of the natural course of family life, the tears in the marital fabric were not, or were not supposed to be, "events" that happened to one. The victims share a voice of betrayal and of outrage quite different from even the most poignant expressions of sorrow and bereavement for which spiritual solace was available.

Victims presented their cases, in the compressed sources that we have, so as to tell their side. When she charged that he "shamelessly committed adultery with divers other women and treated her so cruelly she feared for her person," she was certainly not describing a problem or expressing her anger in a fashion in any way peculiar to fifteenth-century England. Whether she obtained the "judicial separation and dowery restoration that she sought" remains unknown.[4] But such tales quickly elicit our sympathy: do our feelings differ from those of her friends *or* of her judges? Though this couple had had children, what should have been a predictable "happily ever afterwards" proved to fall well short of the model. Who had misled whom?

Wife abuse must have existed in many forms and perhaps up and down the entire social ladder. We are fairly certain that the authorities were not quick to dissolve a marriage just because a woman was unhappy at the way her husband treated her. Nor were they necessarily apt to change their minds, or to move with greater haste, just because her unhappiness stemmed from mental and physical brutality. Again, we do not know if the desired relief ever was forthcoming for the wife whose husband "has so inhumanly beaten and wounded her beyond her desserts, even when she was pregnant, that he caused her to bring forth two still-born children, and has treated her and still treats her so cruelly that she is in fear of her life and cannot any longer remain with him."⁵ At least the church said that if it were shown to be true, relief in this instance would be forthcoming.

A woman's vulnerability was not just physical. She could not be left socially and politically naked, and sometimes her need to be covered could cause problems. Elizabeth, dowager countess of Shrewsbury, married Sir Walter Blount. She had been a widow and in urgent need of protection, because "by the instigation of the enemy of the peace of the human race, very great wars were raging."⁶ A husband was necessary, since she, "a very powerful woman, was without the help of kinsmen." She accepted Blount's offer of marriage, or led him to believe that she did, despite the fact that he was "unequal and inferior to her in nobility and wealth." But she now tells us that her acceptance was no more than "feigned espousals," and she is permitted, freely, to marry as she pleases with "any other man" who is not related within prohibited degrees. Children of further unions will be legitimate. This sounds like another example of special privileges for the specially privileged. Who in this case was the beguiled, whose thoughts of life-long partnership proved to have been built on sand?

Similar tales of treachery, of brutality, and of guile run through the records. Some marriages were perhaps entered into in good faith and then later repented of. As "discovered" ecclesiastical impediments were useful skeletons in the closet, so were discovered instances of abuse, coercion, and ravishment. The wife of Norwich says that John Williamson "violently ravished her and compelled her by force and fear to contract marriage . . . [and that she] left the said John as soon as she could." We long to learn some of the operative dates and intervals. The bishop does not seem to have been impressed, and we pick up the issue when it was appealed to Rome.⁷ Was the church simply anti-feminine? Or rather did it (also) find the forms of these marriages up to its standards, while the search for personal happiness was a lesser matter? A wide variety of cases of this sort, plus all those that revolved around consanguinity and exotic impediments, must have greeted any ecclesiastical court in a typical session.

Men too could see the thread of a predictable and placid future snap before their eyes. Most husbands who found the constraints and expectations of married life to be intolerable probably just took off. Desertion still is the divorce of the poor in modern times, and it must have been common in the traditional but relatively mobile society of Lancastrian and Yorkist

England. Maybe they had both thought the marriage was for life, but if he had his fill, his feet could offer escape. We know that the end of the marriage was not always of his doing, nor was it always his fault, as we saw with Blount and his great widow. In addition, there were other life courses that, once taken, might appear much more secure than they would prove to be. A man who had received permission to leave a marriage and to enter the church might later have his ordination threatened because his wife had committed adultery. But, at least, it was decided that if he had not known of her transgression he could retain his living.[8] Sometimes the married couple cooperated in cutting the thread. Richard and Alice Andrew both took vows to leave their married state and to live lives devoted to religion. He sought for "lyf in fasting, prayer, and werkes of pety, and shal never leve this habit whil I lyf," and her vows were comparable: "to be chaste fro this tyme forwarde; and promitte to lyf stably in this avowe duryng my life."[9] Had they always planned on a mutual withdrawal from the world? And regardless of when the impulse had been planted, who was the instigator? If this was a form of broken marriage, at least we get an impression of consensual dissolution.

These examples are typical of the difficulties that many encountered during the course of the long march. Usually the evidence we have suggests that there was an active partner in the break-up, along with the passive one, the victim or object of the dissolution, and common sense and our experience supports this view. In all these instances we see life's normal course affected by an act of will, an exercise of volition. The human factor removes family life ever further from the biological and demographic factors that governed so much of our inquiry, factors which might be tempered by social strategies but which were largely beyond the world of human control. This seems the note on which to conclude; that life was a mix of forces over which we have no control and of those over which we do. Birth was not asked for. The deaths of others along the way—except for the violence in which one might have a hand—were matters to be borne with whatever variety of emotional and social response one brought to each crisis. Even death was certain and uncertain, or as they were wont to express the cliche, "Quia humane providencie sagacitas sciens nature legibus diffinitum quod cercius nil morte, incercius nil hor mortis."[10]

But this was Edmund Stafford, bishop of Exeter. At the end he was quit of family concerns, and he had no children or heirs to provide for, to worry about. He, we suggest, could rest more easily than the uneasy fathers and mothers who still, with their last breath, were caught in the meshes of family obligation. They went to their deaths, perhaps concerned with the future of a daughter, "if she attain the age of fourteen years," or with a wife, "so long as she remain a chaste widow," or with a young child, "yf she be rulid and wele maried by th'advise of hir moder," or even with a wife, "if she prove enceinte within one-half a year."[11] Such cares outlasted life itself. But then, so did the prayers of those left behind. By the values of the fifteenth century, it may have been an even trade.

Notes

1. For a study of diverse strategies, see Hans Medick and David W. Sabean, eds., *Interest and Emotion: Essays on the Study of Family and Kinship* (Cambridge, 1984); see also Stanley Chojnacki, "Patrician Women in Early Renaissance Venice," *Studies in the Renaissance* 21 (1974), 176–203. For a close look at a relationship that did not "work out," see Gene Brucker, *Giovanni and Lusanna: Love and Marriage in Renaissance Florence* (Berkeley and Los Angeles, 1986).

2. See the works of Michael M. Sheehan and Richard H. Helmholz cited above. Barbara A. Hanawalt, *The Ties That Bound: Peasant Families in Medieval England* (New York, 1986), pp. 205–14. 208: in summing up intra-familiar problems it is gratifying, in the context of a discussion on marriage, to learn that, "it was brothers rather than spouses who tended to come to blows or litigation." Eileen Power, *Medieval Women*, ed. M. M. Postan (Cambridge, 1975), pp. 16–19, on wife-beating.

3. Sanford B. Meech, ed., *The Book of Margery Kempe*, Early English Text Society, 212 (1940); for a recent treatment, see Clarissa W. Atkinson, *Mystic and Pilgrim: The Book and World of Margery Kempe* (Ithaca, N.Y., 1985), with some of the newer studies cited in the bibliography.

4. *CPpL, 1455–64*, 128–29.

5. *CPpL, 1431–47*, 319.

6. *CPpL, 1458–71*, 150–51. The widow was the daughter of James Butler, IV earl of Ormond. John Talbot, V earl of Shrewsbury, was killed (along with his brother) at Northampton, in 1460, and Elizabeth was left with six or seven children. Since her eldest son (VI earl, 1448–1473) was only about 12, there probably was some truth to her plaints about the need for protection—expecially as her husband had been a Lancastrian.

7. *CPpL, 1471–84*, 797; also, *CPpL, 1484–92*, 427–28: she had been held prisoner and forced into a marriage, though without sexual intercourse. She fled and then (re)married. Now she was ordered to resume cohabitation with the "first" husband. On such difficulties, Eric W. Ives," 'Agaynst Taking Awaye of Women': The Inception and Operation of the Abduction Act of 1487," in *Wealth and Power in Tudor England: Essays Presented to S. T. Bindoff*, ed. E. W. Ives, R. J. Knecht, and J. J. Scarisbrick (London, 1978), pp. 21–44. See also Sue Sheridan Walker. "Common

Law Juries and Feudal Marriage Customs in Medieval England: The Pleas of Ravishment," *University of Illinois Law Journal* (1984, 3), 705–18.

8. *CPpL, 1404–15*, 286.
9. *TE*, III, 343–44.
10. *Chichele*, 153–54.
11. *Sharpe*, I, 393; 390; *SMW*, I, 317–18; *Sharpe*, I, 354.

Bibliography

PRIMARY SOURCES: UNPUBLISHED

British Library, London, Additional Manuscripts 27,402, 28,209
Lambeth Palace: Archepiscopal Registers: Arundel I and II, Stafford
Public Record Office, London: E/327/774, E/41/364
Wills of the Prerogative Court of Canterbury: Marche, Horne, Vox, Bennett, Fettiplace, Godyn, Stokton, Wattys, Luffenam.

PRIMARY SOURCES: PUBLISHED

Archer, Margaret, ed. *The Register of Philip Repingdon, Bishop of Lincoln, 1405–19.* Lincoln Record Society, 57–58 (1960–63).
Baildon, William Paley, and John W. Clay, eds. *Inquisitions Relating to Yorkshire of the Reigns of Henry IV and Henry V.* Yorkshire Archaeological Society, 59 (1918).
Bannister, Arthur T., ed. *Registrum Caroli Bothe, Episcopi Herefordensis a.d. mdxvi–mdxxxv.* Canterbury and York Society, 1921.
Barker, E. E., ed. *The Register of Thomas Rotherham, Archbishop of York, 1480–1500.* Canterbury and York Society, 69 (1976).
Bentley, Samuel, *Excerpta Historica.* London, 1833.
Brewer, John S., James Gairdner, and R. H. Brodie, eds. *Letters and Papers of the Reign of Henry VIII.* 4 vols., London, 1862.
Calendar of Inquisitions Miscellaneous, VII (1399–1422). London, HMSO, 1969.
Calendar of Inquisitions Post Mortem, 7–15 Richard II. London, HMSO, 1975.
Calendar of Papal Letters, 1362–1498. London, HMSO, and Dublin, 1902–1986.
Calendar of the Close Rolls, 1377–1509. London, HMSO, 1914–63.
Calendar of the Fine Rolls, 1377–1509. London, HMSO, 1927–63.
Calendar of the Patent Rolls, 1377–1509. London, HMSO, 1895–1916.
Campbell, William, ed. *Materials for a History of the Reign of Henry VII.* Rolls Series, 60, 2 vols. London, 1873–77.
Clarke, Andrew, ed. *Lincoln Diocesan Documents, 1450–1544.* Early English Text Society, o.s. 149, 1914.
Collectanea Topographica et Genealogica. 6 vols. London, 1834–43.
Davis, Norman, ed. *Paston Letters and Papers of the Fifteenth Century.* Vols. I–II, Oxford, 1971–76.
Elvey, E. M., ed. *The Courts of the Archdeaconry of Buckingham, 1483–1523.* Buckinghamshire Record Society, 19 (1975).

Furnivall, Frederick J., ed. *The Fifty Earliest English Wills*. Early English Text Society, o.s. 78 (1882).

———. *Child Marriages, Divorce, and Ratification . . . 1561–66*. Early English Text Society, 108 (1897).

Gairdner, James, ed. *The Paston Letters*. 6 vols. London, 1895.

Gibbons, Alfred. *Early Lincoln Wills*. Lincoln, 1888.

Hanham, Alison, ed. *The Cely Letters, 1472–1488*. Early English Text Society, 273 (1975).

Harvey, John H., ed. *William of Worcester: Itineraries*. Oxford, 1969.

Hope, William St. John, ed. "The Last Testament of John de Vere," *Achaeologia* 66 (1914–15), 275–348.

Jacob, Ernest F., ed. *The Register of Henry Chichele, Archbishop of Canterbury, 1414–1443*. Vol. II. Oxford, 1938.

Jones, Philip E., ed. *Calendar of the Plea and Memoranda Rolls*. 1413–37 (Cambridge, 1949): 1437–57 (Cambridge, 1954): 1458–1482 (Cambridge, 1961).

Kingsford, Charles L., ed. *Chronicles of London*. Oxford, 1905: repr, Trowbridge, 1977.

———, ed. *The Stonor Letters and Papers, 1290–1483*. Camden Society, 3rd series 29 (1919).

Langton, William, ed. *Abstracts of Inquisitions Post Mortem*. Chetham Society, o.s. 95, 99 (1875–76).

McGregor, Margaret, ed. *Bedfordshire Wills Proved in the Prerogative Court of Canterbury 1383–1548*. Bedfordshire Historical Record Society 58 (1979).

Meech, Sanford B., ed. *The Book of Margery Kempe*. Early English Text Society 212 (1940).

Nelson, William, ed. *A Fifteenth-Century School Book*. Oxford, 1956.

Nichols, John G., ed. *A Collection of the Wills . . . of the Kings and Queens*. London, 1780. repr. New York, 1969.

Nichols, John G. and John Bruce, eds. *Wills from the Doctor's Commons*. Camden Society, 1863.

Nicolas, Nicholas Harris, ed. *Testamenta Vetusta*. 2 vols. London, 1830.

———. *The Controversy Between Sir Richard Scrope and Sir Robert Grosvenor*. 2 vols. London, 1832.

Pantin, William A., ed. *Documents Illustrating the . . . General and Provincial Chapters of the English Black Monks, 1215–1540*. Camden Society, 3rd series 57 (vol. 3: 1937).

Power, Eileen, ed. and trans. *The Goodman of Paris*. London, 1928.

Raine, James, and James Raine, Jr., eds. *Testamenta Eboracensia, I, II, III, IV*. Surtees Society, 4, 31, 45, 53 (1836–69).

———. *A History of the Chantries Within the County Palatine of Lancashire*. Chetham Society 59–60 (1862).

Redstone, Vincent B., and Marian K. Dale. *The Household Book of Alice de Bryene*. Suffolk Institute of Archaeology and Natural History, 1931.

Renshaw, Mary A., ed. *Abstracts of Inquisitions Post Mortem Relating to Nottinghamshire, 1437–1485*. Thoroton Society, 17 (1956).

Rickert, Edith. *Chaucer's World*. New York, 1948.

Rotuli Parliamentorum. 6 vols., London, 1832.

Rous, John. *The Rous Roll*, intro. Charles Ross. Gloucester, 1980.

Sharpe, Reginald R., ed. *Calendar of Wills in the Court of Hustings, London, A.D. 1258–1688.* 2 vols, London, 1889–90.

——. *Calendar of the Letter Books . . . of the City of London.* London, 1899–1912: Letter Book I, 1901: Letter Book K, 1911: Letter Book L, (1912).

Smith, Sydney Armitage, ed. *John of Gaunt's Register.* Camden Society, 3rd series 20–21 (1911).

Smith, Waldo E. L., ed. *The Register of Richard Clifford, Bishop of Worcester, 1401–1407: A Calendar.* Toronto, 1976.

Society of Antiquaries. *A Collection of Ordinances and Regulations for the Governing of the Royal Household.* London, 1790.

Storey, Robin L., ed. *The Register of Thomas Langley, Bishop of Durham, 1407–37.* Surtees Society, 6 vols. (1956–71).

Taylor, Frank, and John S. Roskell, eds. and trans. *Gesta Henrici Quinti: The Deeds of Henry the Fifth.* Oxford, 1975.

Train, K. S., ed. *Abstracts of Inquisitions Post Mortem Relating to Nottinghamshire, 1350–1436.* Thoroton Society, 12 (1952).

Weaver, F. W., ed. *Somerset Medieval Wills, 1383–1500.* Somerset Record Society 16 (1901); and *Somerset Medieval Wills, 1501–1530,* 19 (1903).

Weaver, J. R. H., and Alice Beardwood, eds. *Some Oxfordshire Wills, Proved in the PCC, 1393–1510.* Oxfordshire Record Society, 39 (1958).

SECONDARY SOURCES

Alberti, Leon Battista. *Della Famiolia,* trans. A. Guarino. Lewisburg, Pa., 1971.

Amussen, Susan D. *An Ordered Society: Gender and Class in Early Modern England.* Oxford, 1988.

Anderson, Michael. *Approaches to the History of the Western Family, 1500–1914.* London, 1980.

Archer, Rowena E. "Rich Old Ladies: The Problems of Late Medieval Dowagers." In *Property and Politics: Essays in Later Medieval English History,* ed. Anthony J. Pollard, pp. 15–35. Gloucester, 1984.

Archer, Rowena E. and B. E. Ferme. "Testamentary Procedure with Special Reference to the Executrix." *Reading Medieval Studies* 15 (1989), 3–34.

Ariès, Philippe. *Centuries of Childhood,* trans. Robert Baldick. New York, 1962.

Armstrong, Charles A. J. "The Piety of Cicely, Duchess of York: A Study in Late Mediaeval Culture." In *For Hilaire Belloc: Essays in Honour of his 72nd Birthday,* ed. Douglass Woodruff, pp. 73–94. London, 1942.

Atkinson, Clarissa W. *Mystic and Pilgrim: The Book and World of Margery Kempe.* Ithaca, N.Y., 1985.

Axon, Ernest. "The Family of Bothe (Booth) and the Church in the 15th and 16th Centuries." *Transactions of the Lancashire and Cheshire Antiquarian Society* 53 (1938), 32–82.

Bakan, David. *And They Took Themselves Wives: The Emergence of Patriarchy in Western Civilization*. New York, 1979.

Barron, Caroline M. "The Parish Fraternities of Medieval London." In *The Church in Pre-Reformation Society*, ed. Caroline M. Barron and Christopher Harper-Bill, pp. 13–37. Woodbridge, Suffolk, 1985.

———. "The 'Golden Age' of Women in Medieval London." *Reading Medieval Studies* 15 (1989), 35–58.

Barton, J. L. "The Medieval Use." *Law Quarterly Review* 81 (1965), 562–77.

Bean, John M. W. *The Estates of the Percy Family, 1416–1537*. Oxford, 1958.

———. *The Decline of English Feudalism, 1215–1540*. Manchester, 1968.

Beauroy, Jacques. "Family Patterns in Bishop's Lynn Will-Makers in the Fourteenth Century." In *The World We Have Gained*, ed. Lloyd Bonfield, Richard M. Smith, and Keith Wrightson, pp. 32–42. Oxford, 1986.

Beech, Beatrice H. "Women Printers in Paris in the Sixteenth Century." *Medieval Prosopography* 10,1 (1989), 75–93.

Bellamy, John. *Crime and Public Order in England in the Later Middle Ages*. London, 1973.

Bennett, Henry S. *The Pastons and Their England*. 2nd ed. Cambridge, 1932.

Bennett, Judith M. *Women in the Medieval English Countryside*. New York and Oxford, 1987.

Bennett, Michael J. "Spiritual Kinship and the Baptismal Name in Traditional European Societies." In *Principalities, Power, and the State*, ed. L. O. Frappell, pp. 1–13. Adelaide, 1979.

———. *Community, Class, and Careerism*. Cambridge, 1983.

———. *The Battle of Bosworth*. Gloucester, 1985.

Bloch, Marc. *Feudal Society*, trans. L. A. Manyon. Chicago, 1961.

Bossy, John. "Blood and Baptism: Kinship, Community, and Christianity in Western Europe from the Fourteenth to the Seventeenth Centuries." *Studies in Church History* 10 (1973), 129–43.

———. "Some Elementary Forms of Durkheim." *Past and Present* 95 (1982), 3–18.

Breitscher, Jane K. "As the Twig Is Bent: Children and Their Parents in an Aristocratic Society." *Journal of Medieval History* 2 (1976), 181–91.

Brooke, Christopher N. L. "Marriage and Society in the Central Middle Ages." In *Marriage and Society: Studies in the Social History of Marriage*, ed. R. B. Outhwaite, pp. 17–34. New York, 1981.

———. *The Medieval Idea of Marriage*. Oxford, 1988.

Brown, Elizabeth A. R. *The Oxford Collection of the Drawings of Roger de Gaignières and the Royal Tombs of Saint-Denis*. Transactions of the American Philosophical Society, 78, part 5. Philadelphia, 1988.

Brucker, Gene, ed. *Two Memoirs of Renaissance Florence: The Diaries of Buonaccorso Pitti and Gregorio Dati*, trans. Julia Martines. New York, 1967.

Brucker, Gene. *Giovanni and Lusanna: Love and Marriage in Renaissance Florence*. Berkeley and Los Angeles, 1986.

Brundage, James A. *Law, Sex, and Christian Society in Medieval Europe*. Chicago, 1987.

Bullough, Vern. *The Subordinate Sex*. New York, 1974.

Burson, Malcolm C. ". . . For the Sake of My Soul: Activities of a Medieval Executor." *Archives* 13, 59 (1978), 131–36.

Cherry, Martin. "The Struggle for Power in Mid-Fifteenth-Century Devonshire." In *Patronage, the Crown and the Provinces in Later Medieval England*, ed. Ralph A. Griffiths, pp. 123–44. Gloucester, 1981.

Chojnacki, Stanley. "Patrician Women in Early Renaissance Venice." *Studies in the Renaissance* 21 (1974), 176–203.

Clark, Linda and Carole Rawcliffe. "The History of Parliament, 1386–1422: A Progress Report." *Medieval Prosopography* 4,2 (1983), 9–41.

Clay, John W. *Extinct and Dormant Peerages in the Northern Counties of England*. London, 1913.

Clay, Rotha M. *The Mediaeval Hospitals of England*. Cambridge, 1909; repr. London, 1966.

Cokayne, George E. *The Complete Peerage*, ed. Vicary Gibbs et al. 12 volumes in 13. London, 1910–59.

Collomp, Alain. "Tensions, Dissension, and Ruptures Inside the Family in Seventeenth and Eighteenth Century Haute Provence," In *Interest and Emotion*, ed. Hans Medick and David W. Sabean, pp. 145–70. Cambridge, 1984.

Coward, Barry. *The Stanleys, Lords Stanley and Earls of Derby, 1385–1672*. Chetham Society, 3rd series 30 (1983).

Crawford, Anne. "The King's Burden? The Consequences of Royal Marriage in Fifteenth-Century England." In *Patronage, the Crown and the Provinces*, ed. Ralph A. Griffiths, pp. 33–56. Gloucester, 1981.

———. "Victims of Attainder: The Howard and de Vere Women in the Late Fifteenth Century." *Reading Medieval Studies* 15 (1989), 59–74.

Davis, Godfrey R. C. *Medieval Cartularies of Great Britain: A Short Catalogue*. London, 1958.

Davis, Norman. "The *Litera Troili* and English Letters." *Review of English Studies* n.s. 16 (1965), 233–44.

de Beauvoir, Simone. *The Second Sex*, trans. H. M. Parshleg. New York, 1952.

Demos, John. *A Little Commonwealth: Family Life in Plymouth Colony*. London, 1970.

Denholm-Young, Noel. *The Country Gentry in the Fourteenth Century*. Oxford, 1969.

Denton, William. *England in the Fifteenth Century*. London, 1888.

Dictionary of National Biography.

Dillard, Heath. *Daughters of the Reconquest: Women in Castilian Town Society, 1100–1300*. Cambridge, 1984.

Dillon, (Harold T.), Viscount, and William St. John Hope, eds. *Pageant of the Birth, Life, and Death of Richard Beauchamp, Earl of Warwick*. London, 1914.

DuBoulay, Francis R. H. *An Age of Ambition*. London, 1970.

Duby, Georges. *Medieval Marriage: Two Models from Twelfth Century France*, trans. E. Forster. Baltimore, 1978.

———. *The Knight, the Lady, and the Priest: The Making of Marriage in Medieval France*, trans. Barbara Bray. Harmondsworth, 1985.

Duby, Georges, and Philippe Braunstein. "The Emergence of the Individual," In *A History of Private Life: II. Revelation of the Medieval World*, ed. Georges Duby, trans. Arthur Goldhammer, pp. 54–57. Cambridge, Mass., 1988.

Emden, Alfred B. *A Biographical Register of the University of Cambridge to 1500*. Cambridge, 1963.

———. *A Biographical Register of the University of Oxford to 1500*. 3 vols. Oxford, 1957–59.

———. *A Biographical Register of the University of Oxford, A.D. 1501 to 1540*. Oxford, 1974.

"Enumeration and Explanation of Devices of the House of York." *Archaeologia* 17 (1914), 226–27.

Facinger, Marion R. "A Study of Medieval Queenship: Capetian France, 987–1237." *Studies in Medieval and Renaissance History* 5 (1968), 1–48.

Filmer, Robert. *Patriarchia and Other Political Writings*, ed. Peter Laslett. Oxford, 1949.

Fisher, Herbert A. L. *A History of Europe*. Rev. ed. Boston, 1930.

Fleming, Peter W. "Charity, Faith, and the Gentry of Kent, 1422–1529," In *Property and Politics: Essays in Later Medieval English History*, ed. Anthony J. Pollard, pp. 36–58. Gloucester, 1984.

Fourastie, Jean. "From the Traditional to the 'Tertiary' Life Cycle." In *Readings in Population*, ed. William Peterson, pp. 29–38. New York, 1972.

Fuller, Thomas. *A History of the Worthies of England*, ed. P. A. Nuttall. Cambridge, 1840. Repr. New York, 1965.

Gairdner, James. *A History of the Life and Reign of Richard the Third*. Cambridge, 1989. Repr. New York, 1969.

Gies, Frances, and Joseph Gies. *Women in the Middle Ages*. New York, 1978.

———. *Marriage and the Family in the Middle Ages*. New York, 1987.

Given, James B. *Society and Homicide in Thirteenth Century England*. Stanford, Ca., 1977.

Goodman, Anthony. *The Wars of the Roses: Military Activity and English Society, 1452–97*. London, 1981.

Gransden, Antonia. *Historical Writing in England. II. c. 1307 to the Early Sixteenth Century*. Ithaca, N.Y., 1982.

Gray, Howard L. "Incomes from Land in England in 1436." *English Historical Review* 49 (1934), 607–39.

Griffiths, Ralph A. "William Wawe and His Gang, 1427." *Hampshire Field Club and Archaeological Society* 33 (1977), 89–93.

———. "Queen Katherine of Valois and a Missing Statute of the Realm." *Law Quarterly Review* 93 (1977), 248–58.

———. "The Sense of Dynasty in the Reign of Henry VI." In *Patronage, Pedigree and Power in Late Medieval England*, ed. Charles Ross, pp. 13–36. Gloucester, 1979.

Griffiths, Ralph A. and Roger S. Thomas. *The Making of the Tudor Dynasty*. Gloucester, 1985.

Guth, DeLloyd J. *Late Medieval England, 1377–1485*. Cambridge, 1976.

Haas, Louis. "Social Connections Between Parents and Godparents in Late Medieval Yorkshire." *Medieval Prosopography* 10,1 (spring 1989), 1–21.

Hajnal, John. "Two Kinds of Pre-Industrial Household Formation Systems." In *Family Forms in Historic Europe*, ed. Richard Wall, Jean Robin, and Peter Laslett, pp. 65–104. Cambridge, 1983.

Hall, Edward. *The Hidden Dimension*. New York, 1969.

Hanawalt, Barbara A. *Crime and Conflict in English Communities, 1300–1348*. Cambridge, Mass., 1979.

———. "Keepers of Lights: Late Medieval English Parish Gilds." *Journal of Medieval and Renaissance Studies* 14 (1984), 21–37.

———. *The Ties That Bound: Peasant Families in Medieval England*. New York, 1986.

———, ed. *Women and Work in Pre-Industrial Europe*. Bloomington, Ind., 1986.

Hanham, Alison. *The Celys and Their World: An English Merchant Family of the Fifteenth Century*. Cambridge, 1985.

Haskell, Ann S. "The Paston Women on Marriage in Fifteenth- Century England." *Viator* 4 (1973), 459–71.

Helmholz, Richard H. *Marriage Litigation in Medieval England*. Cambridge, 1974.

———. "Infanticide in the Province of Canterbury During the Fifteenth Century." *History of Childhood Quarterly* 2 (1975), 379–90.

Herlihy, David, and Christiane Klapisch-Zuber, *Tuscans and their Families*. New Haven, Conn. and London, 1985.

Herlihy, David. *Medieval Households*. Cambridge, Mass., 1985.

Hicks, Michael A. "Descent, Partition and Extinction: The 'Warwick Inheritance'." *Bulletin of the Institute of Historical Research* 52 (1979), 116–28.

———. "The Changing Role of the Wydevilles in Yorkist Politics to 1483." In *Patronage, Pedigree, and Power in Later Medieval England*, ed. Charles Ross, pp. 60–86. Gloucester, 1979.

———. "The Beauchamp Trust, 1439–87," *Bulletin of the Institute of Historical Research* 54 (1981), 135–49.

———. "Attainder, Resumption, and Coercion, 1461–1529." *Parliamentary History* 3 (1984), 15–31.

———. "Piety and Lineage in the Wars of the Roses: The Hungerford Experience." In *Kings and Nobles in the Later Middle Ages*, ed. Ralph A. Griffiths and James Sherborne, pp. 90–108. Gloucester, 1986.

Hill, J. E. Christopher. "Sex, Marriage, and the Family in England." *Economic History Review* 2nd series, 31 (1978), 450–63.

Hilton, Rodney. "Peasant Women." In *The English Peasantry in the Later Middle Ages*, pp. 95–110. Oxford, 1975.

Hollingsworth, Thomas H. *The Demography of the British Peerage*. Population Studies suppl. vol. 18, no. 2 1964.

———. *Historical Demography*. London, 1969.

———. "A Note on the Mediaeval Longevity of the Secular Peerage, 1350–1500." *Population Studies* 29 (1975), 155–59.

Holmes, George A. *The Estates of the Higher Nobility in Fourteenth-Century England*. Cambridge, 1957.

Homans, George C. *English Villagers of the Thirteenth Century*. Cambridge, Mass., 1941.

Houlbrooke, Ralph A. *The English Family*, 1450–1700. London, 1984.

Howell, Cicely. "Peasant Inheritance Custom in the Midlands, 1280–1700." In *Family and Inheritance*, ed. Jack Goody, Joan Thirsk, and Edward P. Thompson, pp. 112–55. Cambridge, 1976.

Howell, Martha C. *Women, Production and Patriarchy in Late Medieval Cities*. Chicago, 1986.

Hughes, Diane Owen. "Urban Growth and Family Structure in Medieval Genoa." *Past and Present* 66 (1975), 3–28.

Huneycutt, Lois L. "Images of Queenship in the High Middle Ages." *Haskins Society Journal* 1 (1989), 61–71.

Hunnisett, Roy H. "The Reliability of Inquisitions as Historical Evidence." In *The Study of Medieval Records: Essays in Honour of Kathleen Major*, ed. D. A. Bullough and Robin L. Storey, pp. 206–37. Oxford, 1971.

Ives, Eric W. " 'Agaynst Taking Awaye of Women': The Inception and Operation of the Abduction Act of 1487." In *Wealth and Power in Tudor England: Essays Presented to S. T. Bindoff*, ed. E. W. Ives, R. J. Knecht, and J. J. Scarisbrick, pp. 21–44. London, 1978.

Jack, R. Ian. "Entail and Descent: The Hastings Inheritance." *Bulletin of the Institute of Historical Research* 38 (1965), 1–17.

Jacob, Ernest F. "An Early Book List of All Souls College." *Bulletin of the John Rylands Library* 16 (1932), 469–81.

———. "Two Lives of Archbishop Chichele." *Bulletin of the John Rylands Library* 16 (1932), 428–68.

———. "The Building of All Souls College, 1438–43." In *Essays in Honour of James Tait*, ed. J. G. Edwards, V. H. Galbraith, and Ernest F. Jacob, pp. 121–33. Manchester, 1933.

———. "The Warden's Text of the Foundation Statutes of All Souls College, Oxford." *Antiquaries Journal* 15 (1935), 420–31.

———. *The Fifteenth Century*. Oxford, 1961.

———. *Archbishop Henry Chichele*. London, 1967.

Jeffs, Robin. "The Poynings-Percy Dispute: An Example of the Interplay of Open Strife and Legal Action in the Fifteenth Century." *Bulletin of the Institute of Historical Research* 34 (1961), 148–64.

Jewell, Helen. "English Bishops as Educational Benefactors in the Later Fifteenth Century." In *The Church, Politics, and Patronage in the Fifteenth Century*, ed. R. B. Dobson, pp. 146–67. Gloucester, 1984.

Johnson, P. A. *Duke Richard of York, 1411–1460*. Oxford, 1988.

Keen, Maurice. "Brotherhoods in Arms." *History* 47 (1962), 1–17.

Keightley, Thomas. *The History of England*, II, New York, 1840.

Kekewich, Margaret. "The Attainder of the Yorkists in 1459: Two Contemporary Accounts." *Bulletin of the Institute of Historical Research* 55 (1982), 25–34.

Kelly, Henry A. *Love and Marriage in the Age of Chaucer*. Ithaca, N.Y., 1975.

Kelso, Ruth. *Doctrine for A Lady of the Renaissance*. Urbana, Ill., 1956.

Kent, Francis W. *Household and Lineage in Renaissance Florence*. Princeton, N.J., 1979.

Kingsford, Charles L. *Prejudice and Promise in Fifteenth Century England*. Oxford, 1925. Repr. London, 1962.

Klapisch-Zuber, Christiane. "Parrains et filleuls. Une approche comparée de la France, l'Angleterre et l'Italie médiévales," *Medieval Prosopography* 6,2 (1985), 51–77.

Labarge, Margaret Wade. *A Baronial Household of the Thirteenth Century*. London, 1965.

———. *A Small Sound of the Trumpet: Women in Medieval Life*. Boston, 1986.

Lamborn, E. A. G. "The Arms on the Chaucer Tomb at Ewelme." *Oxoniensia* 5 (1940), 78–93.

Lander, Jack R. *Conflict and Stability in Fifteenth-Century England*. London, 1969.

———. "Marriage and Politics in the Fifteenth Century: the Nevilles and the Wydevilles." In *Crown and Nobility, 1450–1509*, pp. 94–126. London, 1976.

———. *Government and Community: England, 1450–1509*. Cambridge, Mass., 1980.

———. "Family, Friends, and Politics in Fifteenth-Century England." In *Kings and Nobles in the Later Middle Ages*, ed. Ralph A. Griffiths and James Sherborne, pp. 27–40. Gloucester and New York, 1986.

Laslett, Peter. *The World We Have Lost*. 2nd ed. New York, 1971.

Laslett, Peter, and Richard Wall. *Household and Family in Past Time*. Cambridge, 1972.

Levett, Ada E. *Studies in Manorial History*, ed. Helen Maude Cam, M. Corte, and L. Sutherland. Oxford, 1938. Repr. New York, 1963.

Lynch, Joseph. *Godparents and Kinship in Early Medieval Europe*. Princeton, N.J., 1988.

MacFarlane, Alan. *The Family Life of Ralph Josselin*. Cambridge, 1970.

———. *The Origins of English Individualism*. Oxford, 1978.

———. "Review of Lawrence Stone. *Family, Sex, and Marriage*." *History and Theory* 18 (1979), 103–26.

McFarlane, Kenneth B. *The Nobility of Later Medieval England*. Oxford, 1973.

———. *England in the Fifteenth Century*. London, 1981.

McKenna, John W. "Henry VI of England and the Dual Monarchy: Aspects of Royal Political Propaganda." *Journal of the Warburg and Courtauld Institute* 28 (1965), 145–62.

———. "Piety and Propaganda: The Cult of Henry VI." In *Chaucer and Middle English Studies in Honour of Rossell Hope Robbins*, ed. Beryl Rowland, pp. 72–88. London, 1974.

McRee, Ben R. "Religious Gilds and Regulation of Behavior in Late Medieval Towns." In *People, Politics and Community in the Later Middle Ages*, ed. Joel T. Rosenthal and Colin F. Richmond, pp. 108–22. Gloucester, 1987.

Madden, Philippa. "Honour Among the Pastons: Gender and Integrity in Fifteenth-Century English Provincial Life." *Journal of Medieval History* 14 (1988), 357–71.

Makowski, Elizabeth M. "The Conjugal Debt and Medieval Canon Law." *Journal of Medieval History* 3 (1977), 98–114.

Medick, Hans, and David W. Sabean. "Interest and Emotion in Family and Kinship Studies: A Critique of Social History and Anthropology." in *Interest and Emotion: Essays on the Study of Family and Kinship*, ed. Hans Medick and David W. Sabean, pp. 9–27. Cambridge, 1984.

Mertes, R. G. K. A. "The Household as a Religious Community." In *People, Politics and Community in the Later Middle Ages*, ed. Joel T. Rosenthal and Colin F. Richmond, pp. 123–39. Gloucester, 1987.

————. *The English Noble Household, 1250–1600*. Oxford, 1988.

Milner, Edith. *The Lumleys of Lumley Castle*. London, 1904.

Milsom/Stroud F. C. *The Legal Framework of English Feudalism*. Cambridge, 1976.

Mitchell, Rosamund J., and M. P. R. Leys. *A History of the English People*. London, 1950.

Mitterauer, Michael, and Reinhard Sieder. *The European Family*, trans. Karla Oosterveen and Manfred Hurzinger. Oxford, 1982.

Moran, Jo Ann Hoeppner. *The Growth of English Schooling, 1340–1548*. Princeton, N.J., 1985.

Morgan, D. A. L. "The King's Affinity in the Polity of Yorkist England." *Transactions of the Royal Historical Society* 5th series, 23 (1973), 1–25.

Myers, Alec R. "The Captivity of a Royal Witch: The Household Accounts of Queen Joan of Navarre, 1419–21." *Bulletin of the John Rylands Library* 24 (1940), 69–84; 26 (1941), 82–100.

Newman, J. *The Buildings of England: West Kent and The Weald*. Harmondsworth, 1969.

Niles, Philip. "Baptism and the Naming of Children in Late Medieval England." *Medieval Prosopography* 3,1 (1982), 95–108.

Oliphant, T. L. Kingston. "Was the Old English Aristocracy Destroyed by the Wars of the Roses?" *Transactions of the Royal Historical Society* 1 (1871), 351–56.

"On the Heraldry at South Kilrington." *Yorkshire Archaeological Journal* 11 (1913), 226–27.

Orme, Nicholas. *From Childhood to Chivalry: The Education of the English Kings and Aristocracy, 1066–1500*. London, 1984.

Ozment, Steven. *When Fathers Ruled: Family Life in Reformation Europe*. Cambridge, Mass., 1983.

Paget, Hugh. "The Youth of Anne Boleyn." *Bulletin of the Institute of Historical Research* 54 (1981), 162–70.

Pollard, Anthony J. "The Richmondshire Community of Gentry during the Wars of the Roses." In *Patronage, Pedigree and Power in Later Medieval England*, ed. Charles Ross, pp. 37–59. Gloucester, 1979.

Pollock, Frederick and Frederic William Maitland. *The History of English Law*. Vol. II, Cambridge, 1885. Repr. Cambridge, 1968.

Poos, L. R. "Life Expectancy and 'Age of First Appearance' in Medieval Manorial Court Rolls." *Local Population Studies* 37 (autumn 1986), 45–52.

Powell, John Enoch and Keith Wallis. *The House of Lords in the Middle Ages*. London, 1968.

Power, Eileen. *English Medieval Nunneries, c. 1275 to 1535*. Cambridge, 1922.

————. *Medieval Women*, ed., M. M. Postan. Cambridge, 1975.

Pugh, Thomas B. "The Magnates, Knights, and Gentry." In *Fifteenth-Century England*, ed. S. B. Chrimes, Charles D. Ross, and Ralph A. Griffiths, pp. 86–128. Manchester, 1972.

———. "The Southampton Plot of 1415." In *Kings and Nobles in the Later Middle Ages*, ed. Ralph A. Griffiths and James Sherborne, pp. 62–89. Gloucester, 1986.

———. *Henry V and the Southampton Plot of 1415.* Southampton Record Series 30 (1988).

Ramsay, James H. *Lancaster and York.* 2 vols. Oxford, 1892.

Rawcliffe, Carole. *The Staffords, Earls of Stafford, and Dukes of Buckingham, 1394–1521.* Cambridge, 1978.

Razi, Zvi. "Family, Land and the Village Community in Later Medieval England." *Past and Present* 93 (1981), 3–36.

Reeves, Albert Compton. *Lancastrian Englishmen.* Washington, D.C., 1981.

Richmond, Colin F. "The Nobility and the Wars of the Roses, 1459–61." *Nottingham Mediaeval Studies* 21 (1977), 71–86.

———. *John Hopton, A Fifteenth Century Suffolk Gentleman.* Cambridge, 1981.

———. "Religion and the Fifteenth-Century English Gentleman." In *The Church, Politics and Patronage*, ed. R. B. Dobson, pp. 193–208. Gloucester, 1984.

———. "The Pastons Revisited: Marriage and the Family in Fifteenth-Century England." *Bulletin of the Institute of Historical Research* 58 (1985), 25–36.

Rosenthal, Joel T. *The Purchase of Paradise.* London, 1972.

———. "Mediaeval Longevity and the Secular Peerage, 1350–1500." *Population Studies* 27 (1973), 287–93.

———. "Aristocratic Widows in Fifteenth-Century England." In *Women and the Structure of Society*, ed. B. J. Harris and Jo Ann K. McNamara, pp. 36–47, 259–60. Durham, N.C., 1984.

———. "Heirs' Ages and Family Succession in Yorkshire, 1399–1422." *Yorkshire Archaeological Journal* 56 (1984), 87–94.

———. "Aristocratic Marriage and the English Peerage, 1350–1500: Social Institution and Personal Bond." *Journal of Medieval History* 10 (1984), 181–94.

———. "Lancastrian Bishops and Educational Benefaction." In *The Church in Pre-Reformation Society*, ed. Caroline M. Barron and Christopher Harper-Bill, pp. 199–210. Woodbridge, 1985.

———. "Other Victims: Peeresses as War Widows, 1450–1500." *History* 72 (1987), 212–30.

———. "Down the Up Staircase: Quondam Peers and Downward Mobility in Late Medieval England." *Mediaevalia*, forthcoming.

Roskell, John S. *Parliament and Politics in Late Medieval England.* Vols. 2–3. London, 1981–83.

———. *The Impeachment of Michael de la Pole, Earl of Suffolk in 1386.* Manchester, 1984.

Ross, Charles D. "The Yorkshire Baronage, 1399–1435." Oxford University, D.Phil. thesis, 1951.

———. *Edward IV.* London, 1975.

———. *The Wars of the Roses.* London, 1976.

———. *Richard III.* London, 1981.

Routh, E. M. G. *Lady Margaret: A Memoir*. London, 1924.

Russell, Josiah C. *British Medieval Population*. Albuquerque, N.M., 1948.

Sanders, Ivor J. *English Baronies: A Study of Their Origins and Descent, 1086–1327*. Oxford, 1960.

Sandford, F. *Genealogical History of the Kings and Queens of England*. London, 1707.

Saul, Nigel. *Scenes from Provincial Life: Knightly Families in Sussex, 1280–1400*. Oxford, 1986.

Schochet, Gordon J. *Patriarchalism in Political Thought*. Oxford, 1975.

Schofield, Cora. *The Life and Reign of Edward the Fourth*. 2 vols. London, 1923.

Scott, Joan W. *Gender and the Politics of History*. New York, 1988.

Sharpe, J. A. *Defamation and Sexual Slander in Early Modern England: The Church Courts at York*. Borthwick Papers 58, York, 1980.

Sheehan, Michael M. *The Will in Medieval England*. Toronto, 1963.

———. "The Formation and Stability of Marriage in the Fourteenth Century: Evidence of an Ely Register." *Mediaeval Studies* 33 (1971), 228–64.

———. "Choice of Partners in the Middle Ages: Development and Mode of Application to a Theory of Marriage." *Studies in Medieval and Renaissance History* n.s., 1 (1978), 1–34.

———. "Marriage Theory and Practice in the Conciliar Legislation and Diocesan Statutes of Medieval England." *Mediaeval Studies* 40 (1978), 408–60.

———. "Theory and Practice: Marriage of the Unfree and the Poor in Medieval Society." *Medieval Studies* 50 (1988), 457–87.

Sherborne, James. *William Cannynges, 1402–72*. Bristol Branch of the Historical Association, pamphlet 59 (1984).

Shorter, Edward. *The Making of the Modern Family*. New York, 1975.

Sinclair, Alexander. "The Great Berkeley Law–Suit Revisited, 1417–39." *Southern History* 9 (1987), 34–50.

Slater, Miriam. *Family Life in the Seventeenth Century: The Verneys of Claydon House*. London, 1984.

Smyth, John, of Nibley. *The Lives of the Berkeleys*, ed. J. Maclean. Bristol and Gloucester Archaeological Society. Bristol, 1883.

Stevenson, E. R. "The Escheator." In *The English Government at Work, 1327–36: Vol. II: Fiscal Administration*, ed. W. A. Morris and J. R. Strayer, pp. 109–67. Cambridge, Mass., 1947.

Stone, Lawrence. *The Crisis of the Aristocracy, 1558–1641*. Oxford, 1965.

———. "The Rise of the Nuclear Family in Early Modern England: The Patriarchal Stage." In *The Family in History*, ed. Charles Rosenberg, pp. 13–57. Philadelphia, 1975.

———. *Family, Sex and Marriage in England, 1500–1800*. New York, 1977.

Stones, Edward L. G. "The Folvilles of Ashby-Folville, Leicestershire, and Their Associates in Crime, 1326–47." *Transactions of the Royal Historical Society* 5th series, 7 (1957), 117–36.

Strickland, Agnes. *Lives of the Queens of England*. Vol. III, London, 1905.

Stuard, Susan Mosher, ed. *Women in Medieval Society*. Philadelphia, 1976.

Thompson, E. Margaret. *The Carthusian Order in England*. London, 1930.

Thompson, Edward P. "Review of Lawrence Stone, *Sex, Family, and Marriage*." *New Society*. (7 September, 1977), 500–501.

Thrupp, Sulvia, *The Merchant Class of Medieval London*. Ann Arbor, Mich., 1948.

———. "The Problem of Replacement Rates in Late Medieval England." *Economic History Review* 2nd series, 18 (1965), 101–19.

Todd, Barbara J. "The Remarrying Widows: A Stereotype Reconsidered." In *Women in English Society, 1500–1800*, ed. Mary Prior, pp. 54–92. London, 1985.

Tout, Thomas F. *Chapters in the Administrative History of Medieval England*. 6 vols. Manchester, 1920–37.

Trevor-Roper, Hugh R. "Up and Down in the Country: The Paston Letters." In *Historical Essays*. New York, 1966.

Trumbach, Randolph. *The Rise of the Egalitarian Family*. New York, 1978.

Turner, Ralph V. *The English Judiciary in the Age of Glanvill and Bracton, c. 1176–1239*. Cambridge, 1985.

———. "The Children of Anglo-Norman Royalty and Their Upbringing." *Medieval Prosopography* 11,2 (1990), 17–52.

Utley, Frances Lee. *The Crooked Rib*. Columbus, Oh., 1944.

Victoria County History: Northamtonshire, vol. 2.

Wagner, Anthony R. *English Geneology*. Oxford, 1960.

———. *Pedigree and Progress*. London and Chichester, 1979.

Walker, Sue Sheridan. "Proofs of Age of Feudal Heirs in Medieval England." *Mediaeval Studies* 35 (1973), 306–23.

———. "Widow and Ward: The Feudal Law of Child Custody in Medieval England." In *Women in Medieval Society*, ed. Susan Mosher Stuard, pp. 159–72. Philadelphia, 1976.

———. "Free Consent and Marriage of Feudal Wards in Medieval England." *Journal of Medieval History* 8 (1982), 123–34.

———. "Common Law Juries and Feudal Marriage Customs in Medieval England: The Pleas of Ravishment." *University of Illinois Law Review* (1984, 3), 705–18.

———. "The Feudal Family and the Common Law Courts: The Pleas Protecting Rights of Wardship and Marriage, c. 1225–1375," *Journal of Medieval History* 14 (1988), 13–31.

Wall, Richard, Jean Robin, and Peter Laslett. *Family Forms in Historic Europe*. Cambridge, 1983.

Wallace-Hadrill, John M. "The Blood Feud of the Franks." In *The Long-Haired Kings*, pp. 121–47. London, 1962.

Warren, Ann K. *Anchorites and their Patrons in Medieval England*. Berkeley and Los Angeles, 1985.

Wedgewood, Josiah C. *History of Parliament, 1439–1509: Biographies of Members*. London, 1936.

Wrigley, Edward Anthony. *Population in History*. New York, 1969.

Zell, Michael L. "Fifteenth and Sixteenth Century Wills as Historical Sources." *Archives* 14, 62 (autumn 1979), 67–74.

Index

Adultery, 203, 261

Aristocracy: death of peers, 47–48, 52–57, 114–17, 182–83; extinction of families, 47–55, 114–17, 257–58; family estates, held by widows, 197–200; fertility, 43–50; patrilineal chains and transmission of titles, 35, 40–42; remarriage of peers, 116–17; remarriage of aristocratic widows, 206, 214–15

Arundel. *See* Fitzalan

Attainder and forfeiture, 55–57

Audley, family of, 45, 58, 197

Bardolf, family of, 49, 55, 194

Beauchamp, family of (earls of Warwick and lords Abergavenny), 40, 42, 48, 117, 157–58, 163, 184, 194, 211, 223–25

Beaufort, family of (earl of Somerset and marquis Dorset), 110, 123–24, 131, 151–52, 156, 202, 228, 245

Beaumont, family of, 45–46, 50, 151, 199, 208, 220

Bedford, dukedom of, 48–49; George Neville, 48; Jasper Tudor, 49; John, 48

Bennett, Judith, xiv

Berkeley, family of, 7, 47, 50–51, 207, 209

Bible (on patriarchy and family links), 6, 23–25, 29–30, 61, 68, 196

Bloch, Marc, xiii, 4

Blount, family of (lord Mountjoy), 49

Bonville, William lord, 49

Booth (Bothe), family of, 142, 145–50, 158, 163–64; Charles, bishop of Hereford, 145; John, bishop of Exeter, 145–50; Laurence, archbishop of York, 145–50; William, archbishop of York, 145–50; burials, wills, and benefactions, 148–50; common projects and family cooperation, 147–48; ecclesiastical offices held by, 145–48; other members of the family, 146–49; relatives by marriage, 147–49; secular and ecclesiastical offices held, 145–48

Botreaux, family of, 49

Bourgchier, family of (earls of Essex and lords Fitzwarin), 70, 131, 138, 163, 184

Bourn, barony of, 51

Bromflete, family of (lord Vescy), 213

Brooke, family of (lord Cobham), 208, 212

Bryene, Alice de: household of, 232–33, 243

Burnell, family of, 49

Burgh, family of, 126

Butler, family of (earls of Ormond), 45, 47, 117

Camoys, Thomas lord, 49–50

Cannings-Young family network, 104

Cecilly, duchess of York (wife of Richard, III duke), 161, 165, 238–46; benefactions and alms, 243; household of, 242–43; income, 239, 241; patronage of, 242; piety of, 239, 243–44; as a survivor, 239–41; will and bequests, 245–46

Cely, family of, and family letters, 60, 64–65

Chantries and masses for the dead, 12–13, 59, 120–21, 223, 225–26

Charity, hospitals, and public works, 226

Charleton of Powis, family of, 49

Chaucer, family of, 26

Chaucer's Wife of Bath, 17, 175, 208

Chaundeler, John, bishop of Salisbury, 135

Chester, earls and earldom of, 52

Chichele family, 140–45, 150, 158, 163–64, 227; Henry, archbishop of Canterbury, 141–45; Robert, 141–43, 145; Thomas, father of the brothers, 141; William, 141–45; burial sites, 141; other members of family, 142–44; relatives by marriage, 144; wills and benefactions, 143–45

Children, mortality and emotional ties with, 10–13, 62–63

This book has been set in Linotron Galliard. Galliard
was designed for Mergenthaler in 1978 by Matthew
Carter. Galliard retains many of the features of a sixteenth
century typeface cut by Robert Granjon but has some
modifications that give it a more contemporary look.

Printed on acid-free paper.